MR SIMSON'S KNOTTY CASE:
Divinity, Politics, and Due Process
in Early Eighteenth-Century Scotland

McGill-Queen's Studies in the History of Ideas

MR SIMSON'S KNOTTY CASE

Divinity, Politics, and Due Process in Early Eighteenth-Century Scotland

Anne Skoczylas

McGill-Queen's University Press

Montreal & Kingston · London · Ithaca

© McGill-Queen's University Press 2001
ISBN 0-7735-1029-X

Legal deposit third quarter 2001
Bibliothèque nationale du Québec

Printed in Canada on acid-free paper

This book has been published with the help of a grant
from the Humanities and Social Sciences Federation of
Canada, using funds provided by the Social Sciences and
Humanities Research Council of Canada. Funding has
also been received from the J.B. Smallman Fund, Faculty
of Social Sciences, University of Western Ontario.

McGill-Queen's University Press acknowledges the
financial support of the Government of Canada through
the Book Publishing Industry Development Program
(BPIDP) for its activities. It also acknowledges the support
of the Canada Council for the Arts for its publishing
program.

Canadian Cataloguing in Publication Data

Skoczylas, Anne, 1938-
Mr. Simson's knotty case: divinity, politics, and due
process in early eighteenth-century Scotland
(McGill-Queen's studies in the history of ideas; 31)
Includes bibliographical references and index.
ISBN 0-7735-1029-X
1. Simson, John, 1667-1740. 2. Church of Scotland –
Doctrines – History – 18th century. 3. Church of Scotland
– Discipline – History – 18th century. I. Title.   II. Series.
BX9225.S46S59 2001   230'.5233'092   C00-901078-5

This book was typeset by Typo Litho Composition Inc.
in 10/12 Baskerville.

Contents

Contents

Acknowledgments

Many libraries and librarians provided me with bibliographical assistance, for which I am grateful. The staff in the libraries of the University of Western Ontario deserve my special thanks, with particular appreciation going to David Murphy for his efforts at locating eighteenth-century material for me.

I wish to thank the Church of Scotland for permission to quote from various presbytery, synod, and assembly records and manuscripts; Sir John Clerk of Penicuik, for letters in the Clerk of Penicuik Collection; the Duke of Montrose, for letters in the Montrose Muniments; and Miss P. Skelton, for correspondence in the Lawrie Papers. For giving me permission to quote from documents in their collections, I am also grateful to the Keeper of the Records of Scotland, the Trustees of the National Library of Scotland, the archivists of the Glasgow University Archives and Business Records Centre, the librarians in the Department of Special Collections, Glasgow University Library, and the librarians of Edinburgh University Library. Permission is granted by the Director of Dr Williams's Library to use and quote from the The Wodrow–Kenrick Correspondence. Quotations from the Benson Papers are reproduced by courtesy of the Director and University Librarian, the John Rylands University Library of Manchester.

While I enjoyed the advice and assistance given by many members of the History Department at the University of Western Ontario, I owe my deepest thanks to Professor Roger L. Emerson, whose expertise was my main stay in all areas of my work. His encyclopaedic knowledge of both manuscript and published sources was an invaluable bibliographical aid to my research. Through him I received further useful suggestions on unprinted sources from Professors M.A. Stewart, J. Moore, and Paul Wood, which I much appreciated.

My husband, Henry, read, commented on, and edited my second draft, which helped me to clarify many of my ideas. I pay tribute to the consistent and generous way in which he endorsed my efforts and to the friendly moral support offered by my children.

Finally, in appreciation of her influence, I dedicate this book to the memory of my mother, Frances De Vere Key, who encouraged me to study history.

Abbreviations Used in the Notes

EUL	Edinburgh University Library
GUA	Glasgow University Archives and Business Records Centre
GUL	Glasgow University Library
HMC	Historical Manuscripts Commission
NAS	National Archives of Scotland, Edinburgh
NCL	New College Library, University of Edinburgh
NLS	National Library of Scotland, Edinburgh

MR SIMSON'S KNOTTY CASE

1

Introduction:
Scotland after 1707

In May 1729 the General Assembly of the Church of Scotland declared
that it was not safe for John Simson, professor of divinity at Glasgow University, to teach prospective ministers. Its members agreed not only that
Simson had uttered theologically unsound statements but that he had
also disturbed the peace of the church. In response, a mild but unre-
pentant Simson took his suspension "out of the hand of his heavenly
Father, ... declared he was ... of the same opinion with this Church, in
point of doctrine, and prayed what was done to him might not be to the
prejudice of this Church."[1]

   Simson's enforced retirement from all ecclesiastical functions was the
last act in a drama that began over twenty years earlier. In April 1708 the
masters of Glasgow University elected a new professor of divinity. Their
chosen candidate was John Simson, a man whose family was distinguished by service to the church and whose personal reputation was
unblemished. Studies in Holland as well as in Scotland had opened
Simson's eyes to contemporary continental philosophy and Calvinist
thought, which he planned to incorporate into his theological teaching.

   Shortly after his arrival in Glasgow from his country parish, however,
Simson's innovations to the traditional divinity curriculum began to
cause controversy among more conservative Presbyterians. As opposition to his teaching style and doctrinal exposition grew, these men
considered charging him with error before the church courts. Finally
in 1714, James Webster (c. 1659–1720), minister of Edinburgh's Tol-
booth Church and an evangelical ex-Covenanter whose disapproval of
eighteenth-century trends encompassed the Union, Episcopalianism,

---

1 Wodrow, *Correspondence*, 3:444.

Erastianism, deism, and modern theology, made specific accusations about Simson. His charges led to Simson's first case, which took three years to work its way through the Scottish ecclesiastical courts. At its conclusion in 1717, Simson was warned to be more careful about his choice of words and expressions.

After new rumours sprang up about his theology in the mid-1720s, Simson was again charged with disseminating heterodox ideas. Once more the issues were complicated and remained under consideration for several years. In 1727 clamorous criticism of the professor resulted in his suspension from teaching and preaching. Public opinion became so heated that both Simson's supporters and his opponents were constrained to agree to leave his suspension in force after 1729. In this way, the church managers circumvented the major religious and political repercussions which would have followed either Simson's return to the lecture hall or his actual deposition. Still nominally professor of divinity, Simson lived on peacefully in Glasgow until his death in 1740.

THE UNION OF 1707 AND SCOTTISH POLITICS

John Simson's generation laid the foundations for the growth of modern Scotland, in spite of political mutations and ecclesiological uncertainty. The economic prosperity and enlightened thought of the second half of the eighteenth century grew from the efforts of the magnates, merchants, and ministers who embraced the opportunities offered between 1688 and 1745. Radical change naturally brought societal stress, in the form of riots and strikes. Similarly the philosophical innovation and theological modernization which Simson and his friends welcomed in the first decades of the eighteenth century presented a threat to conservatives in the universities and the church. The confrontation between Simson and these men significantly affected the development of Scottish intellectual life.

While Scots Presbyterians welcomed the religious and political freedoms brought by the Glorious Revolution, they faced economic disappointment and disastrous famine in the 1690s. English interests denied Scotland a share in the growth of colonial trade and forced the imposition of internal tariffs. An attempt by the Company of Scotland Trading to Africa and the Indies to redress the commercial imbalance through its settlement at Darien proved a disastrous failure. After Anne's accession in 1702, the problems of the succession and the continued continental wars against France exacerbated the unhappy economic relations between Scotland and England. Since the English feared that Scotland could form a base for a Stuart invasion of England, the Scottish Parliament tried to use the Queen's lack of a direct heir as a bargaining tool. In 1703 it passed the Act of Security, which specified that, unless stringent conditions were met, Anne's successor as sovereign of Scotland should be a different member of the Stuart family from the one chosen by England. A second act specified that Scotland could not be forced to embark on wars without the consent of the Scottish Parliament.

These challenges led to the negotiations which resulted in the Act of Union of 1707, the defining event of the early eighteenth century for Scotland. Although in the long term the union marked the beginning of greater prosperity for Scotland at the expense of nominal political independence, it brought speedy disillusionment to those who hoped that it would immediately ease the strains between the nations.[2] Archibald Campbell, Earl of Islay (1682–1761), writing from London in 1710 to Principal William Carstares (1649–1715) of Edinburgh University, lamented that "no party here has our country much at heart."[3] The act inevitably modified more than parliamentary structure and increased rather than diminished many problems between the two nations. Although there was a general realization that "on the Union ... depends the peace of the Queen's reigne," the results were profoundly disappointing.[4] Positive changes wrought by the act came slowly, and its early negative aspects were bitterly resented. The small contingent of Scots parliamentarians at Westminster proved unable to use the act to protect the 1690 Presbyterian settlement of the Church of Scotland from interference from London. Fears of English intervention in ecclesiastical affairs affected the deliberations on Simson's case in the 1720s.[5]

In the years after the Act of Union, Scotland seemed unstable to English observers. Jacobites were numerous, but politically proscribed. The Tory ideology of hierarchical power in the hands of Crown and church was unappealing to most Scots, although prior to 1715 individuals might

2 For a brief discussion of the issues involved in the Union, and the controversy which it stirred up, see Young, "The Parliamentary Incorporating Union of 1707: Political Management, Anti-Unionism and Foreign Policy," in Devine and Young, eds., *Eighteenth Century Scotland*.

3 MacCormick, *State-Papers*, 787.

4 Earl of Mar to Ld. Oxford, 10 June 1711. HMC, *Report on MSS of Mar and Kellie*, 490.

5 For a general view of the political history of the early eighteenth century see Ferguson, *Scotland*.

well lend their support to a Tory government in England to gain advantage in the factional battle at home. English statesmen distrusted the
effect of their Scots colleagues on the balance of power; as John Erskine, Earl of Mar (1675–1732), complained in 1712, London politicians "have such an apprehension of the aquisition of strenth the Crown
gets by us, and as it were in opposition to both their parties, that they
will ever treat us as enimies, Whige and Torie being alike affraid of the
power of the Crown."[6] The following year another observer noted that a
Tory majority in the House of Lords very much depended on the Scottish election of peers.[7] In 1713, Scottish constituencies elected fourteen
Tories to the House of Commons, indicating residual support for the
party under Queen Anne. The Jacobite and Tory determination to win
toleration for Scottish Episcopal ministers, along with the return in
1712 to ecclesiastical patronage, which had been officially abolished following the Revolution, and the imposition of the oath of abjuration,
brought widespread unease. These measures showed the Scots the degree to which they had lost control over their own internal policy, a fact
which made some consider the possibility of repealing the Act of Union,
since its provisions might be so easily overturned.

The death of Anne in August 1714 and the peaceful succession of the
elector of Hanover as George I changed the political picture, forcing
many who endorsed a high Tory view of an Episcopal church and a divine right monarchy into Jacobitism. The 1715 Rebellion had a chilling
effect on the remaining Scottish Tory loyalists. Although in that year
seven Tories gained election, in 1722 the party elected only one MP,
who did not outlast the 1727 election.[8] Jacobite George Lockhart explained the 1722 result by the fact that few Tories had bothered to
stand, since the sheriffs in charge of the returns would have nullified
their votes. He added, "Such as were in the Crown's nomination returned those the ministry recommended, and those that were hereditary, as they stood severally affected to the Argyll or Squadrone faction;
so ... the sheriffs and not the barons or burgesses made choice of the
greatest part of the Scots Members that went to the House of Commons."[9] The Whigs returned to prominence in London, and for the
next few years the group led by the Earls of Stanhope and Sunderland

6 HMC, *Report on MSS of Mar and Kellie*, 495.
7 HMC, *Report on MSS of Portland*, 5:303, 304.
8 Sedgwick, *House of Commons 1715–1754*, 1:14, 79.
9 Lockhart, *Lockhart Papers*, 2:82. Quoted in Sedgwick, *House of Commons*, 1:34.

struggled to maintain power against the attacks of Viscount Townshend and Sir Robert Walpole. From 1713 on, the secretary of state for Scotland was the Duke of Roxburgh, who quickly gained the confidence of the new king.

The Jacobite rising of 1715 in Scotland under the command of the Earl of Mar, whose political expectations had been thwarted by George I, left a residue of fear and concern among all supporters of the new dynasty. In 1715, Whigs demonstrated their loyalty to the Hanoverian dynasty by serving as military volunteers or by providing funds for the army. The masters of Glasgow University voted to provide fifty men for the King's service against the rebels. The cost was sixpence per day per man, and by the end of the year the masters had agreed to support this troop for sixty days. Simson, as first-ranking professor, was personally responsible for the costs of five men. His contribution ranked between the eight men paid by the principal and the four supported by professors Gershom Carmichael and Alexander Dunlop.[10] Financial or physical response to the crisis in 1715 continued for a decade to be remembered as a proof of loyalty to the régime. After "the Fifteen," English government leaders perceived the potential instability of Scotland as greater than it really was. Although there were few active Jacobites in the western Lowlands, only after the ultimate failure of the movement in 1746 did government, church, or people feel totally secure from the twin dangers of autocracy and papacy. This underlying concern was a significant incentive for secular and religious community leaders to recoil from controversies which might tend to cause division and dissension. Even if the majority of Lowland Scots saw Jacobitism as a wild card to be played only in the heat of partisan politics, consideration of its use served both to intimidate Presbyterians and to tempt the unprincipled.

As supporters of the Revolution and the Hanoverian succession, most Scots Presbyterians were Whigs. The two major political factions into which they divided both held Whig principles, their membership depending on traditional family loyalties. The Squadrone Volante lived up to its name in that it might support different Whig statesmen from one year to another. Its main leaders were the Duke of Roxburgh, the Duke of Montrose, the Marquis of Tweeddale, and at times others such as the Earl of Rothes. Although lack of consistent local management sometimes rendered Squadrone policies ineffective, the party received firm support from the ministers of the presbytery of Glasgow for the first

10 *Munimenta*, 2:393–4, 416–19.

quarter of the century. The appointment of the Duke of Montrose as chancellor of Glasgow University in 1714 naturally increased his influence there.

The Argathelian party, formed around John Campbell, second Duke of Argyll (1678–1743), and his brother, the Earl of Islay, was also Whig in spirit and, until the rise of Walpole, equally volatile in factional loyalty. The events of 1715 affected Scots politics, since Argyll, the victorious government general, was dismissed for lack of vigour in his treatment of the defeated (as well as for his friendship with the Prince of Wales) – a loss of favour which seemed to cement the position of the Squadrone in the later years of the decade, along with that of the Stanhope–Sunderland Whigs. In the 1720s the Argathelians under Islay moved into Walpole's camp and gained ascendancy in the north. Islay's skilful use of well-chosen underlings in support of Walpole gave his party the essential administrative competence with which to consolidate its influence.

The aristocratic leadership of the two parties followed Scottish traditional practice. Under the later Stuart kings, the dominance of royal servants perpetuated a long-standing custom of mighty subjects wielding quasi-autonomous authority over the populace. Although after 1688 dictatorial royal government lost some power to Parliament, the practical supremacy of the great landowners endured. For the Scots, day-to-day administration still depended on the ascendant noble group. Not only in the Highlands, with their strong clan structures, was the local magnate the administrative and judicial ruler of his people; this pattern also persisted in the Lowlands.

The notion of party loyalty was embryonic in Britain, while in Scotland fealty to family bonds was deeply entrenched. N.T. Phillipson has pointed out that when a seventeenth-century Scottish judge castigated impartial Cromwellian appointees to the bench as "kithless loons," he demonstrated an understanding of "the realities of litigation in a closed, kin-ridden, society."[11] Family interests took precedence in the distribution of places and the allotment of sinecures. Patronage, even of the most insignificant nature, was vital to the maintenance of noble prestige when personal purses were inadequate to purchase factional fidelity. The manoeuvrings of Montrose and Islay over university appointments indicate the importance of each victory and hint at the negotiations which must have been the background to the Simson cases.[12]

11 Phillipson, "Lawyers," 105.
12 For a brief discussion of this, see Emerson, "Politics."

The close interconnection between Scottish burgh and parliamentary politics meant that competing national factions were compelled to interest themselves in the composition of town councils. As a result, the loyalty of burgesses and the politics of popular ministers, who might influence their parishioners, were grist to the mills of party managers. The church records indicate ties between clergy and party, justifying the frequent charges of politics invading the pulpit. Divinity professors were accordingly important pieces in the factional game. While the narrow dimensions of county electorates (ranging from 5 to 103 voters) allowed landowners considerable control over the choice of parliamentary representatives, within the burghs (33 to 124 voters) dominant landlords could also exercise influence over oligarchic councils in the election of burgh members. The reduction of Scottish parliamentary representation after 1707 to sixteen peers and forty-five commoners enhanced the significance of electoral control.[13]

After the Union the town councils of an electoral district chose the delegates who elected burgh members of Parliament, thus controlling their votes. The parliamentary unit of the Glasgow Burghs, in which Glasgow was the dominant partner, comprised Dumbarton, Glasgow, Renfrew, and Rutherglen; its MP was usually a Glasgow councillor. In 1710 it chose Thomas Smith, a Graham adherent. During the election campaign of late 1714 and early 1715, Montrose and the Squadrone seemed firmly in power, so the town council believed it to be in its best interests to have Smith re-elected.

Because of general fear of Jacobite action after Anne's death, even Argyll was prepared to accept Smith, although his faction's candidate, Daniel Campbell of Shawfield, was less agreeable to this arrangement than his chief. Smith's death shortly afterwards necessitated a new election, in which the forces of Argyll outwitted the Squadrone members, partly because of a lack of willing and suitable Squadrone electoral candidates. As a result, Shawfield became the MP in February 1716.[14] After this, the Duke of Argyll and the town council shared the political patronage of the Glasgow Burghs, with the two working in tandem for some years.[15]

The Scottish nobility felt increasingly threatened after 1707. It saw its power endangered by its limited representation in the House of Lords, a

---

13 See Sedgwick, *House of Commons*, 1:381–404.
14 See Sunter, *Patronage and Politics*, 199–210.
15 Sedgwick, *House of Commons*, 1:400.

restriction perpetuated by the precedent set in 1711 when the House of Lords denied the right of the Duke of Hamilton to sit in Parliament under his new English title of Duke of Brandon. To maintain their positions, the great lords continued to manipulate both those dependent on them and the electorate generally, as their correspondence attests. The importance of both university and church patronage in the aristocratic search for political control ensured that Simson's career at Glasgow University was bound up in the rivalry between the Dukes of Montrose and Argyll. Along with the Duke of Hamilton, both these men wielded great influence in the Glasgow area, although their main territorial bases lay outside the town.

The Scots electoral system might be flawed, but Presbyterians saw the settlement reached after 1688 as an enormous improvement over the recent past. Now, a Protestant sovereign and Parliament acted together as protection against autocratic Episcopacy or Catholicism. At least in theory, Scots believed that the contract between governor and governed symbolized by the Claim of Right (1689) could guarantee the liberty of the subject, the sanctity of his freehold property, and the security of the nation. Scots writers such as George Buchanan (1506–1582) and Samuel Rutherford (1660–61) had enunciated these views earlier than John Locke (1632–1704), with whose work all of Simson's contemporaries were familiar. Simson was to state this creed volubly during his defences. His protest against inquisitorial questioning about his opinions by the Presbytery of Glasgow in 1726 invoked the provisions of the Claim of Right and the privileges of the citizen.[16] Although these theories conflicted with the Roman antecedents of Scots law, good Whigs continued to affirm them, despite the different reality of much contemporary practice.

PROFESSORS AND POLITICS

From the early years of the Scottish Reformation, divinity professors had been the focus of criticism from their analytical co-religionists and from their exasperated sovereigns. Academics found it difficult to satisfy simultaneously the theological and ecclesiological demands of Presbyterian extremists, the spiritual needs of middle-of-the-road Calvinists, and the secular requirements of the Crown. Men whose careers exemplified

16 J. Simson to the Committee of Purity of Doctrine, 7 Nov. 1726. Dundas, *Processes*, 29.

such problems include Andrew Melville (1545–1622), who organized Reformed Scottish divinity studies in the sixteenth century before being forced to flee the wrath of James VI; John Cameron (c. 1579–1625), a man favoured by James but not by Glasgow or its university, whose theology had most influence in France, where he taught in exile in the early seventeenth century; and Gilbert Burnet (1643–1715), who moved to the more tolerant climate of England under Charles II and over to Holland in James II's reign. John Simson was no exception to the rule that a Glasgow professor who crossed local or national politicians was often forced to pay dearly.

The immediately post-Union world of Simson's tenure of the divinity chair at Glasgow University was complicated not only by "interest," but also by a more systematic interconnection between politics, religion, and education. To many Scots, the parliamentary union of 1707 had brought only problems, especially in the relations between church and state. Devout ministers found the promise of the Glorious Revolution dimmed by actions taken by the later governments of Queen Anne to negate some clauses of the Presbyterian settlement. To politicians in Edinburgh and London, however, pulpits and chairs represented opportunities for patronage, to be put to use by their increasingly effective political machines.

While the second Simson case, 1726–29, sheds some light on the relative strengths of the adherents of "new" theology and their ultra-conservative opponents, it also illustrates the methods used by politicians to sway ecclesiastical decision-making. Interested parties continued to vie for control of Scottish schools, seminaries, parishes, and church courts. On a secular level, influence over the election of the Glasgow town council and the local member of Parliament had equal importance. Politicians and ministers alike learned lessons from the discord created by the Simson affair. The pettiness, squabbling, partisanship, and legalistic hair-splitting tarnished the reputation of the church. Leading Scots determined not to repeat these mistakes. Because the balance of power changed between 1714 and 1727, both of the rival Scottish Whig factions intervened in the friction between Simson and the "High-Flyers" – the ultra-orthodox evangelical wing of the Church of Scotland. It is perhaps a comment on the good sense and independent thinking of Scots political managers that each party was prepared to intercede in ecclesiastical affairs to prevent extremist action against the Glasgow professor.

We may compare the commotion which the two Simson cases caused in strict Presbyterian circles with the effects of the other two dramas of the first quarter of the eighteenth century – the Jacobite rebellion of 1715 and the malt tax riots of 1725. In some ways the Simson cases engaged the interest of Scots of conservative religious tendencies more personally, since they extended over a lengthy period and since many of these men had voices in kirk affairs as ruling elders. As a result, most histories of the eighteenth century mention Simson. They describe him variously as a rational expositor of "New Light" theology, as a philosophic necessitarian, and as a disseminator of unsound doctrine. The brevity of the comments has led one modern historian to see him as "a rather colourless person," remembered only as the subject of two heresy hunts.[17] Simson's contemporaries had more vigorous adjectives for a man whose innovative instructional methods, combined with his combative personality, biting sarcasm, and irrepressible wilfulness, caused turmoil in the Church of Scotland for fifteen years.

In the end, however, Simson's pedagogical system and forthright views facilitated the growth of enlightened thought in Scotland. His theological and philosophical opinions expanded the outlook of his pupils, of whom Francis Hutcheson (1694–1746) was the most significant. Simson was doctrinally true to his Calvinist ancestors, and his theological conflict with more traditional Presbyterians, far from destroying the Church of Scotland, ultimately permitted it to embrace new attitudes of tolerance, thereby freeing its members to indulge in historical studies and societal conjecture.

17 Burleigh, *Church History,* 287.

2

John Simson:
Historiography and Significance

SOURCES FOR SIMSON

It is Simson's misfortune that the most easily accessible information about him comes from the pen of Robert Wodrow (1679–1734), the son of his predecessor as professor of divinity at Glasgow University. While minister of the parish of Eastwood, a few miles south of Glasgow, Wodrow wrote on Scottish ecclesiastical history and carried on a vast correspondence with friends throughout the British Isles, as well as in Europe and America. His library, which, with his manuscripts, is held by the National Library of Scotland, included many of the pamphlets published in his day. Wodrow's position at the centre of a network of anti-Simson correspondents, and the survival of his papers, mean that the views of this group are widely known. Though a *virtuoso* of broad cultural interests, Wodrow could be prejudiced and credulous, which caused a nineteenth-century historian to pronounce him a man of "inveterate stupidity."[1] A modern description – an "indefatigable Calvinist gossip-columnist"[2] – is fairer and more accurate; his published and manuscript papers make fascinating reading, tempting the researcher to accept his biased conclusions instead of struggling through Simson's own cumbersome prose in search of the professor's true beliefs.

The printed accounts of Simson's two cases give the dry bones of the issues in contention. The polemic literature about these is extensive but focuses on the theological questions. It gives little indication of the personalities who fuelled the fires. Many of the additional surviving details

---

1 Erskine, *Extracts*, 100.
2 M.A. Stewart, "Berkeley," 27.

about Simson are filtered through the eyes of Wodrow's friends, whose ultra-orthodox religious stance caused them to disapprove of the professor's contribution to the education of a new generation of ministers in the Church of Scotland. Hints in these sources point to the political dimension of the Simson cases alongside the purely doctrinal concerns – a secular intrusion into church affairs that further distressed the writers.

The diversity of the verdicts reached on John Simson over the last two hundred and fifty years indicate the challenge which he presents to the historian. The problem is two-fold. On one side is Simson's total conviction of his own Calvinist orthodoxy, which he proclaimed at all times. He was confident that sound Reformed doctrine could accommodate the scientific model of the world revealed by Newtonianism and expressed in theological language designed to counter the deists' arguments. A uniquely Scottish pattern would preserve Calvinist discipline and moral values from the attacks of rival systems. On the other side lies the equally sincere belief of Simson's opponents that he was endangering the purity of faith of the Church of Scotland. The writings of this group present a picture of a heretic who would lie and dissemble to conceal his corrupting tenets. Both the professor and his accusers were honest and upright witnesses who believed in conflicting truths. One was trying to equip young ministers to deal with the perils threatening the early-eighteenth-century Church of Scotland; the others were labouring to free that same church from the hazardous influence of John Simson.

It should not therefore be a surprise to find that Simson has received contradictory treatment from historians of different disciplines. Members of the Secession churches have viewed him as "the Glasgow heresiarch" for much of the two and a half centuries since his death.[3] To Charles M'Crie this epithet was justified by the insidious effects of Simson's teaching on Scottish ministers. Simson often appeared in nineteenth-century ecclesiastical history as a harbinger of the decline of the eighteenth-century Church of Scotland typified by the preaching of moral virtue rather than of free grace and the atonement and of patronage instead of the "call." The "call" was the formal invitation from a congregation to a preacher to act as its minister, while by "patronage" Scots meant clerical appointment by the landowner(s) who had endowed the

---

3 Charles G. M'Crie, "Professor Simson," 254–77. M'Crie (1836–1910) was a Free Church of Scotland minister and historian.

living or who paid taxes in the parish. The question went to the root of what a Presbyterian system ought to entail.

In intellectual history, if Simson gets any mention at all, it is as a forerunner of the Scottish Enlightenment through his connection with the education of Francis Hutcheson. Richard Sher's Glasgow Enlightenment is associated with the age of Hutcheson and includes Simson only as the cause of time-consuming controversy.[4] In Porter and Teich's collection *The Enlightenment in National Context*, Nicholas Phillipson's chapter on the Scottish Enlightenment emphasizes the discourse of civic morality, from Fletcher of Saltoun to Carmichael and Hutcheson at Glasgow, as the defining background to David Hume and his contemporaries. To him a "bitterly divided" church became open to government exploitation, while university education was secularized.[5] In contrast, Samuel S.B. Taylor's understanding of the Swiss Enlightenment owes a debt to Jean-Alphonse Turretin, as well as to other Reformed theologians, such as Pictet and Osterwald. Taylor comments that Switzerland regained "her intellectual role only when she shed the rigorism of the early Calvinist faith," an observation which might equally be made of Scotland.[6] Martin I. Klauber speaks of J.-A. Turretin's "enlightened orthodoxy which attempted to square the Christian faith with the methodology of the Enlightenment."[7]

If we define Enlightenment as an emphasis on reason and on the right of free inquiry, then Simson's theology was as enlightened as that of Turretin. The more tolerant atmosphere of eighteenth-century Scotland was fostered by the instructional tone set by Simson, as well as by some of his colleagues at other divinity schools. This general trend was acknowledged by an early-twentieth-century successor of Simson in the Glasgow divinity chair, H.M.B. Reid, who saw Edinburgh rather than Glasgow as the "centre of the 'new' theology," consisting of "silences and reserve."[8] The numbers of influential young ministers emerging from Edinburgh University suggest that Reid was correct in locating an important part of the movement in the capital, where the silence of William Hamilton (1669–1732, professor of divinity 1706–32, principal 1730–32) on certain doctrinal points led student William Leechman (1706–1785, professor of divinity

4 Sher, "Commerce," 319.
5 Phillipson, "The Scottish Enlightenment," 28.
6 Taylor, "The Enlightenment in Switzerland," 78.
7 Klauber, *Between*, 192.
8 H.M.B. Reid, *Divinity Professors*, 244.

at Glasgow 1743–61, principal 1761–85), to investigate the reasons for his reticence.[9]

Why then was the conservative attack mounted on Professor Simson in Glasgow, rather than on his Edinburgh colleague? The answer must lie in Simson's refusal to be mute on controversial issues, combined with his lack of the powerful family backing possessed by William Hamilton. His outspoken nature and complicated political loyalties may also have led to the assaults on his work and to accusations of his holding "New Light" views. "New Light" was the name that had been given since the mid-seventeenth century to beliefs which encouraged individual choice in religious decisions, particularly in matters of church polity. Because the words "New Light" developed different meanings during the eighteenth century both stressing experience over election and referring to specific church-state relationships, it is impossible for the modern reader to be quite sure what the accusation was intended to imply.

A political historian of the period might view the charges against Simson as elements in the factional struggles of the early eighteenth century, when the Argathelians vied with members of the Squadrone Volante for control of Scottish civil, academic, and clerical patronage. Both of these groups were Whig, Presbyterian, and loyal to the Hanoverian succession, and Jacobites and Tories had little or no support in Glasgow, but these facts did not lessen the intensity of the battle for the nation's political power and its accompanying patronage. Ronald M. Sunter sees university appointments as an appealing patronage source for the central government.[10] Eric Wehrli confirms that the highest levels of power controlled them; by 1728 Islay had gained the right to be consulted on them.[11] The political loyalties of the individual professors in a university also affected the voting for those positions that were internally elected.

On closer investigation, the historiography on Simson shows that opinions about the man have varied widely, depending on the writer's theological conservatism or liberalism. Among Simson's contemporaries, the evangelical preacher and author of popular spiritual guides John Willison (1680–1750) believed that the professor propounded dangerous

9 Wodrow, *Life of Leechman*, 2, quoted in ibid., 244.
10 Sunter, *Patronage*, 72.
11 Wehrli, "Scottish Politics," 250.

errors and unsound doctrine, which fostered similar lapses by other Scottish professors.[12] To a man with admittedly heterodox opinions, William Whiston (1667–1752), Simson was merely "an Athanasian somewhat milder than ordinary."[13] Later in the century, James Wodrow (1730–1810; MA, Glasgow, 1750; DD, Glasgow, 1786), son of Simson's critic and minister of Stevenston, saw Simson in a favourable light. James possessed first-hand information from those who had known Simson. He wrote to fellow Glasgow alumnus Samuel Kenrick that Simson was one of the few ministers of his day who dared both to think and to speak publicly "with any freedom on high theological points."[14] His friend replied approvingly, "there certainly was a bold spirit of liberality then in embryo."[15]

Nineteenth-century writers with sectarian preconceptions continued to find it difficult to pigeonhole John Simson. His opinions became entangled in the various factional conflicts both within the Church of Scotland and between the church and secessionist bodies. In 1827 John Struthers denounced the leniency with which Simson was treated as "flagrant proof" of the Church's "declension from the purity of gospel doctrine." He saw Simson's career as "ample illustration of the inspired declaration, 'Evil men and seducers shall wax worse and worse.'"[16] A Free Church minister, W.M. Hetherington, considered that the contamination of the Church of Scotland by Moderatism was the result of its acceptance of episcopal clergy after 1690. This in turn had led to the "laxity of principle" shown by Simson.[17] "Moderatism" was a term later used to describe the eighteenth-century attitude of acceptance of the Presbyterian settlement of 1690, with its benefits for the Church of Scotland, despite evils such as the reintroduction of patronage in 1712. Although its fruit was a generation of literary clergymen who contributed to the Scottish Enlightenment, the evangelical wing of the church saw patronage as the worm at the core. Rev. T.D.W. Niven, in contrast, saw the careful attention given to the preservation of church doctrine by

12 Willison, *Fair and Impartial Testimony.*

13 Whiston, *Memoirs,* 327.

14 J. Wodrow to S. Kenrick, 18 March 1808, Dr Williams's Library, MS 24.157/259, 2r. I thank Dr Paul Wood for bringing this material to my attention.

15 S. Kenrick to J. Wodrow, 13 April 1808, ibid., MS 24.157/261, 5r.

16 Struthers, *History,* 1:455–6, 569.

17 Hetherington, *History,* 202. Rev. W.M. Hetherington (1803–1865) joined the Free Church on its formation in 1843 and later became professor of apologetics and systemic theology at its college.

those dealing with the Simson affair as "an instance of the exercise of that sober moderation" which, although often "vilified," served to protect the "spiritual economy" of the church.[18]

By the end of the nineteenth century, even Free Church theologians were moderating their tone. James Walker considered Simson "the ablest man of that semi-rationalistic type" then beginning to appear, whose first trial gave "the Church freedom from one or two merely scholastic points."[19] He believed that the first Secession from the church took place because of "the introduction by the semi-rationalists of a utilitarian theory of morality and religion."[20] M'Crie tried to assure his readers, as had Niven, that the church had done everything necessary to protect its doctrine. He noted the virulence of Secession historians against Simson – a natural attitude, since their schism had been partially justified by church inaction against Simson.[21] Two other ministers with philosophical and historical interests mentioned John Simson. James M'Cosh remarked on him as the teacher of Francis Hutcheson, to whom he imparted "liberal sentiments."[22] Henry Grey Graham discussed Simson's agitation of Scottish religious life without committing himself to any decision as to his orthodoxy. He observed that although the Westminster Confession continued to be the rigorous standard of faith accepted by all, the failure of the attempts of strict Presbyterians to depose Simson, and later Archibald Campbell (1691–1756), led to the end of the "old fanaticism."[23] Without this relaxation it would have been impossible for the Moderates to change the tone of religious life; the Moderates "did not deny the old dogmas, probably they did not even doubt them; they simply felt it pleasantest to let sleeping dogmas lie."[24] Slightly different interpretations of Simson appear in two great

18 Story, ed., *Church,* 4:639. The editor of this history, Robert Story (1835–1907), was a prominent Church of Scotland minister, chaplain to Queen Victoria, and professor of church history at Glasgow University. His theological scholarship was unfailingly liberal. Rev. T.D. Niven wrote volume 4.

19 Walker, *Theology,* 29. Walker (1821–1891) was a Free Church minister and ecclesiastical historian.

20 Ibid., 173.

21 M'Crie, "Professor Simson," 269–73.

22 M'Cosh, *Scottish Philosophy,* 52. M'Cosh (1811–1894), ordained in 1853, joined the Free Church in 1843. He became professor of logic and metaphysics in Belfast in 1851 and president and professor of philosophy at Princeton in 1868.

23 Graham, *Social Life,* 355. Graham (1842–1906) was ordained in the Church of Scotland in 1868. He noted, "With the exception of Professor Simson of Glasgow, there was no heretic – if indeed he were a heretic." Ibid., 413.

24 Ibid., 364.

nineteenth-century reference works. Hew Scott in *Fasti Ecclesiae Scotica-nae* called him "the first notable heretic within the Scottish church, the first to strike a blow that woke her from the lethargy of centuries."[25] Alexander Gordon, in the *Dictionary of National Biography*, stated that although Simson had been seen as "a disseminator of unsound doctrine," he had retracted any doubtful expressions and had not been convicted of heresy.[26]

Twentieth-century historians are equally divided. William Robert Scott saw Simson as Hutcheson's teacher, passing on to his pupil "New Light" opinions. He felt that Simson had led the two-pronged attack on "prevailing provincialism" through secular culture and liberal theology.[27] He commented that when Hutcheson was criticized for liberal preaching at Armagh, his sermon was a "verbal reproduction of the heresies of Simpson."[28] Reid, reviewing Glasgow's divinity professors, was noncommittal, commenting only that Simson was "New Light." He quoted John Flint, a contemporary critic of Simson, to the effect that the professor's main problem was excessive rationalism.[29] W.L. Mathieson considered Simson "the true pioneer of constructive liberalism."[30] Only John Macleod uncompromisingly condemned Simson as a heretic, who "was the means of disseminating unsound teaching and was untrue to the cardinal verities of his Church's Confession ... Not only was he tainted with the Neonomianism of England, but he could not be trusted to set forth or defend the mystery of the Trinity in unity. His teaching wrought havoc among the ministers of the Synod of Ulster, the most of whom studied at Glasgow."[31]

We saw above Burleigh's view of Simson's dull personality. He made no judgment on Simson's doctrines, only commenting that "all parties had professed to contend for strict confessional orthodoxy."[32] Andrew Drummond and James Bulloch considered Simson "an obscure, enigmatic, but

---

25 Hew Scott, *Fasti*, 7:400.

26 *Dictionary of National Biography*, 18:285.

27 William Robert Scott, *Francis Hutcheson*, 13.

28 Ibid., 21.

29 John Flint (c. 1660–1730) had originally been a member of the extreme Cameronian Covenanting sect. Joining the Church of Scotland in 1688, he became minister of West St Giles in Edinburgh in 1710. A non-juror, he supported James Webster in his attack on Simson, publishing a Latin condemnation of his doctrine in 1717. Reid, *Divinity Professors*, 217.

30 Mathieson, *Scotland*, 252.

31 Macleod, *Scottish Theology*, 152. Macleod (1872–1948), a highly respected Free Church minister, was professor and principal of the Free Church College.

32 Burleigh, *Church History*, 291.

significant figure ... [who] vanishes without trace."[33] They also avoided commitment by saying that the clamour of the opposition and the evasiveness of the professor prevent any easy assessment of his views. Two recent scholars are more positive on Simson's importance. W.I.P. Hazlett pronounces Simson "one of the triumvirate who were midwives of the new theology in Glasgow and Scotland – the other two being Hutcheson and William Leechman."[34] James K. Cameron feels that Simson's significance lay in his approach to the study of divinity, calling for continuous re-examination of instructional methods in accordance with new scientific knowledge. The Simson cases demonstrated that intellectual and philosophical considerations had an inevitable impact on the education of divinity students.[35] Nevertheless, it is still possible for a scholar of the social history of religion in Scotland to ignore Simson's existence.[36]

SIMSON'S SIGNIFICANCE

This brief review of the historiography of the Simson cases leads to the conclusion that the judgments of later writers were as often the result of sectarian disputes as were those of Simson's contemporaries. While few have been prepared wholeheartedly to absolve Simson of heterodoxy, equally few have seen him as a danger to Christianity. His importance in the ecclesiastical history of eighteenth-century Scotland is generally accepted, but reasons differ. Those theologians who saw Simson as a true heretic, such as Willison, Struthers, and Macleod, had little doubt as to the danger that he represented to Presbyterian doctrine and held him responsible for some of the shortcomings of the later-eighteenth-century church. A second view of Simson, as a man who introduced liberal views into a lethargic church and opened the way for later developments, is embraced by James Wodrow and Samuel Kenrick, Niven, Graham, Hew Scott, and M'Crie. A third school downplays Simson's own innovations, seeing him merely as one who had some influence on the evolution of the thought of his pupil Francis Hutcheson and hence on the kirk and the Scottish Enlightenment. This group would include M'Cosh and W.R. Scott. A final set of historians identi-

33 Drummond and Bulloch, *The Scottish Church*, 31–2.
34 Hazlett, "Religious Subversive," 19.
35 James K. Cameron, "Theological Controversy," 119–22.
36 Callum Brown, *Religion*.

fies Simson as a rationalist or semi-rationalist – Webster and Flint in the eighteenth century, joined later by Walker and Reid.

Cameron's different understanding of the place of John Simson in the Scottish cultural development is the most persuasive and closest to the facts. Simson's importance lies in the instructional innovations which he introduced to the study of divinity because of his knowledge of contemporary philosophical and scientific thought. Unlike William Hamilton, Simson voiced his opinion freely. The self-assured Glasgow professor, confident in the protection afforded by his impeccable Presbyterian lineage, set out to modernize the curriculum in his university. He planned to prepare his students to deal with the theological and moral problems raised by scepticism, deism, and atheism by using unadorned Calvinist doctrine. His determination to insist on proper legal process in his cases helped to modernize the juridical methods as well as the theology of the Church of Scotland away from a Covenanting ideology.

Although the Simson affair transformed the kirk, it neither displaced its dependence on the Westminster Confession of Faith nor introduced radical change into the Presbyterian foundation of Scottish academic life. The prerequisite for pedagogical employment in Scotland continued to be subscription to the Westminster Confession as one's own belief. The evidence suggests that Simson himself approved of this condition and continued to affirm his adherence to the Westminster Confession throughout his life. He considered himself a true Protestant and a faithful Calvinist. At the same time, Simson has a purely ecclesiastical significance, as the seceding authors who saw him as a heretic were fully aware. The second Simson case was a catalyst in persuading the leaders of the first Secession that they had no spiritual home in the Church of Scotland.

An unintended consequence, for the ultra-orthodox, of Simson's two legal ordeals in the ecclesiastical courts may have been to save other academics from being found guilty of heterodoxy in the Church of Scotland's General Assembly. During the 1730s and early 1740s at least four efforts were made in the Church's judicatories to charge university professors with heresy. The outcomes of these cases were different from the suspension which was imposed on Simson after 1727. Each of the accused was vindicated and continued to teach.[37] Three plausible, perhaps related explanations exist: the gradual modernization of the ruling élite

37 The four men were Archibald Campbell, Francis Hutcheson, William Leechman, and William Wishart, Jr, (?1690–1753). See below, 336–9.

in the church through the teaching of men such as Simson in Glasgow and his colleagues elsewhere; the deaths of older ultra-orthodox ministers and the departure from the established church of some of Simson's more extreme opponents in the first Secession in the 1730s; and the ascendancy which the Earl of Islay had gained by 1733 in the political management of Scottish affairs under the English ministry of Sir Robert Walpole, which lasted until the fall of that government in 1742.[38]

In trying to reconstruct the Simson cases I hope to illuminate what was at stake both doctrinally and politically. The challenges faced by Simson illustrate some of the complexities of national life during this period. We may clarify the relationship between changes in the theological climate and the power structure of government after the Act of Union through the detailed examination of his affairs. Between them, John Simson, professor of divinity, and Archibald Campbell, Earl of Islay, consolidated a moderate segment in the Church of Scotland and thereby fertilized the soil from which the Scottish Enlightenment grew. Simson emerges from this close study as a complex and often difficult man – gregarious and capable of inspiring friendship as well as opprobrium. Professionally, he was as innovative as any of his scientific academic contemporaries. A concerned and bookish Calvinist, Simson believed that he could use traditional Christian doctrine to refute the sceptical, deistic trends of his day. He incurred the anger of the conservatives because of his efforts to reword some seventeenth-century Reformed scholastic tenets to present a more optimistic version of Presbyterian Calvinism; nevertheless, he ultimately introduced a more open atmosphere into the academic world of the Scots divinity schools. At the same time, Simson's cases provided the momentum for a gradual relaxation of the control of the Church of Scotland over the country's universities.

By placing Simson in his religious and political context, we can appreciate his role in making the Church of Scotland a seed-bed of philosophical thought. This in turn permitted the Scottish Enlightenment to have a religious foundation. We can relate the ideas and methods which existed in mid-eighteenth-century Scotland, which we call the Scottish Enlightenment, to Simson's teaching. Late in the century, Kant defined Enlightenment as man's emergence from his self-imposed immaturity. John Simson would have appreciated this description of his experience. As a professor he sought to make his students aware of the advances in

38 For Islay's rise to power, see Wehrli, "Scottish Politics."

knowledge which surrounded them and from which they might benefit. For him these lay primarily in natural philosophy, but also in logic, morals, and theology. In his 1715 defence of his teaching, when justifying classroom discussion of the possibility of the existence of extraterrestrial life, Simson said,

I Think it is my Duty, to let my Scholars Know, that there is nothing in Scripture that is Inconsistent with the True Principles of Natural Philosophy, which they are Taught in This, and the Other Universities of this Kingdom, where 'tis Arrived at a far greater Degree of Perfection than in *Holland*; And by what I ever have Observed of its Progress, the more we Advance in the True Knowledg of Nature, Our Philosophy Agrees the better with the True Sense of Scripture, and is the more Serviceable to True Christian Theology, and the more Confounding to its Adversaries, as this Speculation also is. Wherefore, I Think, I Serve the True Interest of Religion, when I Use my Best Endeavours to Remove these Prejudices and Stumbling Blocks.[39]

The scientific discoveries culminating in the work of Isaac Newton had changed people's ideas of the topography of the natural world and of its governing laws. The new natural philosophy was already being taught at Glasgow University, where Simson kept abreast of the work of his colleagues. As he noted in his defence, he saw no contradiction between more accurate knowledge of the physical world and proper understanding of revealed truth. Not all Scots perceived this compatibility as easily as Simson. In 1768 Kenrick remarked that "freedom of debate & Enquiry" had lately been introduced into Scotland, "But it would be highly absurd to call a rational Enquiry after truth, infidelity."[40] Simson's successors had to struggle to preserve freedom of debate, which he had introduced, from the attacks of the religious conservatives, who indeed considered rational inquiry to be heresy.

In Scotland as elsewhere, the formulation of physical laws was accompanied by the classification of natural material, organic, and inorganic. The tangible and textual proofs of historical accuracy were under investigation in religious topics as well as in classical and modern studies. Wodrow corresponded on various subjects with other *virtuosi*; Simson discussed the epigraphs on Roman masonry with Sir John Clerk of Penicuik (1676–1766), Scotland's leading antiquary and *virtuoso*, whom he

39 Simson, *Libel*, 284–5.
40 S. Kenrick to J. Wodrow, 6 Oct. 1768, Dr Williams's Library, MS 24.157/44, 1v.

had met when Clerk was a student at Glasgow.[41] Throughout his life
Simson read the literature produced by his contemporaries on religious
and scientific matters, as well as continuing to deepen his acquaintance
with patristic writers. He discovered that although the works of the early
churchmen were sometimes at variance with those of scholastic Protestants of the seventeenth century, they were often more appealing to
him. He never doubted that such disinterested investigation was perfectly in harmony with orthodox Christian belief. In this he was followed
by all the major figures of the Scottish Enlightenment, with the notable
exception of David Hume.

Simson understood that intellectual growth entailed a departure
from older metaphysical systems and outdated scholasticism. In his answers to Webster's charges, he demanded that men reconsider the
grounds for their faith. When Simson discussed human motives for the
worship of God, he tried to introduce a modified utilitarianism. The answer to the first question in both Westminster Catechisms, "What is the
chief end of man?," is that it is both to glorify God and to enjoy him for-
ever. Scholastic Reformed divines emphasized the first part of the reply;
to Simson, the second phrase was of equal importance. He wrote that if
the whole response was taken to mean that we should prefer the glory
of God to our enjoyment of him, he was "Persuaded, that this is Contrary both to Common Sense, and Sanctified Reason, and is a Piece of
Unsolid and Absurd *Metaphysicks*, which was never Taught, by any of the
Prophets or Apostles, nor by any Person well Skilled in *Philosophy* or
Divinity."[42]

The consequence was a concentration on happiness now and hereafter and on the moral means of obtaining it. John Ramsay of Ochtertyre
understood this emphasis to have been Simson's greatest fault in the
eyes of his fellow Glasgow ministers: "It was alleged that nothing had incensed the reverend body [the presbytery of Glasgow] as much as his
[Simson's] inculcating, in the strongest terms, the necessity of moral virtue, without which there could be no real Christianity."[43] Ten years later
Simson was still demanding that his countrymen cast aside outworn
phraseology and scholastic metaphysics when he dismissed the suggestion that "it could be called either an impugning or denying, or teaching what is inconsistent with, or tending to lessen the Belief of any of the

41 See letters in NAS, GD18/5019, GD18/5041/3, GD18/5047.
42 Simson, *Libel*, 143.
43 Ramsay of Ochtertyre, *Scotland*, 1:273.

great, necessary and fundamental Truths ... tho' he had called several of the School-Terms, that are neither used in Scripture, nor our Confession of Faith, *Ambiguous Terms of Art*; and tho' he had called Debates about them *Philosophical Niceties*."44

Simson's vision of humanity, its nature, and its prospects had wider implications, including some for politics. He championed a Lockean concept of a governmental contract which guaranteed individual liberty from illegal assaults on personal reputation, property, or livelihood. He had notions of the rule of law and the function of government which did not always accord with the Roman roots of Scots civil and canon law. Simson was adamant that he should be treated as innocent until proved otherwise and not forced into any form of self-incrimination. In 1726 he protested to a committee studying complaints against him that it had no right to ask him to reveal his private thoughts. He further suggested that allegations could be proved only by two or three witnesses, as demanded by the Church of Scotland's rules, and that for the church to do otherwise was "contrary to the *Claim of Right*, and Privileges of every free-born Subject in the Kingdom, and was one of the oppressive Methods made use of before the late happy *Revolution*, against which we are secured by the said *Claim of Right*. It is also manifest, that the Method of Inquisition is one of the most mischievous Engines of Popery."45

Simson pointed out that the General Assembly had told its committee to use all proper ways of inquiry in its investigations. He then inquired what, if any, proper means there could be other than those "contained in the *Form of Process* [the church's disciplinary rules], which are framed according to the Rules of the Gospel, to common Equity, to our Protestant Principles, and to our Civil Rights and Privileges, as free Subjects."46 Simson's references to civil privileges struck a sympathetic chord in Scottish society, which proved open to free discussion of the issues raised in his cases. The publication of statements from the principals in these affairs and of propaganda from both sides, despite occasional disapproval from the ecclesiastical authorities, indicates that Scots were prepared to tolerate and even encourage public debate on religious and legal matters. Opinion was unquestionably divided, but everyone agreed that both sides had the right to the unconstrained expression of their arguments.

44 Dundas, *Processes*, 87.
45 Simson, *Libel*, 29.
46 Ibid., 30.

In spite of the frequent references to civil rights, the Simson cases also show how the enterprising use of government patronage could lead to educational improvement and religious liberation. After the 1715 rising, the ruling parties gradually learned the necessity of promoting men of moderation and intelligence who could implement government policy in Scotland. The policies carried out by Walpole and Islay, a man of culture with a particular regard for scientific investigation, included the provision of chairs, livings, and administrative posts for deserving candidates. Between about 1725 and 1733 the traditional support given by the Argyll family to the Covenanters and their heirs came under Islay's scrutiny. He grew to appreciate that the intransigence of such men made them inadequate administrative instruments – a view that the rhetoric of Simson's second case intensified. As a result, Islay began to promote more progressive scholars and ministers. His patronage nourished the conditions for Enlightenment in Scotland and protected men such as Simson. Islay could do this because Simson himself, and his supporters, were good Calvinists, who saw their task as an internal reform of some of the more antiquated aspects of the established church and Presbyterian society.

Part One   Simson, Glasgow, and Calvinism

3

My Great Unfitness for Discharging such ane Office Aright: John Simson and Glasgow University

I follow the career of John Simson in a roughly chronological manner, diverging only to review the relevant background material on the theological and political developments. The evidence presented in his cases clarifies Simson's religious opinions as well as the fears and prejudices of his opponents. By Simson's death in 1740, the intellectual atmosphere in the Church of Scotland had changed dramatically. Simson's ordeals had created an environment in which all the conditions necessary for Enlightenment were present.

Political realities influenced many of the events of John Simson's life, in spite of the confidence that he derived from a lineage of impeccable Presbyterian orthodoxy. Since the Reformation Simson men had been ministers, starting with Andrew (c. 1525–c. 1590), a schoolmaster who was ordained to the parish of Dunbar. Of Andrew's seven sons, six became ministers, while the seventh was a regent in Glasgow University; his three daughters all married ministers. John's father, Patrick (1628–1715), minister of Renfrew, was the grandson of Andrew's eldest son. After his father's early death in 1642, Patrick was educated partly by his cousin, George Gillespie, the son of Lilias Simson, and her husband, Rev. John Gillespie. For a few years during the Commonwealth, he was employed at Inveraray as chaplain and tutor to the family of Archibald Campbell, Marquis of Argyll (1607–1661), the most powerful magnate in the west of Scotland. A fellow resident at Inveraray was David Dickson (c. 1583–1663), professor of divinity at Glasgow University (1640–50), to whom Patrick acted as secretary in the production of the popular spiritual guide *The Sum of Saving Knowledge*.

In 1653 Patrick was ordained to the parish of Renfrew, where he married Elizabeth Hay, daughter of his deposed Episcopal predecessor. The marriage of their daughter Agnes to John Simson of Kirktonhall, a Glasgow merchant, produced Robert Simson (1687–1768), later professor of mathematics at Glasgow University, Patrick (1694–1773), John's father, and Thomas Simson (1696–1764), first professor of medicine at St Andrews University.[1]

With the return of the Stuarts in 1660, life became difficult for the Simson family. After the execution of his patron Argyll in 1661, Patrick refused to celebrate the King's birthday, citing a typically Scottish Presbyterian argument, possible only in a country where the observance of Christmas was seen as papist superstition: "When I keep Christ's birthday, I shall think of keeping the king's birthday."[2] Patrick's ejection from his pulpit in 1663 for refusing to accept prelacy was not surprising, given his intimate connections with Presbyterian theologians and politicians and his willingness to voice such opinions. Like his stiff-necked son later, he believed in his own rectitude.

The next years seem to have been peripatetic for the Simson family. Nevertheless, Patrick remarried in 1664, his first wife having died before his extrusion. His bride was Janet Peadie, daughter of a Glasgow merchant and widow of another Glasgow merchant, Robert Cullen. Their son John Simson was born on 13 July 1667 at Camperstown, near Glasgow. Other surviving children of this marriage included Rev. Matthew (1673–1756), who was a close ally of his brother in his vicissitudes, and Anna (1674–1760), who married Rev. John Paisley (1658–1728), the Squadrone-connected minister of Lochwinnoch.[3] These links with aristocratic, clerical, and commercial circles in the Glasgow area gave John Simson the relationships which were essential for an ambitious young man in eighteenth-century society.

Patrick complied with government demands after the second Act of Indulgence in 1672, serving as minister at Kilmacolm, but suffered extrusion again in 1679 after being detected preaching at conventicles. He probably returned to Renfrew after the Indulgence of 1687 (he was formally restored in 1690); he remained there until his death in 1715. He refused a call to a Glasgow parish shortly after his resettlement at

1 Details about the Simson family can be found in Couper, "The Levitical Family of Simson, II," and in records from a Simson family Bible published privately in Heath, *Records*. For further information about Patrick Simson see Warrick, *Moderators*, 71–91.

2 Warrick, *Moderators*, 74.

3 Wodrow, *Anal.*, 3:496.

Renfrew but kept a friendly association with gown and town, serving as dean of faculty to the University of Glasgow in the 1690s under Principal William Dunlop[4] and being admitted in 1691 a burgess of Glasgow by the town council, allegedly because of his marriage to the daughter of a merchant and "gild brother."[5] His interest in becoming a burgess may have been motivated by the existence of the position of bibliothecary, or librarian, of Glasgow University, for which only sons of burgesses were eligible.

In 1695 Patrick Simson was elected moderator of the General Assembly, an honour awarded to ecclesiastical leaders thoroughly trusted by the somewhat-insecure governments of the 1690s. This assembly is remembered for its decision to establish a school, supported by public financing, in every parish in the country. Patrick Simson showed himself a man of his time in other ways besides his Whiggism and his interest in education. In the 1690s he gave spiritual assistance to witches about to be burned at the stake in the Renfrew area. He preached sermons for the condemned, prayed with them on their last evenings, and attended their executions. None the less he was known for his scholarship and was asked for his views on such matters as what constituted a legal call to a minister. In 1709 he gave advice on the legalities involved in a disputed call to Inchennan, concluding with the sensible suggestion that if neither the elders nor the property-owners in the parish would support the other's nominee, then "both parties would be advised to fall upon some other fit choice, wherein they will all agree."[6]

John and Matthew Simson considered their father their natural adviser in theological matters because of his knowledge of the seventeenth-century church and its great figures. Patrick guided them in stating their reservations about the wording of the Westminster Confession of Faith to the presbytery of Paisley when they were seeking their licences as probationers.[7] Robert Wodrow also considered Patrick a valuable source of information about Scots religious traditions for his *History of the Sufferings of the Church of Scotland from the Restoration to the Revolution*. In 1710 he was surprised to hear Patrick say the Lord's Prayer at a Communion service. Although the prayer had been largely abandoned in Scottish public worship because of Presbyterian disapproval of service books and set forms

4 See J. Wodrow to J. Stirling, 8 Sept. 1701, and P. Simson to J. Stirling, 1701, GUL, MS Murray 204/16,17. See also Warrick, *Moderators*, 79.

5 Scottish Burgh Records Society (SBRS), *Extracts*, 10.

6 *Edinburgh Christian Instructor*, 27 (1828): 684.

7 See below, page 34.

of devotion, Patrick considered that it should be used, not abused. Observing that Christ's name was correctly given to three things – the Lord's Day, the Lord's Supper, and the Lord's Prayer – Patrick reminisced about David Dickson's 1652 comment that all Christians shared three doctrines: the Ten Commandments, the Apostle's Creed, and the Lord's Prayer.[8] Here as elsewhere, Patrick Simson remained close to the principles of Calvin and the early Reformers in his belief in the underlying unity of the Christian world, deep though its doctrinal and ecclesiological divisions might be. He seems to have communicated to his son a belief in the sufficiency of Reformation doctrine and a distaste for later Calvinist scholasticism.

Patrick Simson's relationship with an earlier generation of Scots divines, and his willingness to swim against the current of the times, may well have had a lasting influence on the conduct of his son. John Simson quoted family recollections about the proceedings of the Westminster Assembly in the 1640s in his correspondence with Robert Rowan. Patrick clearly encouraged his sons to think independently about the scriptural basis of their faith and to be prepared to use common Christian forms which were out of favour among contemporary Presbyterians. His Glasgow colleagues must have become aware of Patrick's views during his years as dean of faculty and have appreciated that his son shared some of them. Since John Simson was a mature man when he became professor, it would have been common knowledge that he had also inherited his father's truculence and unbending temperament.

JOHN SIMSON'S EARLY CAREER

Simson's boyhood cannot have been easy. Apart from his father's tribulations as a result of his opposition to prelacy, he appears to have suffered from ill-health throughout much of his life. During the proceedings against him in the late 1720s, his physical condition rendered him *hors de combat* for critical periods. These problems have been suggested as an explanation for the gaps in our knowledge of his life. The weakness which kept John at home as an adolescent would have reinforced his father's influence as role model and teacher.

Either because his health improved, or because of changed political circumstances, Simson entered Edinburgh University in 1687 or 1688 and graduated as master of arts at the mature age of twenty-five in 1692.[9]

8 Wodrow, *Analecta*, 1:287, 296–7.
9 University of Edinburgh, *Catalogue*, 142.

As far as is known, this was his first academic experience, although he was considerably older than the average student. Along with his brother, Matthew, John proceeded to study theology under Professor James Wodrow (1637–1707) at Glasgow University, where he appeared on the divinity rolls in February 1694.[10]

While a student at Glasgow, John Simson served as the university's bibliothecary. This office was held by a theology student for a four-year term, as a form of bursary for the sons of Glasgow burgesses under the Hutcheson bequest.[11] The presentation was made alternately by the town council and by the university. According to the burgh records, Simson was appointed by the magistrates in 1695, the principal and masters of the "Town College" having testified to his "prudent and pious behaviour and of his fittedness for the said office."[12] There are, however, documents in the Glasgow University Archives which suggest that Simson was already acting as "Bibliothecary & Quaestor" in 1693 and 1694, perhaps through the sponsorship of his father, the dean of faculty.[13] The Glasgow burgh records later cited the case of Simson as a precedent for one man's holding the office of library keeper for eight years.[14] Simson appears to have taken over the office from David Ewing in the middle of his term, being reappointed in 1695, when Ewing's four years would have ended. He probably resigned two or three years later to obtain his licence as a preacher.[15] As quaestor, Simson was responsible for minor financial duties such as collecting students' fees. He must have been considered a sensible and trustworthy young man by his teachers and peers.

In September 1696, the Presbytery of Glasgow and the University of Glasgow jointly issued a Latin testimonial of academic ability and moral worth to three men about to study abroad: John Simson, Alexander Wodrow, and John Hamilton.[16] Alexander, Professor James Wodrow's

10 *Munimenta*, 3:242.

11 This word is variously spelled bibliothecar, bibliothecare, bibliothecary, and bibliothecarius. The office was created by Thomas Hutcheson in 1641 "for ordoring, preserving and enlargeing of the common Bibliothec of the said Universitie ... [and] for the maintenance of ane qualifiet Student, being ane Maister of Airts, and ane Burges sone of the name of Hutchesoun ... quhilk failzeand, ane Burges sone of any uther name." Quoted in Hoare, "Librarians," 27–8.

12 SBRS, *Extracts*, 177.

13 Two receipts given by William Dunlop to John Simson, 8 Dec., 1693 and 22 Jan., 1694, GUA 58201. Simson also signed a document as bibliothecary in April 1696; *Munimenta*, 1:446.

14 Renwich, *Extracts*, 446.

15 Hoare, "Librarians," 31, 40.

16 GUA, 30329.

son, was expected to inherit his father's chair, but he died prematurely in 1706; John Hamilton later became Simson's colleague in the Glasgow presbytery and a bitter opponent of his teaching in the 1720s. Simson claimed to have studied at Leiden under Professor Marck, usually referred to by his Latin name of Marckius.[17] The fact that Simson's name does not appear on the matriculation lists at Leiden may be explained by the frequent neglect of this formality by students, although a Matthew Simson is listed in 1699.[18]

After a year abroad, Simson obtained his licence to preach on 13 July 1698 from the Presbytery of Paisley. Candidates subscribed the Confession of Faith according to a formula agreed on by the General Assembly of 1694, declaring the doctrine contained in it to be true and promising to uphold presbyterian church government, worship, and ordinances. A more detailed formula, ratified by the assembly of 1711, demanded that the subscriber "believe the whole doctrine contained in the *Confession of Faith* ... to be the truths of God," as well as accepting it as his own faith. It also required that the subscriber swear to "follow no divisive course from the present establishment in this church; renouncing all doctrines, tenets and opinions ... inconsistent with, the said doctrine, worship, discipline or government of this church."[19] Simson was never required to sign the 1711 formula, with which he might have had difficulty. In 1712 he explained to Robert Rowan that he, and some other ministers and probationers, had had "scruples" about some of the phraseology of the Westminster Confession. His reservations had been allowed by the Presbytery of Paisley. He remained convinced that a work of human devising could be improved, writing to his friend, "Now this Liberty of making our Confession more exact and perfect, the Presbytry of *Paisly* did expresly reserve in their *formula* prefixed to their Names, the draught of which my Father had the charge of."[20]

Almost immediately after being licensed in July 1698, Simson sailed again for Holland as tutor to the eighteen-year-old grandson of the Earl

---

17 Professor Johannes a Marck (1656–1731) of Leyden wrote the *Compendium Theologiæ didactico-elenticum*, which was in its second edition by 1690. The condensed version used by Simson with his students, the *Christianæ Theologiæ medulla, didactico-elantica ex majore opera secundum eius capitae et paragraphos expressa in usos primos Academicæ Juventutis*, was being printed in Amsterdam in an "editio altera et emendata" by 1696. It ran into six editions in that city up to 1742 and had at least two American editions in Philadelphia in 1824–5.

18 *Dictionary of National Biography*, 18:285.

19 [Dunlop], *Preface to the Westminster Confession*, 67–8.

20 Webster, ed., *True Copy*, 7.

of Eglintoun, John Montgomerie of Giffen, who had been listed as a student at Glasgow in 1694 and so would have just completed his studies. Serving as tutor to a young nobleman was part of the normal career path of a preacher before being considered experienced enough for parish ministry. This time, Simson's destination was the University of Utrecht, where his pupil spent two academic years, before travelling slowly back to Scotland via Flanders, France, and England.

Returning to Scotland in 1700, Simson served as assistant to his "aged and infirm" father in Renfrew.[21] Finally, in July 1705, he received a unanimous call to the parish of Troqueer, Kirkcudbrightshire, in the Presbytery of Dumfries, where he was ordained on 20 September, about the same time that Matthew was ordained to Pencaitland, in the Presbytery of Haddington. Pencaitland was under Hamilton influence, and the conditions of Matthew's call tell us something about patronage politics and the patrons other than Argyll to whom this family looked. Robert Maxwell wrote to Wodrow in February 1705 that James Hamilton, Lord Pencaitland, wished Matthew to be appointed, but the Duchess of Hamilton, a forceful woman whom her clansman would not wish to alienate, was manoeuvring to obtain the benefice for "Mr. G. Crafurd." Pencaitland was said to be "a deal better pleased with Mr. Simson, but to avoid offending her Grace, would rather it should stop by the paroches denying their consent than by his own refusal."[22] Maxwell noted that the parish elders were not unanimous about a call to Matthew Simson. Moreover, someone had anonymously informed the presbytery that the young man had Episcopal tendencies. In the end Matthew received the call to Pencaitland. Owing his ordination to Hamilton influence, he could be expected later to follow the Hamilton family's political views, which tended to be pro-Squadrone.

No information about John Simson's activities at Troqueer seems to have survived. However, in later years he is known to have returned to the area to visit friends, even after his orthodoxy was on trial, so he was clearly liked and trusted there.[23] About 1728 his ailing successor, the Rev. John Bowie, asked him to recommend a preacher to act as his assistant, a request which would have been inconceivable had Simson been

21 Heath, *Records*, 115.

22 This may have been George Crawford (?–1730), who was licensed by the Presbytery of Hamilton in 1704 and ordained to Symington in 1709. R. Maxwell to R. Wodrow, 10 Feb. 1705, Maidment, ed., *Analecta Scotica*, 1:240.

23 See for example, T. Mack to R. Wodrow, 18 Oct. 1727, NLS, Wodrow Letters Quarto, XVII, 351r.

seen locally as a propagator of heresy. Since the religious tendencies of the Scottish southwest were fervently orthodox Presbyterian, Simson must have appeared sound in the opinion of his Troqueer acquaintances.[24] Only one hint of deviation on Simson's part from the sternest Calvinist principles emanated from this area. Rev. Thomas Mack of Terregles (c. 1675–1750) reported in a letter of 1728 to Robert Wodrow, "[H]e was a known Baxterian in point of justification I myself can be a voucher of it the first time th[a]t ever I heard him preach at Traqueir."[25] Mack had been a divinity student at Glasgow University while Simson was there. He was ordained to Terregles in 1707 so was briefly a colleague of Simson in the Presbytery of Dumfries. Since there is no record of Mack, a voluble opponent of Simson in the 1720s, complaining about this twenty years earlier, his perceptions may owe something to hindsight. It can be assumed that Simson preached in acceptable language and performed his pastoral duties in an exemplary fashion, since no objection was raised to his performance as a minister, either then or later.

The favourable impression which Simson made on his contemporaries, both in the southwest and around the Clyde, led three years later in 1708 to the offer of the chair of divinity at Glasgow University. The faculty of the university, however, did not rush to make an appointment. Professor Wodrow died on 25 September 1707, but it was not until the next spring that a decision on his successor was reached. The delay may have been the result of an attempt made during the winter by Principal John Stirling (1654–1727, principal 1701–27) of Glasgow to induce Principal James Hadow (1670–1747) of St Mary's College, St Andrews, to take the vacant chair. A letter of March 1708 from Hadow hints that he would accept this offer if Stirling could ensure the appointment of a Squadrone supporter to his position at St Andrews.

Once these negotiations fell through, there is no evidence in the faculty minutes of any opposition to the election of Simson.[26] On the contrary, Daniel Williams, an English dissenting minister with ties to Glasgow

---

24 See letter from J. Simson to Ld. Milton, 9 Feb. 1732. "At his desire I sent him near four years since one of the best young preachers I could find here to be his assistant." NLS, MS 16551/77–8. Simson was interceding (unsuccessfully) with Milton for the presentation of the now-vacant parish to go to this preacher, James Ritchie. When another man was presented, there were serious disturbances in the parish, where Ritchie had become popular. Hew Scott, *Fasti*, 2:303.

25 T. Mack to R. Wodrow, 10 March 1728, NLS, Wodrow Letters Quarto, XVIII, 196–7.

26 J. Hadow to J. Stirling, 16 March 1708, GUL, MS Gen. 205:95.

University, commented to Stirling in May, "I am glad you are so satisfied in a professor of Divinity."[27] If the faculty had considered for the chair James Hadow, a man of impeccable orthodoxy who had been the divinity professor at St Mary's before his appointment as principal, it is highly unlikely that it would have picked as second choice a minister whose doctrinal soundness had been questioned. In 1708 Stirling had been principal of the college for seven years. During his quarter-century at Glasgow, he was responsible for considerable growth in both the faculty and the student body. Although he was a man who aroused antagonism among his colleagues, he worked unremittingly to raise the standards of the university and to obtain funding for the foundation of new chairs. He would never knowingly have allowed an appointment which could jeopardize his work.

On 10 April 1708, Rector Sir John Maxwell of Nether Pollock, Principal Stirling, Dean of Faculty the Rev. Mr James Brown, Regents Mr Gershom Carmichael, Mr Alexander Dunlop, Mr John Law, Mr John Loudoun, and Mr Andrew Rosse unanimously voted to elect Simson. According to the minutes: "The Faculty considering that the Profession of Theology has been for some time vacant and that all concern'd hath had sufficient time to think of a fit person to supply that post Did Judge it now necessary to proceed to the Election of one to be a professor of Theology. And Therefore Did and hereby Doe Nominate and Elect the Reverend Mr John Simsone Minister of Traqueir in the Presbyterie of Drumfreis to be professor of Theology in this university and to bruik [have the use of] and enjoy all the privileges and Emoluments belonging to his predecessors in that office upon his acceptance of the Universities Call and his admission following thereupon."[28] The professor of mathematics, Dr Robert Sinclair, who had not been present at the meeting, was appointed to go to the Presbytery of Dumfries to request the release of Simson from his parish.

In response to the university, Simson showed proper hesitancy, writing to Stirling, "From the knowledge I have of your temper and my own by a long uninterrupted friendship, I have reason to expect, that throu the Lord's Blessing, we might live in as perfect friendship tender sympathie as both of us have done with our only Brother; which wold make the mater very easie to me were it the only thing in view. But at first sight my great unfitness for discharging such ane office aright, the closs

27 D. Williams to J. Stirling, 20 May 1708, ibid., MS Gen. 206:66.
28 GUA 26632, 49.

tye to my poor people, the love & concern I have for them ... appear to be difficulties that cannot be easily if at all surmounted. I do therefore entreat you may make another choice."[29] Despite this reluctance, Simson's appointment went smoothly. The commission of the General Assembly agreed to Simson's transportation on 7 July, although his formal admission did not take place until 10 November 1708.[30] The new professor produced an extract from the records of the Presbytery of Glasgow in proof that he had "qualify'd himself before the said Presbyterie," in conformity with the law demanding subscription to the Westminster Confession of Faith. A magistrate, John Alexander of Blackhouse, was present to administer the oath of allegiance to the Queen, which Simson swore and signed in front of the faculty members.[31] The faculty allowed him five hundred merks (one merk equalled 13/4 Scots, but only 13½d. Sterling), for moving expenses, as well as the latter half of the year's salary as professor, since he had lost six months' stipend from Troqueer.

GLASGOW AND ITS UNIVERSITY

When Simson moved into his Glasgow University house that November, he was familiar with the town in which he was to spend the rest of his life. The years spent in his father's parish of Renfrew and in his divinity studies ensured that he knew both the university faculty and the ministers of the presbytery, while his maternal relations gave him connections to the local business community.

Scotland's return to Presbyterian church government in 1690 had freed Glasgow from the grip of the archbishop as feudal superior, allowing the council to choose its own magistrates. The result was a governing mercantile élite which was not democratic but which represented the interests of the town with vigour and determination.[32] Glasgow's burgh records present a picture of a forward-looking town willing to incur debt to finance new churches or wharfs for the religious and economic well-being of its citizens.

29 J. Simson to J. Stirling, 19 April 1708, GUL, MS Gen. 205, 98.
30 GUA 26632, 50–1. "Transportation" was the normal word ("translation" was a possible alternative) used in eighteenth-century Scotland for the formal movement of a minister from one parish to another or from a parish to a chair.
31 Ibid., 50.
32 See Jackson, "Glasgow in Transition," 65–8.

In 1701, when the burgh council decided that a sixth clergyman was necessary to minister to the spiritual health of the population, there were 9,994 "examinable persons," those old enough to be catechized.[33] According to a town census, in 1708 Glasgow had a population of 12,766, many of whom were anxious to create a centre of local industry and of trade to the New World.[34] The manufacture of beer, glass, iron, rum, soap, sugar, and textiles was an important element in the local economy. Daniel Campbell and his fellow merchants were learning that there was money to be made in the tobacco trade.[35] Glasgow's provosts and magistrates were generally men, like Simson's Peadie relatives, who were active in the town's commerce.[36] T.C. Smout's analysis of the differences in the class structure of Edinburgh and of Glasgow late in the eighteenth century indicates that in the capital one in three entrants in the street directory was a professional man and one in eight a businessman, while in Glasgow these proportions were reversed.[37] The situation cannot have been too different in the first quarter of the century. Inevitably this preponderance of manufacturers, tradespeople, and merchants influenced the development of the college as well as of the town.

The pivotal role of Presbyterian piety in this mercantile community meant that English dissenters such as Rev. Daniel Williams in London promoted Glasgow University as a suitable training ground for ministers, whereas they recommended Edinburgh University to upper-class fathers, since their sons could benefit from the genteel society of the capital. In 1709 Williams explained this perception to Principal Stirling, adding that "I declare to all that Glasgo is the fittest place to educate ministers."[38] Strong ties connected the local worlds of trade, church, and university during the period. Clergymen such as Patrick Simson married the daughters and widows of prosperous merchants and served as deans of faculty to the university; ministers such as Principal William Dunlop acted in partnership with local landowners and merchants to set up industries;[39] town ministers and university professors were frequently

33 SBRS, *Extracts*, 327–8.
34 Eyre-Todd, *History of Glasgow*, 3:74.
35 See Price, "Glasgow."
36 Jackson, "Glagow in Transition," 80–1.
37 Smout, *History*, 357–8.
38 D. Williams to J. Stirling, 4 Sept. 1709, GUL, MS Gen. 206/82.

39 In 1699 Dunlop and others applied to the Privy Council for privileges in setting up a woollen mill in Glasgow. Earlier Dunlop had been a Darien investor. Eyre-Todd, *History of Glasgow*, 3:75.

granted burgess rights.[40] The university as a landlord was in constant negotiation with the townsfolk over leases, rents, and the collection of teinds (tenths, or tithes). Walls, gardens, and causeways all required attention by the faculty.

The importance of the university to the growing town of Glasgow was economic as well as educational. When, during the early eighteenth century, dissension troubled both the faculty and the student body, it was in the interests of the town to co-operate in restoring calm in order to ensure the permanent flow of new students, with their financial contributions to the town's coffers. Then, as now, the income derived from the student body was a valuable addition to a town's revenues. The total revenue of the university as reported to the commission of visitation in 1696 was over £12,000 (Scots), while the expenses incurred were nearly £2,000. Since some five years later the annual income of the town council was just over £20,000, the university's contribution to the economy was significant.

Even poor boys, who arrived with as much food as they could carry from home, spent money in the community. In 1712, rents ranged from 10s. sterling per session for the best rooms in the college to 4s. for the least desirable. At that date Principal Stirling was arranging board (three daily meals "with meat and drink") and lodging within the university for English students, who were to pay £3 sterling each three months.[41]

Better-born and better-off boys arrived at college with a governor (the role that Simson had played for John Montgomerie) and a servant, so the population increased even more than the college enrolment lists suggest. In 1727 Alexander Dunlop, professor of Greek, wrote to Andrew Fletcher, Lord Milton, that Lord Hume was to be lodged at "Mr Harveys" for three months: "His Board is 6£ st: and his brothers as much, and his servants the half, Including washing and every thing else as well as dyet."[42] Other sons of gentry also lodged comfortably in the homes of professors. Neil Campbell (1678–1761, principal 1728–61) replied to an inquiry from Lord Milton in 1737: "The Expence of Students at the

---

40 For examples, see SBRS, *Extracts*, 418, 501.

41 Coutts, *History*, 176.

42 Andrew Fletcher, Lord Milton (1692–1766), was admitted to the bar in 1717 and appointed to the Court of Session in 1724. Astute and knowledgeable, he was the Earl of Islay's right hand man in Scotland from the mid-1720s on. A. Dunlop to [Ld. Milton], 29 Sept. 1727, NLS, MS 16536, f.78.

College is much according to their Character, & places where they lodge, in the professors house the boarding is pretty high. I'm informed that Sr John Anstruthers son payed at Mr Dunlops for himself Govr & servant 40£ from the 20th of Octbr to the 20th of May & 50 for his last year. Mr Dick had a student from England much in the same Design Your Friend has in view, he payed 20£ a quarter but in the ordinary boarding houses in the Town they pay but 5£ a quarter. Gentlemen of Distinction give the professors 3 Ginneyes, & the other College Dues may be payed w[i]t[h] one."[43]

Glasgow had long housed its principal and professor of divinity in the college. In the 1720s, financing was arranged for the construction of a new professors' court to accommodate the expanding faculty. These conveniently located buildings provided an extra source of income for the masters, as Campbell's letter illustrates. They were thus inducements to prospective professors and offered powerful economic incentives for current professors to remain at Glasgow. The houses were part of the emoluments which were seen as lifetime possessions of the holders of these positions.

The upkeep of the university facilities employed tradesmen from gardeners to glaziers. Indoor and outdoor servants looked after professors and students alike. Brewers and tavern keepers supplied sustenance and meeting space for clubs and other social gatherings. Shrewd business-men must have been conscious of the economic value of a successful educational establishment in their midst, since even more other-worldly clerics such as Robert Wodrow thought that the college and town should strive to attract students from afar. In 1710 Edinburgh's university sent a Mr McKean to the Dissenters in England to discuss proposals for the education of their sons at the university. Wodrow was mildly critical of Glasgow for merely writing, rather than sending a personal emissary who might have been as persuasive as McKean had been.[44]

The accusations that surfaced in the mid-1710s against John Simson could have put the reputation of Glasgow's university at risk, affecting the pockets of many who had little understanding of the issues in-volved. At the same time, the growing mercantile prosperity of the citi-zens gave them the confidence to criticize hide-bound ideas in church or government. Both these facts led to divisions of opinion in Glasgow as elsewhere in the country over Simson's divinity teaching.

43 N. Campbell to Ld. Milton, 19 August 1737. NLS, MS 16569, f.225.
44 Wodrow, *Analecta*, 1:236–7.

As professor of divinity, Simson was *ex officio* a member of the Presbytery of Glasgow, as was Principal Stirling. In 1708 there were seventeen parishes in the town and surrounding communities, which comprised the presbytery. The ministers of these churches, along with lay ruling elders from the kirk sessions, met monthly to conduct disciplinary and administrative business for the presbytery. Stirling and Simson played an active role in the affairs of the church; meetings of committees often took place at the principal's or professor's lodgings. Stirling was frequently chosen to represent the presbytery at the General Assembly; Simson proposed his students for their trials for licensing as probationary preachers. During the first fifteen years of Simson's Glasgow career, there is no hint of disagreement between him and his clerical brethren in the town, perhaps because all were supporters of the Squadrone Volante.

As a member of a presbytery in a society with theocratic tendencies, Simson soon became involved in burgh affairs. The town of Glasgow was not a monolithic electoral bloc; its factional loyalties were complicated and shifting. Graham (Montrose), Hamilton, and Campbell (Argyll) interests vied for ascendancy in burgh politics. Throughout Simson's years in Glasgow, neutral pamphleteers deplored the ill effects of factional hostility on religious and legal affairs, calling vainly for town and church to put aside party loyalty in the interests of civic improvement.[45] Town, church, and university were politically connected; Glasgow merchants were ruling elders in the church sessions; professors and ministers were unabashed factional partisans when their personal and professional futures were at stake. The principals of Glasgow University and their professor of divinity seem to have been either unprepared to abandon party, or sensible that nothing could be accomplished without it.

Both university and burgh were on the threshold of a period of expansion in new directions. In the first decade of the eighteenth century, Principal Carstares of Edinburgh University led the group of Scots academics who wished to reorganize the Scottish church and universities on modern Dutch models.[46] His brother-in-law and cousin William Dunlop (1654–1700) had been principal at Glasgow from 1690 till his death. John Stirling, who succeeded Dunlop, was also connected to

45 See *A Seasonable Advice.*
46 See Dunlop, *William Carstares*, 82, 120.

Carstares through his Dunlop mother. All three men worked to renew their institutions and to enhance educational opportunities for Scots youths. Royal grants, principally from the revenues of the bishoprics of Glasgow and Galloway, paid for the salaries of the Glasgow faculty members and for the maintenance of the buildings. These revenues proved inadequate, and Dunlop had negotiated a grant from the teinds (tithes) of the Archbishopric of Glasgow in 1698. Dunlop, and later Stirling, directed much of their energy to ensuring the continuation of financial aid to the university, which grew from around 150 students before 1688 to 400 in 1702.[47]

Stirling seems to have been thoroughly unpopular towards the end of his life. A lampoonist ridiculed, "Others to some faint meaning make pretence / But Stirling never deviates into sense."[48] Contemporaries accused him (probably unfairly) of financial peculation, and historians have criticized him as a man who fomented faction within his faculty.[49] It is clear, however, that Stirling sought to improve the quality of teaching and to increase the number of instructors. He worked tirelessly to obtain grants to support new chairs and to raise the standards of his institution.[50]

When Simson arrived in 1708, he joined an academic staff comprising the principal, the professor of divinity, Regents Gershom Carmichael, John Law, and John Loudoun, Professor of Mathematics Robert Sinclair, Professor of Greek Alexander Dunlop, Professor of Humanity (i.e., Latin) Andrew Rosse, and a semi-official lecturer on civil and ecclesiastical history, William Jameson, who had no voting rights or administrative duties. In 1708 a chair of Oriental languages was established, so that once more the study of Hebrew and other biblical tongues could be a serious part of the education of theologues.[51] The fact that its first holder, Charles Morthland, was forced to go immediately to the Netherlands to improve his knowledge of the languages which he had been appointed to teach may indicate the need for such instruction in Scottish universities or merely underline the fact that his appointment was the result of patronage.

47 Coutts, *History*, 173.
48 Quoted in Warrick, *Moderators*, 204.
49 See John Anderson's accusations in "Pamphlet," 1717, in GUL 2883; and see those of John Smith in 1722, in GUL, Mu 21–d.25. See also Coutts, *History*, 185.
50 For example, see Cairns, "Origins," on his efforts at creating the law chair.
51 GUA 26632, 52, 59.

During Stirling's principalship, the faculty was further augmented by a professor of medicine, John Johnstoun (appointed 1713), a professor of civil law, William Forbes (1714), a professor of botany and anatomy, Thomas Brisbane (c. 1720), and a professor of civil and ecclesiastical history, William Anderson (1721). Robert Simson replaced Sinclair as professor of mathematics in 1711, and Robert Dick succeeded John Law in 1714. The nepotism involved in some of these appointments may have contributed to the ill-feeling against Stirling. Dunlop was a son of Principal Dunlop, Robert Simson was John's nephew, and Dick was related by marriage to both Stirling and Simson.

Regents continued to take their student groups through the three years of the philosophy curriculum, but all other subjects were taught by specialists. During Stirling's principalship the challenging instruction provided by Gershom Carmichael in philosophy, and by Robert Simson in mathematics, meant that Glasgow students were exposed to Newtonian physics and the latest metaphysical and moral thought. "Grotius, Pufendorf, or Locke" formed part of the regular intellectual fare for Glasgow students in Carmichael's classes in the first quarter of the eighteenth century.[52] In 1715 an English student, Jonathan Woodworth, wrote that Carmichael followed Locke in much of his teaching of logic, while "[i]n Ethics he reads *Puffendorff* de officio hominis & civis, with his own theses. He often differs from Puffendorff."[53] Woodworth called Carmichael "the best Philosopher here" and spoke of his physics classes, where modern authors discussed included Derham, LeClerc, Keil, and Whiston.[54] A few years later James Arbuckle commented in verse on the natural and moral philosophy courses of his day. "Virtuous youth" sought out new knowledge, "tracing Nature to her hidden Springs," surveying the motions of the "rolling Orbs above," and considering "How

52 James Arbuckle, an Irish student of Carmichael's just before 1720, wrote of his Glasgow studies: "In which sad Game their Heads they knock – On Grotius, Pufendorf, or Locke." Quoted by M.A. Stewart in "John Smith," 99.

53 Bromley, "Correspondence," 25. I thank Professor M.A. Stewart and Jonathan Westaway, "Scottish Influences," for bringing this correspondence to my attention.

54 John LeClerc (1657–1736) was a Genevan theologian whose Arminian views led to his studying at Saumur and then becoming a Remonstrant professor in Amsterdam. He wrote extensively on religious and philosophical topics. The Oxford lectures of Edinburgh mathematician John Keil (1671–1721, professor of astronomy, Oxford, 1712) on Newtonian physics were published in 1701 as *Introductio ad veram physicam*. William Whiston, *Praelectiones astronomicae*, 1711. William Derham (1657–1735), *Physico-Theology*, 1713, and *Astro-Theology*, 1714.

laws their Force and Sanctity obtain, / How far they reach, and what they should restrain. / Whence flow the Rules the Good and Just obey, / And how themselves all Virtue's Arts repay."[55] Carmichael introduced his students to Newtonian physics through his use of Rohault's volume on Cartesian physics in the translation by Samuel Clarke, which contained a Newtonian commentary on the original.[56]

His colleague Robert Simson was also aware of current trends through his acquaintance with such scientists as Edmund Halley, whom he had met during his year of studies in London (1711–12). Simson based his Glasgow mathematics course on Euclidean geometry; he himself published an "improved" edition of Euclid's work. After regenting ended at Glasgow in 1727, on the recommendation of a committee of visitation, Gershom Carmichael became professor of moral philosophy, Robert Dick professor of natural philosophy, and John Loudoun professor of logic.

Throughout John Simson's years in Glasgow, members of the university faculty struggled to improve the quality of instruction offered to students. In 1709 they determined that professors must give public prelections (lectures) in order to prevent any chairs from deteriorating into sinecures.[57] In 1710 an interested observer commented on the changes, "[T]hey have, at Edinburgh, altered their method of teaching; and restrict a particular Master to a particulare study, and have public praelections, which this month they are beginning at Glasgow likewise, and bringing all things to the modell of the English and Universitys abroad. As to the method, I wish the doctrine come not in likewise."[58] Wodrow's final sentence indicates that conservative Presbyterians were already anticipating the danger of an influx of Continental innovations to Reformed dogma.

Such fears did not change the direction in which Glasgow's faculty was moving. The following year it agreed that students planning to apply for an arts degree or to proceed to the study of divinity should have

55 Arbuckle, *Glotta A Poem*, 13–14.

56 Samuel Clarke (1675–1729) had become interested in Newton's work while a student at Cambridge, where his tutor suggested that he make a Latin translation of Rohault's book, first published in 1697: *Jacobi Rohaulti Physica; Latine vertit, recensuit et ubrioribus jam annotationibus, ex illustrissimi Isaaci Newtoni Philosophia maximam partem huastis, amplificavit et ornavit S. Clarke.* By 1718, this had run into a fourth edition.

57 GUA 26632, 62.

58 Wodrow, *Analecta*, 1:236–7.

to be privately tested by the regent of the magistrand (or senior) class "on the Languages and the several parts of philosophy," before their public examinations, to ensure that their preparation was adequate.[59] The faculty was likewise prepared to strip a student of a bursary if he seemed insufficiently proficient. In 1714, one of the students proposing to study abroad for the fourth year of the King William's Mortification bursary was deemed "utterly unfit to travel abroad as a Student of Divinity" and was refused the necessary testimonials for entry into a foreign university.[60]

In August 1712, the Glasgow faculty decided to review the operational rules of the library and the teaching methods of the masters. It set up a committee consisting of Dunlop, Simson, and Stirling to prepare a new set of library regulations and required each professor "to give in to the Principal and Dean of Faculty in writing An Account of Their ways of Teaching and managing their several provinces."[61] On 2 September, the faculty approved new rules for the library and learned that all the professors except Loudoun, who was away, had given accounts of their teaching to Stirling.[62] Teaching methods were still being discussed at the faculty meeting on 16 October, when it was recorded that anyone with "Overtures with respect to the Method of Teaching" should have them in writing for the next meeting. Accordingly, at the end of that month, the philosophy course was discussed, while in November the Greek and humanity courses were approved.[63] It seems that this initiative may have been less fruitful than Stirling had hoped, since on 31 December 1716 a committee was appointed: "To make such Overtures concerning the way of teaching and the necessary qualifications of the schollars as may tend most to the advancement of learning and good order, And ... to Call for proposals from any of the Professors within the University relating to their several provinces, and Recommends it to the said professors to give in ... such proposals as may most Conduce to the advancement of usefull Learning."[64] Stirling and his teaching masters were anxious to ensure the best learning environment for their pupils, who for their part ought

59 GUA 26632, 68.
60 Ibid., 116.
61 Ibid., 88.
62 Ibid., 89–91.
63 Ibid., 96–8.
64 Ibid., 156.

to be properly prepared in order to obtain the maximum benefits from their studies.

At the same time the faculty at Glasgow was well aware that a university served more than one function. No thoughtful eighteenth-century Briton had any illusions about the role of educational institutions in the inculcation of religious doctrines and political creeds. J.C.D. Clark quotes a mid-century Whig who held that in England the Fifteen was "entirely occasioned by the wicked principles taught in our universities and schools."[65] In Scotland most professors understood their duty towards society. The faculty of Glasgow University was conscious of its responsibility to advance the Protestant cause. The principal and the professor of divinity worked in concert to keep the university steady on a course approved by Montrose, whose 1714 appointment as chancellor followed an interregnum of several years; that course was Whig, moderate, and disciplinarian. This meant keeping order and restraining dissent, whether republican or Jacobite.

Nothing is known about Simson's personal politics before his appointment at Glasgow University in 1708; thereafter, his deep involvement in the academic and ecclesiastical factions of the city is amply documented. Unfailingly, he stood on the side of authorized government and ministerial power. Two years after Simson's arrival in Glasgow, he married Jean Stirling (1691–1782), daughter of James, minister of the Barony parish, and niece of Principal Stirling, who performed the ceremony. This brought Simson further into Stirling's Squadrone-dominated orbit.

For the next fifteen years Simson faithfully supported his principal, even being castigated as "a firm and ready Assistant in all his little tyrannical Designs."[66] In an undated letter from Simson to Stirling, probably from 1708–9, he commented on faculty dissension and promised support to Stirling. He also remarked that the principal's opponents "will not offer to convene a facultie without calling Mr Brown [the Glasgow minister who was dean of faculty] & me." He seems to have already installed himself in the role of assistant to Stirling.[67] Simson invariably

65 *A Blow at the Root* (London, 1749), vi–vii, xv. Quoted in J.C.D. Clark, *English Society 1688–1832*, 151.

66 [Smith], *Short Account*, 7.

67 GUL, MS Gen. 205, 1:109.

upheld Stirling's authority in internal university matters, whether against masters or against students, as is shown by many documents and entries in the faculty minutes, including two dealing with students.[68] He showed no compassion for these boys if their errors were compounded by Jacobitism. No one could accuse the Glasgow faculty of disloyalty to the Protestant Crown.

THE ACTS OF 1712 AND SIMSON'S ATTITUDE

Simson demonstrated his determination to support legal authority early in his career at Glasgow University. In the controversy over the 1712 oath of abjuration, Simson was one of a network of prominent ministers who tried to ease the consciences of those who scrupled at the apparent support which the oath gave to the Church of England. After the Act of Union, Scots quickly became alarmed at the powerlessness of the small group of Scottish representatives in the British Parliament, especially in religious matters. The Church of Scotland was affected by political tensions with England, as were other Scottish national institutions. Worried Presbyterians believed that there was, at worst, a perverse English determination to disturb the Presbyterian Revolution Settlement or, at best, a covert intention to use unrest in the church for political ends. This feeling was bolstered by the series of bills passed by Tory interests in 1712, which had major implications for the Church of Scotland and its ministers. The acts prescribed toleration for Episcopalians, reimposed lay patronage in the selection of parish clergy, reinstated a Christmas vacation in the law courts, and called for all ministers to swear the oath of abjuration. The implied denial of the national stature of the Church of Scotland, the Erastian stigma of patronage, and the endorsement of the pagan festival of Yule distressed both secular and clerical leaders.

In the long run, the issue of patronage was the most serious of these breaches of the Act of Union, because it eventually led to secession by segments of the church. In the short run, the oath of abjuration was particularly divisive in some parishes, since, in addition to its primary purpose of denying the non-Hanoverian Stuarts' right to the British throne, it appeared to demand recognition of the claims of the Church of England, which could not be made in good faith by many Presbyterians. The oath called for the person swearing to maintain the succession as it had been settled by act of Parliament: first on the Protestant heirs of

68 GUA 26632, 81, 105.

Queen Anne and, second, failing these, on the Protestant Electress Sophia of Hanover and her heirs. The acts in question stated that the sovereign should be of the communion of the Church of England. Because of the inclusion of this reference to English acts, many Presbyterians felt that swearing the oath would imply an endorsement of the English church. One evangelical minister, Ralph Erskine (1685–1752), expressed the general feeling in a poem composed in honour of the coronation of George I:

> Redeem us, Sire, from things our country loathes,
> Subverting patronages, ranting oaths.
> Such was the woeful dubious *abjuration*,
> Which gave the clergy ground of speculation.
> Though all could freely, without laws to urge,
> Abjure the popish James, and swear to George;
>
> ...
>
> Some feared to leave their conscience in the lurch,
> And make the *kirk* swear unto the *church*.[69]

Repeated representations for the repeal or amendment of the acts proved unavailing, although the wording of the oath was altered in 1719 to allow more ministers to swear in good conscience

The contentious nature of the issue was clear even to the saintly Thomas Halyburton (1674–1712), professor of divinity at St Andrews, who commented on his deathbed: "There will be faithful ministers on both sides, and on either hand they will act according to their light sincerely."[70] Aware of the ethical dilemma which the oath presented to ministers, ecclesiastical leaders strove to keep the peace between the warring factions in the church. Thomas Boston (1676–1732) recorded that the General Assembly of 1712 was "at the very point of splitting," when Carstares managed to pour oil on troubled waters. Boston respected the arguments put forward by the principal and honoured his pacific stand, while remaining personally opposed to the oath.[71] Scots leaders such as Carstares, Professor William Hamilton of Edinburgh,

---

69 Quoted in Donald Fraser, *The Life and Diary of the Reverend Ralph Erskine*, 149–50.
70 Halyburton, *Memoirs*, 255.
71 Boston, *Memoirs*, 253.

and the lawyer Sir James Steuart assured the Glasgow University masters that the intention of the oath had not been to imply countenance of the English ecclesiastical establishment. In letters to both Simson and Stirling, Steuart suggested a possible wording for declarations which should "be sufficient to all rational men" and which rendered other scruples "groundless."[72]

In the debates about the oath of abjuration, Simson acted as most Squadrone supporters were doing, championing the aims of those who sought conciliation with English opinion and who tried to discourage demonstrations of extremism. He pressed Steuart's views on his acquaintances. To his fellow Glasgow alumnus Robert Rowan, in November 1712, he voiced the recurrent fear of Scots ecclesiastical strategists that internal division was potentially a greater danger to the security of the Presbyterian settlement than external political action: "It was at the Door which Division opened that Prelacy last entered into this Land and Church, and it is by it the Enemy hopes to get it brought in at present, and he thinks it is now wide opened by the different Opinions and Practises of Ministers about this Oath, which I think give no just Ground either to these who have taken it or refused it, for an Uncharitable Thought one of another on that account."[73] Simson's intolerance of what he considered foolishness was clear in his words to Rowan, when he called non-juring scruples mere semantics.

Because of his academic rank, Simson had not been required to sign the oath, but, had it been necessary, he should have done so, "being convinced that the Sense put upon it importing any Approbation ... of the Church of England, is contrair to the plain and common Sense and Understanding of the Express Words of the Oath." He could see no reason why, of everyone who had been asked to take the oath, only a few Scots ministers should understand it in such a sense. He was scathing about this small group, calling its interpretation "Ridiculous and Absurd." While he did not use the words "fanaticism" or "enthusiasm," that implication was clear in his letter. Since the difference between the two parties concerned merely grammar, Simson believed that it was incumbent on ministers to preach reconciliation, rather than claiming, as both sides

72 J. Steuart to J. Simson, 4 Oct. 1712, and J. Steuart to [? Stirling], 11 Oct. 1712, GUL, MS Gen. 205, 1:120–1. Steuart may have been the lord advocate, Sir James Stewart of Goodtrees (1635–1713) but was more likely his son, another James (1681–1727), who was currently solicitor-general.

73 Webster, *True Copy*, 12–13.

had, that the other had fallen into sin.[74] One can hardly blame Rowan for sounding rather insulted in his reply to Simson's letter.[75] Surely Simson was being disingenuous when he wrote back in March 1713: "I cannot conceive from whence could proceed what you Write to me anent *Censuring so highly the Non-jurants*, unless from groundless Jealousie [suspicion] and bad logick."[76]

The connections between politics, religion, and education would result in the mid-century flowering of the Scottish Enlightenment, to the seeds of which John Simson would make his contribution. During Simson's lifetime, however, the Union of 1707 had brought only problems to many Scots, especially in the relations between church and state. To politicians in Edinburgh and London, pulpits and chairs represented opportunities for patronage to be put to use by their increasingly effective political machines. The challenges faced by Simson thus illustrate some of the complexities of national life during this period. The Fifteen resulted in the deferral of a decision on James Webster's libel against Simson, since national attention perforce turned to military and political matters. In the 1720s different political pressures influenced the outcome of Simson's case, as Walpole and Islay came to exercise wider control over Scottish affairs and as Islay began to appreciate the administrative need for enlightened clergymen.

74 Ibid., 14.
75 Ibid., 30.
76 Ibid., 17.

4

I Profess myself only a Student: Simson as Teacher

THE GLASGOW DIVINITY SCHOOL

The views and methods of John Simson during his tenure of the Glasgow divinity chair were in keeping with Glasgow's trend to academic modernization. Simson assumed the direction of the divinity students with the intention of imparting a contemporary tone to his instruction. He was a mature scholar, confident in the rectitude of his own conduct and in the biblical foundation of his opinions. His teaching, the intellectual stature of his colleagues, and the expansion of the university during the period serve to disprove the sweeping denunciations of historians who saw the early eighteenth century as a stagnant period in Scotland, writing that "the University of Glasgow partook of the general lethargy of that half century."[1] Glasgow's principal and faculty met demands for wider scholarship and a broader curriculum as effectively as possible, given the existing teaching staff and limited financial resources.

Scottish universities were closely linked to the church; many of their professors were ministers, and as seminaries these institutions were expected to provide educated clergymen. The settlement of 1690 forced the universities to re-examine their educational facilities for divinity as well as for philosophy. University-trained ministers were needed to replace the ejected Episcopal clergy and to cover normal attrition in Scotland's parishes. There were also pulpits to be filled in new foundations such as Glasgow's North-West Quarter Session Church (the Ramshorn), in meeting-houses in England, in Presbyterian churches in Ireland, and in colonial settlements in America.

1 Innes, *Sketches*, 241.

The divinity professors prepared their students academically for ministry; local presbyteries upheld the standards of orthodoxy when they tested new preachers for their licences. It was thus essential that professors and presbyteries work together harmoniously. For nearly two decades, John Simson and the Presbytery of Glasgow co-operated with little friction, despite the professor's sharp tongue and propensity for using it against perceived enemies. This *modus vivendi* broke down in the mid-1720s, for reasons that are hard to determine. The professor's friends considered that the cause was a personal quarrel between Simson and one or two members of the presbytery; his enemies said that it was his propagation of heresy.

Who were the young men who came under Simson's tutelage, and how did he prepare them for their vocation? Divinity students in eighteenth-century universities varied in age from the late teens to the late twenties, in contrast to undergraduates, who might be as young as twelve or thirteen.[2] Simson himself was in his mid-twenties when he began his theological studies. To improve ministerial education, Act 10 of the General Assembly of 1711 mandated six years of attendance at divinity classes. As a result, some divinity students might have been at a university for as long as ten years. This remained the ideal rather than the norm, since students tended to move in and out of classes as their financial situations allowed.[3] When Simson's students were questioned in 1727, their ages ranged from eighteen to twenty-nine. Several noted that they attended classes only "sometimes."[4] Many were sons of the manse; others were members of the professional and merchant classes. They came largely from the west of Scotland, with a regular contingent of Irish Presbyterians and a sprinkling of English Dissenters.

As elder members of the student body at Glasgow, theologues were leaders in many areas, including rebelling against perceived injustice perpetuated by the principal and faculty. Trained to debate and to defend theses, they could mount an effective opposition to faculty

2 Most of the details about Simson's students come from their depositions in Dundas, *Processes*. The nationality of foreign students is noted in *Munimenta*.

3 On 6 January 1737, Simson and Neil Campbell wrote to Lord. Milton on behalf of a young preacher called James Allan, who was the son of Simson's cousin. They claimed that he had "been here for the last six years at the study of Divinity." NLS, MS 16551/221. Allan was born in 1713, received his MA from Edinburgh University on 12 May 1732, underwent trials and was licensed to preach on 31 August 1736. Even if he left Edinburgh before 1732, it is hard to fit in six years of divinity studies at Glasgow! Hew Scott, *Fasti*, 2:46.

4 Dundas, *Processes*, 111–34.

policy. Despite their interest in controversy, most were serious students. Young men such as the son of Andrew Tait, minister of Carmunnock, who tried to escape from his theological studies by taking the King's shilling, were the exceptions.[5] The typical divinity student was more likely to resemble the devout Jonathan Woodworth, who asked his cousin to pray "th[a]t we may be under divine protection and be Nurrished up in the words of faith, and good Doctrine."[6]

The pedagogical tradition under which John Simson had been trained stemmed from the Reformation. From John Knox on, Scots religious leaders had placed great emphasis on theological education. In 1579 a commission presented to Parliament a plan for a College of Theology at St Andrews, which stressed a full understanding of the text of the Bible, using the original languages, and gave lesser weight to systematic theology, since the texts took precedence over the mere explanations of men.[7] The perennial lack of funds prevented the plan, which called for five divinity professors, from being fully implemented at any Scottish university.

Instead reality resembled the newly established Town College of Edinburgh, where, at the end of the sixteenth century, the first principal, Robert Rollock, taught divinity and headed a total staff of four philosophy regents and one humanity regent.[8] A century later divinity was taught by a single professor at both Edinburgh and Glasgow universities, with the principal technically his senior in the profession.[9] The Reformation's stress on biblical exegesis had given way to the new importance of systemic theology, a trend that would be questioned in the eighteenth century.

We can compare the curriculum of late-seventeenth-century professors such as Gilbert Burnet and James Wodrow with that of Simson. Under

5 In 1725, Andrew Tait, Principal Stirling, and the masters of the university commenced an action to secure the release of John Tait, aged twenty, from the infantry regiment into which he had signed as a recruit. Printed petition to the Lords of Session, 20 Jan. 1725, GUA, 58013.

6 Bromley, "Correspondence," 20.

7 See Sir Alexander Grant, *Story*, 1:93. The first professor was to teach Oriental languages (Chaldean, Hebrew, and Syriac); the second, to apply these to a critical study of the historical books of the Old Testament; the third, to do the same with the prophetical books; the fourth, to compare the Greek and Syriac New Testaments; and the fifth, who would be principal, to teach systematic divinity.

8 Horn, *Short History*, 8.

9 Thus, when Simson was suspended in 1727, the task of teaching the divinity students fell to the principal.

Burnet, divinity professor at Glasgow from 1669 to 1673, the preaching and debating skills of the students were honed. His programme was a combination of lectures and student seminars, all in Latin. On Mondays the students explained a point of divinity and defended theses from it against their fellows, with Burnet as adjudicator. On Tuesdays, the professor lectured on divinity, intending to review a complete system in the space of eight years. On Wednesdays he taught the Gospels. The Thursday class alternated between comparing the Hebrew, Septuagint, Vulgate, and English versions of a psalm and reviewing the practice of the primitive church, using the Apostolic Canons as a text.[10] On Fridays, the students took turns to preach a sermon on a prescribed text, after which Burnet criticized their efforts, "shewing how the text ought to have been opened and applied."[11] Each evening Burnet read and discussed a passage of scripture with the students, examined them on the progress of their studies, and answered questions about their reading.

As well as possessing a firm grasp of Latin, students were expected to have at least some reading knowledge of Hebrew and Greek. An act of the General Assembly of 1696, directing that no one be licensed to preach without proof of proficiency in Greek and Hebrew, suggests that this latter knowledge may sometimes have been shaky. Burnet's curriculum appears to have concentrated on scriptural interpretation and to have avoided controversial matters of church discipline as much as possible. Nevertheless, Presbyterians disliked him for his acceptance of prelacy, and he did not stay long in Glasgow.

In the purge that followed the Revolution of 1688 and the subsequent restoration of presbytery in 1690, all Episcopal supporters were expelled from university faculties. In Glasgow, James Wodrow was elected to succeed the displaced professor of divinity. In a report dated 20 August 1696, a year or two after John Simson joined his students, Wodrow outlined his programme, which followed much the same daily schedule as Burnet's, but with a very different emphasis. On Mondays the students practised exegeses and disputations. On Tuesdays they gave lectures and homilies, which were criticized by both professor and fellow students. On Wednesdays attention was given to *De methodo exegetica et homilectica* or to preaching. Questions about scriptural issues were discussed on Thursdays. Fridays consisted of a lecture by Wodrow explaining a chapter of

10 This series of eighty-five rules of clerical behaviour came from the *Apostolic Constitutions*, a fourth-century Eastern Church legal collection. The first fifty had been translated into Latin and formed part of the canon law of the Catholic church.

11 "The Life of the Author," in Burnet, *History*, 6:261.

Wendelin's system of divinity, followed by accounts given by the students of other systems that they had read.

Wodrow also listed the texts that he used in teaching or with which he expected his students to be familiar. The first on the list, "Wendelinus his minus Systema Theologice," was the theological system from which he lectured on Fridays; the others were presumably the various systems that the students were expected to expound and discuss. These were "Pareus upon Ursin's Catechism," Calvin's Institutes, Turretin's *Institutio theologiae elencticae*, Waleus, Maresius, Essenius, Altingius, Maccovius, *Theses Leidenses*, and Polanus's *Syntagma*.[12] At the same time the university authorities followed the command of the General Assembly of 1696 by including Hebrew in the arts curriculum to enhance students' ability to read the scriptures in their original languages.

These theologians, with the notable exception of the Genevan professor of theology François Turretin (1623–1687), were predominantly German and Dutch divines who had helped to systematize the Reformed faith in the early seventeenth century. The list of texts indicates that Wodrow adhered closely to the accepted authorities of the Continental Reformed churches writing in the aftermath of the Synod of Dort. He does not seem to have recommended that his students read modern theology. The contrast with Burnet's curriculum is striking. No longer was biblical interpretation the focus; Wodrow's intention was to impart a theological system to his students, rather than to expound the scriptures.[13]

A set of student notes from 1702 gives Wodrow's views on constructing a sermon. The method was painstaking and broken up into numerous parts. The aim of preaching was threefold: "to teach distinctly," "to con-

---

12 *Munimenta*, 2:533–4.

13 Markus Friedrich Wendelin (1584–1652) taught at Zerbst, near Berlin, where he created the first systematic Reformed method of instruction in Germany – the Systema Majus – of which the "minus Systema" used by Wodrow was a simplified version. Zacharias Ursinus (1534–1583) was the German professor of dogmatics at Heidelberg who was instrumental in drafting the Heidelberg Catechism (1563). In 1619 this statement of faith was pronounced by the Synod of Dort to be "a most accurate compend of the orthodox Christian faith." David Pareus (1548–1622), whose commentary on this catechism Wodrow used, was another German theologian who taught at Heidelberg. Altingius (Johann Heinrich Alting, 1583–1644), Maresius (Samuel des Marets, 1599–1673) and Maccovius (Jan Makowski, 1588–1644) were respectively German, French, and Polish Reformed divines, who taught at Gröningen and Franeker. Altingius's son, Jacob, published his father's *Methodus Theologiae Didacticae* posthumously in 1650, a few years after Maresius's popular text book, *Systhema Theologiae*, appeared in 1645. *Syntagma Theologiae Christianae* by Amandus Polanus a Polansdorf dated from 1624. Turretin's *Institutio Theologiae Elencticae* was a highly influential complete doctrinal system in three volumes that came out in Geneva in 1688. *Theses Leidenses* also offered more up-to-date material from the University of Leiden.

vince clearly," and "to persuade pourfully [powerfully]."[14] The book, chapter, particular part of the chapter, and finally the text were to be "opened up" to the hearers before the text itself was analysed.[15] The doctrines drawn from the text had six uses for the congregation: information, refutation, reproof, consolation, terror, and exhortation. The conclusion had a two-fold purpose: to jog the memory about what had been said and to move the affections of the listeners. It is not surprising that sermons on such topics as human progress or moral virtue later roused the ire of ministers educated by James Wodrow.

Outside the formal classroom, the divinity students were divided into "societies," or discussion groups. Topics discussed in them were those that concerned late-seventeenth-century Scottish society. When considering the dangers of atheistical temptation and the risk of scepticism, the students were reminded that they could "bear all temptations and overcome them" if they prayed and read their Bibles.[16] The perennial Scots preoccupation with the rights of magistrates and the duties of subjects was prominent. The magistrate should "advance the interest of Religion" among his people. However, subjects should "not obey them when th[ei]r com[man]ds thuart the com[man]ds of God," although otherwise they should offer "due reverence, honour and esteem" to magistrates.[17] Other more pastoral subjects included the marks by which one might know that one had been called to the ministry and the duties of a parish minister. Although all comments were accompanied by the appropriate texts from Old and New Testaments, once again the focus was on problems of faith and matters of sectarian discipline rather than on the message of the Bible.

As a Glasgow student, John Simson followed this pattern of lecture, disputation, and study of systemic texts, but his Continental experience at the turn of the century gave him another educational measure with which to compare his instruction under James Wodrow. From his Dutch professors Simson had learned of new trends in theology, just as from his father he had heard memories of Scots beliefs before the Westminster Assembly. He was to use both of these sources in his own teaching as he attempted to move beyond the limitations of Wodrow's seventeenth-century conservatism.

14 "John How's notes on James Wodrow's methods of Studying theology, 1702," GUL, MS. Murray 218/64.

15 Ibid., 66.

16 "Cases answered, GUL, MS, Gen. 343/41.

17 Ibid., 377–8.

In a 1717 statement of "The Methode of teaching divinity at present in the Universitie at Glasgow," Simson explained that he taught from mid-October to mid-June annually.[18] On Tuesdays, Wednesdays, and Thursdays throughout the year he expounded the system of divinity contained in John Marck's *Christianae theologiae medulla didactico–elenctica*, the shortened version of Marck's theological system prepared for students, the most recent edition of which had been published in 1705. As an introductory text he used Benedict Pictet's "didactick compend," some of which he also reviewed in lectures.[19] Jonathan Woodworth recorded that John Simson esteemed Pictet and "Particularly commends him for avoiding many scolastick terms in the explication of the Trinity."[20] Although Simson was not accused of error in his teaching of the Trinity in 1714, Woodworth's words indicate that the professor's teaching vocabulary had been early set. In the 1720s Simson defended himself against those who complained that he did not use words such as "necessary existence" and "independency" by saying that he was following the terminology of Pictet and the Westminster Confession. He wished to avoid outmoded scholastic usage when possible.

Along with these Dutch and Swiss systems, Simson discussed the Westminster Confession of Faith, considered differences between British and Continental opinions, and proved the superiority of the Confession from scriptural sources. The fact that he pointed out such areas of disagreement and opted for the Confession's doctrine became significant during his trials, when his preference for the language of the Reformers to that of Calvinist scholastic theologians became a charge against him. Woodworth remarked on the respect that Professor Simson showed for the authors of the Westminster Confession.[21] Simson's regard for them reduces the significance of his occasional objections to their specific wording. His preference was for the Bible, the early Fathers, and the work of an assembly of divines over the systems of individual Calvinists. He preferred ancient and modern writers to medieval ones. His conflict with James Webster was sharpened by the divergence

18 Duncan, *Notices*, 122–3.

19 Pictet (1655–1724), educated in Geneva and Leiden, succeeded his uncle, François Turretin, in the Genevan theology chair in 1687. His *Theologia Christiana* (1696) and his *Medulla Theologiae Christianae didacticae et elencticae*, which the Glasgow students presumably used, were published in Geneva. Student lecture notes show that in the late 1740s Professor Leechman was still teaching Pictet's system. See Kennedy, "William Leechman," 58.

20 Bromley, "Correspondence," 24.

21 Ibid., 25.

of their theological inclinations, since Webster clung to an outdated Scottish system and prohibited any departure from its rigour.

Simson's students were required to participate in several group discussions each week. On Mondays they made presentations that were criticized by their fellows. On Fridays, one student delivered an exegesis, followed by a public disputation. Younger students were assigned systems of divinity, and senior men were given heresies to study weekly. Each had to summarize the argument of his author at a "polemick conference," after which Simson refuted errors and clarified the correct thesis for the group. Finally "the students are desired to propose their doubts and have them answered."[22] It was these conferences that gave birth to some of the charges later laid against the professor.

On Saturdays the prospective ministers met in "societies" for prayer and discussion.[23] After they had studied a difficult biblical passage and consulted the appropriate authorities, they produced a group paper for the professor to correct. With Simson's modifications, the paper would be read publicly and "recorded in a book."[24] The cases studied in these papers were naturally controversial, and by the early 1720s there was mounting criticism of the latitude that Simson allowed the students in their written conclusions.[25] Simson had moved beyond the texts used by Wodrow to more modern material. He also devoted more time to discussion of other theological systems and to the refutation of heresy, a change necessitated by the religious upheavals of his day. The collegiate week was completed by attendance on Sunday at the college church, where the divinity students sat together in the expanded seating that Simson had obtained for them at a faculty meeting within months of his arrival in Glasgow.[26]

We learn from Simson's response to allegations made against his orthodoxy in 1726 that the textual basis of his teaching, as well as his vocabulary, remained constant. In a lengthy letter sent to the Presbytery of Glasgow, he gave this "free and ingenuous" account of his curriculum: "Since I had the Honour to teach Divinity here, I have yearly explained Professor *Mark*'s little Compend called his *Medulla*; and also

22 Duncan, *Notices*, 123.

23 Prayer societies were common in the early eighteenth century among all classes in Scotland. Simson was following the method of his predecessor, James Wodrow, and using the normal terminology for a group meeting for religious purposes.

24 Duncan, *Notices*, 123.

25 For cases discussed in 1724–5, see Wodrow, *Analecta*, 3:171, 175, 179, 181–2.

26 GUA 26632, 53.

some Chapters of Professor *Pictet*'s little Compend, and among others that of the Doctrine of the *Trinity*; together with these, I yearly read over and explain our *Confession of Faith*, and compare the several Articles of it, with what is taught in the *Latin* System; some Mistakes in which I find Reason to correct, by what is more clearly and exactly taught in our Confession."[27]

While the manuals from which Simson expounded a standard Reformed system of theology did not change from 1708 to 1727, he admitted freely during the second set of hearings on his work that he had shifted his emphasis during the later years. Furthermore, while after 1717 he may have not used the examples of which the orthodox had disapproved, he frequently referred his students to the published account of his arguments against James Webster, with the obvious intention of bringing such examples to their attention.

Simson made a point of keeping abreast of the latest theological developments, particularly in the other British churches. Along with his colleagues in other disciplines, he was modernizing divinity instruction at Glasgow. He considered it his duty to lay any controversial matters before his class and to contest changes that seemed to him undesirable. In spite of being a man of authoritarian temperament, he continued and even broadened the tradition of disputation and discussion of all aspects of Christianity among his students. From his letters and from the minutes taken during hearings, Simson emerges as a man with a biting tongue, so it is likely that sometimes his students misunderstood his actual position in some of these debates. His propensity to irony and sarcasm, coupled with the fact that he seems to have made himself unpopular with certain students through his disciplinary actions, may have contributed to the reports about his teaching that led to his eventual suspension.

THE PATH TO ORDINATION AND SIMSON'S STUDENTS

The purpose of the student exercises was preparation not only for a life of ministry and preaching, but more immediately for the "trials" that a prospective minister underwent, first to be licensed to preach, and then to be ordained to a parish. We can trace the method by which a presbytery approved the qualifications of a divinity student through the testing of some of Simson's scholars by the Presbytery of Glasgow. The process

27 Dundas, *Processes*, 15–16.

illustrates both the administration of the church with regard to postulants and the general acceptance of the results of Simson's pedagogy. The argument of Simson's opponents that he was a menace to the doctrine of the Church of Scotland cannot be empirically proved by any heterodoxy shown by his students, who were invariably examined by presbyteries and found suitable for the ministry. During neither of Simson's cases was any Glasgow alumnus cited as demonstrating unsound tendencies. The older generation might grumble about dubious young ministers, but they had usually been trained by Hamilton in Edinburgh.

The licensing procedure began with the professor of divinity announcing at a regular presbytery meeting that a young man was ready to enter on trials, after which a committee examined the candidate privately. If the student was properly prepared, as was generally the case, formal trials were prescribed. The prospective preacher was given a text, usually from the New Testament, from which to deliver a homily, or sermon for spiritual enlightenment, to the assembled presbytery. In 1708, for example, Robert Higgenbottom was asked to preach from Acts 11:23: "and exhorted them all, that with purpose of heart they would cleave unto the Lord."[28]

The next test was an exegesis, or exposition of a statement of Calvinist doctrine. These tended to be straightforward: "Whether divine grace is absolutely necessary for salvation" was used for one student in 1715, with minimal change in wording for another in 1716, and again with slight alterations in 1723.[29] Questions concerning Presbyterian church government were also common; "Whether Presbyterian government is by divine right?" or "Whether Christ is the only head of the Church?" fell into this category between 1708 and 1710.[30] After the student had successfully given his exegesis, he would be asked to lecture on, or expound, a chapter of the Bible, often from Isaiah.[31]

Two other test sermons generally followed. The first was a "presbyterial exercise," which demonstrated the type of preaching suitable for the assembled brethren at presbytery meetings. In January 1724, for

28 GCA, CH2/171/8, 16.

29 *Num gratia supernaturalis sit absolute necessaria ad salutem.* ibid., 9A, 16r, 21r; 10, 23v.

30 *Num Regimen Presbyteriale sit Jure Divino. Num solus Christus caput Ecclesia,* ibid., 8 18r, 57.

31 Ibid., 18v; ibid., 9A, 12r. In Scots church services there was a lecture, or scriptural exposition, as well as the main sermon, which was a homily. Woodworth described a Glasgow public service for his cousin: "(1) Singing 2[ly] prayer 3[ly] exposition (in the forenoon) singing, prayer, sermon, intercession, benediction, singing." Bromley, "Correspondence," 20.

instance, William Maxwell delivered a presbyterial exercise on Ephesians 4. This text seems most apposite: it commences with Paul's exhorting his reader to "walk worthy of the vocation wherewith ye are called" and goes on to list the qualifications for the life of service.[32] The second test was a "popular sermon," which might be shorter (half an hour was the time limit suggested to one student) and would presumably be less erudite.[33] In one case, in December 1723, John Deans was assigned verses from Exodus 20 for his popular sermon. In this chapter Moses told the children of Israel what God had said to him on Sinai and listed the Ten Commandments.[34] While this was on the surface a straightforward and appropriate topic on which a young minister could preach, in fact it was probably a genuine test of the candidate's orthodoxy (and that of his professor), since the Church of Scotland had recently condemned Antinomianism, or the view that divine grace sets Christians free from the constrictions of moral law.

Further tests included answering extempore questions, preparing and defending theses, and giving proof of skill in Hebrew and Greek.[35] A man from outside the district would have to provide a testimonial from his home presbytery as well as undergoing tests to obtain a licence.

The student who passed all the trials then subscribed the Westminster Confession of Faith and swore subjection to the judicatories of the church. He promised to try to maintain unity in the church and to "guard against whatsoever had a tendency to cause a breach therein."[36] Once he had so sworn, the newly qualified pastor received his licence to preach, becoming a "preacher of the Gospel," or "probationer," eligible to take services and perform ministerial tasks.

His next challenge was to find a parish willing to call him, or after 1712 a patron willing to present him for ordination, since the Scottish church refused to ordain a man without a parish. Security and a steady salary came only with a parish; a probationer was dependent on fees earned for acting in the absence of a minister and on what he might earn as private chaplain or tutor in a great house. When he received a call to a parish, the probationer would repeat many of these trials to ensure that his message was acceptable to his prospective congregation, especially to its more influential members, and to his future presbytery brethren.

32 Maxwell was being ordained to serve in Carolina. GCA, CH2/171/10, 24r.
33 GCA, CH2/171/8, 19.
34 Deans was going to Carolina along with Maxwell. GCA, CH2/171/10, 23v.
35 GCA, CH2/171/8, 19–20; CH2/171/9A, 19–21.
36 GCA, CH2/171/8, 20r.

Simson's students had few recorded problems during their trials and appear to have had average luck in finding patronage. They were received into trials by the Presbytery of Glasgow and licensed regularly. There is no instance in the presbytery records of a student failing his trials. The one known Simson theologue who claimed to have been refused trials by the Presbytery of Glasgow was William Wilson, a member of Simson's first class in 1708, who sought a licence in 1712. In his case, the problem seems to have been political. Wilson, a grave and diligent student, felt that his problems with the Glasgow ministers stemmed from his refusal to take the recently demanded oath of abjuration. "The Presbytery of Glasgow were dissatisfied with my conduct about the Oath, and I had not the prospect then of entering on trials any where else, and did not know what Presbytery would receive me."[37] In its stand, the presbytery supported the opinions of both the principal of Glasgow University and Professor Simson, who were exhorting their correspondents to take the oath.

The following year Wilson received his licence from the more evangelical and anti-Erastian members of the Presbytery of Dunfermline. He went on to become a leading member of a group that later seceded from the Church of Scotland, partly over the issue of patronage. Clearly Wilson was not infected with heresy by his professor, although the first rumours of Simson's dangerous opinions were already circulating by 1712.

Despite the fears of James Webster and his friends that Simson was "spreading the Contagion of his New and False Divinity, and pouring it into the Minds of such as stand Candidates for the Ministry,"[38] a cursory review of the later conduct of known students of Simson does not identify any single theological trend inculcated by him.[39] On the contrary, his doctrinal interests seem to have been eclectic and cognizant of the latest research. His influence would appear to have been to produce good scholars, concerned ministers, and some men of tolerant vision.

37 Ferrier, *Memoirs of the Rev. William Wilson*, 75.

38 Webster, *Short Abstract*, 13.

39 I have tracked as many of Simson's Scots students as I could identify in Hew Scott, *Fasti*, and can find no evidence of heterodoxy among them. I have been able to confirm only four non-subscribers among the thirty-nine divinity students listed as Irish (1708–27) in *Munimenta*, although four more were at least sympathetic to that cause, while in England George Benson became Socinian. This still suggests that Simson's proportion of "unsound" pupils was no higher than that of James Wodrow.

The Glasgow matriculation lists demonstrate the diversity of opinion among Simson's students. Among the men who can be positively identified in the class of February 1710 are both Michael McTaggart, whose enthusiasm for his professor's teaching was to alarm Robert Rowan, and William Dunlop, son of the late principal, who became an enlightened, but theologically conservative professor at Edinburgh University. The class of February 1713 contained both John McLaurin, a later ultra-orthodox Glasgow minister, and Francis Hutcheson, the future professor, whose philosophical views differed widely. William Wilson (January 1708), the Secession stalwart, disagreed with Simson for reasons presumably quite different from those of the student rebel Peter Butler (January 1717).[40] If James Arbuckle (February 1721) disliked his professor for reasons that were disciplinary and personal, not doctrinal, Simson's lifelong friendship with his pupil Archibald Campbell (February 1712), and the various examples of his attempts to recommend young men for posts, demonstrate that he could also develop cordial relationships with his students. Some of the Glasgow alumni indeed embraced the rational trends of the eighteenth century, but so did some ministers emerging from Edinburgh University, and probably from Aberdeen and St Andrews as well.

Simson's teaching methods seem to have entailed presenting all sides to a question and giving some latitude to his hearers in their choice of which to follow. He believed that a class of Scottish theological students would select Calvinist doctrine based on biblical texts, but that each should be free to adopt whatever line of persuasive argument he chose. A pedagogy that centred on the Westminster Confession of Faith and the terminology of the Bible contained no inherent conflict with Simson's own adherence to an increasingly rational theology and worship of a benevolent Creator. The God of the Confession was "most loving, gracious, merciful, long-suffering, abundant in goodness and truth, forgiving iniquity, transgression, and sin."[41] In the Covenant of Grace "he freely offered unto sinners life and salvation by Jesus Christ."[42] This was the Creator whom Simson stressed, along with the necessity for His creature, man, to use his God-given reason to understand the divine Revelation.

40 *Munimenta*, 3:250–6.
41 "Westminster Confession of Faith," 2:1.
42 Ibid., 7:3.

JAMES WEBSTER'S ATTACK

Opposition to such teaching arose swiftly. In 1714 matters became serious enough for Simson to bring to the attention of the faculty of Glasgow University charges of error against him made by the Edinburgh minister James Webster, a man of inflexible religious conservatism. Because of its "regard to the Reputation and Credit of the University," the faculty, as we see in its minute book, demanded that Webster repair to Glasgow to substantiate the accusations of Arminianism, Socinianism, and Jesuitism that he was casting at the divinity professor.[43] To explain this entry we have to go back a few years and consider Simson's relationship with James Webster and other ultra-orthodox Presbyterians.

Webster was strongly anti-Erastian in his vision of the established church in Scotland, disapproving of any governmental interference in ecclesiastical affairs and resolutely refusing to take the oath of abjuration.[44] He had been known to criticize the right of the Crown to impose fasts or thanksgivings and had prayed for divine guidance to prevent the Queen taking another "wrong step."[45] Simson's contempt for the ideological position of the non-jurors must have exacerbated Webster's dislike of the professor's theology. It seems likely that Webster's attacks on Simson in this decade were influenced by his non-juring stance and his bitter rejection of the Erastian co-operation that Simson endorsed by calling for his acquaintances to sign the oath of abjuration.

There was, however, an additional political factor involved. During the slow progress of the first case through the church judicatories, the Squadrone was in favour in London. Consequently, in the acerbic words of Grange, "[M]ost of the clergy, with the usual honesty of clergymen … servily crouched to the prevailing. The Argathelians, of consequence, favoured Mr. Webster in his prosecution of a court minister and professor of divinity, Simson."[46] Since Simson and Stirling were committed to the Squadrone, and had the open support of both the Court and the church leaders, it was understandable that Argyll's ecclesiastical supporters saw the affair as an opportunity to make political ground. Their inclination to favour Webster was in accordance with the long-standing

43 GUA 26632, 121.
44 Wodrow, *Correspondence*, 2:515, 517.
45 Wodrow, *Analecta*, 1:260, 1:286–7, 2:5.
46 Erskine, "Letters," 27.

support given by the Campbells of Argyll to evangelical Presbyterianism. Argyll and Islay had not yet come to appreciate that a partnership with fanatics involved unproductive complications.

Reports about the teaching of Professor Simson at Glasgow began to circulate about 1710, disseminated swiftly by the orthodox. Simson himself claimed that such stories were "chiefly spread" by James Webster.[47] By 1711, they had reached the ears of Robert Wodrow in his country parish south of the Clyde near Glasgow. Since Simson was middle-aged when he began teaching in the academic year 1708–9, his theology must have developed during his earlier experiences as preacher, "bear-leader," and parish minister. If his lectures were arousing comment beyond the university doors this early, then from the time of his appointment they must have incorporated a more rational doctrine than had those of his predecessor, James Wodrow. Simson continued to read widely, maintaining in 1715, "I Pretend not to Perfection or Infallibility; On the Contrary, I Profess my Self only a Student, and hope to do so while on Earth."[48] From his own statements during the second case, it is evident that Simson's spiritual understanding continued to evolve, and his approach to his exposition of theology altered at least once during his academic career, although his textbooks were unchanged.

Webster, however, remained one of the most fanatical ministers of his day and relished castigating fellow clerics for back-sliding. Edmund Calamy (1671–1732), a Dissenting minister in London, pronounced him "over-orthodox, as great a bigot as any in the country."[49] During a visit to Scotland in 1709, Calamy was given an opportunity to preach in Edinburgh. Webster disapproved of his sermon and later, from the pulpit, made "some peevish and angry reflections" on it.[50] Calamy thought the Edinburgh minister mean-spirited and prone to ill-temper.

Other recorded episodes featuring Webster were similar in character. Prominent Edinburgh ministers William Hamilton and William Wishart were condemned by Webster in church, and then before the Presbytery of Edinburgh, for travelling on a Sunday, although the intention of that journey was to reach an English town where they might hear a sermon by

---

47 Simson, *Libel*, "Speech to the Presbytery of Glasgow, March 29, 1715," 64.
48 Ibid., 228.
49 Calamy, *Historical Account*, 2:161.
50 Ibid., 2:179.

a Dissenting preacher![51] When both men, along with their presbyterial colleagues, represented to Webster that his behaviour was unbrotherly and indeed slanderous, Webster took offence and professed himself injured. A Jacobite wit, Dr Archibald Pitcairne (1652–1713), was a thorn in the side of Presbyterian Whigs in Edinburgh. When Pitcairne could not resist a Latin pun about a Bible, Webster flew into a rage and called him an atheist.[52] That episode led to Pitcairne's suing Webster for slander, a case that was eventually settled through the mediation of Lord Grange.[53]

Webster's orthodoxy, strong convictions, and emotional intensity were captured in a 1720 obituary by Ralph Erskine: "This heavenly zealot for the Gospel-scheme / Taught without fear, and argued without shame. / His active zeal 'gainst error all did flash, / And burnt up anti-evangelic trash."[54] In contrast, an earlier, anonymous verse indicates that popular opinion thought the minister deranged rather than merely enthusiastic: "There is a man, whom God ne'er made / A Minister nor Webster, / Who has a crack'd distracted head; / There is a man, whom God ne'er made; / Lord, cure him with his cape of lead, / Or knock him like a labster."[55]

Webster protected his vision of religious purity with hot-headed acts and reckless words. Although in the first years of the century he had published sermons and treatises on presbyterian church government, in his fifties he seemed unfocused in his abuse of prominent ministers. Simson hinted that Webster had wanted a divinity chair himself and that his sense of rejection caused him to accuse professors of error.[56] Bitterness might explain his ill-considered attacks on Simson and Hamilton.

Had prosecution not been forced on him by Simson himself, the University of Glasgow, and the church courts, Webster would almost certainly

51 NAS, CH2/121/9, 555–91.

52 Attending an auction, Pitcairne noticed that a Bible remained unsold when secular volumes went quickly; "Verbum Dei manet in æternum" (The word of God endures for ever), he jested. Erskine, *Extracts*, 101–8.

53 Wodrow, *Correspondence*, 1:437, has preserved a contemporary verse supposedly sent to Pitcairne: "You'll rally oaths, and thunder down religion; / This is the air of Satan and his legion. / ... Till Bacchus knock thee down thou'lt never rest, / Thou art But Webster's Atheist at the best."

54 Quoted in Donald Fraser, *The Life and Diary of Rev. Ralph Erskine*, 146.

55 A "Roundell" on Webster published in Maidment, ed., *A Second Book*.

56 See Simson, *Libel*, 66; [?Simson], *Answer*, 8.

have been content to let his inflammatory comments circulate in gossip and pamphlet form without taking further action. Perhaps because of its pressure on him to substantiate his libellous statements about Simson, in 1716 Webster issued a challenge in print to the General Assembly of the Church of Scotland: "I do offer ... if they will allow this Affair of Mr. *Simsons* but one Hour of their Time, to make evident that he is guilty of *Arminianism, Jesuitism,* and *Socinianism*; and that not be any strain'd Consequences, but in plain categorick Expressions under his own Hand. Further, after comparing his Scheme with that of *Placaeus* ... I do think they are both the same."[57] His offer was not taken up.

Although Webster's public denunciations of Simson were stronger than his determination to sustain his charges, his pursuit of John Simson between 1714 and 1717 before the courts of the Church of Scotland was endorsed by like-minded conservative Presbyterians such as Robert Wodrow and by political followers of the Duke of Argyll. Had it not been for this support, his claims might have failed quickly, and John Simson might have faded from history. For Simson and his university, however, it was essential to vindicate both his own reputation and that of the divinity school. They resolved to challenge Webster to make good his threats and to defend themselves – through three years of committee hearings, as it turned out.

Not only had the classroom methods and texts used by Simson altered from those of Professor James Wodrow, but his very understanding of the basis of his faith was different. The Simson–Rowan correspondence[58] shows that the two men had dissimilar beliefs about the precision with which the Westminster Confession of Faith expressed Presbyterian dogma. Simson hoped that new critical principles could be followed to improve men's perception of scriptural truth. He saw it as his duty to empower his students to follow such principles. Under Simson and his colleagues at the other Scottish universities, Presbyterians were emulating their Continental brethren in abandoning the restraints of Reformed scholasticism. For the next two decades Simson was opposed by many conservative ministers and laymen who were apprehensive about the dangers that appeared to threaten Scottish Presbyterianism.

57 Webster, *True Copy*, 37.
58 See below, chapter 6.

Simson's defiance of their efforts to control theological education was an important stage in the development of the Church of Scotland into a vital component of the Scottish Enlightenment. Without its eventual commitment to free discussion involving new findings in all areas of learning, Scotland would have been less welcoming to eighteenth-century ideas. In that case, the Scottish Enlightenment would have lacked the support of the church and universities that contributed so much to it.

5

So Unspotted a Church: Challenges to Scottish Calvinism

CALVINIST ORTHODOXY AND SIMSON'S USE OF REASON

James Webster and his friends believed wrongly that the Church of Scotland had never been troubled by disputes over dogma. In fact Scots had contended over doctrinal issues as well as over ecclesiology ever since the Reformation. Cartesian scepticism, Dutch Arminianism, Socinianism, French universalism, and antinomianism had all agitated the Scots church despite its rigid adherence to the Westminster Confession. New challenges appeared in Simson's lifetime, both homegrown and imported from the Continent. These heterodoxies alarmed many and increased their determination to restrain Simson's teaching at Glasgow.

The departure of the Stuarts from England in 1688 had opened a new chapter for the Church of Scotland. In 1690 William of Orange permitted the Scottish Parliament to re-establish Presbyterianism and abolish patronage for church livings. Bishops were expelled, and parish ministers faced the double quandary of the oath of allegiance and Presbyterian church government. The consequent purge of Episcopalian ministers from church pulpits and professors from university chairs led enlightened spirits such as Dr Archibald Pitcairne to see the Presbyterian Settlement as the triumph of the "religious Non-sensical Cant of the Right Reverend Godly Blockheads of the Phanatick Order."[1]

Nevertheless, the considerable independence of the church's governing bodies created a more relaxed atmosphere, in which academic consideration of contemporary issues became possible, as we can see by the

---

1 Pitcairne, *The Assembly*, 60.

speed with which John Simson implemented a new divinity curriculum at Glasgow. Although after 1707 the change to a more open attitude, welcomed by the theology professors at Glasgow and Edinburgh, became anathema to many who feared the Erastian threat that the parliamentary union seemed to embody, a new freedom of theological discussion began to prevail in some Scottish circles. This atmosphere was threatened, but not eradicated, by the anxiety caused by Tory legislation in 1712, a contributing cause of the first Simson case. While Presbyterians enjoyed a sense of security for the first time in a century, their church found itself facing challenges in doctrine, ministry, and organization as philosophical perils quickly emerged to replace the ecclesiological dangers of prelacy. The opposition that Simson faced during his years in the Glasgow divinity chair must be considered in the light of fears raised by events of the 1690s and of the extreme theological stance of many in the victorious church.

Descartes had dug "deep pits of Scepticism and material Atheism" that trapped many of Pitcairne's contemporaries.[2] Apprehension lest scepticism might lead the unwary to Socinianism or atheism had spawned draconian laws in the past. In 1648 the English Parliament made death "without benefit of Clergy" the penalty for anti-Trinitarian statements.[3] The Act of Toleration of 1689 covered neither Roman Catholic nor anti-Trinitarian dissent. A new wave of contention about the nature of the Trinity emanated from Oxford in the 1690s, drawing in Bishop George Bull, whom Simson was later to cite, as a defender of orthodoxy.[4] As a result, a law passed in 1698 dealt expressly with anti-Trinitarianism. Under a Scots law of 1661, blasphemers, including those who speculated on Christology, were to receive capital punishment. A revised act of 1695 specified imprisonment and public repentance for a first offence, a fine for the second, and death only for the third. Echoing the civil law, the twenty-first act of the General Assembly of 1696 warned against the danger of the atheistical principles of deists. In particular, the act mentioned the denial of "The doctrine of the Trinity, the incarnation of the Messiah ... justification by his imputed righteousness to them who believe in his name ... the certainty and authority of scripture revelation: As also, their asserting, that there must be a mathematical evidence for each purpose, before we can be obliged

2 Hogg, *Memoirs*, 13.
3 Florida, "British Law," 206.
4 See Redwood, *Reason*, chap. 7.

to assent to any proposition thereanent; and that natural light is suffi-cient to salvation."[5] Ministers were instructed to pay attention to saving the seduced but also to proceed against the seducers "as scandalous and heretical apostates."[6]

Unlike many of his peers, Simson does not seem to have had sceptical doubts, but he must have been aware of why they were feared. By the late 1690s, individuals as diverse as Rev. James Hogg of Carnock, Profes-sor Thomas Halyburton of St Andrews, and Glasgow Provost John Aird had encountered the temptations of sceptical philosophy. Men who had attended university spoke of the dangers inherent in the philosophy course that they studied. An unanswered question of the period is whether the outspoken deist John Toland (1670–1722), who passed through Glasgow and Edinburgh Universities between 1687 and 1690, was exposed to new ideas in Scotland or whether his ideas influenced others. The unfortunate Edinburgh student Thomas Aikenhead, who expounded his sceptical discoveries to some ill-chosen drinking com-panions, was charged and tried for blasphemy in December 1696. A few weeks later he was hanged, despite the stated 1695 punishment for a first offence.[7] Aikenhead's final wish – that his death might put an end to the "rageing spirit of atheism which hath taken such footing in Brit-tain" – was not entirely fulfilled.[8] Elsewhere in the kingdom the Dublin Arian Thomas Emlyn (1663–1741) was gaoled and fined for blasphemy in the early years of the eighteenth century.

In England there was reluctance to prosecute men for heterodox opinions, but the care with which John Locke disguised his opinions, and the lack of evidence about the rumoured views of Sir Isaac Newton, may be ascribed to the danger under which such public figures felt they laboured. When William Whiston made himself notorious for Arianism, he lost his Lucasian chair of mathematics at Cambridge in 1711.[9] As late as 1721, a bill was introduced in the House of Lords to suppress any de-nial of the Trinity, as defined by the Thirty-Nine Articles of the Church of England. Anyone convicted of such blasphemy was to be imprisoned until he formally recanted. Edmund Calamy expressed his shock at the lords who voted in favour of this bill and mentioned that Argyll and Islay voted against it.[10]

5 Stewart of Pardovan, *Abridgement*, 23–4.
6 Ibid., 24.
7 See Michael Hunter, "'Aikenhead the Atheist.'"
8 Cobbett, Howell, et al., *Complete Collection*, 13:933.
9 See Duffy, "'Whiston's Affair.'"
10 Calamy, *Historical Account*, 2:451.

The heterodoxies listed in the General Assembly's act of 1696 remained the topics of philosophical inquiry for the ensuing decades. John Simson and his friends continued to debate the evidence for scripture revelation and the sufficiency of natural light for salvation. In the 1720s Simson engaged in lively discussion about the Trinity with his Glasgow acquaintances. While his conclusions were by no means necessarily contrary to orthodox Calvinist dogma, the frankness with which he publicly scrutinized the issues led to disapproving criticism from the extreme party in the church. Although it seems likely that he and his friends were all orthodox Athanasian Christians, Simson incurred the wrath of many of his ministerial colleagues. Fortunately the prevailing mood had changed since the execution of Aikenhead; ecclesiastical rather than civil censure was now seen as the appropriate means of dealing with blasphemy. The Simson cases moved opinion yet further, saving future professors from a similar fate.

We must set the uproar over Simson's teaching against the background of the evolution of the Reformed faith in Scotland and abroad. Founded by men who had been impressed by the discipline and devotion of Genevan theocracy, the Church of Scotland based its theology on that of John Calvin (1506–1564) and his more systematic successors, such as Theodore Beza (1519–1605). Seventeenth-century altercations within the Calvinist community had led to a series of important synods and assemblies, whose decisions defined orthodoxy for the faithful. The rigid scholastic Reformed faith that resulted had given spiritual comfort to Scots Presbyterians during the years of persecution under the Stuarts. Such men expected ministers, particularly professors of divinity, to conform to the strictest doctrinal standards. Conservative opponents of Simson claimed that internal divisions on doctrine were unprecedented and that heresy had never before been found in the Church of Scotland. In reality, while seventeenth-century political upheaval had limited the perspective of many Scots Presbyterians to the struggle for the maintenance of their chosen form of church government, the assertion that Scots minds had been closed to theological controversy was disingenuous. Scots had followed, and often participated in, the doctrinal evolution of Reformed Protestantism during the century and a half since the death of Calvin.

Calvin's legal training and organizational skills helped him to create a movement of great power. His theology, based on wide biblical scholarship, was designed to illuminate the mysteries of Scripture for ignorant humanity. Calvin believed that man was the noblest divine creation, endowed with intellect and with free will, but had been corrupted by

Adam's Fall. He agreed with the anti-Pelagian Augustinian argument that Adam was not merely the progenitor of the human race, but also the root through whom it became depraved. Reason, however, was a natural gift that had not been totally destroyed by the Fall, merely weakened in its ability to discern right and wrong; the once-free human will thus required grace to keep it from sin. Nevertheless reason was the property that distinguished man from the animals.

Calvin's interpretation of the Fall separated the sufficiency of reason in temporal matters from its utter inadequacy in soteriology, for divine assistance was essential for salvation. Through Christ as mediator, the elect received the saving gift of faith. Calvin insisted that the Word be preached and offered to all, although he understood that "Some would object that God would be inconsistent with himself, in inviting all without distinction while he elects only a few. Thus, according to them, the universality of the promise destroys the distinction of special grace."[11]

The objection to a universal offer of Christ to sinners remained a contentious topic for Scots Presbyterians and other Calvinists. Throughout the seventeenth century, the issue surfaced in various forms and in different places. Calvin personally considered the message that Christ died for all to be essential, "so that no one at all may think he is excluded."[12] Since only a few would accept the offered gift of grace that was preached, the atonement of Christ was effective only for the elect, though sufficient for all. The gift of faith given by God to his elect was both unconditional and unmerited, but all men should strive to live righteously, since the end of election was holiness of life (Ephesians 1:4).[13] Calvin's view of saving faith has been identified as a passive knowledge in the mind of the believer, whose "assurance of salvation is of the essence of faith, and is grounded *extra nos*, that is outside ourselves in the person and work of Jesus Christ."[14]

The development of Scottish theology in the late sixteenth and early seventeenth centuries led to a different interpretation of faith. It became an act of will, through which assurance was gained as the result of belief attained "through self-examination and syllogistic deduction" – a more self-absorbed faith, which placed the grounds of assurance *intra nos* instead of in Christ.[15]

11 Calvin, *Institutes*, 3:22,10.
12 From Calvin's *Commentary* on John 3:17. Quoted in Bell, *Calvin*, 17.
13 Calvin wrote, "if the end of election is holiness of life, it ought to arouse and stimulate us strenuously to aspire to it, instead of serving as a pretext for sloth." *Institutes*, 3:23,12.
14 Bell, *Calvin*, 8.
15 Ibid.

After Calvin's death, Reformed theologians consolidated his work, a process that left it starker and less flexible. The loss of the enthusiasm of the early reform movement, the necessity for effective ecclesiastical organization, and the internal divisions within some churches meant that, for many Calvinists, "Theology ceased to be in dialogue with the intellectual movements of the time and concentrated upon its own inner development."[16] Calvin had been a humanist who emphasized the biblical promise of salvation and had little interest in philosophical theory.[17]

Other leaders – Beza in Geneva, Peter Ramus (1515–1572) in France, and Peter Martyr (1500–1562) and Jerome Zanchi (1516–1590) in Strasbourg, and counterparts elsewhere in Germany – propounded a new theological scholasticism, which encouraged precision of definition, systematic expression, and logical consistency, often based on Aristotelian principles. Such a theology had fewer dogmatic ambiguities and less of the inner fire of the first Reformers; it appealed to the mind rather than to the emotions. Where Calvin had focused on how a biblical God revealed himself to mankind, Calvinist scholastics speculated on the nature of God, on predestination, and on the exercise of the divine will. Their general nominalism led to an emphasis on man's inability to comprehend God. Divine righteousness and judgment took precedence over fatherly love and forgiveness. They expounded these beliefs in systems that seemed to diminish human will and rationality. The progression of early Reformed faith into that of the mid-seventeenth century is exemplified in the conceptual difference between the humanistic and generic Scots Confession of 1560 and the detailed Westminster Confession of 1647, with its careful citation of texts to prove each point.

It was against the sterile logic of Reformed schoolmen that Simson took his stand. In 1717 a pamphleteer (who was, I suspect, Simson himself) wrote: "Tho' he [Simson] retains all the Orthodox Principles of our Church and Confession, yet it is evident that in his Rational Way, he has freed them from some Difficulty's they are Incumbred with in the Way they are ordinarily treated of, in the common Systems of Theology ... he has the Happiness to unlearn all that Cant, with which the Ignorant are deceiv'd as if it were true Knowledge."[18] He believed that once again theology could become part of the intellectual challenge of his day. He called for a re-examination of Calvin's doctrine of God and for a faith

16 Leith, *Introduction*, 115.
17 See Donnelly, "Italian Influences."
18 [?Simson], *Answer to a Paper*, 9.

that stressed God's benevolence expressed in the world through the gift of His Son.

Simson was convinced that God had so structured his revelation that no man could be without some means of discovering it. Approaching his seventieth birthday, he enthusiastically wrote to a friend that God, as "an All wise Just & Good creator," had revealed himself and given needed rules to newly created man and that furthermore "God & his necessary Laws wer also known to all mankind after the Flood of Noah."[19] It must then have been possible for the knowledge of such rules to have been passed down to all nations on earth. To Simson, as to Calvin, all religion and morality were based on revelation, contrary to the views of most of the deists and rationalists.

SIMSON: ARMINIAN? SOCINIAN? JESUIT? PLACAEAN?

The heresies of which Webster accused Simson were either products of the later Reformation or reactions to developments within it. The systematization of Reformed theology led naturally to the growth of dissident groups that queried the new, unambiguous definitions of the Protestant scholastics. Webster asked for one hour of the General Assembly's time to prove Simson guilty of Arminianism, Socinianism, and Jesuitism and of dangerous similarity to the beliefs of Placaeus, the Latin form of the name of Josué de la Place.

Arminianism was first on Webster's list of Simson's errors. The disturbing teachings on universal grace and free will of Jacob Harmensz, or Arminius (1560–1609), professor of theology at Leiden, caused an uproar in the Dutch church and were condemned at the Synod of Dort in 1619. The Five Remonstrant Articles of 1610 were formulated after Arminius's death but based on his works. First, all will be saved who by grace believe and persevere; this is eternally decreed; it is dependent on foreseen faith or unbelief. Second, Christ died for all; this means universal atonement. The sufficiency of Christ's atonement does not necessarily imply its efficiency. Third, saving faith is possible only through regeneration. Fourth, grace may be resisted, although it is absolutely necessary for salvation. And fifth, it cannot be proved by scripture that grace cannot be lost.

James VI and I sent representatives sent representatives to Dort, as did other European Reformed states, in order to consider the Remon-

---

19 J. Simson to A. Campbell, 3 March 1736, NAS, GD461/15/7, 4.

strant position. Political bias determined the choice of the Dutch delegates, who were overwhelmingly of the orthodox party rather than from the Remonstrant, or Arminian side. This alignment ensured the defeat of the Remonstrants and the subsequent deposition of many Dutch clergymen.

The Canons of Dort stated that election did not depend on foreknowledge, rather it was itself the fountain of faith. The atonement was limited: Christ died for the elect alone, although His sacrifice was sufficient for all. Faith was a gift of God, given to man corrupted by the Fall. The elect would both persevere and receive assurance.[20] Since secular politics had become interwoven with doctrinal controversy, the result of Dort was a foregone conclusion. Perhaps as a result, outside the United Provinces only the French Reformed church made the Canons of Dort authoritative, and even there a dissenting group became entrenched in the college in exile at Sedan.

In Scotland, while the Canons of Dort were treated with esteem and regarded by many as an "infallible test for separating the sheep and the goats," they had no prescriptive power.[21] Since Arminians eventually secured a niche in the normally tolerant Netherlands, where many Scottish youths studying at Leiden or Utrecht were exposed to them, divines in Glasgow and Edinburgh continued to fear their influence. Arminianism also found a home in the church around Aberdeen, where a school formed first around John Forbes (1593–1648) and the "Aberdeen Doctors" (c. 1620–40), then around Henry Scougal (professor 1650–78) and the brothers James Garden (1647–1726) and George Garden (1649–1733), who were also influenced by the Flemish mystic Antoinette Bourignon (1616–1680).[22] This area of the northeast remained the last bastion of Episcopalianism in Scotland. After 1688, great efforts were made to place orthodox Presbyterian ministers in the region's pulpits. The conservative influence of these men becomes clear in the area's responses to the assembly's initiatives in the second Simson case.

The second error charged by Webster against Simson was Socinianism, one of the earliest and most feared heterodoxies. Some radical reformers

---

20 See Arminius, *Works*; Schaff, *Creeds of Christendom*; Bangs, *Arminius*.

21 Drummond, *The Kirk*, 119.

22 George Garden translated Bourignan's *Light of the World* into English in 1696. The General Assembly of the Church of Scotland condemned Bourignianism in 1701, 1709, and 1710. From 1711 on, all prospective ministers had to abjure Bourignianism along with other heterodox tenets.

early became doubtful about Athanasian Christology and its abstruse Trinitarianism. Calvin himself acted swiftly against such heresy. In 1553 he was widely criticised for sending to the stake the anti-Trinitarian Michael Servetus, who had taken refuge in Geneva. Other radical refugees from western European nations found a safer haven in Poland. In Racow a community grew up with tolerant and rational ideas that became known as Socinian from the influences of Lelio Sozzini (1525–1562) and his nephew, Fausto (1539–1604), members of a Siennese Anabaptist family.

The Socinian beliefs expressed in the Racovian Catechism (1605) were execrated throughout the Calvinist world. Socinian doctrine defined God as omnipotent free will. Christ, while conceived by the Holy Ghost and born to a virgin, lived on earth as a mortal, becoming immortal only after the resurrection. His death was not an atoning sacrifice made by a co-equal member of the Trinity; rather He was the willing victim of sin, accepted and rewarded by God. From His example men might also hope for forgiveness of their sins and reconciliation with the Creator.

As Christ did not atone for the sins of men, so Adam did not pass them on to his posterity. In the absence of original sin and of a doctrine of necessary sin, the atonement was not required. Stress was instead laid on morality and intellect. Human reason, through careful exegesis of the New Testament, could reveal everything needed for salvation.[23] Men had free will to make reasoned choices; if they chose evil, God might punish them as He willed.

Most Christians saw Socinianism as a serious threat, against which vigorous defence was essential. The Socinian creed turned the spotlight on humanity, on its ability to use reason to comprehend the world, and on its free will to act ethically. This view of human nature diametrically opposed that of the Calvinist, who saw degenerate mankind as quite unable either to live virtuously on earth or to achieve salvation without the intervention of divine grace. At the end of the seventeenth century, Bayle remarked that the usual objection to Socinians was that "they open a way to Scepticism, Deism, and Atheism."[24] These were precisely the dangers feared by many Scots. The religious controversialists of the late seventeenth and early eighteenth centuries were not always consis-

---

23 The Old Testament was considered merely a guide. See entry "Socinianism" in *Encyclopedia of Religion and Ethics*, 11:650–4; "Socinus" in Bayle's *Dictionary*, 5:168–80.

24 Bayle, *Dictionary*, 5:178.

tent as to what they meant by a charge of Socinianism. While the primary intention might be to suggest a subordinationist challenge to Trinitarian Christology, a secondary meaning of the term implied no more than excessive stres on the use of reason in the interpretation of biblical mysteries.[25]

There seems little doubt that Webster based his allegations against John Simson between 1713 and 1717 on the latter meaning of Socinianism but probably included an assumption that such rationalism led to scepticism or deism, and both to Socinianism in its primary sense. When Simson began to place renewed emphasis on human reason and its place in God's scheme for Creation, he aroused the suspicion that he was rejecting the Calvinist interpretation of man and choosing what could only be Socinianism, Arminianism, or even deism. An accusation of Socinianism, such as Webster levelled at Simson, was dangerous to a layman; to a divinity professor it was perilous or worse. Should such charges be proven, he would automatically lose his position, and possibly even his life, as Aikenhead's case had demonstrated.

Third, in addition to Simson's stress on the use of reason, which might be construed as Socinian, and on the possibility of all mankind having access to divinely revealed knowledge, which was presumably Arminian, Webster condemned Simson's understanding of the relationship between God and Adam. To orthodox Scots, Adam was the federal head of mankind, relating to God through the covenant of works. Adam's posterity entered into a new covenant with its Redeemer after the incarnation – the covenant of grace.

Federal, or covenant, theology developed to temper the stringency of the doctrine of the divine decrees that gained greater prominence after Calvin's death in 1564. Since all of creation exists to realize a divine plan formulated by the Godhead from eternity, reformed theologians formalized theories concerning the order and method by which God implemented His will. The divine purpose became manifest through a series of decrees whereby God predestined the elect to be saved and the reprobate to be damned, with Christ acting as mediator on behalf of the former. From the time of Beza, who was responsible for elevating Calvin's discussion of election and reprobation from a section of the *Institutes* dealing with how man may obtain grace, to being part of the doctrine of God, theologians were divided into infralapsarians and

25 See Reedy, *The Bible*, 119–20.

supralapsarians. Infralapsarians believed that the Fall came before the determination of salvation for the elect. Supralapsarians had a harsher, though more logical, viewpoint in which the decrees were part of the divine plan before creation itself, thus demonstrating that grace preceded election.

The methodology of the decrees led to the belief that Christ died only for the elect – the doctrine of limited atonement – enunciated in the Canons of Dort. Knowing that many were deaf to the preaching of the Word, and believing in a God of inflexible justice and severity whose power would seem diminished should His offer of salvation be rejected, Calvinist theologians denied the possibility that Christ was the universal mediator.[26] Their philosophical delineation of an omnipotent and inscrutable deity who created sinful men, all of whom deserved damnation, had alarming consequences for pastoral ministry. Both Scots and Dutch theologians accordingly began to work out escape clauses to mitigate its severity and give the clergy a means of presenting to their flocks an understanding of God's offer of salvation.

The place of the Fall in the eternal scheme of salvation was redefined in the seventeenth century through federal theology. This shifted attention from the characteristics of the divine decrees themselves to how they were fulfilled in history.[27] A practical understanding of the minutiae of election was more valuable than a knowledge of its theoretical underpinnings to a minister preparing a Sunday sermon for his congregation. Rather than considering how the divine plan for election was determined, the new theology concentrated on God's relationship with His creatures. This was explained by covenants (*foedera*), a concept based on Old Testament history.

The theology developed in various countries including Scotland, but its mature formulation came from another Leiden professor, Johannes Cocceius (1603–1669), whose work Herman Witsius expanded in 1677. Historians have argued that the ideas expressed by Cocceius were already prevalent in Britain. The Scot Robert Rollock had spoken of a covenant of works in 1595, and his ideas were worked out by several seventeenth-century divines. Johannes Wollebius (1586–1629) in Basel and the English Puritan exile William Ames (1576–1633) in Holland published theological writings that included the topic. In

---

26 For further discussion on this see Armstrong, *Calvinism.*
27 Leith, *Introduction,* 116.

England the subject was being discussed from 1629 on and played a major role in the framing of the Westminster Confession.[28] The concept of the covenant was particularly powerful in seventeenth-century Scotland, where it served a politico-religious purpose in the strife between church and Crown.

Scots divines sometimes identified three scriptural covenants. The covenant of works was a pact between God and Adam before the Fall, whereby the Creator promised His creature eternal life in return for perfect obedience. The covenant of redemption existed eternally between God the Father and God the Son to obtain salvation for the elect. This was sometimes merged with the covenant of grace, between the Father and the Son as the representative of the elect, just as Adam had been the representative of mankind, to assure grace through His mediation. This scheme meant that the role of Adam, not merely as progenitor but as legal representative of mankind, was pivotal; Christ appeared as the Second Adam, bringing the "gift of righteousness" (Rom. 6:17): "For as in Adam all die, even so in Christ shall all be made alive" (1 Cor. 15:22). Adam represented all mankind, not merely the Christian community; but only those who could and did believe in Christ would be saved.

The difficulty in such an explanation of the working of divine providence is the apparently legalistic and conditional nature of divine grace. Rollock made both covenants conditional, thus implying "that God is related to all of humanity by nature and law, but relates in love only to the elect, for only the elect are effectually called in the covenant of grace, whereas all humanity are born under the covenant of works."[29] It became a common Scottish spiritual exercise for an individual to make a covenant personally with the Lord in preparation for such events as communion, marriage, or the beginning of an educational or professional venture.[30] Many evangelical ministers had trouble with the conception of a covenant between God and man stated as a contractual agreement. Thomas Boston and others were concerned about the legalism of these

28 See Bell, *Calvin* for a Scottish context for federal theology.

29 Ibid., 57.

30 An example is found in Ferrier, *Memoirs of the Rev. William Wilson*, 43–4. Wilson, about to enter Glasgow University's divinity school, declared that his intention in undertaking his studies was "God's Glory, and the good of souls," and asked for divine assistance. In return he promised not to waste his time, as he had in the past, and to devote himself to the divine service.

practices, fearing that the free gift of grace was being treated as a commercial transaction.[31] Even worse, an element of salvation by works seemed to be implicit in the idea of individuals' bargaining with God with promises of a devout and virtuous life.

Simson likewise objected to the explicitly legal language of "Stipulation, Restipulation and Ad-stipulation."[32] He also condemned those who suggested that under the Gospel there was "A *Covenant of Duties*."[33] Aware that there was no direct scriptural basis for this theology, Simson was anxious to return to the biblical interpretation of Adam as the ancestor of man through natural generation and, as such, the channel for natural corruption. His studies had led to his insistence on the use of clear language for doctrinal discussion. He was in no way denying the doctrine of original sin; rather he was trying to make it intelligible to all and to remove any contractual implications.

In his attributing a non-federal role to Adam, Simson was accused of falling into the error of Placaeus of Saumur (Josué de la Place, 1596–1655).[34] In the seventeenth century, French Huguenots had formulated defences against the challenge from a new Catholic Pyrrhonism. The Saumur school had been a leader in this effort, influenced by a Scottish professor, John Cameron (c. 1579–1625), a Glasgow graduate who had furthered his education in France, Geneva, and Heidelberg. At Geneva he disagreed with Beza on some issues, and when he spoke of three covenants between God and man, he was suspected of Arminianism. At Saumur he taught the most distinguished representative of the school, Moyse Amyraut (1596–1664), and Josué de la Place, who created new theological excitement in the French church, as well as the innovative biblical critic Louis Cappel (1585–1658).

In the stimulating milieu of Saumur, Amyraut, de la Place, and Cappel defended their vision of the meaning of Calvin from the scholasticism inherited from Beza. Amyraut used a modified form of covenant

31 Boston wrote of being influenced by Rev. James Fraser of Brea and, more particularly, by Fraser's colleague at Culross, Rev. George Mair. Even before he came across Fisher's *The Marrow of Modern Divinity*, he "had several convictions of legality in my own practise," and in 1704 he objected to an affirmative argument in a trial exegesis by a young preacher on *An foedus gratiae fit conditionatum?* Boston, *Memoirs*, 160–2. Modern scholars have agreed with Boston. Geoffrey W. Bromiley noted that the covenant of works "becomes a contract with appropriate rewards and penalties for observance or non-observance"; *Historical Theology*, 316.

32 Webster, *True Copy*, 18.

33 Simson, *Libel*, 169.

34 Webster, *True Copy*, 28.

theology in an attempt to return to Calvin's original scheme and to counteract the scholastic tendencies that he felt were mere speculations not based on the Bible.[35] He postulated three covenants that were successive revelations of God's relations with man: a covenant of nature, a legal covenant, and a covenant of grace; through these God showed His mercy to His people.[36] The covenant of grace had a universal application; a loving Father "sent his Son to be the propitiation for our sins" (1 John 4:10), and that Son commanded his disciples: "Go ye therefore and teach all nations" (Matt. 28:19).

Amyraut followed Calvin in believing that predestination should be understood only as an explanation of why not all believe. Combining the facts that Christ died for all and yet that only some are elect, he claimed that even though God willed the grace of universal salvation to be common to all, it was "in such a way conditional that without the accomplishment of the condition [of belief] it is completely inefficacious."[37]

Josué de la Place's thought moderated contemporary ideas of original sin. His work was attacked for his view of the imputation of Adam's sin. Seventeenth-century Calvinists were divided as to whether the imputation of Adam's sin should be considered immediate and antecedent or mediate and consequent. Immediate imputation made Adam's descendants responsible for participation in his actions: hereditary guilt preceded hereditary sin. Mediate imputation made the inherent depravity of man, which was derived from Adam, the ground for imputation and damnation. A majority of Reformed theologians called for actual participation of men in the Fall of Adam; he, as a natural, organic head, transmitted the corruption incurred by his personal sin to his posterity through physical generation. During the seventeenth century the theory was elaborated that Adam vicariously represented his posterity legally, via the covenant of works; therefore his disobedience and its consequences are judicially imputed to them (Hos. 6:7: "But they like men have transgressed the covenant: there have they dealt treacherously against me"). Supralapsarians and federalists believed in immediate imputation, which left men responsible for Adam's disobedience as participants and condemned them independently of and prior to personal depravity. Orthodox Scots placed great stress on Adam's federal headship of his posterity.

---

35 Armstrong, *Calvinism*, 142.
36 Ibid., 151.
37 Amyraut, *Brief Traitté*, quoted in Armstrong, *Calvinism*, 169–70.

De la Place replaced this stance with mediate imputation: the inherent depravity inherited from Adam was the only ground for imputation of sin. He thus rejected an inherent human predisposition to sin, while accepting the reality of the degeneration of mankind since Adam. This view was denounced at the Synod of Charenton in 1644–45, which "condemneth the said Doctrine as far as it restraineth the Nature of Original Sin to the sole Hereditary Corruption of *Adam's* Posterity, to the excluding of the Imputation of that first Sin by which he fell."[38] When Simson queried the notion of Adam's being the federal head of his posterity, it was logical for his opponents to suggest that he was leaning towards a Placean belief in mediate imputation.

THE WESTMINSTER CONFESSION
AND SIMSON'S POSITION

When he was licensed to preach, John Simson had to subscribe the Westminster Confession of Faith. Twice more, on his ordination and on his formal admittance to the Glasgow faculty, he had to provide proof of this subscription. By 1700 this confession was seen as the pre-eminent standard of Scottish faith, although it had been drawn up by a gathering of English churchmen in the 1640s. The Westminster Assembly (1643–52) had been appointed by Parliament to create a new foundation for the Church of England and to promote unity with the Church of Scotland, which sent advisory delegates to the meeting at Westminster. The issues that had been discussed at the Synod of Charenton were examined further at Westminster. Letters from Scots delegates underscored the concern felt by all Reformed churches about the influences emanating from Saumur, proving that later orthodox Scots were simply misinformed when they denied any previous division over doctrine in the church. Continual argument marked the early stages of the assembly; when the delegates tried to create a form of presbyterian church government for the whole island, Erastians, Independents, Anabaptists, and Antinomians all objected.

This last group – Antinomians – may be briefly introduced here, since it represented what seemed a significant danger to orthodox Scottish Presbyterians, both in the seventeenth and in the early eighteenth centuries. Antinomianism was the belief that grace set Christians free from servitude to law: "for ye are not under the law, but under grace"

38 From John Quick, *Synodicon in Gallia Reformata*, 2 vols. (London, 1692), 2:473–4. Quoted in Armstrong, *Calvinism*, 104–5.

(Rom. 6:14). Although this did not mean that the devout Christian was exempt from obedience to the Ten Commandments or to the law of his nation, some saw it as a slackening of such controls. Antinomianism flourished in the relaxed atmosphere of the Civil War, but the opportunity that social disruption gave for the expression of such radical views was relatively short-lived. With the resumption of firm government, measures were taken to bring extremists under control. Looking back, men of Simson's generation saw Antinomianism as a product of the disorderly sectarianism of the Commonwealth in Scotland. Nevertheless, in reaction to excessive legalism in interpreting the Gospel message, a form of it re-emerged in the early eighteenth century, when it found itself enmeshed in the aftermath of Simson's first case.[39]

One Scottish delegate to the Westminster Assembly, Robert Baillie, regretted that Amyrauldism had affected some members of the assembly. "Many more loves these fancies here than I did expect ... Amyraut's treatise goes in the assemblie from hand to hand."[40] In the end Baillie pronounced that the Assembly had produced "a very gracious and satisfactorie Confession."[41] Back in Edimburgh, a younger colleague of his, Patrick Simson's cousin George Gillespie, told the General Assembly of 1647, "The Confession of Faith is framed, so as it is of great use against the floods of heresies and errors that overflow that land; nay, their intention of framing of it was to meet with all the considerable Errors of the present tyme, the Socinian, Arminian, Popish, Antinomian, Anabaptistian, Independent errors, &c. The Confession of Faith sets them out, and refutes them."[42] Despite this confident assertion, the documents produced by the Westminster Assembly suggest that its members wanted to express a broad Reformed theology that would allow for some individual interpretation.[43] The theology of the Westminster Confession was based on Calvinist predestination, on the idea of decrees as containing the divine plan, and on the covenants, but since its premises were backed by biblical citations, it was mute on the notion of double predestination.

Many members sympathized with Amyraut's hypothetical universalism, as Bailie's concern showed. They favoured the idea of a real intention by God for universal salvation: Christ actually died for all, but not everyone

39 For a discussion of this, see below, chapter 9.
40 Baillie, *Letters*, 2:324.
41 Ibid., 2:379.
42 Ibid., 3:451.
43 See S.B. Ferguson, "Westminster Assembly and Documents," in Nigel Cameron, ed., *Dictionary*.

accepts his sacrifice. The Westminster Confession recognized freedom of will in articles 3:1 and 9:1. It contained contradictions in its interpretation of the divine intention. Article 3:6 seems to suggest limited redemption, article 8 is generally ambiguous, and in article 7:3 sinners are freely offered life in return for faith. Even in this last article, however, there is an element of limitation in the fact that God will give this faith only to "all those that are ordained unto life." The scriptural references used to back this up are also equivocal: the Old Testament passage from Ezekiel is a generous promise to the House of Israel (Ezek. 36:26, 27), while the Gospel text from John demanded that the Father draw sinners to Christ, but adds: "And they shall all be taught of God. Every man therefore that hath heard, and hath learned of the Father, cometh unto me" (John 6:44, 45). This last section may have been a compromise between both positions, as in Saumur.

The confession and catechisms define two covenants, of works (7:2) and of grace (7:3). Covenant theology differed from that of the decrees in that it saw man as a "free responsible agent, not as a machine for the execution of absolute divine decrees."[44] God was carefully sheltered from being the author of sin in any way (5:4). This final point was difficult to resolve in a philosophical world in which the will of God was operative. While all temporal actions were controlled within the divine plan, God "neither is nor can be the author or approver of sin" (5:4). The eighteenth-century debate on this question is considered below in the discussion of issues raised by Webster in Simson's first case, when the two men were to clash over their interpretation of God's responsibility for sin. Here it may be said briefly that the subject was central to the Calvinism of many seventeenth-century Scots. Principal John Strang (1584–1654) of Glasgow University was forced to resign his position in 1650 because he attacked the prevalent opinion, which taught that God, in order to encompass His desired end, used sin to demonstrate His justice. Thus, although God warned man of the dangers, He did nothing to prevent him from committing sinful acts and punished him for their execution, a doctrine illustrated by the story of the Fall.

Since the signing of the National Covenant in 1638, Scots Presbyterians had been concerned primarily with issues of ecclesiology rather than with doctrine. The covenant was designed to elicit support from the nation against the religious innovations decreed by Charles I and his

44 Schaff, *Creeds of Christendom*, 1:773.

archbishop of Canterbury, William Laud. Subscribers committed themselves to opposing civil control of the church and to defend Reformed forms of worship. Writing to Simson in 1711, Robert Rowan noted: "It hath been the Exercise of this Church to wrestle against *Erastian* Prelacie since the Reformation began, and she never had any considerable struggle about her Doctrine within her self."[45] Scots representatives to the Westminster Assembly had stressed the significance of extending presbyterian church organization throughout the British Isles, while warmly accepting the confession and catechisms produced by the English delegates. Although both Presbyterian ecclesiology and the Westminster theological documents fell on stony ground in England, in Scotland the Westminster system became the foundation of faith for the future. Professor James Wodrow, who had studied under Baillie at Glasgow University, taught his divinity students that the Westminster Assembly had the status of a general council of the Reformed churches because representatives had been present from all British churches and Calvinists abroad had been consulted. It thus followed that to Wodrow's students: "Our *Confession* is justly to be esteemed the Doctrine of all the *Calvinist* Churches in *Europe* or any where else."[46] In view of the persistent threats from the Crown to the integrity of the Church of Scotland in the latter half of the seventeenth century, and of the consequent struggles to uphold the headship of Christ against the usurpation of kings and bishops, devout patriotic Presbyterians saw the Westminster standards as sure ground on which a stand might be safely taken.

Simson chose to differ, not in his claims of adherence to the Westminster Confession, but in his understanding of the perfection that it represented. Defending himself to the Presbytery of Glasgow in March 1715, Simson stated that he had "in the first Place, taken for my Rule the Holy Scriptures, which are the Perfect Rule of Faith and Manners. I do, in the Second place, for a help to follow this Rule aright, set before me that Excellent Sum of the Doctrine of the Gospel, which is Contained in Our *Confession* of Faith and *Catechisms*; Having, after frequent Examination, and Mature Deliberation been Convinced that it was agreeable to the Word of God, the Supreme Rule."[47] In Simson's eyes, the Bible represented the only perfect code for human conduct. The

45 Webster, *True Copy*, 24.
46 Robert Rowan, in ibid., 31.
47 *Libel*, 60.

confession was a document of earthly derivation, which could and should be studied with care, in order to form a reasonable judgment as to its applicability as a guide to assist sinful mortals in obeying the divine commands. Simson claimed that he had determined that it was indeed "a help to follow this Rule." He would have agreed with Baillie that the confession was "a very sweet and orthodoxe peice, much better than any Confession *yet extant*."[48]

To both men the Westminster document represented only an improvement on previous confessions. As Simson pointed out to Rowan, their forebears had originally signed the "Old-Confession," or Scotch Confession of Faith, of 1560. When the Westminster divines produced "the same Doctrine with the old more fully explained and better expressed," they signed it willingly.[49] It was Simson's view, as it was that of his student William Dunlop, that public confession was necessary if the church was to maintain its standards. This code would state the basic doctrines of the members in a way that could be understood by all and would be taught in its seminaries. Like the civil law, however, such a code was not infallible, and it could be changed, should its subscribers so desire.

Simson rejected any restrictions on a professor's right to re-evaluate man-made creeds or canons. For him they were all comments on the Bible and on church history, which every Protestant theologian (and indeed every individual) was required to consider personally. He was thus free to voice the opinion that various articles might have been better phrased, particularly that of the covenant of works. He and his brother had discussed these issues with their father when they were undergoing trials to become preachers. Accordingly, before John Simson signed the confession to obtain his licence, he informed the Presbytery of Paisley of his scruples about its wording. The ministers present accepted his qualms and allowed him to sign notwithstanding his reservations. In consequence he felt no doubt about continuing to examine the confession critically, noting, "There are several Truths in it, which I do not believe upon the Common Proofs used in Systems: nor dare I stop Inquiry or fair Examination of any Proposition that Differs from or contradicts it, or any other humane Composure. Neither do I think it cannot be amended to the Better, both as to Thoughts and Expressions: Which Ministers signing of it does not bar up."[50]

48 Baillie, *Letters*, 2:397, emphasis added.
49 Webster, *True Copy*, 7.
50 Ibid.

Simson added that his father, who had known Dickson and Gillespie, two of the Scottish representatives at Westminster, had told him that "there were different Sentiments among the Members of that Assembly, and that they expressed some Articles in general Terms to take in both Parties or exclude neither."[51] If this should make the Westminster Assembly seem as like the Council of Trent "as one Egg is like another," it did not alter the facts.[52] The records of that assembly uphold Simson's contentions, but for Webster these arguments represented an ominous attack on the foundations of the doctrine of the church.

CONTINENTAL CORRUPTION
AND SIMSON'S BALANCE

Continental developments in Simson's lifetime underscore the balanced position that he held in terms of contemporary Calvinism. By the 1710s, even Swiss Calvinists were rejecting the strict Helvetic Consensus Formula of 1675, which had stated that the Gospel call to salvation was never intended to be general: in the Old Testament God's message was directed to the children of Israel; in the new dispensation of the Gospel, it is limited to Christians. To conservative Scots, however, the document still represented a clear statement of their faith. When Simson and his friends wished to break down the walls of dogma, the orthodox saw them as foxes breaching the hedge surrounding the Lord's Vineyard. There was real concern that Scotland was following the lax pattern observed elsewhere.

Thomas Harvie, a graduate of Simson's programme studying in Leiden, wrote in 1715: "[T]he Church in Switzerland and at Geneva, I think, is generally thought to be corrupting by degrees, both as to doctrine, worship, and government, which is imputed to a triumvirate of their ministers who have correspondence with the Church of England, viz, Mr Turretine at Geneva, who is much reflected against by the people; another at Neuschattel, whose name I know not, and one at Basil called Werenfelsius."[53]

By 1730, the Scots feared that Jean-Alphonse Turretin (1671–1737) "had quite overturned everything in Geneva," where he was professor

51 Ibid., 16.
52 Ibid.
53 Wodrow, *Correspondence*, 2:18. Harvie is listed in the Glasgow divinity class of January 1708 and received a King William bursary to study theology abroad in June 1714. *Munimenta*, 3:250, 296.

of divinity.[54] The Swiss professor was allowed more latitude than his Glasgow counterpart, publishing in 1719 a work that stated that all humans were capable of salvation.[55] Unlike his father, the theologian François, Jean-Alphonse Turretin espoused rational theology, publishing defences of it with the apparent approval of the majority of Swiss Calvinists. As early as 1706, J.-A. Turretin had championed the rights of ministers who hesitated to subscribe the Helvetic Consensus Formula, dealing the formula a deathblow as a prerequisite for admission to the Genevan Company of Pastors.[56]

The unnamed corrupting influence at Neuchâtel was presumably its professor of theology, Jean-Frédéric Osterwald (1663–1747), who busied himself both with liturgical reform and with the writing of a new, simplified catechism to promote orthodox theology against Socinians and deists. He shared liberal opinions with J.-A. Turretin and joined him in the campaign against the Helvetic Formula Consensus.

Samuel Werenfels (1657–1740) taught theology from 1696 to 1720 at Basel, where he attempted to minimize the emphasis on doctrinal systems and stress the Christian life. All three men were teachers whose ideology agreed with that of Simson and who condemned the scholasticism of seventeenth-century Calvinism. Klauber notes that "the so-called Swiss triumvirate were seen as champions of enlightened orthodoxy," a distinction that would certainly make them suspect in the eyes of conservative Scots.[57]

During much of the later seventeenth century, exiled Scots ministers had been exposed to Continental influences as the result of Stuart religious persecution. After 1688, many other Scots, including John Simson, discovered Dutch theology and learning through their studies at Leiden, Utrecht, or Gröningen. For the first decades of the next century, Scots divinity students continued to study in Holland, where they received a message of liberal Remonstrant theology and secular toleration. Conservatives complained about Dutch Reformed church members accepting wild theological notions, as well as being apparently under the control of the secular authorities.[58] They also had problems with heterodox ministers such as Herman Roëll, a teacher who pre-

---

54 Wodrow, *Analecta*, 4:149.
55 See Beardslee, "Introduction," 21–2.
56 See Klauber, *Between*, 146–8.
57 Ibid., 173.
58 See Wodrow, *Analecta*, 2:283, for Holland. See also Wodrow, *Correspondence*, 2:4–9, 2:351–4, letters from Thomas Harvie and William Wright on Dutch church affairs.

sented some interesting parallels to John Simson and whose ideas Simson would have heard during his residence in Holland.[59]

J.-A. Turretin became acquainted with Roëll when he studied in Holland in the early 1690s, but we have no evidence that Simson met the controversial professor.[60] Roëll (1653–1718), professor of theology at Franeker and then at Utrecht, aroused orthodox concern for his views both on the role of reason and on the Trinity. From 1686 on he was criticized for his efforts to reconcile the roles of reason and revelation in the human search for salvation. He also became embroiled in controversy over his views on the generation of the Son, believing that the orthodox terminology was simply a code to explain the relationship of the co-eternal and consubstantial partners in the Trinity. In 1691 several Dutch synods condemned these teachings, forbidding all ministers and professors to refer to them. Nevertheless, Roëll continued in his career as professor and suffered no lasting injury. The suggestion that such clement treatment could be ascribed to Roëll's "gentle disposition" might offer at least a partial explanation of the difference in the punishment meted out to Simson in the late 1720s.[61] The similarity between Roëll's theology and Simson's indicates clearly the central position taken by the Scot in the doctrinal advances of his time.

A good Presbyterian could not remedy foreign shortcomings in theology or ecclesiology, but he could be roused to a pitch of indignation about dangers within the Church of Scotland. The tenets of orthodox Calvinism, as upheld by the Synod of Dort, the Westminster Assembly, and the Helvetic Consensus Formula, had met with little opposition in seventeenth-century Scotland outside the northeast. A strict interpretation of Calvin's message was the crux of Webster's faith; it represented the theological foundation of his attack on Simson. The Westminster Confession, with its scriptural basis, seemed to obviate any need for further theological speculation. That a belief in the freedom from doctrinal disagreement was a misconception that ignored the debates of the early seventeenth century, the exile of John Cameron, and the resignation of John Strang did not lessen the conviction of those who held it.

59 See T. Harvie to R. Wodrow, Leiden, 22 March 1715. "Roell is not thought Arian or Socinian in the great point of the Deity of Christ, but rather a Tritheist, though I am informed, in the matter of justification, he goes in to them and in other things." Wodrow, *Correspondence*, 2:17. Also NLS 2.246/6.

60 Klauber, *Between*, 59.

61 See article on Roëll by S.D. van Veen in *New Schaff-Herzog Encyclopedia*, 10:65.

The teaching of the Glasgow professor might introduce foreign heresy into Scotland. Webster and his friends knew that it was their duty to save their countrymen from the errors experienced by the Continental churches. Despite their efforts, however, the world of the eighteenth-century Scottish universities was to belong to the more open-minded Presbyterians who followed Simson.

John Simson's eagerness to adopt new concepts and his openness to conjecture presaged later Scottish Enlightenment standards. Just as he accepted the Lockean premises of the Glorious Revolution and the political compromises implicit in the Act of Union, so Simson adopted a broader Reformed orthodoxy which encompassed the thought of the new century. The significance of the theological philosophy which he embraced lay in its pastoral applications for dealing with the religious and philosophical controversies of the day. Libertinism, scepticism, and deism must be confronted by a theology which would allow ministers to reconquer wavering souls. Simson believed that a rejuvenated church would be strong enough to withstand sceptical conjectures if some natural theology and a form of hypothetical universalism could be incorporated into the often-carping body of Scottish orthodox doctrine. While he tried to avoid the dangerous pitfalls of explicit Arminianism or Amyrauldism, he wished to introduce a more compassionate view of Christ's offer of salvation in order to counteract the risks of infiltrating deism. A review of the charges against Simson and of his defences leads to the conclusion that the professor was a sound adherent of a more inclusive form of Calvinism than had become current in Scotland. Unfortunately this was exactly what Simson's antagonists feared.

Scotland was in close and continuous contact with London and the intellectual centres of the Continent through printed material and personal relationships. Many Scots professors and ministers had studied abroad and often maintained the friendships formed at that time. The well-to-do normally sent their sons overseas to finish their education under the law professors of the Netherlands, while scholarships existed for less privileged students to study theology in Holland or for a few to widen their horizons at Balliol College in Oxford. Newspapers, books, and letters flowed north from England, west from Holland and France, and east from Ireland. Glasgow University had subscriptions to London papers which were available for all to read at specific times daily.[62] Students abroad were bombarded with letters of requests for particular books or for general information as to what was current in the religious world elsewhere.[63]

Decreasing emphasis was placed on the sceptical risks posed by Cartesianism, as Newtonianism began to replace it at Glasgow and other schools. Although the works of English deists were read and largely rejected, the broader issues raised by them were harder to resist. To Webster and his orthodox friends, Simson was part of a widespread trend to propagate error throughout the British Isles. Webster felt that it was imperative to prevent the contagion of English deism from entering the Scottish church. While finding an adequate definition of deism has long challenged historians, I take it to be a system of natural religion employing reason to dispense with revelation.[64]

The contemporary English debate on the relationship between Christianity and reason had been stimulated by John Locke's *The Reasonableness of Christianity* (1695) and John Toland's *Christianity not Mysterious* (1696). Locke's epistemology denied the existence of innate ideas, but it permitted human knowledge of God through the exercise of reason. Toland argued that Christianity contained only what could be understood by human reason and that its mysterious aspects were perversions of its purity. Thirty years later Matthew Tindal summarized the deistic viewpoint in *Christianity as Old as the Creation, or The Gospel, a Republication of the Religion of Nature* (1730). During the intervening decades it was common to assert that those who sincerely used their reason to find truth would be successful in their search. Since divine law was instrumental in the promotion of human happiness, religious duty must always harmonize with the real wants and spiritual welfare of the individual. It

62 Letters from Postmaster James Anderson to Principal Stirling discuss stopping the college's subscription to the *Flying Post* in November 1716 and paying for the *London Gazette* and the *Evening Post* in November 1717. NLS, Advocates MS, 29.1.2, Anderson Papers Vol. VII, 81, 120. In 1722 the newspapers were on the table of the forehall of the college from noon to 2 p.m. and from 4 p.m. to 6 p.m. on each post day during the session and from 2 p.m. to 6 p.m. in the vacation. GUA 26632, 61.

63 Simson wrote to John Clerk of Penicuik, in Italy on the grand tour, expressing interest in Clerk's hopes of getting a copy of the foundation charter of the University of Bologna. J. Simson to J. Clerk, 7 Feb. 1698, NAS, GD18/5212. Wodrow made many requests to friends for foreign intelligence. Letters between him and the Glasgow student Thomas Harvie in 1714–15 demonstrate his wide interests; Wodrow, *Correspondence*, 2:4–18.

64 See Emerson, "Latitudinarianism," 19–48.

becomes evident below that while John Simson was in agreement with these propositions, he always tried to express them within the framework of orthodox Reformed theology based on revelation, and he accepted the intervention of Divine Providence.

Since the 1690s the Boyle lecturers in London had annually affirmed the foundations of revealed Christianity against various unbelievers, including deists, and had set forth the proofs for the being and attributes of God. Samuel Clarke, the Anglican priest who had written the Newtonian commentary on Rohault's physics text admired by John Simson, gave the Boyle lectures in 1704 and 1705, eloquently presenting fashionable arguments. Clarke's interest in the basis of Christian faith led him to publish *The Scripture Doctrine of the Trinity* (1712), a study of the textual origins of Trinitarian theory. Since he found none, he left himself open to accusations of Arianism, but ecclesiastical charges against him were dropped when he declared his orthodoxy and promised neither to preach nor to write again on the subject. A different fate befell Clarke's friend William Whiston, who had inherited Newton's Cambridge chair in 1703. Dabbling in patristic criticism proved more dangerous for Whiston; he was ejected as an Arian from the university in 1710. His *Primitive Christianity Revived* appeared in 1711, but Queen Anne's death in 1714 brought proceedings against him to an end.

Scots were early alarmed about the effect of deistic developments on organized religion. In 1701 Sir William Anstruther (d. 1711) published *Essays Moral and Divine* against some of the vices and dangers of his day. In response to Toland and Aikenhead, he testified against "the Spreading Contagion of Atheism" and spoke with some approval of Locke.[65] Thomas Blackwell (1660?–1728), professor of divinity and later principal of Marischal College, Aberdeen, produced his *Ratio Sacra, or an appeal unto the Rational World about the reasonableness of Revealed Religion* in 1710. Its lengthy title defined its purpose of refuting "the three grand prevailing errors of Atheism, Deism, and Bourignonism." Bourignianism, a set of beliefs borrowed from the teaching of Antoinette Bourignon and particularly influential in the northeast, was one of the few contemporary heterodoxies of which Simson was not accused. Blackwell's book first established the power of the intellect, then proved the reasonableness and divine origin of revealed religion in a rational way. A second volume, explaining the divine scheme of natural and revealed religion, appeared shortly afterwards. Thomas

65 Anstruther, *Essays*, preface, no pagination.

Halyburton rebutted deistic arguments in *Natural Religion Insufficient* (posthumously published in 1714).

Simson, along with other educated Scots, followed the English controversies, eagerly reading the books which they spawned and agreeing that the authors generally erred in their conclusions. Robert Wodrow corresponded with Simson in 1711 about a Whiston publication regarding the actions of Convocation (the Church of England's assembly) against him. Wodrow felt that Convocation's weak handling of the matter would merely strengthen "the hands of Deists, Atheists, and Unitarians in England."[66] He clearly considered that the recipient of his letter would share his views. Simson found the research and techniques of the English scholars interesting and worthy of further study, even if their conclusions were erroneous. His own examination of patristic texts in the early 1720s may have stemmed from his reading of Clarke and Whiston. Professors such as Blackwell and Simson met in the course of church and university affairs and shared a belief in the ability of reason to elucidate revelation. However, Webster and like-minded Presbyterians, who were afraid of English deistic influences, saw as dangerous innovation Simson's efforts to expand the range of his divinity instruction to include a reliance on rational discovery and to promote belief in a generous God. Nevertheless, the biblical scholarship initiated by Locke and continued by Clarke appealed to Presbyterian scholars, with their intimate Bible knowledge. Locke's work in paraphrasing the Pauline epistles was carried on by two English Presbyterian scholars.[67] One, James Peirce, was the centre of the Arian controversy in Exeter; the second, George Benson, had studied with John Simson at Glasgow University.[68]

Although Wodrow in 1713 lamented the fact that the sons of the nobility and gentry were no longer following the recommendation of the General Assembly to attend divinity lessons for a year,[69] his correspondence illustrates the knowledgeable concern possessed by many in the upper strata of society. Younger sons of the aristocracy such as James Erskine, Lord Grange (1679–1764), brother of the Earl of Mar, had the theological skills to argue with ministers on points of doctrine. Educated abroad, and later corresponding with foreign friends, they rapidly

---

66 Wodrow, *Correspondence*, 1:251.
67 Thomas, in Bolam, *The English Presbyterians*, 147.
68 Moore, "Theological Politics," 79.
69 Wodrow, *Analecta*, 2:267.

learned of trends in Paris, Amsterdam, London, or Belfast. This awareness of the world caused considerable distress to conservative Scots, who
listened to established and dissenting churches elsewhere in Britain
vigorously debating theological and organizational questions. The English dissenters were little more united than they had been in the 1640s;
the Presbyterians of Ireland were also divided. Orthodox Scots Presbyterians sensed the importance of suppressing the transmission of any
dubious doctrines which might produce similar dissension.

　　Already there were signs of theological discord in Edinburgh. In a
1711 letter to Simson, Robert Rowan hinted of something political and
Erastian when he stated that "not long since" a professor had been "vigorously supported" by those in power in the church when he taught
Baxterian principles, with an ill influence on young ministers.[70] Rev.
Richard Baxter (1615–1691) had left the Church of England in 1662 to
preach as a moderate Presbyterian. His theological writings stated that
Christ died for all and stressed the need for regeneration and repentance, through grace. Orthodox Scots Presbyterians disapproved of his
views, seeing them as similar to those of Amyraut. The professor in question was probably George Meldrum, professor of divinity at Edinburgh
University from 1701 to 1709. Meldrum moved to Edinburgh from
Aberdeen in 1692. He had been a regent at Marischal College as a very
young man and had as a minister frequently served as rector of the college. With this background in the episcopalian northeast, he might be
expected to be both more Arminian in doctrine than Webster and more
accepting of state interference in ecclesiastical affairs. Elizabeth West
remembered hearing Meldrum preach at the Tron Church in 1695,
when he "came with one of the largest offers of Christ that ever I heard,
to all that would accept of it."[71] Meldrum taught in Edinburgh under
the tolerant Principal Carstares, who presumably was one of the powerful supporters mentioned by Rowan. Simson considered that Webster
himself taught a variety of Baxterianism, along with his friends Alexander Hamilton (1663–1738), minister of Airth, and George Mair
(d. 1716), minister of the second charge at Culross.[72] As we see below, a
conflict over Mair's career was a precipitating factor in Webster's pursuit
of Simson, while the church took Hamilton to task in 1720 for his publi-

---

70 Simson, *Libel*, 25. Appendix to Fisher, *Marrow of Modern Divinity*, 364.
71 West, *Memoirs*, 18.
72 Webster, *True Copy*, 3.

cation of *A Short Catechism, Concerning the Three Special Divine Covenants* (1714), which implied approval of a form of universal atonement.

In 1709 William Hamilton succeeded Meldrum in the Edinburgh chair of divinity. Webster relied on innuendo to malign the well-connected and discreet Hamilton. In his speech of 29 March 1715 to the Presbytery of Glasgow, Simson commented on Webster's belief that professors of divinity taught error, adding " 'tis also well known, what Mean Arts he used to Defame the Present Worthy Professor [of divinity at Edinburgh]."[73] In 1713 Webster accused an Edinburgh probationer called Doucat of "laxness" and tried to stop his trials.[74] Doucat was subsequently given a royal presentation to Burntisland, where the fight put up by the parish to reject him caused a considerable stir in the church. In July of the same year, the Presbytery of Edinburgh learned that another probationer, Robert Yule, had published an unsound book, entitled *The Nature and Extent of the Covenant of Grace*.[75] Between July and October 1713, three different committees of local ministers tried to persuade Yule to admit that his views were unorthodox. Despite (or perhaps because of) Webster's presence on two of these, their efforts were unavailing. At the presbytery meeting on 7 October, the third committee reported that "after all the pains taken to Reclame him, he adhered to what he asserts in the said book as his Judgement."[76]

The records of the Presbytery of Edinburgh describe Yule's errors briefly, citing five claims that he allegedly made. First, all men were to some degree under the covenant of grace, and "no man is properly under the Covenant of Works."[77] Second, there was one general reconciliation, and one peculiar to believers. Third, faith and repentance, strictly speaking, were conditions of man's first justification; furthermore, perseverance in faith, repentance, and sincere obedience was the condition of the covenant of grace. Fourth, God ruled the world and conveyed salvation to the elect through the law of grace and the law of nature. Fifth, Christ in His sufferings and death did not take the place of all mankind or of any individual man. Yet He died for all men in that He procured grace and mercy; thus God is the God of all through both

73 Simson, *Libel*, 66.
74 Wodrow, *Analecta*, 2:198.
75 NAS, CH2/121/8, 377. Book title given in CH1/1/24, 277.
76 NAS, CH2/121/8, 409.
77 Ibid., 396.

creation and redemption, although election and redemption "are not of the same Latitude or extent."[78]

These statements and Webster's accusations against Simson had features in common. Both downplayed the divine decrees and permitted some form of universalism. They also stressed the merits of Christ and the more general intention of His atonement, although the federal role of Adam was not explicitly mentioned by Yule.

All of this raises questions about the divinity school at Edinburgh. We may assume that the divinity professors at both Glasgow and Edinburgh had absorbed many of the new ideas of international Calvinism and were gradually trying to introduce them to Scotland. Hamilton was considered by many to be a man of moderate opinions, who maintained an ominous silence on various doctrines.[79] His reticence was a more effective protective strategy than Simson's public conversations on religion; or perhaps his more powerful family connections saved him from open attack. Although Hamilton was later the subject of dubious comments by Robert Wodrow and his friends, he was never directly accused of unsound teaching. For the first half of the century the zealots had serious doubts about the performance of the Scottish university professors of divinity. Simson's willingness to speak openly to his students about his liberal opinions left him more open to attack than his colleagues in other divinity schools who were more discreet. Simson was the only one whom the zealots managed to silence, although their waning power was insufficient to destroy him utterly. Nevertheless, it is possible that Simson also would have been left unimpeded in his work had he not made a personal enemy of the unbalanced James Webster over church appointments.

The controversy raised over Simson's teaching has left enough literature to allow some assessment of the positions taken by both sides. The evidence from the prosecutions of John Simson suggests that, in both Glasgow and Edinburgh, the foundations were being firmly laid for the connection which developed between the Moderates in the Church of Scotland and the ideas of the Scottish Enlightenment. Like-minded men were forced to co-operate to preserve the autonomy of the kirk and the independence of its courts against political encroachments and fanatical demands. The professors were aided by Scottish political managers, who used their patronage to improve educational standards while

78 Ibid., 410.
79 See, for instance, Killen, *History*, 3:327.

creating a loyal clientage in church and university. From a partisan point of view, an educated man of moderate opinions was a much more flexible agent than a fanatic. Scottish politics in the first quarter of the eighteenth century formed the backcloth before which the drama of the Simson cases was acted out. Political agents served as unseen prompters to the performers in the play, while their principals were the producers whose coffers helped to finance the production through patronage. For both sides in the quasi-judicial ecclesiastical investigations into Simson's theological opinions, the issue was not entirely one of truth or justice. The cases revealed the continuation of patronage and paternalism within the legal structures of Scotland. Scottish legal proceedings had traditionally been swayed by family and interest. Both the zealots and the politicians saw the Simson cases in similar terms; to the former, the honour of God was at stake, to the latter, the issue was party pride. There could be no shame in using whatever influence was available to secure a victory in such a contest.

Part Two   Simson's First Case

6

A General Inclination to Novelties in Doctrine: Letters, Negotiations, Skirmishes, 1711–1715

James Webster first made accusations against Simson in the summer of 1710, when they were taking the waters at Moffat, a spa with sulphur springs in the high Border country of Ettrick.[1] On that occasion, after the two men debated some of the contentious issues, Webster accepted Simson's explanation of his teaching. Simson recorded that Webster had further said: "He would Defend Me against all that He should find Blaming Me" for statements on the covenant of works.[2] When the two men met again the following summer, they were still on good terms. This suggests that their early disagreement rested on their differing opinions of how original sin was to be imputed. Simson had expressed scruples about the Westminster Confession to the Presbytery of Paisley ten years earlier, when he had "conversed with [his father] about the meaning of all Places of it that appeared Doubtful, whereof the Covenant of Works was One."[3] Evidently he had not seen any reason to change his views since then, and for the moment he had managed to persuade Webster to accept his position.

By the autumn of 1711, however, another orthodox clergyman was expressing concern. Robert Rowan, minister of the southwestern country parish of Penningham, had been eighteen months ahead of Simson

---

1 Webster was fond of taking the waters at Moffat; on 29 May 1717, after the stress of the General Assembly, the Presbytery of Edinburgh minutes noted that Mr James Webster was allowed to spend some weeks at Moffat well for his health, since he had provided a supply for his pulpit during his absence. NAS, CH2/121/9, 531.

2 Simson, *Libel*, 67.

3 Webster, *True Copy*, 7.

in Professor Wodrow's divinity classes at Glasgow and had been a member of the same presbytery (Dumfries) when Simson was minister at Troqueer. Simson considered him a friend and evidently hoped to reassure him on the doctrinal questions that had alarmed him. *A True and Authentick Copy of Mr. John Simson's Letters to Mr. Robert Rowan,* published by Webster in 1716, contains seven of Simson's letters dating from the period from 4 October (misdated September) 1711 to 23 November 1713, which constitute the earliest expositions of Simson's theology. Although the material printed by Webster in 1716 did not contain all of Rowan's side of the correspondence, Rowan seems to have learned of the professor's "unsound Doctrine" through reports from students at Glasgow and from the "Table Discourse at Kells" of a group of ministers.[4] Michael McTaggart "was the occasion, accidentally, of Mr Simson's first process; being born in the parish of Penningham, and 1714, a student with Mr Simson, and Mr Rouan had his informations from him, and communicat them with Mr Webster and Mr Simson himself."[5] McTaggart, whose name appears on the divinity list of 15 February 1710, expounded Simson's exciting ideas to the disturbed Rowan during his summer vacation in his home town.[6] Other students included "Mr Daes," who matriculated in divinity in February 1711 and was the bearer of Rowan's letter of 23 October 1711 to Simson. In August 1713, Simson and Webster met at the house of Mr Kell, vintner in Edinburgh, so the earlier meeting was likely at the same establishment, presumably a tavern patronized by members of the clergy when attending meetings of the assembly or its commission.

Simson heard that Rowan was thinking of requesting his synod to censure some articles taken from his teaching in the late summer of 1711. His first letter to Rowan is a pained note wondering why he had not been asked personally for an explanation of the divinity taught at Glasgow University. Rowan's reply listed the doctrinal positions that he found offensive. In the remaining letters, Simson tried to set his old acquaintance's mind at rest, although he realized that "a Letter is like

4 Ibid., 1–2. This man is called variously Kell, Kello, and Kellie. The statement that he was a vintner comes from Simson, *Libel,* 9.

5 Wodrow, *Analecta,* 4:202–3.

6 *Munimenta,* 3: 251. The "Mr Campbel" also employed as a letter carrier by Simson in 1712 may have been his student Archibald Campbell, later professor of ecclesiastical history at St Andrews University and a life-long friend and correspondent of Simson. Campbell was cited by Webster as a witness against Simson. Webster, *True Copy,* 21. Simson, *Libel,* 8.

the *Cucow* that can only tell over the same thing, not being able to tell when its Meaning is mistaken."[7] He failed, and so Rowan's apprehensions became the basis for a 1713 conference at Kell's house in 1713 and Webster's libel of 1714 against him.

Rowan charged Simson with teaching false principles, namely:

1. The Word of God is not the only Principle of Theology: Human Reason is likewise a Principle, and the Ultimate Foundation of theology.
2. The Gospel is promulgate to all the Race of Mankind, explicitly or implicitly, that they may obtain eternal life, through the use of prayer and study.
3. There was no Covenant of Works in a proper Sense between God and Adam before the Fall, only a law given to Man. If no remedy for the Fall had been provided, Adam and Eve would have had no posterity.
4. Christ by or with his Merit, is the Cause why there is an Election, but is not the Cause why this man rather than another is Elected.
5. There is no physical concourse of God with Man in sinful Actions, our natural Powers are sufficient to produce them: Nevertheless there is a Divine Predetermination about them.
7. The first Justification of the Elect is by Faith in Christ, our last Justification at the day of Judgment is from our good Works, but not by Merit.
10. The Christian magistrate hath a full power of calling Synods, appointing Fasts and Thanksgivings, but not the Sole power.

Three other points (presumably 6, 8, and 9 in the series) were mentioned as being controversial: that organs are lawful in the worship of God, that beasts have immaterial souls, and an apparent refutation of Marck's system.[8] The general effect of such a catalogue of rational notions shocked the conservative Mr Rowan.

Although Rowan demonstrated "the fervour of a Preposterous Zeal,"[9] Simson intended his barbed responses to be private. He concluded Letter III with the comment that he had used a cousin as secretary, since he did not wish Rowan's acquaintance McTaggart to see his criticism of the Penningham minister: "I thought [it] unfit to let him or

7 Webster, *True Copy*, 13.
8 Ibid., 23–4.
9 Ibid., 3.

any that understood to whom I am writing, know."[10] In November 1713 Simson told Rowan that he had no intention of publishing their correspondence, unless Webster carried out his expressed intention of formally accusing him and calling Rowan as a witness. Because of this possibility, he asked Rowan for copies of those of his letters of which he had not previously made his own version. Webster might then be sent the originals, to "let him have all the Evidence he can get out of them against me."[11] Rowan died before Webster published his edited version of the letters, presumably without Simson's permission.

Simson defended himself vigorously against Rowan's charges in his written responses to his old friend and later in public meetings and published material. His first pedagogical concern was to promote an appreciation of "the Justice and Goodness of God." His second priority was to refute enemies of Reformed theology, which sometimes proved difficult when a teacher used conventional arguments against common Arminian positions.[12] Simson seems to have tried to instruct his students in a way that would be true to Calvin's original intention, but which would place less emphasis on exclusion than was commonly the case, and more on inclusion. In his speech of 1716 to the General Assembly, Simson indicated that the terms "Calvinism" and "orthodoxy" were sometimes ambiguous, "for these who are called *Calvinists*, are not all of the same Mind with Respect to the Orthodoxy or Hetrodoxy, of several of the Propositions" stated to be erroneous by Webster.[13] Rowan and Webster did not ask whether Simson reflected the faith of Calvin and Knox; they directed their criticism at Simson's betrayal of late-seventeenth-century Reformed orthodoxy.

Simson's dependence on reason as a fundamental principle of theology headed Rowan's list of complaints against his teaching and is worthy of detailed examination here.[14] The scholastic Calvinist doctrine of the corruption of human reason since the Fall was stressed in both the manu-

---

10 Ibid., 11. Simson frequently used students as secretaries. Jonathan Woodworth mentions writing out material for him (see below, note 86), and in 1729 Simson said to Archibald Campbell, "It was a misfortune that the papers came to me in the summer vacancy when I ... had none to assist me either in reading or writing." NAS, GD461/15/13.

11 Webster, *True Copy*, 22.

12 For examples of his views, see Webster, *Propositions*, 17, and Simson, *Libel*, 61–4.

13 Webster, *Propositions*, 9.

14 In Webster's libel Simson's beliefs about reason were downgraded to no. 11 on the second list of items.

script and printed documents of Webster's partisans. Calvin himself had written that "sound reason in man was seriously injured by sin, and the will greatly entangled by vicious desire."[15] He had found that many patristic writers, such as Origen, to whom reason was "a power to discern between good and evil; of will to choose the one or the other," exalted the power of human reason in order to harmonize with classical philosophers.[16] Calvin preferred the Augustinian view that man's supernatural gifts were withdrawn after the Fall and that thereafter individuals could not use reason to know God. He concluded, however, that weakened reason remained an essential property of human nature.[17] Its function was to regulate conduct, since here the mind still had some discernment of natural law, although its perception of good and evil was flawed.[18]

Late-seventeenth-century Anglican Latitudinarians gave considerable thought to the theological significance of reason. Some central mysteries of the Christian religion are known only through revelation, but once they are revealed, reason may prove that they are possible.[19] Simson's own statements echoed those of John Locke, who, when reviewing the relationship of faith and reason, had defined the latter as "the discovery of the certainty or probability of such propositions or truths, which the mind arrives at by deductions made from such ideas which it has got by the use of its natural faculties, viz., by sensation or reflection," while faith was "an assent to any proposition, not thus made out by the deductions of reason, but upon the credit of the proposer, as coming from God by some extraordinary way of communication."[20] Revelation could not contradict reasonable evidence, and when it dealt with matters outside the direct knowledge of human beings, reason was essential in judging its probable truth. Locke concluded that "nothing that is contrary to, and inconsistent with, the clear and self-evident dictates of reason, has a right to be urged or assented to, as a matter of faith, wherein reason hath nothing to do."[21]

15 Calvin, *Institutes*, vol. 2, chap. 2, para. 4, p. 225, usually rendered 2, 2:4, 225.

16 Ibid., 2, 2:4, 227.

17 Ibid., 2, 2:12, 233.

18 Ibid., 2, 2:22, 241–2.

19 Reedy, *The Bible*, 34.

20 Locke, *Essay*, 355.

21 Ibid., 358. Following Locke would not enhance Simson's image in the eyes of the orthodox. In 1703, Wodrow commented in the *Analecta* that he had heard reports that "Mr Lock" was studying the Bible. "It's a most eminent instance of God's soveraigne dealing with one of the main propes of the Socinians and Deists, and may be a mean to engage his admirers to value the Scriptures." *Analecta*, 1:40.

While this conception had an influence on Simson and younger Scots, orthodox Scottish thought in the early years of the eighteenth century adhered to the conclusions of Calvin. James Hogg (c. 1658–1734), the ultra-orthodox minister of Carnock and a controversialist with a fertile pen, in 1716 contributed a pamphlet to the discussion on reason, in which he defined reason as primarily "our rational Faculty, as the Principle of Perception" and, secondly, "the Rules and Maxims, which are clear by what we call Nature's Light, even in our fallen Estate."[22] This faculty of reason had been corrupted by the fall, when it was "overwhelm'd with ... spiritual death."[23] As a result, corrupt reason could not explain *"revealed Religion,* which is all Mystery."[24]

Agreeing with Calvin, Hogg stressed that only through divine guidance could man have any knowledge of spiritual matters. In the eyes of conservatives such as Hogg, the functions of this debased sense of reason were strictly limited. Reason could be used "to detect & refute the Mistakes and Blunders of pretended Matters of Reason, to discover the Danger of their false and vain philosophical Schemes, and what therein consisteth not with sound Reason, and genuine Philosophy."[25] Alternatively, reason might be used to create a system of natural theology built on clear principles from which deductions might be made.[26] The dependence of man might be proved from his creation by an independent God, although the early Christians had only been able to do this in order to refute Pelagianism "owing to a merciful Conduct, and the tender Regard they had ... to Revelation contain'd in the Scriptures of Truth. Otherwise corrupt Reason left to its own Byass, would with a full Stream have run in a Self-exalting, and Pelagian Channel."[27] Hogg felt that to use reason as a means of deciding scriptural meaning would be to debase faith and the Word itself. Hogg was holding firm to the rule laid down by Calvin, who said that only by faith could one know that the scriptures were the Word of God.[28] For him, the proof of revelation lay in revelation, a circular argument that Simson despised and had denounced to Rowan.

22 Hogg, *Letter Concerning Interest,* 5.
23 Ibid., 8.
24 Ibid.
25 Ibid., 10.
26 Ibid., 12.
27 Ibid., 13.
28 Calvin, *Institutes,* 1, 8:13, 82–3.

The published views of Thomas Blackwell on reason had much in common with those of Simson and countered those of Hogg. Blackwell stated clearly that although, since the Fall, human reason was but a dim reflection of its original light, nevertheless, he believed "Reason with its Intellectual Abilities, to be an excellent Instrument, in the Hand of the Spirit of God, for discovering and finding out, what Doctrines are truly revealed in the Holy Scriptures, together with the literal Import and Sense of the same."[29] Even the damage done to the human intellect by the Fall was mitigated in the regenerate Christian. Blackwell considered that sanctified reason could be nearly restored to its original purity "in Relation to divine Truths," thus making it the greatest friend of faith.[30] The slightly younger Edinburgh minister John McLaren (1667–1734), though also a polemicist against Simson, took a position closer to the two professors than to Hogg. He claimed that reason had three uses: to understand and judge scripture truths, to draw arguments from scripture, and to confirm scripture truths by rational deductions.[31] Simson, Blackwell, and McLaren were venturing beyond normal orthodoxy. Simson believed that one should be able to convert the heathen by a rational proof of the divine origin of revelation, although Calvin had said that it was foolish to make such an attempt.

In his letter to Rowan of 21 November 1711, Simson tried to clarify his definition of reason. Using a mixture of Latin and English, he contended that the Word of God was not the sole principle of theology; indeed human reason was its ultimate foundation. He told Rowan that he considered that reason meant propositions naturally revealed, while a principle or foundation was the argument that proved a conclusion. He hastened to add "That the Scriptures are the immediate Foundation of Revealed Theologie, and the Perfect Rule of Faith and Manners, which are to be believed and obeyed, because the Word of GOD, and can receive their Authority from no Creature," as was proved in the Westminster Confession, which he taught. Having made this clear, he continued,

It is true the Scriptures are to be believed only because the Word of GOD; but none can be obliged to believe them to be GOD's Word without Proof.... Now Reason in this sense being the proper and ultimat proof by which we know every

29 Blackwell, *Ratio Sacra*, 101.
30 Ibid., 108.
31 McClaren, *New Scheme*, chap. 12.

Revelation of God to be his, it is truly and properly said to be *Principium ultimum Theolo*.... As I take Reason, (for evident Propositions naturally revealed,) I think a true Proposition taught by all; That evident Truths do not contradict Scripture, nor can, and that nothing in Scripture, can contradict them. Nor can that be the true sense of Scripture that does: And consequently I think also the other Inference; *Nothing is to be admitted in Religion, but is agreeable to Reason and determined by Reason to be so ...* to be true, as do all Orthodox Divines that I ever read; only some *Papists* and *Lutherians* deny it.[32]

Simson's opinions stemmed probably from a combination of Locke's thought and the older scholastic tradition descending from Thomas Aquinas via Hooker about the use of reason in establishing biblical meaning. He stressed that since truth could not contradict truth, and circular arguments could prove nothing (or anything), our belief in God and His revelation must be demonstrated by natural revelation and our reason. Speaking to the General Assembly in 1716, Simson reiterated his definitions: "By *Reason* I understand Evident Propositions naturally revealed, and by *Principium* or *Fundamentum*, the Argument by which any Proposition is proved."[33] He emphasized his traditional Calvinist stance when he added that no man could therefore be obliged to believe anything contradicting an evidently true proposition. To avoid any appearance of rejecting original sin and human corruption, however, he added, "if *Ratio* be taken for *Science* falsly so called, or false Notions and Principles supposed to be true, then the Proposition is manifestly absurd; and if it be taken for our darkened Understandings misled by Prejudice and corrupt Affections, it is ridiculous."[34]

The suggestion that seventeenth-century Scots attached little importance to historical arguments, considering the Bible to be its own evidence, is borne out by some statements of Simson's adversaries, who considered that his objection to circular arguments was sophistical.[35] They saw the Bible as "the most glorious of God's works, and the highest proof of Deity," and judged that reason, however logical, could not convince an unbeliever as well as could scriptural argument. "In proving the Scriptures to be the word of God by such proofs as found and beget a divine faith," they declared, "the ultimate proof is drawn from

32 Webster, *True Copy*, 4.
33 Webster, *Propositions*, 12.
34 Ibid., 15.
35 Walker, *Theology*, 40.

the Scriptures themselves."[36] Simson demanded a more logically structured argument. He refused to accept that human reason, despite being corrupt, was necessarily an enemy in spiritual matters. Although the
Westminster Confession stated, "The infallible rule of interpretation of
scripture is the scripture itself; and therefore, when there is a question
about the true and full sense of any scripture … it must be searched
and known by other places that speak more clearly,"[37] Simson did not
feel that this negated the use of reason in interpretation. The very acts
of searching the scriptures and determining which text displayed greatest clarity involved the use of human intellectual faculties. Simson
asked his adversaries how they would prove the Bible to be the word of
God to someone in China. To the response that the proof lay in the
divine axiomata, or intrinsic characters of divinity, he further questioned how one would decide what intrinsic properties were the true
characters of a divine revelation. He believed that the determination
must be made by reason or natural revelation. In his opinion it was a
circular argument to say that proof lay in scripture taken to be of divine
authority.[38] Simson's appreciation of the importance of proving divine
Revelation to the heathen, when Calvin dismissed it as foolish, is a further indication of his emphasis on pastoral training. He knew that his
students might find themselves defending their faith to non-believers
whether in the Highlands or in the Carolinas.

Simson told his inquisitors in 1728, when these charges were being
re-examined, that professors of divinity must be careful about ascribing
too little to reason as well as too much. The mortal danger of scepticism
was real to his generation, both spiritually and physically. Writing on
the spiritual risks presented by the "universal dubitation" urged by
René Descartes,[39] Hogg pointed out how, after doubt had been cast on
everything, many young people could find no map by which to escape
from the pits of scepticism and atheism in which they found themselves
trapped. As divinity professor, Simson perceived this problem and struggled to augment his pupils' ability to differentiate between real and
seeming contradictions in their reading, lest "all Certainty, both in Philosophy and Religion" be destroyed. He feared the introduction of
"universal Scepticism, and so we cannot tell, whether the Books of the

36 Quoted in ibid., 41.
37 "Westminster Confession," chap. 1:9.
38 Webster, *True Copy*, 20.
39 Hogg, *Memoirs*, 13.

Old and New Testament, or the Alcoran of Mahomet, or the Dictates of Confucius, or the Decrees of the Roman Pontif, or the Dreams of St. Bridget, and the like be the true Oracles of God."[40]

In his reliance on reason to prevent scepticism, Simson leaned heavily on orthodox Continental theologians, though of a generally more recent generation than those whose works James Wodrow had used. Simson's experts were François Turretin, Witsius, and especially Benedict Pictet, whose system he taught.[41] Among these, there was a consensus that reason must be used to combat scepticism and to tell the differences between real and seeming contradictions. Pictet wrote that man should use his reason to examine any proposition, "so he may not take errors for truths, and allow himself to be imposed upon, and seduced."[42] Although nothing should be admitted contrary to reason, faith and reason could never be opposites. François Turretin also believed that conscience, enlightened by reason, must make the ultimate judgment for each individual, although no one should assume that reason is above faith or think "that human reason is the judge of controversies, and the interpreter of Scripture as the Socinians teach."[43]

François's son, Jean-Alphonse Turretin, professor of theology at Geneva from 1705, taught a doctrine that further enlarged the role of reason. Its place was to provide substance for the preliminaries to faith. J.-A. Turretin divided theology into two parts, natural and revealed. Each originated in God, and together they formed a consistent whole: "For natural religion is the foundation of revealed, which cannot be known and explained but by principles drawn from it.... For the Existence and perfections of God ... are plainly deduced and demonstrated from reason.... For as God is most benevolent ... it necessarily follows that he must render himself capable of being known by men whom he had himself created and endowed with intelligence, in order to lead them to wisdom and happiness, provided they make a proper use of the light he has favoured them with."[44]

40 Dundas, *Processes*, 260.

41 Herman Witsius (1636–1708) was ordained in 1657 after an education at several Dutch universities. He became professor of divinity at successively the universities of Franeker (1675), Utrecht (1680), and Leiden (1698). His best-known work was his *Economy*.

42 Pictet, *True and False*, 3.

43 Turretin, "Doctrine," 224.

44 Turretine, *Dissertations*, 1–4.

These were exactly the principles being propounded by Simson in Glasgow. Some Reformed church members looked askance at the younger Turretin, as well as at Simson. The dividing line between using reason to determine the divine nature of scripture and using it to reveal the nature of salvation was a fine one. Hogg wrote, "Reason in its present corrupt State is our Arch-enemy in all the Concerns of Religion, but when subdued to the Obedience of Faith, it proves [a] choice Friend."[45] To him, knowledge of the Mysteries of religion "is intirely owing to special and divine Revelation."[46] Any suggestion that reason could elucidate the nature of God and His intentions towards men was seen as a Socinian denial of the effects of the Fall. Indeed, "Whatsoever may be said of Principles, or Maxims, naturally known, or clear Positions naturally revealed ... yet ... sound Divines, in Opposition to *Socinians*, do own, *First*, That these Maxims ... naturally revealed ... as they are understood by Men in a corrupt natural Estate, have ... scarce any Thing common with *revealed Religion*, which is all Mystery, and wholly above us; and far less can they amount to any Principle or Foundation of it, into which it may be ultimately resolved."[47]

Hogg laid bare the Protestant paradox. Reformed churches expected their individual members to interpret Holy Writ according to their own consciences and rejected giving credence to tradition or human authority. They assumed that divine grace would guide an individual's conscience to a correct rendition of any cryptic or inconsistent passages. Webster, Rowan, Hogg, and their friends believed that "orthodox divines" spoke in a united voice, that of late-seventeenth-century Covenanted Scotland. They assumed that since revealed religion was wholly mysterious and its only foundation lay in biblical texts, there must be a single orthodox dogma to which men were spiritually directed.

Simson tried to show them that even within their own church such unanimity did not exist. In response to Rowan's concern about his views of the Westminster Confession and catechisms, Simson denied saying that the documents contained error but admitted that they could be better worded. Furthermore, he said, "I allow both Ministers and People a Discretive Judgment."[48] It is questionable how many of his colleagues would have gone so far.

---

45 Hogg, *Letter Concerning Interest*, 19.
46 Ibid., 6.
47 Ibid., 8.
48 Webster, *True Copy*, 21.

NEGOTIATIONS WITH WEBSTER, 1713

In spite of the chasm between his views and those of his adversaries, initially Simson seems to have believed that the issues in question could be quickly settled by friendly discussion and personal explanation. He pointed out to Rowan that any proposition could be construed in an unsound sense when taken out of context. "To sense" was a verb used frequently in Scottish clerical circles, referring to the ways in which a given word or phrase could be understood. Since many scriptural expressions had more than one possible interpretation, preachers prided themselves on being able to give a series of sermons on a single text considered in different lights. In both Simson cases, the orthodoxy or otherwise of the professor's words often depended on how the hearer "sensed" them. Simson blamed those who debated his teaching "at a publick Table" for not first asking him to clarify his sense.[49] Rowan, however, in his letter of 23 October 1711, said that he had learned of the assertions that he found distasteful from talking to McTaggart, a young man who was remarkably enthusiastic about his professor's classes. Responding to Rowan's allegations, Simson denied placing an undue emphasis on the efficacy of works. On the contrary, he warned his students against following "Baxter's scheme." He then counterattacked by accusing Webster, Hamilton, and Mair of being the only ministers he knew teaching some form of this.[50] In his address to the Presbytery of Glasgow in 1715, Simson mentioned that Webster's approval of his instructional method changed after he had opposed Rev. George Mair's transportation to Closeburn.

Mair's problems began in March 1710, when the Synod of Dumfries refused to approve his call from the parishioners of Closeburn. The matter went to the General Assembly of 1710, which was unable to resolve it. In 1711, the assembly again tried to deal with the fact that the Synod of Dumfries did not want Mair. Typically, there were three parties involved: the congregation, the synod, and the Duke of Queensberry. Eventually a committee, which included Webster, was formed to review the case with the Presbytery of Penpont. The result was that Mair did not go to Closeburn but in 1714 was transported to Tulliallan.

Simson pointed out that although Webster had accepted his views earlier, in 1712 he "took the Liberty to Slander me in very publick Compa-

49 Ibid., 2.
50 Ibid., 3.

nies, for *Teaching Gross Errors.*"[51] He implied that Webster made his slander in revenge for his antagonism to Mair's move. In fact, Simson's approach to ministerial calls was consistent; he supported the higher authority. His alignment with the Synod of Dumfries in its refusal to admit the evangelical Mair, when Closeburn had given him a call, fore-shadowed his attitude in Glasgow to John Anderson's call, when he voted with his own presbytery to bar the pastoral choice of a church session. The passing of the oath of abjuration, and Simson's public sup-port for jurants, must have been major contributory factors in Webster's change of attitude in 1712. As the letters to Rowan prove, Simson had little sympathy for the premises of those whose consciences prohibited them from signing the oath.

The correspondence between Simson and Rowan continued until No-vember 1713. Even then Simson seemed to believe that Rowan could be brought to his point of view by further argument. By this date, however, Webster was deeply involved and was determined to bring Simson's name into disrepute. Simson was confident that "neither he nor any else can Prove that I Teach one Proposition contrar our Confession" and "dared him to pursue me."[52]

In February 1713, he had written to Webster explaining his views on four doctrinal points and calling for him either to answer the argu-ments or to prosecute him formally.[53] To this, Webster sent the follow-ing pugnacious reply, which in Simson's words "smelled ranker of something els than of the Spirit of Christ"[54]:

Ed[inbu]r[gh] 13 March 1713

R.S. In Answer to your Letter of the 23d of D[ecem]ber I know no Injury done to you by, R[everend] S[ir] your humble S[er]v[a]nt.
Ja. Webster.
P.S. I'm resolvd by Grace to stand for the Defence of Christs Truth and the Purity of the Doctrine profess'd in this Church ag[ain]st any Man who vents Errours destructive of the same; against Errours that touch near the Foundation: and no threats, no insolence, and no rude treatment shall I hope ever move me to change my firm and fixd resolution. Therefore there is no Man shall make me

---

51 Simson, *Libel*, 67.
52 Webster, *True Copy*, 22.
53 Simson, *Libel*, 67.
54 NAS, CH2/121/9, 92.

singe a Palinodiam, and eat in what I have said. You may for me take what Methods you thinke fitt for your own Vindication, if you thinke your Reputation hurt. Our Good Lord keepe this Church from Baxterian, Arminian and Pelagian Errours.[55]

Even the salutation on this missive was peremptory: "Reverend Sir" rather than the normal greeting from one minister to another of "Reverend & Dear Brother."

When Simson attended the meetings of the Commission of the General Assembly in Edinburgh in August 1713, a group of local ministers arranged a conference between him and Webster at Kell's house in the presence of William Carstares, William Wishart, John Flint, John McLaren, James Grierson, John Stirling, William Hamilton, and James Smith. This list suggests that the restraining hand of Carstares was at work. Perhaps the leading Edinburgh ministers believed that they could persuade Webster to tone down his rhetoric against Simson. Certainly the group seems carefully chosen – a majority of moderate men along with the hard-liners Flint and McLaren, whose presence might reassure the unstable Webster that fairness would prevail.

The discussion opened with Webster's demand that nothing said at the meeting should be used in any future process: "Which both the Brethren present, and I [Simson] thought very Reasonable, seeing we were met for a Friendly Conference, to Remove Mistakes, and Prevent any Process; wherefore, I heartily agreed to it."[56] After this agreement, the tone of the meeting deteriorated rapidly. Webster read a libel of twelve articles, to which Simson replied that some were "utterly false" and that others, though indeed his opinions, were not heterodox. His proposal to review them in a friendly fashion came to nothing because of the "wrangling" that ensued. When Webster began to speak heatedly of prosecuting the professor for error, Simson challenged him to do so speedily. The other ministers tried to persuade the combatants to reconcile their differences peacefully "and prevent further Noise," since that had been the purpose of the meeting.[57] Most of these men were ecclesiastical managers whose aim was to ensure that clerical squabbles did not

---

55 Simson comments that the date of the letter to which Webster referred was in fact February. A palinodiam or palinode is a poem in which the poet recants the viewpoint of a previous poem. Simson, *Libel*, 68.

56 Ibid., 69

57 Ibid., 70.

endanger the church. In the aftermath of the Tory acts of 1712 that had caused so much strife, the last thing that leading clergymen needed was a public washing of theological dirty linen which might produce further repercussions from London. Carstares and Stirling must also have been specifically concerned about the preservation of the reputation of Glasgow University and its divinity professor.

After this altercation Simson felt that it was impossible to resume amicable dialogue with Webster. Instead he offered to read his written responses to the accusations at a subsequent meeting of the same group the following week. The two men shook hands on this agreement, and, on 20 August, Simson read his answers to thirteen queries asked by Webster. To Simson's irritation, these answers later became the basis from which Webster constructed a second class of errors in the libel to the Presbytery of Glasgow, in direct violation of the initial understanding between the two men.

Webster, however, delayed charging Simson until 1714, finally bringing his accusations to the attention of the Presbytery of Edinburgh on 14 April, when an overture was passed asking the General Assembly to inquire into the fact that "a minister of this Church doth vent some Errors, contrary to our Confession of Faith, and known principles."[58] The Synod of Lothian and Tweeddale, on examining the minutes of the Presbytery of Edinburgh at its next meeting, asked the identity of the minister in the overture. Webster responded that the minister was Professor John Simson, "who as he could prove had vented both Socinian and Arminian errours."[59] The synod directed Webster to follow the correct procedure by taking the matter to the accused's own presbytery. Webster then protested this decision, considering himself to be "lesed" (legally injured) by it and appealed to the General Assembly for redress. Once again Webster's touchy personality inhibited his capacity for effective action. The synod appointed commissioners to defend its sentence at the General Assembly and named a committee to draw up answers to Webster's reasons for appeal.[60]

Of course, all this became quickly known in Glasgow. On 6 May 1714 Simson wrote at length to the Presbytery of Edinburgh expressing his entire adherence to the Confession of Faith and catechisms of the

58 In his speech to the Presbytery of Glasgow on 29 March 1715, Simson states that Webster accused him to the Presbytery of Edinburgh on 17 March 1714. However, the entry of 14 April contains the charge. NAS, CH2/121/9, 68.

59 30 April 1714. NAS, CH2/252/8, 148.

60 Ibid., 149.

church and his distress that "one who would be thought eminent for Christian Zeal" should treat him in a manner contrary to the normal procedure of the church.[61] From the outset, Simson was determined that Webster should be forced to follow due process. He tabled complaints against Webster for defamation before the Presbytery of Edinburgh and before the Synod of Lothian and Tweeddale. His letter concluded with the plea that "the Reverend presbytery will take such measures according to the Rules of the Gospel and of this Church, as may put a stop to so scandalous a practice, and repair the injurie done to me, and to the Society wherof I have the honour to be a member by the decree of this Church, and above all the injurie done to the whole Church, by so unchristian a treatment of one Minister by another."[62] By this time it was imperative for the welfare of Glasgow's divinity school that Simson be vindicated. The university was in danger, along with its professor.

THE FORM OF PROCESS

When Simson spoke of the rules of the Gospel and the church, he had specific legislation in mind. Mindful of the need to be meticulous in dealing with charges against ministers and others, the General Assembly of the Church of Scotland had recently ratified a formula for dealing with discipline in 1707. This *Form of Process* was published in 1709 by John Stirling's brother-in-law, Walter Stewart of Pardovan, along with other acts passed by the General Assembly relating to worship, discipline, and church government. To ensure that all ministers familiarized themselves with its provisions, the Synod of Glasgow and Ayr ruled in October 1710 that each minister and parish session should buy a copy.[63]

Scots civil and canon law had originally been founded on the Roman legal model. Although the Act of Union had confirmed the Scottish legal system, the approval of the *Form of Process* indicates that ecclesiastical legal scholars felt a need for clarified rules that would limit the inquisitorial procedures of Roman law. Whig political theories of individual liberty and contractual government demanded that men be free from

---

61 Ibid., CH2/121/9, 91–2.

62 Ibid., 93.

63 While this guaranteed the sale of Pardovan's book, ministers proved tardy debtors. A year later Pardovan complained to the synod that he had not yet received payment from all who had received copies, and in 1724 his widow was still alleging that she was owed money by synod members. NAS, CH2/464/2, 248, 267; CH2/364/3, 125.

groundless accusations and self-incrimination. The formulation of the appropriate means of dealing with spiritual error and physical wrong-doing by church members showed a divergence from Scots principles of civil law and a considerable debt to Whig ideology. The cases of John Simson and James Hogg, to note but two in the next quarter-century, proved that ecclesiastical courts found it difficult to adapt to these precepts of legal method. The objectives of political factions and the aspirations of fanatical Calvinists conspired to limit the application of the rules approved in 1707 and set out by Walter Stewart.

The *Form of Process* contained clear instructions for initiating proceedings against both ministers and laymen. It took into account the fact that the Reformed churches had tried to model their methods where possible on the Bible, noting the admonition in 1 Tim. 5:19: "Against an elder receive not an accusation, but before two or three witnesses." A minister must be first charged before the presbytery to which he belonged; its members were his natural peers, who might be expected to be aware of rumours or scandals in their area. Such a charge could be the result of either a *libel*, a specific indictment of wrong doctrine or misbehaviour made by an individual who was prepared to stake his reputation on the truth of the charge, or a *fama clamosa*, a rumour of scandal or misdemeanour so widespread that investigation must be made to preserve the good name of the church.

The *Form of Process* specified that no one should formally accuse a minister without first asking him personally for an explanation and then seeking advice from some of the more reliable ministers and elders in his presbytery. In the case of insistent rumour, the presbytery was warned to "be careful, first, to inquire into the rise, occasion, brochers and grounds of this *fama clamosa*."[64] Once a process was under way, testimony could be taken from the written words of the accused and also from witnesses to his public utterances. The assembly's formula tried to balance the influence on his congregation of the example of a minister's private life and the precepts that he expounded from the pulpit with the potential destruction of his reputation and career by a false accusation. The presbytery was to scrutinize informers and allow adequate intervals between the laying of charges and the hearing of the defence. The defendant was to be present at the interrogation of witnesses and might "modestly" cross-examine them.[65] In cases of doctrinal unsoundness,

64 Stewart of Pardovan, *Collections*, 256.
65 Ibid., 257.

"great caution should be used, and the knowledge and understanding of witnesses much looked into."[66]

Whigs of Lockean principles denied the right of a court to question anyone on personal opinions that had not been shared with others, objecting strongly to the use of "queries" designed to elicit such opinions from an accused person. They drew a distinction between public and private speech and also between public and private opinion. The former was always open to investigation; the latter, by its very nature, could not be the subject of a *fama clamosa*. They also stressed that witnesses must quote only the *ipsissima verba*, or exact words, they had heard spoken, on the grounds that if a witness did otherwise, he or she might inadvertently place a new and possibly improper sense on the expression in question, which might have had an orthodox intention. These demands represented a considerable change from the traditional requirements of canon (and Scots) law.

The pyramid of church judicatories permitted a system of appeals from one level to the next. For the laity, the process began at the church session, where parish discipline took place. Above that was the monthly meeting of the presbytery, then the biannual synod, and finally the annual General Assembly. At the parish session, the minister was moderator or chairman, and the ruling elders were members. In each gathering above the parish level, specified numbers of ministers and ruling elders were eligible to attend, and one minister was elected moderator. At the General Assembly, for instance, the rules laid down that approximately twice as many ministers as elders should be present as commissioners from their presbyteries.[67] In practice, these were largely meetings of professional clergy, and the number of ruling elders present was normally small compared to that of ministers. The judgment of any court could be appealed to the next level. Such an appeal would often be accompanied by a protest or counter-appeal by the lower court.

The ecclesiastical judicatories took all charges very seriously and made every effort to consider a problem and resolve it effectively. Unfortunately there were usually many different interests to be balanced, even when the case was a simple one of a disputed ministerial transportation, as the proposed move of George Mair has shown. The wishes of the minister himself, of the patron of the church, of the local heritors or contributing property owners, of the ruling elders, and of the majority

66 Ibid.
67 See table in Wilson, *Index*, 218.

of the congregation had all to be taken into consideration. Their motives in differing from one another might be theological, political, or personal in nature.

The church courts had to weigh these factors and try to make the best decision for the people of the parish, the wishes of the patrons, the government of the day, the state of the national church, and finally for the minister or ministers involved. The members of these judicatories did their best to accomplish all this with the minimum of disruption and the maximum of consensus. The instances where this was not possible generally had implications in several of the areas of concern, and as a result the difficulties in reaching peaceful resolution were insurmountable.

The two cases involving John Simson illustrate many of these issues. In them the combination of personal, doctrinal, academic, and political factors created explosive situations that stirred up the nation.

EARLY LEGAL SKIRMISHES, 1714–15

By April 1714 rumours about Simson's teaching had reached as far north and east as Brechin and Dunfermline, as can be seen from the instructions given by those presbyteries to their commissioners to the General Assembly. Brechin had heard that Simson was "venting and teaching erroneus doctrines in his Colledges or Lessons," while Dunfermline, home presbytery of Webster's friend James Hogg, specified that the "errors of very dangerous consequence" taught by the professor were that the damned do not sin in Hell and that Adam was not the federal head of the human race.[68]

Before the Presbytery of Edinburgh could consider Simson's counter-charge against Webster, the General Assembly met in May 1714 and rejected Webster's appeal. It upheld the decision of the Synod of Lothian and Tweeddale that Webster should take his complaint to the Presbytery of Glasgow, insisting that Webster continue to act individually, rather than accepting the existence of a *fama clamosa* to be investigated.[69] This curious compromise may have been the best that Webster's friends could achieve in view of the political strength of the Squadrone, which was sufficient to prevent united church intervention in the case. Many, both then and later, saw the assembly's ruling as an unfair imposition on

68 NAS, CH1/2/34, 97 and 144.
69 Ibid., CH1/1/24, 257–60.

Webster and believed that the church had shirked its duty to preserve purity of doctrine.[70] One "Elder of the Church" compared unfavourably the relative inaction of the church against Simson with the actions taken by the Presbytery of Edinburgh and the other judicatories against Yule. He noted that the "Errors vented by a late Probationer ... were much of a bind with these alledged against Mr Simson," and yet no "Personal Pursuit" was demanded.[71] Obviously the fact that Yule's thesis had been published made informed criticism and condemnation more straightforward. Simson's oral teaching was harder to probe accurately, while his skill at debate, his academic position, and his political backing combined to make him a more dangerous target.

On 1 June 1714 the faculty of the University of Glasgow heard a memorial by Simson about Webster's accusations against him. Although the text is not in the minutes, it evidently called for Webster to make his charges formally, so that they could be refuted. Simson was determined to silence Webster's continuous murmuring against him in the most public and effective way open to him. The members considered Simson's request reasonable and agreed that the dean of faculty, Rev. John Hamilton, as university judge of doctrine, should ask Webster to bring his evidence before the dean and his assessors on the third Wednesday of June. Simson was to respond to the charges on the first Wednesday of July, when the dean and his assessors would make their judgment. The dean was also to tell Webster that if he did not either answer at this time or bring his charges before the Presbytery of Glasgow, "his said Accusation will be looked upon as false and slanderous," leaving him liable to the appropriate censure.[72]

When the third Wednesday arrived with no appearance by Webster, the faculty recommended that the dean should inform the moderator of the Presbytery of Edinburgh of the facts, a recommendation that was repeated at the next faculty meeting on 10 August 1714.[73] The following spring, Simson accused Webster of never having intended to lay formal charges, since "he not only Delay'd, but when Required, did Refuse to come hither, and prove me Guilty of *Socinian* and *Arminian* Errors,

---

70 Elder, *Memorial*, 2. Willison also commented that it was hard on Webster to have been burdened with a libel that should have been the affair of the whole church; *Fair and Impartial*, 86.

71 Elder, *Memorial*, 7.

72 1 June 1714, GUA 26632, 121.

73 Ibid., 123, 125.

which he had to Publickly Undertaken to do; as may be seen by his Letter ... to the Reverend Presbytry of *Edinburgh* from Kinnoul, July 13th
1714. In which He says, He had no Call from God, to come to *Glasgow,*
and Prosecute me, and that it was his Fixed Purpose that he would not
come."74 This passage supports the idea that Webster's pursuit of Simson had a personal element. Surely a zealot would have heard the divine
summons to action had his main incentive been danger to the church?
It required Simson's threat of prosecution for slander to force Webster
to comply with the synod's instructions to take the matter before the
Presbytery of Glasgow.

Given Webster's concern at laxity and error in the church, the dilato-
riness with which he approached his pursuit of Simson is hard to understand if he really believed that Simson was disseminating false doctrine.
He seems to have been a man who often spoke without thought of the
consequences, and perhaps his choleric temperament prevented him
from following up his efforts in a logical manner. Fiery preacher and
rash accuser though Webster might be, he lacked the legalistic attention
to detail required to follow the procedure of the *Form of Process.* Webster's unstable behaviour must have been a considerable trial to his
brethren in the Presbytery of Edinburgh, making it understandable
that, in the words of one of Wodrow's correspondents in April 1716,
some committee members "would be content to have the prof[essor]r
assoilat [acquitted] to have a hit at Mr W[ebster]."75

Slow though he might be in pursuing formal charges, Webster was
stirring up his friends against Simson. In September 1714 James Hogg
distributed a "Letter concerning our natural Enmity," in which he refuted the belief that there was no sinning in hell, without identifying the
propagator of such an error.76 Nevertheless Simson complained in
November that he was "weel enough described; considdering what
Mr Webster & oth[e]rs have spread of me throw toun & country, & all
the Gentlewomen who should read yo[u]r Letter were, if ignorant,
doubtless to be informed th[a]t I was the person meant."77 Hogg replied, first relatively briefly on 6 December, then in an undated, expanded version of his criticism of Simson's teaching on sinning in Hell.
In the correspondence that followed, other writers became involved,

74 Simson, *Libel,* 71.

75 NLS, Wodrow Letters Quarto, XI, 137.

76 J. Simson to J. Hogg, 23 Nov., 1714, NLS, Wodrow Folios, XXXIX, 104.

77 Ibid., XXXIX, 104. The remark about "gentlewomen" is intriguing. Did Hogg publish a regular religious letter that had a primarily female readership?

copies of whose epistles survive in Wodrow's collections and in New College, Edinburgh. One, identified as "Mr. Logan" in the New College manuscript – presumably Alan Logan of that Ilk (d. 1733), minister of Torryburn and then of Culross – replied to a minister in the Presbytery of Dunfermline, presumably Hogg, who had given him access to a letter from Simson, which he rebutted.[78] It is significant that Dunfermline was one of the presbyteries calling for action against Simson at the General Assembly of 1714. Hogg had a strong influence in his own district and would have been supported by Wodrow's young friend William Wilson, who had recently been licensed by the Presbytery of Dunfermline.[79]

The records of the Presbytery of Glasgow were damaged by fire in the late eighteenth century and as a result are missing some portions, one of which runs from early 1712 to the beginning of 1715. The first mention of Webster's accusations thus appears in the minutes of a February 1715 meeting of the presbytery, called to hear Simson's answers to Webster's libel against him. The text indicates that Webster had formally laid his charges on 29 September 1714 (see Appendix A) but that the libel was legally incorrect. As a result Simson did not receive a copy of the complete libel until 3 December.[80] In early 1715 the presbytery had determined a timetable for action.[81] Since Simson had asked various Edinburgh ministers to be cited as witnesses, a letter from the Presbytery of Edinburgh, dated 2 March 1715, suggested that they be examined in the capital, a request that Simson refused.[82] The professor's reluctance to travel to Edinburgh during the academic year is understandable, especially when he considered the accusations against him to be caused by personal animosity rather than by unsound theology.

On 16 March 1715 the Glasgow ministers held their normal presbytery meeting for privy censures, at which the members were sent out of the room one by one, while their fellows scrutinized any individual frailties in personal or professional behaviour that might be worthy of reprimand. On this occasion Simson was present, and the record reports:

78 New College Library (NCL), Box 11.2.6, 7. NLS, Wodrow Folios, XXXIX, 123–52.

79 The material in this correspondence is discussed below in chapter 7, along with the article on sinning in Hell in the libel.

80 GCA, CH2/171/9A, 7r.

81 "Mr John Hamilton ... Reported that ... he had acquainted Mr Webster with the Presbyteries procedure at their Last Meeting in the affair betwixt him and the Professor, and of their Appointment to meet this day to Receive the Professor's answers." Ibid., 2r.

82 Ibid., 3r.

"The whole Brethren … were one after another Removed, In order to privie Censure, Each of them was well Reported of, being Called in … They were encouraged."[83] This finding emphasizes the legal inadequacy of Webster's efforts to libel Simson. The *Form of Process* demanded that an accuser should seek advice from reliable members of the accused's presbytery. Had Webster done this, he would have learned that in the eyes of Simson's brethren, who might be expected to have personal knowledge of the matter, the professor had committed no error in 1715. His students similarly felt that Simson was being misunderstood. Jonathan Woodworth told his cousin that while the case was *sub judice* he should say little, but he went on, "At present it seemes to come from misrepresentation. We see our weakness both in not understanding another's meanings and in disagreeing when the meaning is understood."[84]

The same month Webster received a letter from the Presbytery of Glasgow assuring him that nothing would be done in his absence but noting that, since the last papers on the libel had reached Glasgow only on 30 December 1714, the accusation of wilful delay was unfounded. Webster must have suggested that the presbytery's tardiness was a contravention of the normal rules of the church, to which its clerk responded, "As for the other reflexion in y[ou]rs that our conduct is a direct counteracting of the forme of process ye and thes with you may be easie for we shall take care to show a regard to the forme of processe and our own reputation in that behalf and I persuade my self when you are heer ye shall alter your thoughts or at least differ from thos with you of that sentiment."[85]

On 29 March 1715 James Webster and many of the witnesses finally appeared in Glasgow. The presbytery meeting, moderated by John Gray (d. 1729), minister of the Inner High Church in Glasgow, was attended by Simson's divinity students, who had been acting as his secretaries, copying papers for distribution to presbytery members.[86] After some discussion, the presbytery determined, from the wording of the acts of the

---

83 Ibid., 3v.
84 Bromley, "Correspondence," 22.
85 J. Gray to J. Webster, 9 March 1715, NAS, CH1/5/11, no pagination.
86 J. Woodworth to P. Walkden, 5 March 1715. "15 of us are writeing coppies of the Professor's answer to be given to so many members of the presbitery … The accuser is appointed to be here about the 29th of March the students of divinity have liberty to attend the Presbitery. Soe I expect we shall see the proceedings, as we have seen what has been done hitherto." Bromley, "Correspondence," 22.

General Assembly and the Synod of Lothian on Webster's charges against Simson, that it should begin by considering Socinian and Arminian errors. Webster demanded that the libel be considered as a whole and that he be allowed to question his witnesses on every point of the libel, in whatever order he chose. Although the records suffer from fire damage here, it seems clear that the presbytery chose to adhere to its method and to go through the articles of the libel in order.[87] The clerk was ordered to read the first paragraph of the libel, to which Simson gave his answer in the form of a speech. Webster interrupted to protest against the reading of previously unmentioned material before answers were given to the libel. In his words, the professor "had shuffled in a paper ... and because [of] this his Conduct was disagreeable to several of the Reverend Members."[88] Webster's irritation may have stemmed from the fact that the speech was generally uncomplimentary about him, since the majority of the presbytery voted to ignore his protest and to let the reading continue.

Reproduced in full in Simson's printed *Libel*, the speech explained Simson's methods of teaching divinity, admitting to the use of hypotheses or propositions that were speculative in nature and which served merely to silence the "Cavills of Adversaries," and justifying his use of such controversial arguments as ways "to Convince Gainsayers, and Stop the Mouths of Unruly and Vain Talkers, and Deceivers."[89] These arguments had nothing to do with the doctrine or practice of the Reformed church, would not be preached, and had been used by theologians from other Reformed churches, none of whom had been challenged. Simson went further, however, and claimed that, even had his teaching been innovative, as a good Protestant he had the right to advance any proposition in agreement with scripture and reason. He denied that he taught anything contrary to the Westminster Confession or the Westminster Catechisms.[90]

Shifting to the attack, Simson accused Webster of habitually quarrelling with divinity professors: he had censured the previous professor of divinity at Edinburgh for error and had defamed the present occupant of that chair. The reason for this animosity was well known, Simson continued, and few believed that it was merely zeal for the Gospel. While

87　The meeting of the presbytery is reported in GCA, CH2/171/9A, 4r.
88　Ibid., 4v.
89　Simson, *Libel*, 60–1.
90　Ibid., 62–3.

Edinburgh's political infighting might be a plausible explanation for Simson's innuendoes, an anonymous 1717 pamphlet, written perhaps by Simson, contains an alternative explanation. Webster had been disappointed in his own expectations of a university chair – "some Men will aspire to *Preeminence* in the Church and shew their Resentment if they are neglected; that Merit which could not be discern'd by those who raise Professours to their Chairs must be (at any Rate) made Plain and visible to the World."[91] Simson then explained that Webster had turned against him only after a disagreement between them over Mair's translation to Closeburn.

In August 1712 – a significant date in view of their differences over the oath of abjuration – Simson had heard that Webster was openly defaming him. He alleged now that Webster had not wanted to cite him for error to the Presbytery of Glasgow; only the threat of an action for slander had made him bring the charges – Webster's enthusiasm for truth was rather "*Loud Publishing,* and *Bold Spreading* of *Calumny* and *Slander,* with a design to leave it there."[92] Simson concluded by stating that his own feeling for the preservation of the doctrine of the church and his consciousness of innocence made him ask the Presbytery of Glasgow to insist that Webster lay formal charges that could be answered.

Simson's position in early 1715 as professor of divinity made it imperative both for himself and for the university that rumours be dispelled. Thirty years later William Leechman faced a similar predicament. To a friend in England he wrote that he had been obliged to defend himself against "Industriously spread Rumours of the dreadful Dangers Religion was in from an Erroneous Professor of Divinity. Tho' this could not have hurt my Interest or my Reputation with people of moderation, yet it would have brought a Suspicion of Heresy on the Young men who studied under me, & so both prov'd an obstruction to my Usefulness, & have hurt the Interest of the University."[93] Simson's position at this time was analogous to that of Leechman, and his reasons for forcing Webster into the open must have been comparable.

91 ?Simson, *Answer,* 7–8

92 Simson, *Libel,* 72.

93 W. Leechman to G. Benson, 14 July 1744, John Rylands Library, University of Manchester. I am grateful to Professor J. Moore for this reference.

7

A *Speedy Trial*:
Libel, Committee, Trial, 1715–1717

The course of events for the next two years, from March 1715 to May 1717, defies rapid summary. Although James Webster claimed that he could prove his case in one hour of the General Assembly's time and John Simson wanted "a speedy Trial,"[1] the interplay of ecclesiastical, political, and personal factors in the Scottish church courts, complicated by the effects of the 1715 Rebellion, led to countless hours of hearings. The significance of the Simson case to Scots ecclesiastical and academic life meant that many important Presbyterians were involved in its time-consuming investigation – men who had other calls on their time during these eventful years. Ecclesiastical politics still seemed precarious in the first quarter of the century, causing moderate members of the church to wish to avoid any conflict that might cause state intercession in church affairs. For its part, the ultra-orthodox group suspected Erastian mischief on all sides. Whether actual or feared, interventions of secular politics stiffened the positions of both sides in this early confrontation between traditional Covenanting piety and the emerging world of the Enlightenment.

To understand why Scots found this affair so momentous, we need to consider not only the General Assembly and committee process that the church employed, but the theology involved. Fortunately there is a wealth of manuscript and printed material on the Simson case. Simson's printed *Libel*, which contains Webster's original charges of 27 September 1714, Simson's speech of March 1715 to the Presbytery of Glasgow, and his defence of his doctrinal stance, is 288 pages long (see excerpts in

1 Webster, *Propositions*, 8.

Appendix A). Simson presumably published it in 1716, since that summer he apologized to the Committee for Purity of Doctrine for printing his case.[2] It represented his response to a flurry of pamphleteering against him, including Webster's publication of Simson's *Letters to Rowan* (*A True and Authentick Copy*), which ended with Webster's call for the rooting up of evil. Webster reacted to Simson's *Libel* by printing a *Short Abstract* from it in 1716, with brief quotations from the statements that he considered most abhorrent. He completed the *Short Abstract* with a further condemnation of the degeneracy of the times. Along with Simson's speech of 11 May 1716 to the General Assembly, these publications constitute the main sources for his theological opinions in this decade. His opponents' viewpoints come from both printed and manuscript sources. Details of the ecclesiastical process against Simson come from the records of the Presbytery of Glasgow (Glasgow City Archives), the records of the General Assembly (National Archives of Scotland), and a copy of the register of proceedings of the Committee for Preserving Purity of Doctrine (New College Library, Edinburgh).

Webster's charges and Simson's published defences provide a picture of the theological rifts in early-eighteenth-century Scotland. They illustrate how the Church of Scotland related to other Reformed bodies and how the Scots were familiar with, and reacted to, opinions beyond their borders. Despite the furore that they produced among the conservatives in the church, Simson's innovations in teaching were not explicitly condemned at the end of his first case. Leading churchmen appreciated the pastoral necessities of contemporary ministerial training, which Webster and his supporters ignored in their determination to restrict university teaching to seventeenth-century systems. In addition, the members of the Presbytery of Glasgow championed Simson, using whatever legal strategies were necessary to support his case. The change in the theological climate of opinion effected by Simson's strong advocacy of his doctrine and pedagogy was such that by mid-century no minister or teacher would have to defend himself from censure on similar issues. Simson was instrumental in forcing the church to accept a more liberal form of Calvinism.

When we consider the charges against Simson and his defence against them, we can appreciate why the Church of Scotland found the resolution of the case so problematic. Although Webster had refused to

2 The copy of Simson, *Libel* that I have used is bound with another volume and has no title page.

categorize his accusations into Arminian, Jesuit, and Socinian errors as he was frequently requested to do, several articles in his libel seemed to imply some form of Arminian universalism, an error abhorred by Scots Presbyterians for the past century. Scots saw themselves as a chosen people – their Reformation, their covenants, their adherence to Calvinism, and their century-long battle against prelacy had all served to create a sense of being set apart. They used covenant theology to strengthen this idea of a special divine bond between themselves and God, in which they replaced Israel as God's covenanted people.[3] By the late seventeenth century orthodox Reformed divines taught a very limited form of election conferred only on those within the covenant.

The English trend of reducing the centrality of the atonement to Christianity led Scots to fear that religion was degenerating into a morality experienced by following the example of Jesus as teacher in place of a spirituality characterized by an acceptance of the gift of the divine satisfaction. Wodrow was "afraid the steps of defection are but very short from the doctrine, relative to the grace and Spirit of Christ, to direct attacks upon his person," which would inevitably undermine revelation and lead to deism and atheism in "an overflowing flood."[4] When Professor Leechman ran into difficulties with the Presbytery of Glasgow in 1744, the issue was again his lack of emphasis on Christ as mediator when praying to the Father. The doctrines of a limited atonement and a restricted number of elect went together with a focus on the sacrifice of the Son. Any diminution of either of the first two elements seemed to conservative Scots to detract from the third.

Undeterred by such considerations and never a man to mince words, John Simson was scathing about the wording of the libel drawn up by Webster: "If these Articles ... have been wrote by a Scholar of mine, as they are pretended to be, he has certainly been One, who wanted a Competency either of Common Sense, or Honesty; Or, if he hath given a true Account of what I Teach on these Heads, then certainly some Body void of Sense, or Common Honesty, has reduced them to the Form they now have" – a conclusion scarcely flattering either to Webster or to his supposed informant![5] Simson wanted it to be clearly under-

3 See Burrell, "Covenant Idea" and "Apocalyptic Vision."

4 R. Wodrow to Rev. A. Taylor, 7 June 1729, Wodrow, *Correspondence*, 3:449. From about 1712 on, Wodrow commented regularly on English Arianism and atheism. Wodrow, *Analecta*, 2:133, 285–90, 323, and 341.

5 Simson, *Libel*, 86.

stood that the quoted phrases were none of his and that he queried the veracity of both Webster and his spies.

The libel accused him of a lengthy list of errors ranging from central issues of Calvinist dogma to philosophical ponderings about extraterrestrial life. They fall into four main categories, each of which I examine in this chapter. Various questions dealing with salvation generally and election and reprobation specifically were at the root of the disagreement between Simson and Webster. They included the possibility of salvation outside the church, the fate of baptized infants, the baptism of infants of non-Christians, and the relative numbers of elect and reprobate. The second major topic that can be identified among the charges is pastoral and stemmed from the direction in which Simson was guiding his divinity students as future Scottish ministers. It comprised such questions as the problem of evil, man's right to seek salvation, the means by which he might employ to find it, and the nature of the eternal punishment meted out to he who fails in his quest. The third group of charges dealt with dogmatic minutiae such as the covenants, Adam's role as federal head of the church, the divine decrees, the *filioque* clause, and the nature of sin. Finally, there was a series of assertions about Simson's views on such doctrinally unimportant matters as the eating of blood and whether the moon was inhabited. We examine each group in turn before turning to the legal process that followed.

THE NUMBER OF THE ELECT

Simson had told Rowan in March 1713 that he felt that "Natural Revelation" was the only "solide" proof that the scriptures were divine and that "It is a Notorious Untruth, that I Teach another way to Heaven than by CHRIST: *Though I Teach, that God may by his Spirit reveal that way to some who want the Scriptures.*"[6] He felt that Paul's proclamation of his mission to the gentiles indicated the possibility of salvation outside the church, should God choose to reveal himself to the heathen. Incorporating some phrases from the Westminster Confession, he explained, "By the Light of Nature, and the Works of Creation, and Providence, including Tradition, God has given an Obscure Objective Revelation unto all Men, of his being Reconcileablc to sinners; which the Heathen may come to the Knowledg of, if they observe and consider it."[7] Simson did not

6 Webster, *True Copy*, 20.
7 Simson, *Libel*, 77–8. The Westminster Confession words are from 1:1.

believe that God would make "known the Remedy to some Heathen Nations and not to others."[8] He merely considered the possibility of salvation to all individual sinners, since Christ had commanded the apostles to preach to all nations and since in Revelation (7:9) the saved were "a great multitude ... of all nations, and kindreds, and people, and tongues."[9] This was a possibility that Continental contemporaries such as Turretin also accepted.[10]

McLaren, the "Private Christian," and Webster saw any suggestion of salvation outside the church as Arminian heresy. Each antagonist quoted selectively from the relevant sections of scripture and the Westminster Confession and repudiated the meaning extracted by the other. One pro-Simson author – perhaps, from his style, the professor himself – asked rhetorically, "Is there no Hope of the poor virtuous Heathens? Are those that did, in so many Things, resemble God, altogether abandon'd by him? Is this the received Doctrine of our Church, and must all who maintain it be stigmatiz'd as hereticks?"[11] On the contrary, the doctrine of the possibility of the regeneration of the heathen was stated in the Westminster Confession 10:3, which accepted the salvation through the Spirit of "all other elect Persons who are uncapable of being outwardly called by the Ministry of the Word."[12]

This line of argument ended with a topical simile, which would have been meaningful to all Scots readers in 1717 – the virtuous heathen were like Jacobites who had been taken captive in the Fifteen. Such prisoners were aware that the King was both just and merciful. Their knowledge of his justice would make them fear punishment; their knowledge of his mercy would allow them to hope for clemency. Should the King choose the latter, they could not know by what process he had reached his verdict. He might decide himself, or he might accede to the pleas of his son or to those of a "prime Favourite." The author concluded: "I do not think that Rebels will be admitted to the King's Cabin–Councils, and consequently must be ignorant of many Circumstances relating to this and other State-Affairs: Yet I believe there is not one of the Rebels but is persuaded that the King is Reconcileable to them, and that they will obtain an Indemnity."[13]

8 Webster, *Propositions*, 10–11.
9 Simson, *Libel*, 78.
10 Klauber, *Between*, 111.
11 Simson, *Answer*, 17.
12 Ibid., 18.
13 Ibid., 21.

Webster accused Simson of interpreting scripture in an unorthodox fashion, calling the argument about the publication of the divine remedy to Adam, and subsequently to Noah, an Arminian gloss and charging him with teaching that more of humanity were saved than damned.[14] Simson responded that he had lectured annually against the Arminian notion that Christ was the universal remedy for all mankind. Nevertheless the assertion that fewer were saved than damned could not be supported by scripture, and both Calvin and Gomar considered that the statement that many were called but few chosen could refer only to adults.[15]

Since Webster was accusing him of Arminianism, Simson cleverly introduced the name of Arminius's chief adversary at Leiden, the orthodox professor of theology Francis Gomar (1563–1641). Simson cited the Helvetian Confession and pointed out that the Westminster Confession made no decisive statement on the matter. His knowledge of the older documents of the Reformed faith seems almost to have worked against him in the eyes of some of his colleagues. Bullinger's Second Helvetic Confession of 1566 may well have been much more to Simson's taste than more recent compilations. Unaffected by Reformed scholasticism, it had a charitable attitude towards sinners and tended to focus on the generous texts of the Gospels. "Come unto me all ye that labour and are heavy laden, and I will give you rest" (Matt. 11:28) was quoted in section 10:8, on predestination and election. "And although God knows who are his," the confession stated, "and somewhere or other the small number of the elect are mentioned, nevertheless, all may properly hope for election, and no-one will be numbered among the reprobate without cause."[16] Bullinger's creed expressed the conviction that Calvinist Christianity is in harmony with the catholic faith of all time, especially that of the ancient Greek and Latin churches.[17] Since there was another area in the libel where Simson leaned towards the opinions of the Greek church, this may be significant.

To bolster his argument about the greater number of the elect, Simson had postulated that baptized infants dying without actual sin would be saved. The Westminster Confession provided no decisive guideline: "Elect infants, dying in infancy, are regenerated and saved by Christ

14 Webster, *Short Abstract*, 2.
15 Simson, *Libel*, 108–9.
16 Second Helvetic Confession 10:4, in Schaff, *Creeds*, 3:252.
17 See Schaff, *Creeds*, 1:394–5.

through the Spirit, who worketh when, and where, and how he pleaseth. So are all other elect persons, who are incapable of being outwardly called by the ministry of the word."[18] This carefully worded clause served as the confessional basis for Simson's belief about the possible election of some outside the church. Calvin and his early Scottish followers did not demand baptism as a prerequisite for salvation. Indeed the Second Scotch Confession deplored the Roman Catholic doctrine of the damnation of unbaptized infants.[19] Baptism represented admission into the visible church and the seal of regeneration, but it was neither essential to salvation nor a proof of election. Following Wallaeus and Pictet, Simson felt that baptized infants "are Probably of the Number of the Elect ... and Nothing in Scripture, that I know, shews that any of them are Reprobate: Wherefore, the Probability lies on the Favourable Side."[20]

Oddly, since their letters and memoirs show that they found comfort in the belief that their many dead children were saved, the ultra-orthodox were roused to fury by this issue. James Hogg went to far as to suggest that if this were indeed the case, loving parents would be obliged to slaughter their children immediately after baptism to ensure their salvation. Since such action was clearly immoral, not to mention absurd, the automatic salvation of baptized infants must be impossible.[21] McLaren criticized Simson on the grounds that his view of salvation negated the effects of original sin. With no scriptural proof either way, McLaren concluded, "I grant it is a great Mystery concerning Infants; but I think there is no Ground to be so charitable in our Judgment this way."[22] The words of Simson and McLaren encapsulate their conflicting opinions about the divine intentions. To Simson "the probability lies on the favourable side," while to McLaren "there is no ground to be so charitable."

Simson had also taught that heathen infants dying without actual sin might be saved. To Webster these children were outside the covenant and therefore reprobate, while Simson thought that "we should Judge Charitably, and Hope the Best of the Children of Heathens ... it being very Agreeable to the Nature of our Gracious God" to save all those who die in infancy, regardless of the beliefs of their parents.[23] Simson argued

18 "Westminster Confession," 10:3.
19 Schaff, *Creeds*, 3:482.
20 Simson, *Libel*, 111.
21 Hog[g], *Letter Detecting Gangrene.*
22 McLaren, *New Scheme*, 80.
23 Simson, *Libel*, 112.

that should God do otherwise He would be treating them more severely than He had the rebel angels, who had actually sinned. Since neither the Bible nor the Westminster Confession gave any decisive answer about the salvation of infant heathens, nothing he taught could be considered contrary to them, nor could it be made an article of faith.

Simson even believed that all might be saved, except those who excluded themselves by their actions or by their wilful rejection of either the Gospel or "that obscure Discovery and offer of Grace, made to all without the Church."[24] This was indeed a "New Scheme of Doctrine" to McLaren and to most orthodox Reformed believers. McLaren protested that positing the offer of a remedy to pagans was the model of universal grace that the church had condemned, making Simson guilty of the "smoothing of that Arminian Error."[25] Simson retorted that, while it was indeed Arminian to state that God could not justly condemn a person for original sin, his proposition was different: God would probably not cast sinners into Hell solely on account of original sin. God had told Adam and Noah about the remedy for sin; through their children they transmitted the knowledge to the rest of mankind. Simson held this position for the remainder of his life, as his correspondence with Archibald Campbell in the late 1720s and 1730s proves.[26] He admitted that it had also been held by Arminians, but he argued that because something had been said by a heterodox group did not necessarily make it untrue.

On a related question, Simson saw no reason why infidel infants adopted by Christians should not be baptized: the practice had been accepted by Wallaeus and Marck. Here he was confronting the extreme care with which contemporary Scots "fenced" their two sacraments. Communion could be offered only to parishioners who had been carefully prepared by their minister and been given tokens of permission to participate. The dispensing of communion tokens could be used to discipline the unruly and effect political aims. Similarly in the case of baptism, ministers expected compliance to church discipline by parents asking for their children to be received. A family that moved from one congregation to another might have to obtain a testimonial from its previous minister or other considerable citizen before its new pastor

24 Ibid., 115.
25 McLaren, *New Scheme*, 93.
26 See NAS, GD461/15.

would baptize a child.[27] McLaren identified only two ways for any person to be accepted within the covenant through baptism: a personal profession of faith and natural descent from Christians.[28] Simson, in contract, believed that, with proper education, a child could become a son of God by adoption. He rejected any suggestion that this contradicted the Westminster Confession's chapters on the church or on baptism. Simson's arguments on the matter are entirely in keeping with his general views about the benevolence of God and the possibility of salvation for humanity. In this, as in the other libelled articles, Simson was enlarging the compass of Scots Presbyterian thought to include as many sincere seekers as possible.

The libel charged Simson with having said that human souls were created as pure as Adam's had been, contracting wicked qualities only by being united to corrupt bodies. When teaching that original sin deprived Adam and Eve's descendants of original righteousness from the moment of creation, Simson was said to have added the libelled words with a statement that this deprivation was hard to justify as the act of a just and good God. Simson admitted this to be his opinion, believing that it was inconsistent with divine justice to create rational creatures with an inclination to evil. There was no need for God to prejudge a soul, since the corrupting influence of the body would immediately cancel out any righteousness. The souls of infants were thus perfectly innocent; pollution came from union with the body. Simson accepted the imputation of Adam's sin to his posterity, which "is the Reason why Corrupt Bodies, that Vitiat the Souls United to them, are Propagated," and denied that his teaching was contrary to Scripture.[29] Once again Simson appears to have been trying to palliate the rigours of the Reformed doctrine of original sin, without denying the Fall and its consequences.

Webster further objected to Simson's understanding of the order of the divine decrees. Simson disapproved of both supralapsarian and infralapsarian positions. He avoided any reference to Adam and the Fall in his discussion of the divine decrees, limiting his review to the attributes

27 See below, chapter 8, for instances of withholding communion tokens. The papers of William Wishart, Jr, in Edinburgh University Library (EUL) contain the following note, apparently from a lay landlord: "Glasgow 24 Decebr 1726. Sir   The Bearer William Bennie lives in my proportion in Stockweell his [sic] a child to be Baptized tomorrow he his had children before Alowed the Benefit of that sacrament   I know nothing to hinder him now   I am Sir Your most humble servt Ja: Smith." EUL, La. II 114, 212v.

28 See McLaren's discussion in *New Scheme*, chap. 3.

29 Simson, *Libel*, 228.

of God, the display of His glory in creation, the appointment of a mediator, and the salvation of the elect. The eternal decree of God had two parts – one determined the purpose, which was to manifest the glory of God through His works, and the other comprehended the means for attaining that end: creation, providence, and redemption. The conception that one was prior to the other "flows not from any such Way or Order, wherein God Decreed them, but from the Imperfection of our Understanding, and the Relation of End and Means, which the Objects of that One Decree gave to One Another."[30] The totality of God's works made up the means of manifesting His glory and wisdom. The explanation of the salvation of man was further broken down:

So, Mankind is Considered as lying in a State of Sin and Misery, from which the Infinite Love, Mercy, and Free Grace of God in Christ alone can Relieve him, and thereby is a fit Object, by which God may display the Glory of his Excellent Perfections, mentioned in the former Part of this Decree of Man's Salvation. For the Manifestation of which, he first Chuses a Certain Number out of the Corrupt Mass of Sinfull Mankind, Equally Sinful and Miserable as the Rest, whom he gives to the Son Appointed Mediator, to be Saved by Him; whereby the Infinite Free Love of God the Father is Glorified in Chusing them to Salvation; And the Love and Kindness of the Son, in Undertaking to Satisfy for them.[31]

Election must therefore be subordinate to the constitution of Christ as mediator. This was the reason why Rowan and Webster had misunderstood Simson's teaching on the merit of Christ being the cause of election. Simson warned his students against the error that Christ was "the Meritorious Cause of Election."[32] The decrees are simultaneous in the divine mind, but the human intellect, lacking the capacity to understand this, must invent a temporal order for them. The order that seemed to Simson easiest for human comprehension was that God first gave grace to the elect, to cleanse them from sin, and then granted them eternal glory.

Simson stressed that Webster, misunderstanding what his informant had told him about this, had assumed that Simson was teaching that men were predestined on their foreseen use of means – faith and repentance. This was an Arminian error contrary to scripture (Acts 13:48,

30 Ibid., 87–8.
31 Ibid., 89–90.
32 Ibid., 91.

"and as many as were ordained to eternal life believed"), to the Westminster Confession, and to the Canons of Dort. He, however, believed himself to be in accord with the Canons of Dort, which he quoted, "Election is the fountain of all saving [literally, health-bearing] good, from which flow faith, holiness, &c."[33] Webster claimed to have understood from Simson's letter that the professor considered that men would receive regenerating grace if they used the means provided.[34] It is possible that he misunderstood Simson's arguments. Simson was convinced that God provided the means to accomplish His predestined ends, in this as in the matter of the salvation of the heathen. Simson's lengthy explanation of his opinions about the order of the divine decrees seems entirely within the bounds of the normal Reformed tradition, and quite unexceptionable. Furthermore, his elect are "a certain number out of the corrupt mass," which, while indefinite, still represents a limited number.[35]

Simson's optimistic soteriological teaching ran counter to the worldview of early-eighteenth-century Scots Presbyterians, for whom the persecutions of the previous century had proved only too plainly the inherent sinfulness of man. Despite the problems that this divergence of interpretation brought upon him, Simson's belief in the love and benevolence of God remained unchanged. In the mid 1730s he wrote movingly that disinterested human love was but "a faint resemblement of the Love of God & of our Saviour."[36] Perhaps Simson's reflective reading both of patristic literature and of the works of the early Reformers helped to inoculate him against the prevalent Scottish fear of Arminianism. He remarked that he did not find cogent the reasons given by modern divines for their pessimistic views. He accused Webster of expecting everyone to take the current interpretation of the Bible as infallible, which he considered "more Absurd than the Popish" demands on the faithful.[37]

PASTORAL CONCERNS

The second category of charges against Simson dealt with matters of pastoral importance to prospective ministers. Simson was preparing his students to deal with real problems of human sin. His intention seems

33 Ibid., 95. "Electio est fons omnis Salutiferi Boni, ex qua Fides, Sanctitas &c. fluunt."
34 Ibid., 19.
35 Ibid., 90.
36 J. Simson to A. Campbell, undated c. 1735–6. NAS, GD461/15/14, 5.
37 Simson, *Libel*, 107.

to have been to counter the fire-and-brimstone approach of the orthodox, as expressed in so many of their sermons.

Webster presumably considered Jesuitical an article dealing with
God's providence with respect to human actions. He charged Simson
with teaching that "Concursus then is nothing else, but the Lord's ...
puting the Creature in such Circumstances in which the Creatures being placed, does without any previous or predetermining Instance upon
it, freely, yet Infallibly produce the Decreed Effect."[38] *Concursus Divinus*,
or *physicus concursus*, is God's immediate concurrence in the actions of
all created beings – the world is conserved and governed through the
continuous involvement of providence. It was a doctrine that had provoked debate within the church from the time of Augustine and which
had divided Catholics in the sixteenth century. Dominicans and other
Thomists followed the views of the Council of Trent that divine providence governed the world and impelled all creation to action through
physicus concursus. Jesuits, after Luis de Molina (1535–1600), held that
God possessed foreseen knowledge of individual action (*scientia media*).

For Protestants, divine concursus was an effective ideology to support
predestination. To doubt it was to risk being accused of placing a Pelagian gloss on the doctrine of human free will. It was particularly important to the orthodox to maintain the doctrine of *physicus concursus* at a
time when the deist idea of a clockmaker god was prevalent. Conservative Presbyterians therefore stressed the continuous effects of divine
providence on all aspects of life, as stated in the Westminster Confession.
The Molinist notion that men acted freely with God's foreknowledge
seemed to the orthodox to be a hazardous attack on the sovereignty of
God. "Private Christian," who wrote in 1722 contrasting the Church of
Scotland's differing reactions to Simson and to the twelve ministers (discussed below) who supported the *Marrow*, noted that Simson's thesis on
divine concursus "seems to debase the Almighty and Infinite God, that
he should be at such pains to solicite Men outwardly, for securing the
Infallibility of his Decree."[39]

The second significant feature of the belief in *physicus concursus* lay in
the problem of evil. Reformed stress on predestination and the decrees
did not solve the difficulty of divine responsibility for human wickedness. In common with Continental writers such as Bayle, seventeenth-
century Scots theologians continued to ponder the enigma of theodicy.

38 Ibid., 5.
39 Private Christian, *Videte apologiam*, 11.

The theory of sin followed by Webster and his friends saw God as being "efficient in all entitive acts about sin" but "not efficient in the production of sin."[40] If sin were a reality, then it existed either by God's will, which would cast doubt on His holiness, or against His will, which would deny His omnipotence. Walker pointed out the danger of making the problem of sin metaphysical rather than moral – a distinction that must have been difficult to explain to, for example, a loose-living parishioner, and one that was impossible to justify in biblical terms, since in scripture sin is a very real human concern, against which God urges man to struggle.[41] This seems to be another instance in which Simson found that the scholasticism of seventeenth-century Reformed theology was inconsistent with pastoral ministry. He thought it impossible to instruct his students without softening the precepts of *physicus concursus*.

Nevertheless Simson, in the *Libel* and to the presbytery, denied teaching that God merely permitted sinful action or lacked full dominion over free human efforts. He refuted annually the Pelagian schemes that disallowed *physicus concursus*, just as he did the Jesuit *scientia media*. Simson thought "that, as God had Eternally and Unchangeably Decreed ... So as All Things come to pass Immutably and Infallibly, according to his Foreknowledg and Decree: Yet, by the same Providence He Ordereth them to fall out according to the Nature of Second Causes."[42] The libel, however, quoted Simson as disagreeing with the text that he was teaching, which said, "Rational Creatures are like passive Instruments in the hand of God." The professor was quoted as saying, "This way of Explaining it, seems to be inconsistent with the Rational Nature."[43] This sentiment is close to many of his admitted views on the relationship of God and man. The words of the libel ring true to his normal speech patterns. Simson had been accused of teaching that God placed individuals in such circumstances as would infallibly produce the decreed actions, which was presumably the charge that led Walker to see Simson as a philosophic necessitarian. Nevertheless, in the course of his defence, Simson did not deviate from the words of the Westminster Confession, which separated those things that came to pass through God as first cause from those that were contingent on second causes (5:2). The first

40 Walker, *Scottish Theology*, 59. In scholastic terms, an "entitive act" was one that was actual or material rather than merely potential or formal.

41 Ibid., 60.

42 Simson, *Libel*, 122.

43 Ibid., 4.

form of providence repudiated Pelagianism; the second permitted sin through free will.

At issue for Simson was the reconciliation of a benevolent and just God with the Presbyterian covenanting deity of inflexible power, omniscience, and righteousness. With his familiarity with contemporary scholarship, and his irritation at what he considered the outdated language of the "quibbling Schoolmen," he was again trying to modulate late-seventeenth-century doctrine.[44] Parish ministers would meet human weakness in their flocks. They needed the tools to rehabilitate the unrighteous, who must first be brought to admit their faults. Although the life of the individual was known and foreordained, yet, within the custody of providence, man still had freedom to sin. He must be led to acknowledge and repent his errors for the greater good of his community, as well as for the salvation of his soul.

Simson's eloquent testimony to human ability to seek grace gave considerable anguish to the orthodox, who debated the matter for hours during the General Assembly of 1717. Quoting liberally from the Sermon on the Mount, Simson explained his belief in a generous God, who "was not only the Father of them all ... but ... was now Offering them His Richest Grace ... Exhorting them to Seek, and Promising, that, upon Asking, they should Receive Good Things from Him, and Find, that He was a more Loving and Bountiful Father, than any Father among them was to his Children."[45] Since Christ preached in this vein to a multitude of different races and backgrounds, so also should His ministers to their congregations. God had provided men with the means of obtaining grace – diligent Bible study, attentive attendance at sermons, meditation and prayer – and the power to use them, although in practice only the elect would do so. "For," Simson pointed out logically, "it seems very Unaccountable, to say, that People should Use Means, for Obtaining the First Grace, which yet they cannot Use until they have got it, because it is above their Natural Ability to make Use of them."[46] While no merit could be ascribed to it, some "Preparatory Work" must take place in sinners' souls before, and necessarily connected with, regeneration and conversion. Through this step-by-step argument, Simson in 1715 assured the Presbytery of Glasgow that he upheld the

44 Webster, *Propositions*, 23.
45 Simson, *Libel*, 215.
46 Ibid., 216.

doctrines of election, reprobation, and providence and refuted Pelagian and Arminian objections.[47]

The pastoral dilemma implicit in Webster's idea of the elect person as passive in regeneration lay in the fact that it discouraged sinners from prayer, study, church attendance, or ethical habits until they were sure of regeneration. Simson saw these activities as the divinely appointed means of regeneration. As a professor, dealing with the training of young ministers, he needed a doctrine that would enable them to preach the Gospel wholeheartedly to the black sheep of their parishes as well as to the apparently elect and which could work towards raising moral standards in Scotland. It is a tribute to the concern of the members of the 1717 assembly for this reality that they treated the issue of moral seriousness as one of the most consequential of Webster's charges. The fact that at the same time they faced an example of apparent Antinomianism in Auchterarder probably drove the significance of the issue home to them.[48]

None of Simson's arguments to the presbytery or in print on such pastoral matters seems to have been heterodox or even unusual in Calvinist circles, but discussion continued to rage. The strength of his feelings may be deduced from his lifelong interest in the possibility of the redemption of all of mankind. Writing to his friend Archibald Campbell in 1732, Simson spoke of a revelation coming "between the universal Revelation to all men by Noah & that by Christ," in which God made Himself known to Abraham's posterity. The dwelling place of this favoured tribe was at the centre of the known world, "by which means all nations might have access to know the true God & the way of worshiping him."[49] Through his own previous experience and his current membership of the Presbytery of Glasgow, Simson as a teacher was alert to the problems facing parish ministers in summoning their flocks to repentance. He believed that his students should be prepared to make the Gospel offer to all their hearers and that congregations should actively seek redemption through rational examination of their own lives and the use of the means that God proffered them.

A connected group of accusations in Webster's libel charged Simson with including good works and obedience in his teaching on the nature

47 Ibid., 220–1.
48 See below, chapter 9, for an overview of this affair.
49 J. Simson to A. Campbell, 26 Feb. 1732, NAS, GD461/15/3, 5.

of justifying faith. The danger in this proposition lay in considering that works, in the form of obedience to the moral law, were a constituent part of justifying faith. In 1713 Webster had questioned Simson about a possible antecedent condition of the covenant of grace. Although he found the question obscurely worded, Simson tried at that time to give a full answer, which he repeated to the presbytery in 1715. The crux of his belief was that "we must Receive a Whole Christ, or Accept of Him, and His Righteousness, not only for Pardon and Glory, but also *for Wisdom and Sanctification*: and (must) Engage in the Strength of His Grace, to Study sincere Obedience to the whole Law, before we be Pardoned or Justified."[50] This statement must be scanned carefully. If it is read to assume that prevenient grace precedes the study of obedience ("Engage in the Strength of His Grace, to Study ... Obedience to ... Law"), then it is orthodox. Simson felt that saving faith worked through love, which would naturally command obedience, but he firmly denied that justification could be found in works or in anything outside the satisfaction of Christ.

The argument again revolves around the duty of a minister to preach repentance and rectitude. Simson's disapproval of Antinomianism, combined with his insistence on moral values, meant that his theology was more tolerant of certain aspects of Arminianism than was that of his opponents. For Webster, justification came before regeneration. Simson disagreed with this position, calling it Antinomian and arguing that an unregenerate person was incapable of accepting Christ and repenting. McLaren had no sympathy with Simson's opinion on justification. He made short work of his arguments, saying, "it's plain, he makes Repentance; a Prerequisite to Justification."[51] Simson's convoluted defence centred on the belief that through grace the elect will find faith and obedience. The elect accept Christ, and through Him try to lead good lives, before they are justified. Simson felt that Webster went "pretty far in the *Antinomian* Way," in his belief that justification preceded regeneration.[52] To Simson justifying faith could not exist without a determination "*to Obey GOD in all things*," a position that he supported by several biblical texts, particularly Christ's words in Luke 13:3, "I tell you, Nay: but, except ye repent, ye shall all likewise perish."[53] Simson

50 Simson, *Libel*, 247–8.
51 McLaren, *New Scheme*, 376.
52 Simson, *Libel*, 252.
53 Ibid.

referred to a sermon that he had preached two years earlier, in 1713, to the members of the Presbytery of Glasgow on Acts 20:20–21, verses in which the apostle says, "I kept back nothing that was profitable unto you, but ... have taught you publickly ... testifying ... repentance toward God, and faith toward our Lord Jesus Christ." The message that he had shared with the assembled ministers had not been challenged by any of them; only Webster had ever accused him of error about faith and justification.

Webster had another grievance against Simson on the head of justification – the teaching of a two-fold justification, one part through faith, the other by works. Simson explained to the presbytery in 1715 that he had correlated the justification taught in Romans 3:23, 24, where "all have sinned, and come short of the glory of God; Being justified freely by his grace through the redemption that is in Christ Jesus," with that in James 2:22: "Seest thou how faith wrought with his works, and by works was faith made perfect?" Once again he saw works as the fruit of faith working by love. He referred Webster to Pictet, who had reconciled the apparently differing visions of Paul and James, by suggesting that they were responses to different accusations, and pointed out that at the Last Judgment, according to the Gospel, the evidence of a man's true faith would be found in his works. He deplored the tendency of Webster's friends to play down repentance and Webster's own Antinomian turn of phrase.

Simson told the presbytery in 1715 that Webster's complaints about his teaching on the imputation of Christ's righteousness were totally false. In the interests of both morality and common sense, he taught that ministers should try to check any tendency to place excessive trust in Christ's righteousness being imputed to humans. Such a tendency was a disincentive to living an ethical life and led again to Antinomianism. Simson was bothered by ministers' remarks such as: "The Gospel is only a Bundle of Absolute Promises, and Contains neither Precepts nor Threatnings," which could easily be taken in a wrong sense.[54] He was also concerned about the effect on the "Vulgar" of such sentiments from the pulpit as: "*That the pressing them to the Study of Holiness in the Strength of Christ, as a Necessary Mean and Condition of Salvation, tho' not of Justification, is Legal Preaching.* The plain Scotch of which, I think, is, *that it is the Preaching up of the Covenant of Works, in stead of Preaching the Gospel.*"[55] The pastoral concerns behind Simson's arguments were shared by the majority of

54 Ibid., 276.
55 Ibid., 276–7.

his fellows. The controversy over Antinomian tendencies in Scotland came to a head in 1717 and had repercussions in the succeeding years. It may be suggested that the open discussion of the issue created by the Simson case led to the later condemnation of Antinomianism, which tendency the enlightened would later equate with enthusiasm and fanatic madness.

The first question of the Westminster Larger Catechism asked, "What is the chief and highest end of man?" The answer was two-fold: "to glorify God, and fully to enjoy him for ever." Expounding this in 1715, Simson understood it in the light of the recent philosophy of human understanding. When teaching the class text – presumably Marck – he was alleged to have said that, for rational creatures, the desire for reward and fear of punishment were the chief motives in worshipping God, since God had created them to seek their own good and happiness. Defending himself against this incorrect version of his opinion, Simson laid out a logical series of steps that illustrated his views: God's purpose in creating the world was to display His perfections; a rational being loves for reasons of real or apparent good and hates for reasons of real or apparent evil; he strives to obtain that which he sees as his greatest good; when he makes a correct choice, he "Chooses that which God its creator has proposed as its Greatest Good and Chief End; whereby its Real and apparent Good are the same."[56] This greatest good is assumed to be eternal enjoyment of God and His glory, to obtain which man must both worship reverently and live morally. Human beings could not be obliged to abandon the struggle towards everlasting life. Simson agreed that both divine purpose and common sense urged men to venerate God. If, however, Webster thought that anyone would prefer the glory of God over his eternal enjoyment of Him, "then I Own, I am not of His Mind; Being Persuaded, that this is Contrary both to Common Sense, and Sanctified Reason, and is a Peice of Unsolid and Absurd *Metaphysicks*, which was never Taught, by any of the Prophets or Apostles, not by any Person well Skilled in *Philosophy* or *Divinity*."[57]

Simson then charged Webster with Antinomianism and mysticism – accusations that seem remarkably mild in view of his next request, which was that a "Timeous Stop may be put to the Spreading of this *Antinomian* Gangrene ... because, not only some of the People are Tainted

56 Ibid., 136.
57 Ibid., 143.

with it, but it is Preached on the most Solemn Occasions, by some Ministers as a *Necessary Branch of Self Denyal, that we be Denyed to our own Salvation.*"⁵⁸ When Simson argued that his students should avoid such
theological contortions, his adversaries felt that his doctrine ran contrary to the true nature of Calvinist Christianity. They granted that desire of reward and fear of punishment might be motives for the worship
of God but denied that they could be the chief motives. One wrote to a
friend, "I do not like this strain of teaching, it savors little of the spirit of
a christian, & speaks little sense of the meanness and emptiness of the
creature."⁵⁹ In this, as in other parts of his defence, Simson's views corresponded with contemporary interest in natural law. Simson was trying
to phrase the moral concerns expressed by many British philosophers in
language that might be acceptable to his Calvinist countrymen. Ultimately, it may be said that he was successful; but in the short term, he
faced powerful opposition from prominent preachers whose apocalyptic vision of the Almighty must have struck terror into the hearts of their
parishioners every Sunday.

RETREAT FROM SCHOLASTICISM

Another series of charges against Simson in 1715 was dogmatic in
nature and flowed from his rejection of seventeenth-century scholasticism. The accusations illustrate the remote nature of the theology of the
conservative Presbyterians and its detachment from the intellectual
world of Locke and Newton, into which Simson was introducing his students. Federal theology placed a new gloss on original sin and the precise nature of Adam's responsibility for the corruption of humanity.
Simson felt that a simpler, more scriptural doctrine of Adam, as both
progenitor and corruptor of his race, was more helpful in championing
Calvinist theology against "those who Impugn it with Arguments not
Easy to be Answered."⁶⁰ Neither the Bible nor the early Reformers
called Adam the federal head of mankind. Like Boston, Simson rejected
the contractual language of the federal covenants, with its implication
of mutual obligations between God and man. Disliking the misuse of
legal terms in theology, he rejected the use of the word "covenant" in an

58 Ibid., 155.
59 Anonymous layman to Hogg[?], minister in Presbytery of Dunfermline. NLS,
Wodrow Folios, XXXIX, f.134v.
60 Simson, *Libel,* 175.

"improper," or legal sense. Webster, however, was less precise. He had defined "covenant" at the Edinburgh meeting in the summer of 1713 as "a Law with a Double Sanction." When Simson asked for further explanation, Webster had said it was "A Law Enforced with Rewards and Punishments." Simson commented that if this were really Webster's belief, then their only difference lay in names.[61]

Denying many of Webster's charges entirely, Simson insisted to the presbytery that he believed and taught the doctrine of the Westminster Confession, including the covenant of works made by God with Adam. The word "covenant" in that context was not "called a Covenant in the Proper and Strict Sense, as a Covenant is Distinct from, and Opposed to a Law."[62] By taking its meaning as law rather than as contract, one could base the imputation of sin on a natural rather than on a federal relationship with Adam. His father's personal ties to Gillespie gave Simson an understanding of the difficulties that the members of the Westminster Assembly had faced in formulating the confession and catechisms. Simson quoted the Westminster Confession to prove that the guilt of original sin was imputed through ordinary generation; its clauses contained no hint of a federal relationship. "I grant," Simson said in his *Libel*, that "Our *Catechisms* seem to fix it on the Federal Relation, if the Word *Covenant* be taken in the *Strict Sense*; and so *They* will Differ from the *Confession*.... But, if the Word *Covenant* be taken *Improperly*, then they will *Agree*."[63] His explanation of the intended meaning of "covenant" allowed the confession and catechisms to conform with each other, which a federal reading rendered problematic. Any contradictions were the result of doctrinal differences among the assembly's members and of the inevitable compromises required to reach a consensus.

Simson explained that three years earlier (presumably in 1712) he had made an addition to his dictates defining the legal meaning of "law" and "covenant" to ensure that his students did not fall into error. The former was an "Obligation laid on by the Authority of a Lawful Superior," while the latter was a general idea denoting a mutually agreed pact, which Simson termed "An Obligation Contracted by Promise and Acceptance between Two Parties."[64] In both scripture and other literature, "covenant" was sometimes used "in a Large Improper Sense," for

61 Ibid., 170.
62 Ibid., 158.
63 Ibid., 159.
64 Ibid., 161–2.

obligations, or the contracting of obligations, and often meant the same as "law." Simson believed that the rationale behind the use of "covenant" by the Westminster Assembly was that the law of God was unique in that it contained a promise of reward to the obedient: "it hath something of the Nature of a Covenant or Paction, seing God Obliges Himself to Man by his Promise."[65] In a secular metaphor, the satisfaction of the subjects of an absolute monarch with the good laws imposed by him no more turned such laws into contracts than did Adam's acquiescence in God's law. Moreover, the critical verses in Romans, 5:12–20, consistently used the term "law," not the word "covenant." Simson concluded that since his understanding of the word was the same as that of the compilers of the confession and catechisms, he could not be regarded as teaching anything contrary to them, and he cited the provisos of both Scottish and Continental theologians as to the correct meaning of "covenant."

Having disposed of the covenant issue, Simson proceeded to justify his view of Adam's relationship to his posterity. While fully admitting that Adam was a public representative of mankind in his sense of law, he preferred to follow the first Reformers in choosing explanations that were closer to both the Bible and reason. Since God gave Adam and his race a law, not a covenant, there was no need for the first man to have represented his posterity as federal head in any pact with the Creator. The doctrine of original sin, which depended on the belief that degenerate human nature derived its corruption directly from Adam, provided a satisfactory rationale for the otherwise inexplicable actions of human beings, as Simson, with his concern for pastoral training, was well aware.[66]

Webster had accused Simson of Socinian error in denying the imputed guilt of Adam's sin. Simson now poured scorn on this "sorry Shift," saying that he was neither an Arminian nor a Placean in his understanding of the imputation of Adam's sin.[67] Advocating the necessity of maintaining divinely appointed civil authority, he was unlikely to disavow the inevitable repercussions of disobedience to God's laws. His teaching on the imputation of sin stated that Adam's posterity was justly charged with the guilt of his sin and was thus liable to be punished for it, although the divine purpose of this was beyond its understanding. The

65 Ibid., 162.
66 Ibid., 180.
67 Ibid., 182.

invention of covenants "Contributes Nothing at all, to Remove Difficulties, brought against the Justice of GOD, in Imputing Adams Sin" to his posterity, since Adam, as a parent, had no right to make engagements in their name that he could not fulfil.[68] The Bible did not state that Adam had been appointed to transact affairs in the name of his descendants prior to the making of the covenant of works. Furthermore, Simson pointed out that even had Adam been "placed in the Relation of a *Tutor Dative* to his Posterity," his errors would not have been imputed to them, since in legal terms no ward should suffer from his guardian's mismanagement.[69] In such a case, the ward could seek redress from any magistrate who had appointed a tutor known to be likely to mismanage his pupil's affairs.

The emphasis on rights and duties implicit in this passage shows Simson's familiarity with the legal and political thought of his day. In 1718, Simson's colleague Gershom Carmichael published an edition of Samuel Pufendorf's *De officio hominis et civis iuxta legem naturalem* (1673), with supplements indicating Carmichael's own judgment on moral philosophy. Supplement IV, dealing specifically with contract theory, agrees with Simson's interpretation.[70] The members of the Glasgow faculty had a similar approach to ethical teaching and a shared understanding of divine and natural law, as had many Continental theologians by 1715.

In his 1716 speech to the General Assembly, Simson indicated that "every Intelligent Divine" would acknowledge that reconciling the idea of a good and just God with His appointment of Adam as federal head was "one of the greatest Difficulties in Divinity"; his interpretation, which other theologians had used, allowed a reconciliation that was "Comparatively easie."[71] To counter the implication that only an unjust God would command fallen man to obey His Law when he had no power to do so, Simson argued that humanity had received the means with which to obey through revelation and the strength with which to comply by the Gospel. Webster had heard that Simson taught that Adam had no power to believe in Christ; untrue, said Simson, "Nor do I see any use to Divinity by determining such a question."[72] He had, however, told Webster that it was both inconsistent with a state of innocence and

68 Ibid., 186.

69 Ibid., 187. A "tutor dative" was the guardian and administrator of the estate of a minor, or "pupil."

70 Carmichael, *Gershom Carmichael.*

71 Webster, *Propositions*, 17.

72 Simson, *Libel*, 194.

unnecessary for Adam to have such power. He felt that if Adam had known that a remedy would be provided, the divine threat of death would have been weakened. For Webster the importance of the issue lay in the necessity of Adam's obligation to believe in Christ so that his posterity should have a similar obligation.

This quibble seems to have been typical of the finicky nature of the orthodox Calvinist dogma from which Simson was trying to escape. No light could be cast on the deeper meaning of original sin or on the amelioration of the human condition by speculation on the exact nature of Adam's knowledge before the Fall. Each man claimed that the Protestant authorities were on his side, but Simson embarked on a risky course when he added, "If it be an Error Taught by Arminius, I am not Guilty of it, seeing I do not Teach it, and think the Arguments he adduces for it, to be Naught: Yet, I will not Grant, that a Proposition is Erroneous, because Arminius Taught it."[73]

Simson's generation of Scottish ministers had been brought up on the works of Dutch divines. Hogg, Webster, and Wodrow might still consider Marck and Witsius the most effective theologians in the continuing battle against scepticism and deism, but Simson had doubts about their universal applicability against Pelagian and Universalist arguments. Protestants had an obligation to find a personal doctrinal message in the Bible, not to follow blindly the interpretation of their predecessors. If they were not free to think for themselves, they might "introduce by the back-gate a dangerous branch of popery."[74] Simson was trying to offer to his students a flexible doctrine with which they could promote Christian values and ethics, while countering sceptical or deistic arguments. He accepted the dogma of original sin without question – he merely rejected the legalist structure of federal theology, which he felt had served its purpose and was no longer a practical tool for the explanation of human evil.

The two final charges in Webster's main libel dealt with eternal punishment. Simson was participating in a vigorous and long-lasting controversy, which may have received new life from Protestants' shocked disapproval of Louis XIV's *dragonnades* in the seventeenth century.[75] Socinians, Arminians, and deists had queried this doctrine, which had been the subject of a controversial sermon by John Tillotson (1630–1694,

73 Ibid., 200.
74 Ibid., 189.
75 See Briggs, "Mysticism."

archbishop of Canterbury 1691) before Queen Mary in 1690. Tillotson had suggested that more might be threatened by God than He actually intended to execute, since the point of sanctions is to prevent sin rather than necessarily to punish it. While he himself did not endorse such a view, he closed his sermon with the remark that the wise man would not run the risk of finding out. Copies of Tillotson's *Works* were bought for the Glasgow University Library in 1723, but the list of books bequeathed to it by Principal Stirling contained volumes by Tillotson with publication dates of 1707 and 1712.[76] It is possible that Simson had access to these if the library did not already possess them.

Englishmen who probably rejected the idea of eternal punishment included Locke, Newton, and Whiston, while on the Continent both orthodox Calvinists such as Pierre Jurieu (1637–1713) and Arminians such as Jean LeClerc wrote and preached in favour of mitigating the doctrine of Hell. John Simson's views were thus akin to those of the more advanced thinkers of his day. His compatriot Dr. George Cheyne (1671–1743), while working in London, had published *Philosophical Principles of Natural Religion* in 1705.[77] One of the arguments in this volume was that a god of infinite perfections could make intelligent beings only for the end of happiness, consisting of reunion with the mystic centre. Simson was no mystic but would have agreed with the first part of this argument. Whether he was exposed to the current debate during his visits to Holland, or whether he encountered it during his reading, is less important than the reality that he early incorporated a distinctive interpretation of Hell into his lectures.

Webster claimed that Simson had denied that the necessity for eternal punishment flowed from sin's offending the majesty of God. Simson felt that this charge was based on a student's inability to follow his Latin.[78] Since the slightest sin was an unpardonable affront to the divine Legislator, it was necessary to have sanctions to the law. A wise and just God might certainly threaten eternal punishment for sin, though not necessarily from His Majesty, but perhaps from "a Free and Arbitrary Act of His Will."[79]

Webster also deplored Simson's gloss on his text book's treatment of the fate of the damned. The bitter debate that followed on this issue

76 GUA 43121 (Stirling's bequest), 58024 (receipt for books purchased 26 Nov., 1723).
77 George Cheyne, *Philosophical Principles of Natural Religion*, appeared in 1705. An enlarged second edition came out in 1715, and re-editions in 1716, 1724, and 1736.
78 Simson, *Libel*, 229.
79 Ibid., 230.

illustrates again the opaque complexity of Reformed doctrine and the scholastic knots into which its adherents could tie themselves. Scottish theological opinion held that sinners continued to sin in Hell, in thought if not in deed, for eternity. Enlightened opinion, however, was suggesting that eternal damnation should mean annihilation rather than suffering. Simson stayed close to the orthodox Presbyterian doctrine, but he had original ideas about the moral state of the damned. When asked to clarify his views in 1713, he had stated that God, after the Last Judgment, would restrain the damned from further sin. Speaking to the presbytery, he agreed that sinners would indeed cease to sin, not from their own volition, "But, because They will then, by the Power of God, be put in a State Purely Passive." In this condition, they would be aware of only three things: "the Tormenting Flames of Divine Vengeance," perplexity and horror at their earthly wickedness, and "Clear and Silencing Convictions of the Equity and Justice of Gods Sentence."[80] Where Webster and his friends saw the necessity of perpetual sin to emphasize the evil of the sinners and the appropriate nature of perpetual punishment, Simson preferred a stance of accepting, passive penitence.

Defining his epistemology with respect to the damned, Simson further explained that he sometimes called the exercise of the human reasoning faculty "action," in order to distinguish it from the passivity of inanimate objects such as stones. In other words, he said, he used the word "action" "to Signify any Perception, Agreeing to an Intelligent Creature."[81] If, however, action was taken to mean something done willingly, or by choice, then it would be inconsistent with the passive state of the damned, in which there could be no voluntary mental processes. He further defined the three forms of understanding for the damned: for the first, passive sensations, and for the second and third, passive reflections. Simson considered that this was entirely in keeping with the scriptural descriptions of Hell. He felt that it was necessary that sin should cease in Hell, since the honour of the Judge could be upheld only if sin received appropriate retribution, but no greater punishment could be inflicted on the damned than they already suffered.

In 1714 James Hogg printed an energetic rebuttal of the idea that there was no sinning in Hell. When the aggrieved Simson wrote to complain about his being clearly misrepresented in this publication, although his name was not disclosed, Hogg wrote back with a further list

80 Ibid., 223–4.
81 Ibid., 234.

of queries. Perhaps the heart of his objection to Simson's thesis lay in Query 12, where he asked, "Such a Submissive temper of Spirit, is a sure presage, and happy beginning of the best of Issues upon Earth, doth not this tend to give some sort of hope to the Damned of their being delivered from that State at the long run. This would open the gate to Execrable Athiesm."[82] To men of a deeply spiritual nature, such as Hogg and his friends, living in a state of sin would be *per se* the most painful condition that a soul could suffer. The greatest gift possible would therefore be relief from the burden of actual sin. The notion of the passive and sinless damned thus represented to them "some sort of hope" and certainly a deliverance from the worst of their punishment.[83] Simson and his students were closer to everyday human reality in their conviction that most sinful people did not find their impure thoughts or blasphemous ideas the worst trial that life offered. Simson must have suggested this to Hogg in explanation of his teaching, for Hogg replied, "I confess sinners in time propose to themselves pleasure in Sining, yet they often cannot attain it, no not in the most evanide [fleeting] Shadows thereof ... but in hell matters are quite otherwayes, Sin there is separated from pleasure & inseparably joined with pain & anguish."[84]

Hogg and Webster were also disquieted by the fact that the damned seemed to equal Christ in their acceptance of their fate, which was impossible, since it was "a priviledge peculiar to the Lord Jesus, He reflected not in the least against the Righteous Judge."[85] Suffering, but totally passive, damned souls might be deemed more virtuous than Christ, who cried out, "My God, my God, why hast thou forsaken me?" (Matt. 27:46). As one critic of Simson queried, "Is the keeping the soul back from the least sinfull motion a fruit of vindictive wrath? Is the reformation of the damn'd a part of their damnation?"[86] "Mr. Logan" commented, "If there be such a Reformation in Hell, God has not thought fitt to reveal it to us in Scripture."[87] Simson's error in "Setting the Suffering of the Devils on a levell with these of Jesus Christ" must be universally abhorred.[88] The problem was not merely that the damned seemed

82 J. Hogg to J. Simson, 6 Dec. 1714, NLS, Wodrow Folios, XXXIX, 107v.
83 Ibid., 110v.
84 Ibid., 119v.
85 Ibid., 111v.
86 (My punctuation.) Anonymous, to a minister in Presbytery of Dunfermline, presumably Hogg, no date, ibid., 134r.
87 Ibid., 151r.
88 Ibid., 150r.

to have as much or greater powers of endurance than Christ, but also that they had more virtue than was natural for human beings. On earth even the saints were known to have been "found murmuring, quarrelling, repining, and charging God foolishly" in situations of far less desperation than those of the damned in Hell.[89]

Hogg's correspondent felt that God was "destroying the nature of rationall creatures & making them passive instruments" in Simson's notion of the damned after the last trump. This seemed to impose a greater constriction on human will than "predeterminatio physica is or can be."[90] The writer discussed the nature of spontaneous and voluntary actions, noticing that even the actions of animals were considered spontaneous. "I hope," he said, "Mr S. doth not think the brutes mere machines, he is a more fashionable divine than to be a Cartesian as matters are now stated in the learned world especiallie among the witts, & have the damn'd less of what is spontaneous than the brutes."[91] He pointed out the contradictions between any belief in the passive state of damned souls and a denial of immediate physical predetermination of human action (*physicus concursus*).[92] "I suspect Mr S. has the same notion of free will and human libertie with the Jesuits, Socinians & remonstrants, would he open his mind clearly. perhaps I might consider his thoughts about human liberty on Earth, as I have his human necessitie in hell."[93] He accused Simson of straying into dangerous territory by denying spontaneous actions to the damned, which might permit others to argue against spontaneous actions on earth, as Spinoza and Hobbes had done, to the encouragement of atheists.

Scots preachers often used texts from Romans, especially 5:12–14, "By one man sin entered the world … but sin is not imputed when there is no law," and they continued to consider the implications of the last phrase to the damned in Hell. "Mr. Logan" mused, "If he [Simson] say the Law of God reacheth man only in a state militant, then it will follow there are no good actions in Heaven, for there is no goodness of actions among creatures, where the Rule of goodness ceaseth to oblige, as where there is no Law among creatures, there's no transgression."[94] The legalism of the necessary connections made between the existence

89 Ibid., 151r.
90 Ibid., 138v.
91 Ibid., 139r.
92 Ibid., 127v–128r.
93 Ibid., 140r–v.
94 Ibid., 150v.

of law and good or bad actions seems to have been typical of much of Calvinist thinking in this period.

For Simson, there were several kinds of law. He compared the "Law of Creation given to Adam" – the kind of law that Mr Logan described – with "the true Notions of the Eternal Law, by which all Rational Creatures, while they have a Being, are Subjected to the Soveraign Dominion of God." The two could be reconciled only if "the Final Sentence Inflicted on Sinners, lays them under the most Dreadful Sufferings, and perfectly Restrains them from the least Act of Sin."[95] Simson may have shared the theories of his colleague Carmichael, who wrote that the will of God, which he called "Divine Law," demanded certain actions from men and prohibited others and was "the highest rule of human actions."[96] This divine law is manifested through express signs and through "the very constitution of Human Nature and of other things." In the latter mode, the will of God is known as Natural Law.[97] Simson's "Eternal Law" seems to be the same as Carmichael's "divine law."

One article of the libel related to Simson's teaching of the procession of the Holy Ghost. According to the *Representation*, "He doubts of the Procession of the Holy Ghost from the Son, and will not Condemn the *Greek* Church for the Denial of it."[98] In reply, Simson cited teaching from John 15:26, which stated that Christ would send the Comforter, "which proceedeth from the Father," and Galatians 4:6, "God hath sent forth the Spirit of his Son into your hearts, crying Abba, Father." Since nowhere in scripture did it explicitly say that the Holy Ghost proceeded from the Son, Simson taught that the procession was from the Father and the Son, as stated in the Westminster Confession 2:3. He felt that the difference between the Greek and Latin churches on this issue was mainly one of words and concluded with suggesting that Webster read Isaac Vossius's (1618–1689) *de Tribus Symbolis* on the subject, where he would see that the *filioque* clause was rather the excuse for the division between the Eastern and Western churches than the cause of it. During the next decade, Simson studied carefully the works of the early church fathers after Samuel Clarke had stimulated his interest in Trinitarian theology. Even in middle and old age, he was always prepared to return to the available sources and to expand his knowledge when possible.

95 Simson, *Libel*, 242.
96 Carmichael, *Gershom Carmichael*, 4.
97 Ibid., 7.
98 Simson, *Libel*, 279.

The contradictions to which his opponents in the mid-1710s pointed in Simson's teaching may be explained by the fact that his divinity curriculum was developing with his beliefs. While Simson consistently denied Arminian views, he felt that orthodox Calvinism could encompass a more generous attitude to eternal punishment. The vocabulary used by each side highlighted the differing theological stances. To Simson, divine justice was not "the fruit of vindictive wrath" – instead the reprobate would have "Clear ... Convictions of the Equity and Justice of Gods Sentence." Disparate beliefs about providence and eternity derived from dissimilar images of God. Simson was too imbued with Scots Presbyterian traditions to embrace the full range of Arminian beliefs. As he said, however, he refused to reject a dogma simply because it had been held by Arminians. Once again it seems that Simson was trying to teach a body of theology that would be appropriate for the inquiring minds of a new century, but which would keep Scots true to their fathers' faith.

PHILOSOPHICAL "TRIFFLES"

Webster's libel ended with many minor cavils about ideas thrown out by Simson to elucidate or elaborate an argument. Simson had, for instance, suggested that God might animate several bodies through one soul, as an example to clarify the orthodox Nicene statement of the Trinity. To demonstrate his point, Simson used the example of the soul's giving motion to several bodily functions simultaneously. He asked why, if God could "Create a Spirit that can be Present in a Place that is of the Largeness of the Eight Part of an Inch Square, and can Move Four Bodies, Placed at the Four Sides of that Square, in a Line Perpendicular to each of its Four Sides, at the Same Instant of Time," He could not make one that could move four bodies at the four angles of a square mile? And if that were possible, then logically that soul could "Perform Vital and Rational Actions in Three Different Bodies" within the square mile.[99] We do not know if he presented this interesting notion in Latin or in English. If in the former, then it is hardly surprising that Simson was misrepresented!

The two men accused each other of using "the Old Jargon of the Schoolmen."[100] Simson claimed that Webster believed that some body functions were performed without the mediation of the soul, which was either contrary to the (Newtonian) "Laws of Mechanism," since the body

99 Ibid., 261–2.
100 Ibid., 257.

needed new impulses to keep it in motion, or was a "Groundless Fancy of Malbranch," which was "Built on an Absurd Supposition, 'That God either Cannot or Will not give to the Human Soul a Power to Produce these Motions in a due Subjection to His Own Supreme Government.'" He added that modern philosophers had "Clearly Demonstrated, that this Shred of Cartesian Tattle is Contrary to the Establish'd Laws of Motion."[101] In portraying Webster as out of date in his philosophical knowledge, Simson drew attention to the fact that he himself had kept abreast of current trends in scientific and medical thought. Scots universities were teaching Newtonian science by the early eighteenth century. In Glasgow it may be assumed that the masters, including the professor of divinity, were conversant with the latest ideas in natural philosophy. Many conservative ministers, however, were less likely to be familiar with the new science, whose methods and metaphysics they tended to distrust.

Simson was similarly brief in his rejection before the presbytery of Webster's allegations on four other topics that did not have serious doctrinal implications. First, given his own preconceptions, it was inevitable that Webster should criticize Simson's exposition on the powers of secular rulers in ecclesiastical affairs. He accused the professor of teaching that civil magistrates had the power to call synods and to appoint fast days and days of thanksgiving. He also charged Simson with teaching that if the magistrate were an open enemy to the church, ministers might call private meetings themselves. In reply Simson merely commented that the Latin of the charge had not been used by him but had come from Rowan. His teaching followed the Westminster Confession, chapters 23 and 31, with regard to synods, and the Acts of Assembly of 1647 and 1710, on fast and thanksgiving days.

Webster must have consulted his copy of the confession before he arranged to print his *Short Abstract* of Simson's version of the *Libel*. Although the *Short Abstract* contains nearly thirteen pages of Simson quotations from the *Libel* that contributed to "spreading the Contagion of his New and False Divinity," Webster dropped any mention of this particular error.[102]

Second, Simson neither admitted nor denied teaching that the New Testament forbade the eating of blood. He merely said that the article was irrelevant and that all ministers should be careful about stressing

101 Ibid., 258–9.
102 Webster, *Short Abstract*, 13.

passages of scripture where particular foods might be mentioned that were unobtainable.

Third, and on a more controversial point, Simson said, "I Own, I do Think it Probable, that there may be Rational Creatures Inhabiting the Moon and other Planets."[103] He could see no danger to religion in this viewpoint. The question of extraterrestrial life was raised by many writers, including Marck in the *Medulla*, which was Simson's text book, so it was necessary to discuss it. Since the days of classical Greece, there had been intermittent debate about the possibility of a plurality of worlds. Seventeenth-century natural philosophers popularized the topic, while fully appreciating the theological pitfalls that it contained. In England, John Wilkin's *Discovery of a World in the Moone* (1638) was republished in 1640, 1684, and 1707, and the Cambridge Platonist Henry More also wrote on the subject. Bernard le Bovier de Fontenelle's *Entretiens sur la pluralité des mondes* (1686) received nine English editions between 1687 and 1719.[104] In his 1693 Boyle lectures, Richard Bentley argued for inhabited planets on the basis of final causes, as did William Derham in his *Astro-Theology* of 1715: the existence of other heavenly bodies required the existence of other beings, just as earth had people. Scots such as David Gregory (1661–1708) and John Keill likewise entered into the fray, teaching pluralism.[105] Jonathan Woodward's letters testify that Glasgow students had studied Derham and Keill and therefore might be interested in the question of the possibility of life in space.

The debates formed part of the development of a new science dependent on natural theology – a subject that Simson clearly found interesting. He presumably had read some of these writers and agreed with them. His Newtonian friends had also kept him up to date with their work. He instructed his students that scripture was consistent with the known principles of natural philosophy, which they were learning at Glasgow. They could use their knowledge of the accord between revelation and natural philosophy to refute deists and atheists. In contrast to Simson's scientific interests, McLaren was typical of conservative commentators when he called such discussion "Idle speculation."[106] To him these topics were unacceptable in the divinity hall, however appropriate they might be in a philosophy class. He argued from Genesis that rea-

---

103 Simson, *Libel*, 284.
104 See Dick, *Plurality*, 136–7.
105 See Crowe, *Extraterrestrial Life*, 30–1, and Dick, *Plurality*, 155.
106 McLaren, *New Scheme*, 448.

soning by final causes could have a different outcome; the moon and stars had been created for the benefit of humans, and any inhabitants would have been mentioned in the Bible.

Fourth and finally, Simson scorned Webster's suggestion that he had been not merely rude but also heterodox when he called Marck a "Halucinatur Author."[107] On the contrary, *halucinator* was a normal adjective meaning mistaken, which Gomar had used of Calvin. He remembered Marck with gratitude and would never use a rude term about him, although he was perfectly prepared to differ from him on philosophical grounds. Simson observed justly that "Mr Webster Discovers more Ill Will to Me, than True Zeal for the Truth, when he makes such Triffles an *Article* of a *Libel* against me."[108] Webster himself thought Marck unsound on the subjects of church government and of the use of organs and so could hardly complain if Simson did not always agree with the learned Dutch professor.[109]

Although Webster believed Simson to be pouring "New and False Divinity" into the minds of the next generation of ministers, "and they swallowing down full Draughts thereof," his libel mentioned few if any departures from doctrines that were widely accepted in Reformed circles.[110] The fact that many of the charges were contentious stemmed less from Simson's Calvinist theology than from Scots Presbyterians' differing understandings of scripture and divergent interpretations of the decisions of Dort, Charenton, and Westminster. Simson's own convictions and pedagogical intentions led him to teach a faith that was in keeping with the beliefs of the early church, with the works of Calvin, and with current Reformed opinion in Europe, but which did not always correspond to that of Scottish orthodoxy.

1715–16: COMMENCEMENT OF THE CASE

When the Presbytery of Glasgow met in March 1715, the principals hoped to determine the truth of Webster's accusations promptly – a hope that was quickly dispelled. From 29 to 31 March 1715, the assembled

107 Simson, *Libel*, 285.
108 Ibid., 286.
109 Rowan had complained about Simson's support of the use of organs, again presumably because the subject was raised in the *Medulla*. Webster was wise enough not to include this issue in his libel.
110 Webster, *Short Abstract*, 13.

witnesses waited while the presbytery, Simson, and Webster wrangled about procedure, terminology, scriptural interpretation, and orthodox doctrine. Even when the presbytery began to consider the charges, it became bogged down by its inability to agree on the meaning of the words of the libel. Webster demanded that the libel be taken in its "natural sense,"[111] but Simson pointed out that many propositions were capable of such differing interpretations "that unless Mr Webster agree to the Determining the sense of such propositions ... He stops the progress of the Trial, and hinders this affair to be Legally Cleared."[112] After an *in camera* discussion, the presbytery agreed with Simson. Furious, Webster protested formally.

When Simson asked for the witnesses to be heard to prove his innocence, Webster, losing patience, accused the presbytery of partiality, declared his inability to accept its jurisdiction, and appealed to the Synod of Glasgow and Ayr.[113] Since the next synod meeting was on 5 April, leaving scant time to prepare documents and call witnesses under the provisions of the *Form of Process*, which called for ten days between the delivery of a citation to appear in court and the opening of the hearing, he declared himself ready to waive a synod hearing and take his case to the General Assembly meeting in May. He then summoned the whole Presbytery of Glasgow, including John Simson and the witnesses, to appear before whichever judicatory should hear the case.[114] In reply, Simson declared himself willing to defend himself immediately, accusing Webster of seeking a technical victory rather than the maintenance of orthodoxy. If the case could not be concluded without Webster's consent, and if that consent were withheld, he demanded "that Mr Webster be esteemed and repute, according to the Rules of equity and Justice, by this Rev[erend] presbytery, and all persons of piety, sense and probity, an Infamous Calumniator."[115]

At its April meeting, the Synod of Glasgow and Ayr received a notarized document from the presbytery clerk of Glasgow explaining that there had not been time to make copies of "about fourtie sheets of paper written bookwayes" of extracts from the minutes for the synod.[116] The

111 GCA, CH2/171/9A, 5v.
112 Ibid., 6r.
113 Ibid., 6v.
114 Ibid.
115 Ibid., 7r.
116 NAS, CH2/464/2, 351.

synod therefore concluded that, lacking both Webster's presence and the relevant documents, it could make no judgment and passed the appeal on to the General Assembly.[117]

The General Assembly of 1715 met in May, with the Earl of Rothes as royal commissioner. He had been chosen for his loyalty to the Crown but was known to have "good affection to the interest of the Church of Scotland."[118] William Carstares was elected moderator. The assembly decided to send the whole question of Webster's appeal to a special committee of thirty ministers and six ruling elders, whose quorum was set at twenty. This "Committee for Preserving the Purity of Doctrine" – the standard name for such a body – was to consider the process of Webster versus Simson, prepare a full statement, and present the necessary overture for the next assembly for decision.[119] It was carefully constructed to include men of all points of view, ensuring that its conclusions would carry weight within the church.

Its clerical members were headed by Carstares as moderator and consisted – in order as given by church records – of Principal James Hadow (New College, St Andrews), Professor William Hamilton (Edinburgh), Professor Thomas Blackwell (Marischal College, Aberdeen), Professor David Anderson (King's College, Aberdeen), Thomas Linning, William Mitchell, John Anderson, Andrew Cameron, James Ramsay, John Hunter, William Wishart, James Smith, John Currie, John Gray, John Ritchie, Andrew Rodger, Alexander Lauder, John Hamilton, Robert Horseburgh, John Brand, George Turnbull, James Alston, Thomas Black, James Cuthbert, William M'George, George Chalmers, Allan Logan, William Miller, and John Flint. Carstares had worked with Simson for years in state affairs; the other university professors might be expected to be sympathetic to him, while men such as Flint and Linning were likely to support the hyper-orthodox contentions of Webster. The influence of the ministers on the committee may be measured by the fact that no fewer than eight of them were past or future moderators of the General Assembly.

The six ruling elders included the lord president, Hugh Dalrymple of North Berwick; the lord justice-clerk, Adam Cockburn of Ormiston; and

117 Ibid., CH1/5/11.
118 Wodrow, *Correspondence*, 2:29.
119 Church of Scotland, General Assembly, *Principal Acts of the General Assembly*, Act 8, 1715, 13–14.

the solicitor-general, James Stewart of Goodtrees – government appointees who could be trusted to keep the proceedings firmly on prescribed lines. The others were John Clerk, a baron of the exchequer and an old acquaintance of Simson; Dr Dundas, a member of the Squadrone Arniston family; and Col. John Erskine of Carnock, a Presbyterian of highly orthodox opinions, who could be expected to side with Webster.

Apart from the Aberdeen professors, the ministers came from accessible lowland parishes and would be able to attend committee meetings with reasonable facility. The elders likewise led lives centred on Edinburgh. The thoughtful composition of this committee, appointed during a busy week of meetings, leaves the impression that Carstares and his advisers had been planning ahead to deal with the eventuality of Webster's appeal.

Cockburn reported to Montrose that while the assembly was dealing with Webster's appeal, that belligerent minister had managed to get into "a very unpleasant dialogue" with the solicitor-general, Sir James Steuart. The assembly was in his opinion "ye angryest and most peremptor ... ever I saw."[120] When it ended, Rothes was relieved to be able to tell Montrose that the "hott brethren" had been privately dissuaded from formally making a dissenting declaration. He had been able to induce Cameron, Linning, Logan, and others to send the matter to the commission; only Col. Erskine had held out against persuasion.[121] Between them Rothes and Carstares had managed to defuse a dangerous confrontation and avert any open split in the church ranks. Unfortunately it is not clear what subject prompted Rothes's problems. It may have been disagreement over the specifics of grievances to be brought to the notice of the King, rather than over the Simson affair.[122]

The committee soon received instructions as to how it should proceed. Those (if any) parts of the libel that constituted error were to be stated as "distinct Propositions," which were to be classed as, first, contrary to the word of God, the Confession of Faith, and the catechisms of the church; second, the subject of controversy among "orthodox divines," but which were not determined by either the confession or the catechisms; or third, not clearly mentioned in either Scripture or the works of orthodox Reformed theologians. The committee should then proceed "according

120 A. Cockburn to Montrose, 17 May 1715, NAS, GD220/5/454, 40.
121 Rothes to Montrose, 14 May 1715, NAS, GD220/5/258, 23.
122 See Wodrow *Correspondence*, 2:40–41.

to the Weight and Import of these Propositions so classed."[123] It was further to distinguish between what had been taught in divinity classes and what had been said in private conversation.

These directions suggest that the managers of the church were aware that while unsound teaching was a legitimate basis for censure, personal opinions mentioned in confidence were not. By determining which, if any, of the libelled articles were actually heretical, and by clearly noting which others were merely questions for debate among Reformed divines, they were trying to ensure that logical argument would take the place of orthodox enthusiasm, so that a consensus could be reached that the whole church would accept.

Once the classification was complete, Simson and Webster were to be interrogated and witnesses heard for both parties. Each might cross-examine the other's witnesses. A full report was to be ready for the next General Assembly. The committee was empowered to accept information about heterodox opinions held or published by any other teacher or minister and, if necessary, to prepare an overture on it (a power that might be applied to the errant Scrimgeour at St Andrews).

While Webster announced that he no longer considered himself "a pursuer ... having sufficiently exonerated himself,"[124] Simson tried to help the committee with its daunting task, arranging for copies of the libel to be printed and distributed to the committee members. Anxious about accuracy, he told Nicol Spence, the agent for the General Assembly, that Robert Wodrow had "corrected the extract by the original & also collated the print with both & all the errors of the print are corrected in this sheet enclosed."[125] Simson also informed Spence of the whereabouts of witnesses who might have moved.[126] He radiated confidence in his case and eagerness for a proper hearing to vindicate his name.

The committee received its instructions on 20 July 1715. The number of votes recorded suggest a group of about twenty-one members, who continued to meet daily until 23 July, when the committee adjourned until 21 September. The timing of the projected September meeting was unlucky – on 6 September, the Earl of Mar raised the Stuart standard to begin the 1715 Rebellion. Few Whig Presbyterian ministers

123 Dundas, *Processes*, 3–4.
124 Church, *Principal Acts*, Act 10, 1715, 18.
125 J. Simson to N. Spence, 22 June 1715, NAS, CH1/5/11.
126 J. Simson to N. Spence, 22 June 1715; same to same, date illeg., 1715, ibid.

were going to desert their pulpits when their presence was needed to bolster their parishioners' loyalty to the House of Hanover. The minutes of the meeting state briefly that there was no quorum because of "a Rebellion in the North."[127] With the interruption in normal life caused by the Fifteen, and the arrival of poor travelling conditions in winter, the committee members abandoned their efforts until the spring.

When the group sat down to business on 12 April 1716 it was obvious that it could not complete its mandate before the General Assembly in May. William Wilson condemned the committee for its pro-Simson stance, "The greatest part of the Committee laboured to bring the Professor off, by palliating his errors, and coining senses upon his erroneous propositions ... [But] The Lord left not himself without a witness. He helped six members of the Committee to give faithful witness ... against these errors, and ... when they were not condemned, they immediately entered their dissent."[128] Cameron, Flint, Linning, and Logan consistently interpreted the libel as Webster had done, and Thomas Black sometimes voted with them; the sixth man was probably Hadow. They wanted the committee to condemn the libelled propositions. When outvoted by others who wished to leave decisions to the assembly, they registered protests.[129] On April 28 it was noted that there had been no quorum, since "many of Mr. S's friends had thought fit to goe out of the toun," and, as a result, nothing had been prepared for the assembly. "Thus our com[mittee] is ended, but alas w[i]t[h] little credit to truth or to the Ch[urch] of Sc[otland] except what the few dissenters have done."[130] The 1715 Rebellion had prevented any decisive action by the committee. Since the Pretender did not leave Scotland until 4 February 1716, the committee cannot be accused of excessive delay in not meeting until early April. By then not enough time remained for the members to complete their task before the assembly's meeting.

1716: GENERAL ASSEMBLY AND COMMITTEE

The General Assembly of 1716 found the Simson matter time-consuming; objections to Simson sitting as a member, committee reports, complaints, motions, and debates on his affair absorbed the attention of

---

127 Minute in ibid.

128 Ferrier, *Memoirs of Wilson*, 129–30.

129 This pattern can be seen in NCL, CHU 10.1, various pages; NLS, Wodrow Letters Quarto, XI, 128, 136, 147, 209, etc.

130 A.P. to R. Wodrow, 28 April 1716, NLS, Wodrow Letters Quarto, XI, 147.

members in six of the fourteen sessions. The aftermath of the Rebellion left this assembly particularly riven by political differences; the contest for supremacy between the Squadrone and the Argathelians led to tests of strength. The Argathelians were anxious that a congratulatory address on the royal success be sent to the King, in which they intended to mention favourably the Duke of Argyll. To counter this plan, the Squadrone proposed that the names of other military leaders, including Gen. Cadogan, who had succeeded Argyll as commander-in-chief in Scotland, should be added, which heightened political feelings. Wodrow deprecated the "two or three ruling elders, all of them our hearty friends, and two ministers ... [who] carried their party business to the open Assembly, after such a fair trial in private committees. The Lord preserve us from party heats and heights, for I never saw so much, when the matter was not conscience but compliment!"[131]

With factional strife so much in evidence, the Simson case was "like to breed a dreadful heat in the Assembly," since it could be seen as another party conflict.[132] It was impossible that the charges could be properly sifted in the available hours. On 14 May, after "Many long speeches were made, some panegyrics, and some satires,"[133] it was proposed that the three divinity professors present should decide whether the assembly could judge on the propositions on the use of reason and on predetermination. Hadow refused to participate, while the other two decided that the matter should be referred to a committee. Simson made a declaration of his complete adherence to the Bible, the Westminster Confession, and the catechisms. Tempers began to fray. Hogg said that the propositions contained "the very soul of Pelagianism," whereupon Hamilton demanded that he should be made to prove this and to join Webster as libeller. After an extra day, 16 May, had been allotted to the assembly to complete its business,[134] it passed Act 7, which renewed for another year the powers given to the Committee for Purity of Doctrine. Meanwhile Simson was instructed to discontinue teaching the propositions charged as heretical by Webster. At the same time all ministers were ordered to desist from claiming that Simson was guilty of error. They might, however, continue to preach against the propositions that he was alleged to have taught.[135]

131 Wodrow, *Correspondence*, 2:186.
132 Ibid., 2:173.
133 Ibid., 2:186.
134 Ibid., 2:191.
135 Church, *Principal Acts*, 1716, 16–18. The act notes Simson's denial of having taught error.

Other vital national problems absorbed the General Assembly in 1716. The Rebellion had again brought to the fore the question of episcopal dissent in the northeast. The presbyteries of Arbroath and Meigle worried about the "corrupt principles" of the masters at the colleges in Aberdeen.[136] The assembly decided to refer the matter of the condition of universities to the commission for further study. If it should see cause, the commission had permission to apply to the Crown for a visitation.[137] This recommendation in fact resulted in the visitation of the Aberdeen and Glasgow universities in the following years. The Aberdeen visitation began in September 1716 and constituted a conflict of priorities for some Scottish notables. Cockburn of Ormiston, Stewart of Goodtrees, and Principals Hadow and Stirling were all involved in both the visitation and the Simson committee.[138] In Aberdeen the visitors had to deal with Jacobite sympathizers. The situation differed in the south, where the predominantly Squadrone Glasgow visitors saw little reason to question the wisdom of Principal Stirling's administration and made few changes in the established order of the university. The dual roles of committee member and visitor in areas geographically distant created further difficulties in achieving a quorum in the committee in the following months.[139]

None the less, and perhaps because of the pressing political problems exposed by the Rebellion, 1716 was a more fruitful year for the Committee for Purity of Doctrine. Although some members evaded meetings when possible, the general feeling seems to have been urgency to finish the task. For four weeks during the summer (10 August–3 September) the committee convened in Edinburgh at considerable expense and inconvenience to its members. Only a case of unusual significance could have moved the church to demand such effort. Witnesses were interrogated, although Webster was difficult as usual, saying that he would no longer appear as a party in the case because of the manner in which these examinations were being conducted.

The witnesses were asked such questions as: "In what words, to the best of your remembrance did you hear Mr Simson, defender, express

136 NAS, CH1/2/36, 79, 81.
137 Church, *Principal Acts*, 14 May 1716; unprinted act listed in index, no pagination.
138 For Aberdeen information, see Wodrow, *Correspondence*, 2:211–2.
139 Cockburn of Ormiston, James Hadow, and the Revs. Gray, Hamilton, Mitchell, Ramsay, and Smith were all visitors to Glasgow University. Since the distances involved were not great, their work was probably less time-consuming.

himself upon the subject of the severale articles of the Lybells sustained relevant, and placed in the first class?" "Did you hear him deny or impugn any of ye articles of ye Confession of faith relating tow articles libelled?" "Have you read printed Libell ... and do you remember yt yow heard him teach any of ye propositions which he there denyes?"[140]

Many of those summoned as witnesses made their excuses. Stirling, for instance, wrote that he had to go to Aberdeen on the visitation, adding that the reasons he had given for refusing to act as judge in the case also applied to his being a witness. He had a surprisingly short memory: "Besides I can ingenuously declare that albeit I were the most proper evidence I can witness nothing as to the Conference at Edinburgh having forgot the particulars so that for me to depone with respect to that which is the only thing I'm called to be a witness about were to emitt an oath in vain especially since ther's no penury of witnesses as to what concerns that Conference."[141]

Most of the witnesses who did depose could not remember that Simson taught error. The committee had decided that the witnesses should be asked to respond with the *ipsissima verba*, or specific words used by Simson, despite dissent from Cameron, Linning, and Logan.[142] At least one witness refused to depone because he could not recall the exact words used by the professor.[143] Simson rejected William Wilson as a witness on the grounds that he had provided Webster with material about the Glasgow divinity classes, that he had personally preached against Simson, and that he had written to friends complaining of the committee's procedure and saying that "some of the members were endeavouring to wash the Ethiopian white."[144] Despite problems maintaining a quorum and frequent dissent by Webster and his supporters from the conclusions reached by their fellow members, the committee forged on. On 20 August a vote was taken to request the ruling elders to attend more regularly to avoid wasted time.[145]

Possessing few depositions of Simson's words, the committee voted to place many of the libelled articles in the second, or controverted, category if it could not simply declare them safe. Thus Simson's teaching on the nature of justifying faith was voted orthodox, while his views on

140 NAS, CH1/5/11.
141 J. Stirling to W. Hamilton, 20 Aug. 1716, ibid.
142 Wodrow, *Correspondence*, 1:257.
143 Mr W. Henderson, a probationer at Dunblane. See NCL, CHU.10.1, 151–3.
144 Wodrow, *Correspondence*, 2:188.
145 NCL, CHU.10.1, 112.

sinning in Hell and the eating of blood were placed in the second category. In late August the committee decided to "sense" Simson's statements on reason in an orthodox way rather than put them in the first category.[146] The broad spectrum of opinion represented in the committee meant that the different meanings of some of the expressions libelled by Webster received full consideration. While in a Socinian sense an article might belong in the first class, in other senses, it might be in the second or even the third – a classification from which Black, Cameron, Flint, Hadow, Linning, and Logan frequently dissented.[147] Sunk in gloom about the failings of his church, William Wilson wrote in his diary: "The greatest part of the Committee were set on bringing off the Professor; and, in the end, came to this conclusion, that he was free of the errors charged against him by Mr. Webster."[148]

Towards the end of this protracted series of meetings it proved hard to persuade even the committee members to attend meetings. Anderson of Aberdeen announced that he too had to go home because of the university visitation; there were problems with his salary that he had to discuss. Alston wrote that, at great inconvenience to himself, he had already spent thirty-six days at committee meetings – he was now too ill to attend. Hunter was persuaded that he would not be missed. Rogers was called away by "business of consequence."[149] By early September even Linning was complaining; the orders to attend were peremptory, and he was sick.[150] The minor officials of the court were equally restless. In 1716 the beadles William Graham and Matthew Machan petitioned three times for extra compensation for "our long and tedious service" at the Simson deliberations. In late August, Hamilton told Nicol Spence to give them ten shillings for their pains.[151]

On 1 September 1716, Webster recorded six specific protests against the following committee actions: the *ipsissima verba* for witnesses, the committee's "laying aside the plain Grammatical sense of my Lybell and fixing a Sense of their own upon it," the fact that he was forced to prove the libel, the committee's adding of further material, its rejection of

146 See NLS, Wodrow Letters, Quarto, XI, 208–9.

147 Ibid., XI, 208–13.

148 Ferrier, *Memoirs of Wilson*, 131.

149 The committee member Andrew Rogers (d. 1735) had been ordained to Galston in 1692. This note came presumably from him.

150 Letters from all these men in NAS, CH1/5/11.

151 18 April 1716, n.d., and 24 Aug. 1716, ibid.

branches of the libel, and its procedure.[152] Simson, perhaps seeing which way the wind was blowing, apologized for printing his version of the process. The committee now felt that it had classed the articles as directed by the General Assembly and could begin to write its report.[153]

When there was no quorum at a meeting held on 15 March 1717, the decision was reached to send the final report as it stood to the assembly. The committee's final report indeed recommended that "Mr Simson ought to be assoilzied by the venerable Assembly."[154] None of the propositions in the first class had been proved by the depositions of the witnesses; Simson had apologized for publishing his account of the proceedings; Webster had not proved his charges of "Arminianism, Socinianism and Jesuitism"; and the injustice of his accusations had been aggravated by his publication of a pamphlet stating his case. The committee accepted Simson's argument that he had used the questionable words and phrases at issue as ways of solving contentious theological problems or of countering the "objections of adversaries," although it recommended that in future all teachers be prohibited from using such methods.[155] The committee, which had heard the witnesses and studied the evidence, sustained Simson's claims of orthodoxy.

1717: SPEEDY TRIAL

The committee's report went to the General Assembly on 6 May 1717, with the Earl of Rothes as royal commissioner and William Mitchell as moderator. Most lay and even clerical members were ill-equipped to deal with subtle theological nuances, and their political differences inevitably coloured their responses to the Simson case. Wodrow thought the affair lamentable and wished "to see no more processes of this nature in this Church, and particularly in the supreme numerous judicatory. There necessarily falls in so much heat, and so many irregularities, that agree not well to so grave a subject."[156] He felt that the assembly was being manipulated to avoid votes when feelings were running high – a belief that was borne out by Lord Grange. Although Grange seldom looked favourably on Simson, his blend of theological

152 NCL, CHU.10.1, 189–92.
153 Ibid., 192–3.
154 Report partially printed in Wodrow, *Correspondence*, 2:691–3, 2:692.
155 Ibid., 2:692.
156 Ibid., 2:258.

and legal expertise made him valuable to all. He was requested by influential men on Simson's side to meet after the daily sessions ended "to concert how to manadge things in the Assembly."[157] The objective was to negotiate a solution that would prevent further division and heal the present rifts among churchmen. Grange considered that the opposition to Simson was wrong on issues concerning the procedure of the committee, with the single important exception of the examination of witnesses as to *ipsissima verba*. In this, however, he voted with the pro-Simson faction, because he felt that if the vote went the other way the whole affair would have been referred back to committee for another divisive year.

On 6 May the assembly voted 87 to 60 to approve the method of taking the witnesses' testimony.[158] On 7 May Mitchell asked the assembly to appoint a committee to study Simson's own answers and letters. When it was proposed that the old committee members should form this group, some refused on the grounds that "they were abundantly wearied already."[159] To Wodrow's surprise (he assumed that the purpose was to prevent further acrimony), an anti-Simson group was named to form a committee.[160] After the first six propositions were debated and passed in full assembly, a lengthy discussion of the salvation of infants took place. In the end a committee was asked to compare Simson's passages with a proposition classed contrary to the Confession of Faith. Wodrow believed that if a vote had been taken then, it would have gone against Simson. By the next morning, however, Simson had explained the passages in contention.

Webster was furious about this and "broke out in a dreadful sally."[161] The committee's register reported that he "uttered several undutiful and disrespectful expressions" in announcing that, even if forbidden by the assembly, he would print Simson's offending words.[162] Grange was aware that many were delighted at the opportunity to rebuke the unruly Webster for using "most insolent and impertinent expressions" to the assembly. He considered that, for the peace of the church, Webster must be pacified. Here Grange met opposition from Rothes, who hoped "that

---

157 Erskine, *Extracts*, 1.

158 Wodrow, *Correspondence*, 2:257.

159 Ibid., 2:260.

160 These were "Mr Allan Logan, Mr Cameron, Mr Hog, Mr Black of Perth, Mr John Logan of Alloa, Mr Brough, and two others." Ibid.

161 Ibid., 2:261.

162 NCL, CHU.10.1, 245.

Mr. Webster might be roundly taken to task."[163] Grange felt that Rothes was showing unfortunate party spirit, since Squadrone members, including "the President of the Session, and all the lawyers and men of business of any figure in this country, who medle in ecclesiastick matters," were opposed to the non-jurors, while "the Duke of Argylle and his party favour them."[164] Webster's friends succeeded in bringing him to his senses; on the following day he made his apologies to the assembly.

Underlining the accusations of party spirit over the case is the fact that one of the authors who published against Professor Simson in 1717 was the Edinburgh minister John Flint. His ponderous Latin volume, according to the Simson camp, was designed to present the orthodox side to foreign observers.[165] However, its preface contained a fulsome dedication to Provost John Campbell and the town council of Edinburgh, commending the provost for his illustrious Campbell blood and praising Argyll for his military heroism and Islay for his eloquence and legal skill.[166] Flint clearly assumed Campbell support for Webster and disapproval of Simson when he penned his dedication in January 1717. Flint, Hogg, and Webster had certainly tried to enlist overseas as well as Argathelian support. Pamphlets printed by them include copies of two letters from foreign clergymen. One condemned the demands made on Webster to prosecute Simson personally. He compared this case with that of Roëll, who had been censured by the Dutch church. The writer denounced use of "the Pretence of Moderation" to palliate error, a practice that could only hurt the church.[167] The second, from a Utrecht theology professor, was much less extreme in tone.[168]

On 9 May the members spent six hours discussing Simson's statements on the connection between moral seriousness and grace. Wodrow again commented that, had a vote been taken at the end, Simson would have been condemned. The following day, however, Simson produced a paper explaining his meaning, which proved him innocent of Pelagian or Arminian leanings in this connection. Wodrow still felt that the feeling in the assembly was against Simson. Adept management came into

---

163 Erskine, *Extracts*, 12.

164 Ibid., 16–17.

165 "The Reverend Mr. W[ebste]r threatencd us, last Assembly, with an Appeal to the Foreign churches. I am afraid this Book of the Reverend Mr. F[lint]'s is publish'd with that Design, else I cannot understand why it should be in *Latin*." [Simson?], *Answer*, 23.

166 Flint, *Examen*, preface unpaginated.

167 *Copy of a Letter*.

168 Leideker, *Copy of a Letter*.

play once more with the proposal for a committee to produce an overture on which the assembly could vote. The problem was seen to be the reconciliation of Simson's current stance with his libelled words (even though he had denied using many of them). Even in their libelled form, Simson's opinions were scarcely heretical by normal early-eighteenth-century Reformed standards. The assembly's difficulty lay perhaps more in how to phrase Simson's views in language that could be accepted by the extremists who supported Webster. It nominated Dr Dundas, Grange, Hadow, Hamilton, Allan Logan, Mitchell, and Smith to solve this riddle. Over the weekend they managed to hammer out a compromise, which went to the assembly on 14 May.

Although their overture was much more severe on Simson than the report of the committee had been, it was a statement that could be accepted by the assembly, bringing to an end the tedious and divisive four-year process. The motion, which became Act 9 of the General Assembly of 1717, stated that although Simson had disowned any error contrary to the Confession of Faith, yet he had given offence in printed material and letters. In these he had "vented some opinions not necessary to be taught in Divinity, and that have given more occasion to strife than to the promoting of edification," through the use of "some expressions that bear and are used by adversaries in a bad and unsound sense, though he doth disown that unsound sense." He had employed hypotheses that "tend[ed] to attribute too much to natural reason and the power of corrupt nature."[169] The act merely prohibited Simson from using such propositions or hypotheses in the future and made no comment on his pedagogical methods. While the professor's printed material and his letters to Rowan were found offensive, they were not found specifically unorthodox or heretical. The act called for all parties in the process to accept each other's faults and avoid further prosecutions on the matter to prevent "contentious Debates."[170] A majority in the church clearly believed that Simson's work was orthodox, provided that he exercised due care in his choice of words. It was determined to end the misunderstanding and discord that the case had produced. While

169 14 May 1717, Act 9 "for Maintaining the Purity of the Doctrine of this Church, and determining the process, Mr James Webster against Mr John Simson," Church, *Principal Acts*, 1717, 16.

170 Ibid., 17.

political exigencies prevented the full exoneration of John Simson, the act cleared him of unsound teaching.

Critical perceptions varied on how to interpret the assembly's decision, although its long-term significance is clear. Aggrieved, Webster showed his distaste at the result, while "Mr Simson said nothing, and was the wiser."[171] Thirty years later John Willison, looking back over the ecclesiastical developments of his lifetime, shared Webster's feeling that the censure imposed was "very gentle." He attributed this outcome to the fact that the assembly contained "so many members ... who either had been his scholars, or were his relations, comrades or acquaintances, who stood up for saving him."[172] Certainly the Squadrone faction had greater political strength in 1715–17, claiming the loyalty of most of the managers of the church. To these men, Simson deserved compensation for his efforts to encourage his friends to take the oath of abjuration and for his assistance to Principal Stirling in the university and presbytery. Many church leaders agreed with the tendency of Simson's teaching and were unwilling to see all modern theological trends suppressed. They were also anxious to preserve the reputation of the University of Glasgow and the credit of its teaching.

Wodrow commented: "In the West country, the act will appear harsh on Mr Simson, and it was evidently with reluctancy that such who appeared most for him came in to it. But what brought them to this was an open dissent, threatened not in public, but in private, they say actually signed by a good many, which would no doubt have broke the peace of this Church."[173] This is an an interesting statement, which indicates that Glasgow was at least as polarized in its religious opinions as the rest of Scotland. Evidence from the church records of the 1720s accords with Wodrow's views, putting the ultra-orthodox camp firmly in the east. The Cambuslang revival of 1742 notwithstanding, the Clyde valley was no longer the exclusive habitat of covenanting enthusiasts. It was developing into a nursery for empirical natural philosophy and commercial enterprise. The zealots now generally could be found north of the Firth of Forth. Despite the portrait of a cantankerous and sarcastic professor drawn by those who disliked Simson, often on political grounds, he

171 Wodrow, *Correspondence*, 2:269.
172 Willison, *Fair and Impartial*, 87.
173 Wodrow, *Correspondence*, 2:268.

must have made himself popular with the majority of those with whom he came in contact in church and university circles in Dumfries and Glasgow. This regard allowed him to gather and conserve influential support during this case, and again ten years later.

Simson's theology was both in keeping with that of the sixteenth-century Reformers and appropriate to meeting eighteenth-century demands. His view of works through grace eliminated Antinomianism; his belief in divine mediation refuted Socinianism; his acceptance of some limitation of the number of the elect, and their need for prevenient grace, saved him from Arminianism. After 1717 Simson continued to teach as he had done but advised students to look at his published defences against Webster in place of actually discussing the arguments that had inflamed the orthodox. His habits of study stayed constant; his reading persuaded him that some of his examples could be better chosen and that his stress on the dangers of Arianism could potentially lead to other errors. When transformed into lectures, this development in his thought brought a second libel against him in the next decade and caused his extremist adversaries to demand a new investigation into his obedience to the assembly's ruling.

Simson's theological teaching, like the philosophical teaching of Carmichael, compared favourably with the most enlightened systems in Continental universities. Carstares had been remarkably successful in his efforts to modernize the outdated instruction in Scottish lecture halls. The fruits of those efforts were becoming evident to all by the 1710s – a fact that alarmed the covenanting remnant. This group's fears were probably exacerbated by the fact that new ideas and methods had permeated much of the teaching in Aberdeen, Edinburgh, and Glasgow, while at St Andrews, the church had been unable to oust the lay Episcopalian divinity professor, Scrimgeour. The rear-guard action that the ultra-orthodox undertook against Simson between 1714 and 1717 represented a desperate attempt to stem the flow of religious change into Scotland. Benevolence, utilitarianism, and a minor degree of universalism were the features of enlightened theology; Simson offered them all to his students.

*Part Three   Simson and the Struggles
in Scotland, 1717–1726*

8

Adiew to the Piece and Unity of this place: Simson and Glasgow Politics

GLASGOW POLITICS, 1717–1727

The Act of Union of 1707 forced Scotland to adapt to new conditions of government and obliged aspiring politicians to modify their managerial methods to a new system. The political conditions in the increasingly important urban area of Glasgow and in its university created the secular background to Simson's later problems with the conservatives in the church and may account for his altered factional loyalty. Ten years after his partial exoneration in 1717, facing more serious difficulties, Simson was to claim adherence to the Argyll faction. The anti-Simson charges of the mid-1720s emerged at a time when a renewed contest for power in Scotland was in progress. By then, the university had experienced a decade of unrest, while the town was in turmoil over economic and legal issues arising from Robert Walpole's administrative measures from London. These factors may have contributed to the breakdown of unanimity within the Presbytery of Glasgow. As both political factions sought to use university patronage to strengthen their positions during this struggle for power, faculty members manoeuvred for advantage between them. Although evidence of Simson's shift in allegiance does not exist prior to the charges against him in 1726, suspicions of such a change might explain the documented ill-will that existed by that date between the professor and a few of his Glasgow ministerial colleagues.[1]

---

1 Simson quarrelled publicly with John Gray and Charles Coats in January 1725, when he accused Gray of wanting "to take up Mr Webster's cudgell." Wodrow, *Analecta*, 3:182. Simson later noted that Coats had attacked him in a subcommittee of the 1726 assembly. Simson, *Case*, xv.

Simson's political activity during the decade from 1717 to 1727 was that of a natural authoritarian, who did not question his age's belief in social and academic hierarchy. His Presbyterian faith would have ensured his loyalty to the Hanoverian dynasty; his fear of Jacobitism probably drove him to back whichever Whig group seemed ascendant in Scotland. Before 1725, the outcome of the political battle between the Squadrone and the Argyll party was still in doubt. Three years later the Argathelians had clearly prevailed, with the result that, at Glasgow University, Principal Stirling had been succeeded by Principal Campbell. The shift in Simson's political allegiance would have been facilitated by this change and by the fact that his family had had close ties with the Campbells dating from the time of Patrick Simson's service with them. In contrast, most of his brethren in the Glasgow presbytery and many of his academic colleagues had deeper connections to Montrose and greater difficulty accommodating themselves to the new political reality.

During the first part of George I's reign, the Squadrone politicians had the upper hand, especially after Argyll's fall from royal favour in 1715–16. "Hasty and forward" by nature, the duke was not suited to being a party leader. These characteristics, however, were counterbalanced by the "cunning and crafty" nature of his brother Islay, who wrote in 1716, "Politics is a continuall petty war and game, and as at all other games, we will sometimes win and sometimes loose."[2] In Glasgow the Argathelians, encouraged by the 1716 election, continued to challenge the Squadrone. As a result, the political stresses of the decade after 1717 affected ecclesiastical and academic affairs, including Simson's, as well as the financial well-being of the merchant community in Glasgow, as we see in this chapter.

PRESBYTERY OF GLASGOW VERSUS ANDERSON

Although the General Assembly finally resolved his case in early May, other sources of conflict complicated Simson's life in the spring of 1717. As ordained ministers, the principal and the professor of divinity of the university were members of the Presbytery of Glasgow, where party discord tended to spill over into ecclesiastical affairs. One such intervention of politics into church life began at the end of 1716 with the appointment of a new minister for Glasgow's North-West Quarter

2 Comments by Robert Wodrow in Maidment, ed., *The Argyle Papers*, 7. Islay's words in HMC, *Report*, v. (Marquis of Bute), 618.

session. Strong accusations of factional partisanship arose during the struggle over this appointment between the town and the Presbytery of Glasgow, in which Principal Stirling and Professor Simson became the objects of bitter recriminations. Founded in 1701, but lacking its own church, the congregation of the North-West Quarter session had been served by the second minister of the Tron church. When Rev. Alexander Main died in 1711, two other Glasgow pulpits were already vacant. Ministers were found for these in 1713, but the death of the Queen and the rebellion of 1715 delayed the search for a minister for the North-West Quarter session.

Despite the reduced power of the Duke of Argyll in London, the Argathelians had gained ground locally with the election to Parliament of Daniel Campbell of Shawfield. At the end of 1716, the church session of the North-West Quarter gave a call to John Anderson, minister of Dumbarton; the town council voted on 29 December to join the congregation in asking the Presbytery of Glasgow to nominate a minister "to moderate the call," or preside over the election and induction of the new minister.[3] Anderson had served as tutor to the second Duke of Argyll and remained on terms of friendship with the duke's uncle, the Hon. John Campbell of Mamore, MP for Dunbartonshire and local power-broker. Since Anderson was a strong preacher and had appeared in print as a formidable apologist for Presbyterian principles, there could be no question as to his suitability as minister of a major town congregation. In his pamphlet on the difficulties encountered in his transportation, Anderson stated categorically that the opposition to him was rooted in his friendship for the Argyll family. He was thus a "Party Man," and there is a distinct note of sarcasm about the consequent impossibility of his acceptance by ministers "who are well known to be perfectly innocent of all *Party* Views."[4] Certainly the town ministers' aghast reactions indicate that they considered the call to be an attempt by the Argyll faction to assert its authority in the Glasgow presbytery.

In December 1716, a delegation of town and session officials requested the presbytery to provide a minister to moderate the call, as required by church regulations. The ministers of the town responded by tabling the matter until January 1717.[5] At the January meeting, the

3 SBRS, *Extracts*, 606.

4 Anderson also accused Stirling of financial chicanery with regard to university bursaries and complained about the interference in the case of Stewart of Pardovan, Stirling's relative. Anderson, pamphlet, in NLS, Wodrow Folios, XXXIX, 217–21, 8 [f220].

5 GCA, CH2/17, GCA, CH2/171/8, 40.

town commissioners repeated their request and further proposed that Stirling and Simson be barred from voting on the matter. When the presbytery denied both petitions, the Glasgow magistrates and the North-West Quarter session appealed to the Synod of Glasgow and Ayr.[6] A committee consisting of Stirling, Simson, and Andrew Tait drew up a reply to the session's "Reasons for Appeal," which stressed that up to this time all calls had been given by the whole general session of the town.[7] Calls by the general session were important for the independence of the church, since otherwise the town council, with thirty-two members, could overrule any single church session of nine members. Ministers had to collaborate in an urban setting, and the promotion of the Gospel depended on their giving assent to a colleague whom they found congenial.[8] A group of ruling elders also dissented from the call. Their names suggest a party connection to the Squadrone and reinforce the view that the call to Anderson was part of the factional rivalry within Glasgow.[9] The group empowered Hamilton, Hartfield, Luke, and Peadie to act on its behalf.

The Synod of Glasgow and Ayr attempted to conciliate the matter, asking the feuding parties to devise a mutually agreeable overture. A statement by Simson in May, which was rapidly passed around by the town gossips, indicates the scant chance for success that this mediation offered. The professor had just returned from the General Assembly, which had finally dealt with Webster's accusations against him, and was preaching in a city church. Notwithstanding an appeal by the assembly that ministers maintain unity in the church, especially among themselves, Simson caused outrage when he begged the congregation not to "break the Hearts of five Godly Ministers, in favours of one Man [Anderson]."[10] Many felt that Simson had acted inappropriately in thus taking what was essentially a political quarrel into the pulpit. In so doing he reflected the powerful feelings that the affair had produced in the minds of the "five Godly Ministers" and their allies. The date of this con-

6 Ibid., 41r, 42v–44r.

7 Ibid., 171/9A, 44r.

8 Ibid., 55–6.

9 Hugh Montgomerie of Hartfield (Squadrone-supported rector of Glasgow University in 1725), William Anderson, John Crose, Hugh Fulton, John Gillespie, Thomas Hamilton, James Lochhead, John Luke, James Peadie, John Peadie, James Shirer, James Stewart. Ibid., 57r.

10 Church, *Principal Acts*, 17. Anderson, pamphlet, in NLS, Wodrow Folios, XXXIX, 218.

troversy is important in view of Grange's charge of political partisanship in the 1714–17 hearings on Webster's libel. Having been subjected to negative Argathelian activity in committee and assembly, Simson might well have felt strongly opposed to a colleague of that party.

Another indication of the current temper in the town was the narrow election of to the presbytery of an elder from the Middle Quarter session – the merchant James Peadie, who had already registered a dissent over the call to Anderson. On 1 May 1717 the presbytery approved this election, although Rev. John Gray had to use his deciding vote as session moderator to ensure it.[11] Peadie, who became provost of Glasgow in 1727, was John Simson's first cousin through his mother, Janet Peadie, and was also a brother-in-law of the Squadrone gentleman and future rector of Glasgow University, James Hamilton of Aikenhead.[12] Peadie and Pardovan were of use to the principal's party as lay counterbalances to the Argathelian city officials in the North-West Quarter session. Since the 1716 parliamentary election had diminished the Montrose interest in the town, a Squadrone elder was a valuable acquisition to the presbytery. The narrowness of his election indicates that the lay members of the presbytery were by no means as devoted to the Squadrone as their ministers. Meanwhile, on 17 January 1718 the town council voted to commence construction of a church for the North-West session congregation.[13] One may interpret this decision as an attempt to put pressure on the presbytery and the synod. While a new church was needed to serve the growing population and its construction would provide employment and benefit trade, it could easily have been delayed until the desired minister was in possession of the living.

Throughout 1717 there were further recriminations, protests, and appeals. Caught in the cross-fire, the synod tried to extricate itself. In April 1718, by a majority that surprised observers, it voted to transport Anderson.[14] Naturally this decision was appealed,[15] sending the whole unsavoury dispute to the General Assembly of 1718, at which Anderson was translated from Dumbarton to Glasgow by the narrow margin of

11 GCA, CH2/171/9A, f.49v.

12 Lumsden, *Records*, 62.

13 Renwich, *Extracts*, 4.

14 J. Hadow to J. Stirling, 23 April 1718, "I was surprised that the Transportation of Mr. A. was carried in your Synod by so great a plurality." GUA 27165.

15 NAS, CH2/464/3, 41.

86 votes to 72.[16] The Glasgow council expressed its delight at the end of the month by creating Anderson a burgess of the town and determining the site of his new church.[17] On 6 August 1718, the town's provost and magistrates appeared before the presbytery armed with the General Assembly's act transporting Anderson. Michael Robb was appointed to admit the new minister at the Tron church on the last Sunday in August, which he did, preaching ominously on the text, "Take heed to the ministry which thou hast received in the Lord, that thou fulfil it."[18] Writing in September about new propositions to make the oath of abjuration more acceptable, Wodrow spoke of his dislike of church politics and how the "heat" between the Squadrone and the "Agatholians" was said to affect decisions. He explained that "Argyle's party" was said to have been responsible for the assembly's vote in the Anderson case and that the non-jurors had influenced the result.[19]

Once the council had gained its chosen minister, the building of the church for the North-West Quarter session proceeded throughout 1719 and 1720. It ran into various construction problems, the most severe of which involved the rebuilding of the steeple.[20] Nevertheless, John Anderson was able to preach its dedication sermon in 1720, shortly before his death the following year.

A postscript to the protracted tussle between the Glasgow ministers and people over the call to Anderson came in late 1718, when the victorious magistrates took revenge on a Glasgow merchant called James Lowdoun. It illustrates the seamless relationship between religious and secular affairs in early-eighteenth-century Glasgow. The previous April, Lowdoun had written to James Ramsay, minister of Kelso, asking him and other non-jurors to support the ministers of Glasgow in their campaign to keep Anderson from being transported to Glasgow by the upcoming General Assembly, since "the politick at Bottom of this Affair is so plain, that I need not explain it to you; it will be a melancholy thing if the Church of Scotland should truckle to a party of Men who combine to distress our

---

16 Wodrow, *Correspondence*, 2:383. Wodrow blamed the Glasgow ministers' "assuming a power of imposing in the elections" for their loss in this vote. See also A. Ian Dunlop, "The General Session," 227.

17 Renwich, *Extracts*, 30, 32.

18 Text in Col. 4:17, GCA, CH2/171/9A, 78–9.

19 Wodrow, *Correspondence*, 2:288–9.

20 Renwich, *Extracts*, 83.

good King's just government, and who have joyn'd the Tories for that end…. if the Assembly should transport him, then adiew to the Piece & Unity of this place."[21]

The magistrates loyal to Argyll tore up Lowdoun's burgess ticket, casting him out from the ranks of freemen. Since this move prohibited him from carrying on his business, Lowdoun applied to the Lords of Session for a bill of suspension on the action of the magistrates. The magistrates in turn protested that they were within their rights in depriving Lowdoun of the privileges of a burgess. Acting for Lowdoun, the prominent Squadrone lawyer Robert Dundas called the whole attack on his client an infringement on the liberty of a citizen and an act of oppression.[22] The victorious Argathelians were no more conciliatory towards their antagonists than Simson and his friends had been to them.

Finally, relations between the Glasgow ministers and the town's population continued to be uneasy in the following years. In 1721 the register of the Synod of Glasgow and Ayr noted that some out-of-town ministers were attempting to help their brethren in Glasgow find an accommodation to their disagreements with some of the elders and deacons of Glasgow.[23] By 1723, political divisions were once again the subject of debate in the church courts.[24] Throughout the period, Simson can be seen acting in concert with his Squadrone presbytery brethren in all their affairs.

RECTORIAL ELECTIONS AND SIMSON'S ROLE

The presbytery was not the only forum in which Simson encountered and participated in factional conflict in 1717. Concurrent with the troubles over the Anderson call, Simson was involved in problems within the university. Principal Stirling, with Simson's assistance, had tried to administer Glasgow University autocratically. Politically conscious students, however, refused to be brow-beaten by Stirling's efforts to restrain their active participation in college affairs. As a result, although Stirling's administration could resolve routine disciplinary incidents with relative ease, it collided with the student body on several

21 This is an expression of the opinion that Argyll had briefly supported the Tories in his frustration with royal lack of appreciation of his talents. NLS 1.7, no. 156.
22 Ibid., no. 157.
23 NAS, CH2/464/3, 86, 91.
24 See below, chapter 8.

occasions over such matters as the election of the university rector. This officer was responsible for the legal management of students, as well as for many of the financial concerns of the institution and, according to the university's statutes, was to be elected at the beginning of each academic year by the votes of the four nations into which the matriculated students were divided. Since the rector was of equal importance to the administration as to the students, the custom had developed in recent decades for the principal to exercise control over the nominations by drawing up a list of three candidates to be voted on only by the members of the faculty.[25]

Rumblings of discontent among the masters concerning Stirling's methods of government erupted into an electoral battle during the spring of 1717, when rebel members of the faculty refused to reconfirm Stirling's ally, Sir John Maxwell of Pollock, who had been rector since 1691, in his position for the next year. Professor William Forbes explained to Maxwell that the intention of the opposition group was to make a public demonstration of the need to "cross a groundless despotick power" exercised by Stirling, because the principal was attacking the privileges of the university by taking sole management.[26] It is probable that this academic challenge was part of the general Argathelian campaign to take control of Glasgow in the wake of Shawfield's success in the 1716 election, since a minority of the faculty supported Argyll, despite the Squadrone affiliation of Stirling and the majority. The principal reported in an apologetic letter to Maxwell, "all that could be said by the Dean [of faculty, John Hamilton], Professor, and myself, did not prevail on a sett of men who, it seems, were entred into a combination to affront the society."[27] A letter was also sent to Montrose as chancellor signed by Stirling, John Hamilton, John Simson, Morthland, and Rosse; the duke, with a disapproving comment on the dissidents' letters, replied that he hoped to be able to heal "such unlucky divisions" during his forthcoming visit to Scotland.[28]

25 *Munimenta*, Volume of Preface and Index: lxv.

26 W. Forbes to Sir John Maxwell, 4 March 1717, GUL, MS Gen. 205, 2:17. Forbes's position was awkward, since Maxwell had been his patron. In 1717 he was making the first of several subsequent political shifts. See Cairns, "Origins."

27 J. Stirling to Sir John Maxwell, 1 March 1717, William Fraser, *Memoirs of the Maxwells*, 2:367. "The Professor" always indicates the professor of divinity in Glasgow University documents.

28 Montrose to J. Stirling, 12 March 1717, GUL, MS Gen. 204:19.

This internal discord led to a royal visitation of the university in 1717, in which the Duke of Montrose succeeded in protecting his adherents.[29] On 5 November the visitors laid down rules that prevented the students from voting for their rector. The chancellor, rector, principal, and professor of divinity were to form a committee to draw up a list of three names, drawn from men of integrity known to be "well affected to the Government in Church and State," who were neither ministers nor officers of the university. This provision indicates that the recent Rebellion was still a factor in the appointment of any official in Scotland. The election was to take place on the first lawful day of November, and the voters were to be all legally appointed professors.[30] Sir John Maxwell of Pollock was accordingly returned to his customary role as rector, although eight members of the faculty boycotted the election on the grounds that it was "inconsistent with the Rights & Privileges" of the university.[31] Simson stayed firmly on the side of principal and power, being designated as one of the rector's two assessors.

Immediately a group of students, led by Peter Butler, John Edmonston, and Simson's nephew Patrick Simson, unsuccessfully petitioned the chancellor and faculty members to delay the election.[32] The presence of Francis Hutcheson among the dissidents suggests that although the future professor might agree with Simson on theology, he certainly did not follow his views on authority. After this electoral setback, the students, presumably encouraged by the faculty opposition, looked for legal redress.

29 Unsigned letter to J. Stirling from Edinburgh, 10 July 1717, GUA 27130, lists members of the commission of visitation: Duke of Montrose, Earl of Rothes, Earl of Hyndford, the Lord Justice Clerk Adam Cockburn of Ormiston, Sir John Maxwell of Pollock, James Hamilton of Pencaitland, Mr Francis Montgomerie, Sir David Dalrymple, The Solicitor Mr Robert Dundas, Hugh Montgomerie of Hartfield, Rev. Mr Mitchell, Rev. Mr Hamilton, Rev. Mr Ramsay, Rev. Mr Haddow, Rev. Mr Smith, Rev. Mr Gray. The majority of this group could be counted as sympathetic to Stirling's administration. Noteworthy with respect to Simson are Mr Francis Montgomerie, who may have been Montgomerie of Giffen, father of Simson's ex-pupil, and Lord Pencaitland, Simson's brother's sponsor.

30 GUA 26633, C.P.21, 2.

31 The dissidents were Carmichael, Dick, Dunlop, Forbes, Johnston, Loudoun, Rosse, and R. Simson. Ibid., 7.

32 GUA 58013 contains various documents relating to the case. Students of divinity named in these were Peter Butler, Thomas Colthrust [Colethurst], John Edmonston, Francis Hutcheson, John Leitch, John Pedeh [Peadie?], Patrick Simson; students of philosophy were John Naper [Napier], Charles Rosse, and Thomas Whittaker. Copy of Petition in NLS, Wodrow Folios, XXXIX f.252r.

From December 1717 to February 1718, both sides published their petitions and counter-petitions to the court of session. Duncan Forbes of Culloden, an influential Argathelian, appeared for the students; Walter Stewart of Pardovan, Stirling's brother-in-law, and Walter Pringle, who shortly afterwards received a Squadrone appointment to the College of Justice as Lord Newhall, were the legal representatives of the rector and faculty. In an *Information* published by the students on 21 January 1718, Simson was implicated as having been instrumental in the disputed rectorial election. The students also denied the powers of a commission of visitation to alter the statutes of the university and complained that the faculty was creating delays in answering the courts in order to drag the matter out.

Divisions appeared in the university ranks; the Argathelian group of Carmichael, Dick, Dunlop, Forbes, Johnston, Rosse, and Robert Simson disassociated itself from the defence made by the principal and the rector.[33] Furthermore, it published its grievances, much to the disapproval of that other pro-Squadrone supporter of authority, Principal James Hadow of St Andrews, who commented that it "is very unfair & invidious, and I see not how any that has an hand in it can justify the deed."[34] The duel in the courts and in the printing houses had deep political undertones. The university agent in Edinburgh, William Millar, wrote to Stirling on 30 November 1717, "It seems this affair is design'd to be a party business which is pretty palpable from the concern certain people begin already to show in it, and those imployed as advocates too witt Mr Duncan Forbes, Mr Thomas Kenning & Mr Hugh Dalrymple ... there is like to be warm work about it and I think you ought to come in as soon as I shall advise you."[35] Although Montrose's right-hand man, Mungo Graeme of Gorthie (who was to serve as rector from 1718 to 1720), and Walter Pringle advised against such tactics, the university took the position that the royal prerogative was an issue at stake and that it had a duty to obey the orders of a commission of visitation.[36]

33 Document signed by the seven men in GUA 58013.

34 J. Hadow to J. Stirling, 23 April 1718, GUA 27165.

35 GUA 27147. Thomas Kenning was presumably Thomas Kennedy, who held legal positions before being briefly MP for the Ayr burghs from 1720 to 1721, when he was appointed a baron of the exchequer through the influence of Argyll. See Wehrli, "Scottish Politics", 25–7, and Sedgwick, *House of Commons*, 2:186.

36 Correspondence from W. Millar, Nov.–Dec. 1717, GUA 27145, 27147, 27149a.

At the end of the broadsheet printed in February 1718, the students expressed fear about possible proceedings by the rector's assessors against the petitioning suspenders. That this concern was justified is demonstrated by the next publication from the group – Forbes's complaint to the Lords of Session about the disciplinary action taken by Professor Simson against Peter Butler and John Edmonston, students of divinity. When the two men returned from Edinburgh at the beginning of February after an absence of ten weeks, the professor expelled them for the rest of the session. To their demand for a written explanation for their expulsion, Simson replied that their excuse of attending court did not constitute a "Necessary Cause of Absence." This action was further fuel for the opposition. As Millar presciently wrote to Stirling, "However Just your Resentment may be yet I'm affrayed it has been ill timed and that it wound your Cause, you may assure your selfe there will be a summar complaint in ag[ains]t you on mundays night."[37]

Duncan Forbes immediately petitioned the Lords of Session to direct that the students be readmitted into the Divinity School and to censure the professor of divinity for the injury done to them.[38] Millar passed on to the college's advocates the information that he had received about the professor's "Bussines" on 25 February. The advocates had, however, already drawn up answers for Simson that seemed sufficient. Millar added that Matthew Simson, whose parish was just outside Edinburgh, was also attending the hearings to keep a watching brief for his brother.[39] At the end of February, Millar wrote to Glasgow that a vote in the session on the affair had gone against the university administration: "I would have you to Bear this verry Easily for our freinds here make nothing of it att all, tho' it served for a Great triumph to our adversarys, In my humble oppinion and it's the mind of all our advocates that its more advantage to the Cause [than if it had carried] ... I must beg the favour you'll give this Letter to Charles Murthland to be communicated to Bailly Hamilton our folks I know will be most affected with the Rumor as it will come from our adversarys and I would be Glad they knew the truth."[40] These shrewd political operators well understood the importance of keeping friends and followers supplied with positive propaganda. Millar's correspondence

37 W. Millar to J. Stirling, 8 Feb. 1718, GUA 27161.
38 *Petition and Complaint*, 10 Feb. 1718, GUA 58013.
39 W. Millar to J. Stirling, 25 Feb. 1718, GUA 27164.
40 W. Millar to J. Stirling, 25 Feb. 1718, GUA 27155.

makes it clear that party strife had as much or more to do with these legal challenges than any real or perceived injustices.

The question was still before the courts in June 1718, when Walter Stewart petitioned the Lords of Session in the names of John Simson and the Glasgow ministers John Gray and John Hamilton in connection with a disagreement over the dates and places at which examinations of the parties were to be conducted. In the students' counter-petition Duncan Forbes complained of the use being made of delays in legal procedure by Simson and the ministers, accusing them of complicity with the Glasgow magistrate Baillie Thomas Hamilton in the deliberate deferral of the examination of the student's witnesses. The students pointed out as evidence that Baillie Hamilton had adjourned until 12 May an examination arranged for the morning of 6 May, on the grounds of important business, but that very afternoon he "exercised himself at the Bowls."[41] The dates were critical, since all parties were aware that on 12 May Simson, Gray, and Hamilton would be in Edinburgh attending the assembly, which would inevitably bring about yet another postponement.[42]

Plagued by internal dissension, the university was unable to solve its problems. As a result, by September 1718 a new commission of visitation had been appointed.[43] In November, Mungo Graeme of Gorthie declared that the act of visitation of the previous year had not been properly signed and proposed delaying the rectorial election until the current commission of visitation gave direction. The next month the commission confirmed the decision of 1717, and on 18 December Graeme was unanimously elected rector.[44] The Squadrone had again succeeded in neutralizing the opposition within the university.

41 "Answers for the Scholars, and other Matriculated Members of the University of Glasgow, to the Petition of Mr John Simson, Professor of Divinity in the said University, and Mr John Gray, and Mr John Hamilton, Ministers of the Gospel at Glasgow." 11 June 1718. NLS 1.7, no. 25.

42 The students were probably quite correct in their complaints of deliberate delays. If the university could keep the case from being heard until the end of the academic year, the dissidents might be forced to leave town and thus drop their charges.

43 13 Sept. 1718, GUA 27166.

44 The members of the commission of visitation of 1718, meeting in December 1718, were the Earl of Lauderdale, the Earl of Hyndford, Lord Torphichen, Lord Justice Clerk, Lord Pencaitland, Mr Robert Dundas, his Majesty's solicitor, Mr Charles Cockburn, Mungo Graham of Gorthie, Mr William Mitchell, Mr William Hamilton, Mr John Orr. GUA 26633, C.P.21, 11–15.

Simson's involvement in all these legal battles gave him a thorough training in the most effective use of legal tactics. Ten years later he put to good use this expertise in procrastination, prevarication, and obfuscation in his second appearance before the church courts. Even the suggestion that the royal prerogative was under attack would be raised during Simson's second case. Unfortunately, Simson had learned to manipulate the system almost too effectively, and in ecclesiastical circles his legal skills were seen as being nearly as deplorable as his theological innovations.

STUDENT POLITICS AND SIMSON'S USE OF THE LAW

During the next decade, the students continued to display a keen interest in the political affairs of the day. They were of a safely Whiggish persuasion in the 1720s, when no more is heard of men with Jacobite leanings. On occasion, national and academic concerns merged, as the students were prepared to use broader political issues to address educational grievances, and *vice versa*. John Simson remained a steady supporter of Principal Stirling and duly constituted authority.

In 1720 the Glasgow students attempted to stage the popular plays *Cato*, by Joseph Addison, and *Tamerlane*, by Nicholas Rowe. The Irish students James Arbuckle, John Smith, and their friends were known for their provocative intentions. M.A. Stewart argues that their theologically liberal background in Protestant dissent in Ireland, and the civil disabilities that they encountered there, stimulated their interest in liberty and toleration, causing them to distrust dogmatic influence in civil causes.[45] Their productions were not entirely for entertainment: the opinions of the dramatic characters were intended to point out the tyranny of Stirling and his followers. Arbuckle's prologue to Tamerlane comments that "dire Effects" follow "When fiery Zeal gives wild Ambition Wings; / When sacred Names to fraudful Arts are giv'n, / And Priests beat up for GRANADIERS to Heav'n."[46] Forbidden to act on college property, the students moved to the Grammar School. John Smith wrote that "a Riot or some other great Crime could not have been examined with more Solemnity and Earnestness than the grievous Sin of acting Tamerlane." The excitement over the play does not seem to have abated, even after

45 See M.A. Stewart, "Rational Dissent".
46 Arbuckle and Griffith, *Prologue*, prologue, in GUL 2883.

it had been expelled from college property.[47] In January 1721 the council of Glasgow denounced public diversions such as balls, comedies, and plays as being occasions of "great disturbance in the citie" and prohibited them in future "within any of the touns houses." It was particularly concerned about the use of the Grammar School house and ruled that only students of the Grammar School might perform on school property in any plays, which should "have relation to their learning," to confined audiences of masters and other scholars.[48] The university discussed an "overture for an act anent plays" and decided to prohibit students from acting in public unless so directed by the faculty.[49]

The students deplored Simson's actions as an "eccho" of the principal in this affair, as they did his next efforts to prevent them from meeting in clubs. The ruling group in the university administration seems to have become alarmed at the proliferation of student club meetings. The club members suggested that the only reason for the concern was fear lest the masters be the objects of criticism at such gatherings:

Only People of such Penetration as the P[rincipa]l, and P[rofesso]r of D[ivinity] could have discovered any thing Dangerous, or Criminal, in their Meeting. But the true Reasons of their declaring against it were disguised, and a great Outcry raised, that the Members, who were at first chiefly English and Irish Men, were a Set of Latitudinarians, Free-thinkers, Non-subscribers, and Bangorians, and in a Word, Enemies to the Jurisdictions, Powers, and Divine Authority of the Clergy.[50]

It is likely, however, that Stirling and Simson were at least partly correct in their opinions about the students' principles, since two years later Robert Wodrow was also denouncing student clubs in much the same terms.[51] Simson threatened to expel any club members from the Divinity Hall. When challenged on the legality of this stance, he explained that he did not want the senior students of the university setting

47 [Smith], *Short Account*, 16–17.

48 Renwich, *Extracts*, 104.

49 GUA 26634, 28 Feb. 1721, 3 March 1721, 20–1. "The said practice ... is like further to tend to the great diversion of the students therein emplyd from more serious and usefull studies."

50 [Smith], *Short Account*, 21.

51 Wodrow, *Analecta*, 3:129.

a bad example by being seen in public houses, where all club meetings were held.[52] Although this matter blew over, Simson later refused Arbuckle a communion token on the grounds of his having been seen late at a house of ill fame.[53]

Relations between Simson and the youthful lovers of liberty were anything but cordial. Simson's belief in hierarchy, authority, and order was not shaken by his unruly students. He would find his own methods of expressing his displeasure, if he were not permitted to discipline the theologues legally. In Smith's eyes, Professor Simson was a man who would oppose Latitudinarianism and non-subscription. The conflict of opinion between students, who found Simson too rigid in his demands, and religious conservatives, who shortly afterwards found him too lax in his control over his pupils, leads to the conclusion that the fears of the latter were exaggerated.

Animosity still existed between Simson and his students some months later. In autumn 1721, a divinity student called William Morison presented to the rector, Robert Dundas of Arniston, a petition complaining of actions against him by Stirling and Simson. The minutes of faculty report a rectorial meeting at which this petition and a letter to Simson from Morison were produced. On 31 October, Morison was summoned to a faculty meeting to explain himself. There he admitted authorship of the letter, which included the words, "Hoping you'll attone for your villany by the acknowledgement of your faults," and a promise that he would not put up with the affront that he had received.[54] The entry in the minutes briefly cites the unanimous opinion of the faculty that William Morison should be extruded, which was accordingly done. Although there is no hint as to how Simson had offended Morison, their troubled relationship is another instance of his determination to maintain academic order and discipline.

STUDENT POLITICS: THE 1722 ELECTION

For some years after 1716, the outcome of the rivalry between the Squadrone and the Argathelians hung in the balance. During the 1719 debates over the Peerage Bill, both Scottish Whig factions came together

52 [Smith], *Short Account*, 22–3.
53 Ibid., 25–6.
54 GUA 26634, 28.

to support the measure, as the King wished, while Walpole led the successful opposition to the bill in the Commons.[55] Although the Squadrone lost some power with this defeat, it still retained enough strength in 1720 to ensure the replacement of the Argathelian Sir David Dalrymple as lord advocate with the Squadrone lawyer Robert Dundas of Arniston.[56] Since in 1721 both Argyll and Islay received places, the honours were even.

The economic crisis caused by the bursting of the South Sea Bubble in 1720 allowed the Townshend-Walpole faction to take control, with Walpole becoming first lord of the treasury in 1721. The transformation of London politics after Walpole gained power made Scottish Whigs aware of new perspectives in the south. The resulting struggles within the Whig party at this time led to wild excitement at elections that had repercussions in Scottish university life. The election campaign that followed was of importance to the Glasgow council, the students, and the university masters, because of its national significance.[57]

New stresses between faculty and students at Glasgow University developed in the parliamentary election campaign of 1722. It was suggested that the Glasgow citizens were stirring up the students to commit disorders during these elections.[58] The students saw a vocal supporter of Revolution principles, Lord Molesworth (1656–1725), as their patron in the struggle against the tyranny of Principal Stirling.[59] Frustrated by the unwillingness of the college administration to address the increasing level of dissatisfaction among some of the students, the student leaders petitioned the House of Commons for assistance.[60] "Several Honourable Patriots in Parliament" assured the students that they were "so sensible

55 This bill would have limited the royal ability to create peers and given hereditary rights in the House of Lords to twenty-five Scots peers, in place of Scotland's current sixteen elective peers.

56 Dundas also served as rector of Glasgow University from 1720 to 1722. The lord advocate was the Crown's chief legal officer in Scotland. In addition to his legal responsibilities, he performed a political role. He received the large salary of £1,000 – £200 more than that of the top Scottish judge, the lord president of the Court of Session. Riley noted that Dundas was "a firm Squadrone man"; *English Ministers*, 270.

57 See Ferguson, *Scotland*, 137–41, and Riley, *English Ministers*, 264–74.

58 [Smith], *Short Account*, 37.

59 Robert Molesworth became a member of Parliament in 1714. Molesworth was Irish, as were several of the Glasgow student ringleaders. His friend and client the Scottish-educated deist John Toland (1670–1722, MA Edinburgh 1690), could have crossed paths with John Simson either in Glasgow or at Edinburgh University.

60 See GUA 26634, 31, for the students' dissatisfaction with anatomy instruction.

both of the Justice and Importance of the Cause" that they would es-
pouse it.[61] The current Parliament being nearly over, however, they suggested that it would be wise to keep the petition to present to the next
Parliament, in which, if re-elected, they guaranteed their support.

This set the scene for the excitement of the election itself, and the
exhilaration at the arrival of the news (later proved false) of the re-
election of one of the "Patriots," Lord Molesworth. John Smith and
others set out to light a bonfire of celebration outside the college gate
on city property. Smith was assisted by a fellow student, Thomas Cuthbert, while William Stewart and William Hamilton, the Grammar
School rector, drank Molesworth's health beside them. Gershom Carmichael, as the senior master in the principal's absence, took it on himself to interrupt this celebration, ordering the college servants to
extinguish the bonfire. Smith intervened, and the two men struggled
over the hot coals. As the townspeople gathered to watch, before tempers and coals cooled some of the latter had been used as missiles to
break windows in the adjacent houses of Stirling and Simson, which
faced the street near the gate. Carmichael was further angered by the
town magistrates, who refused to accede to his demand for forces to
disperse the crowd with the words, "the Gentlemen might take their
Diversion." His reply to the provost was cast in indignant terms, "I
always thought it the Duty of Magistrates to keep the Peace in their own
Bounds; if your Lordship think otherwise, at lest, I hope, you'll be so
just as to keep this Line as a Proof at whose Door it must lie, whatever
further Mischief may ensue."[62] This insight into the attitude of the
magistrates to political demonstrations makes the accusations against
the council after the 1725 riots more understandable.[63]

In the inquiry that followed, the faculty expressed indignation at the
treatment of Carmichael, while the students equally deplored the abuse
of student rights. When Smith was being questioned by the masters at a
meeting in the principal's house, he refused to reply until he was given a
written statement of the charge against him. The inquiry exposed the
divisions among the masters: "The P[rofesso]r of D[ivinity] who under-
stands every Thing, told him, that what he was seeking was grand Nonsense, and this in the Face of the Professor of Law [William Forbes],
who, the Minute before, had asserted it could not in Justice or Equity be

61 [Smith], *Short Account*, 27–8.
62 Ibid., 27–9, and Appendix 3.
63 See below, 204–6.

refused."[64] At the faculty meeting on 26 April 1722, Thomas Cuthbert emulated Smith's tactics and refused to answer any questions "unless he gott a signd copy of a complaint against him."[65] Cuthbert's fate is unclear, but Smith was extruded from the university on 1 May, at a meeting from which the opposition masters withdrew in dissent.

This event of course was not the end of the matter, for Smith promptly applied to the Lords of Session for redress, both on his own behalf and on that of other students who had been subject to an attempt at wholesale intimidation. The lords suspended the sentence of extrusion while taking the matter under cognizance, much to the disgust of Simson, who was reported to have told Smith, "he might light his Pipe with his Suspension, because (according to that Gentleman's decent Way of making Similies) it was not worth a F--t."[66] On 21 May 1722, Smith tried unsuccessfully to serve Stirling with the suspension of his sentence of extrusion obtained from the Lords of Session. Witnesses to a document detailing Smith's efforts were William Hamilton, rector of the Grammar School, and "Mr. Thomas Hervy," merchant in Glasgow.[67]

This suspension led to another series of legal manoeuvres, involving Duncan Forbes for Smith, and Robert Dundas for the college, with published statements coming from both sides. William Millar again tried to keep Stirling informed of events in Edinburgh, remarking on 7 June that "that foolish boy Smith has given in a Clamorous Bill ag[ains]t you."[68]

Petitioning the Lords of Session in June, Duncan Forbes complained in Smith's name that the principal had refused to acknowledge the suspension of the sentence of extrusion and had continued to exclude Smith from his chambers in college. Smith considered himself punished for "no real Trespass or Offence" and said that he would be unable to move in "virtuous Society" unless his reputation were vindicated.[69] He pointed out that students in divinity and law were grown men, who could not be expected "to enter into such slavery" as Stirling was trying to impose.[70]

---

64 [Smith], *Short Account*, 31.
65 GUA 26634, 41.
66 [Smith], *Short Account*, 33.
67 In GUA 58013.
68 W. Millar to J. Stirling, 7 June 1722, GUA 27199.
69 Petition of Mr John Smith, Student in the University of Glasgow, June 28th, 1722, GUA 58013, 1.
70 Ibid., 3.

The next month Archibald Stewart gave Stirling's response to the Lords of Session, claiming that the university's right to discipline its students was "absolutely necessary for curbing the Licentiousness of the Students in the University, and the maintaining of good Order in the Society,"[71] and suggesting that the political issues raised by the students were red herrings to distract attention from their real faults. A week later, Dundas petitioned the lords on behalf of Stirling and the masters to have the matter returned to the jurisdiction of the university. Although he accepted the powers of the lords over affairs of "Right and Property," he pointed out that "the Matter in Hand is simply Accademick, belonging properly only to the Cognition of an University, and that such Matters ... fall to be tried only by an University, and not by the ordinary Courts of Justice, and such is the Practice all the World over."[72]

These long, drawn-out arguments prevented the case from being heard before the summer recess of the court. Letters from Millar in July indicate that one of the objects of the university administration's tactics had been to prevent the case from going before Lord Dun, who had passed the bill of suspension of Smith's extrusion.[73] These legal expedients appear similar to those employed in the matter of the rectorial election of 1717–18. Since taking disputes to law was so common, "the ability to suspend a legal process or to threaten its resumption [was] a regular tool of the Administration's local managers."[74] Here the tool was probably successful, since Smith does not seem to have returned from Ireland in the autumn.[75]

MR HERVIE'S CASE AND THE PRESBYTERY OF GLASGOW

A year later, another major battle with secular causes raged between lay members of the North-West Quarter session and the ministers of Glasgow. Charges were laid in the Presbytery of Glasgow against Mr Thomas Hervie, or Hervy, who had witnessed John Smith's unsuccessful attempt

71 17 July 1722, GUA 58013, 3.

72 24 July 1722, ibid.

73 Letters from W. Millar, 9 June, 19 July, and 23 July 1718, GUA 27200, 27206, and 27207, respectively.

74 Sunter, *Patronage*, 68. Phillipson notes that while the outcome of a case did not depend solely on party, yet "in a small, turbulent, tightly-knit landed society, it was as difficult to forget a man's politics as his family or his face." "Lawyers," 105.

75 See M.A. Stewart, "John Smith," 98. Stewart also observes that the university lost the jurisdictional battle with the Court of Session over the right to discipline students.

to serve Principal Stirling with a legal document. This new trial of strength between Glasgow's ministers and its merchants, in which Simson played a prominent role, again grew from factional roots. One pamphleteer assumed that Hervie's main fault lay in his support of Anderson's call and his later opposition to changes in the rules about church sessions.[76] It is more than likely that this sin was aggravated by Hervie's championship of the Glasgow students. Once again an individual who had participated in political opposition to Stirling and Simson found himself in trouble.

The charges against Hervie, an elder of the North-West Quarter session, occupied several meetings of the Presbytery of Glasgow and of the Synod of Glasgow and Ayr. They clearly had a political motive, which the Squadrone was using the church courts to pursue. The accusations against Hervie, which were based on remarks passed in various private conversations, were first discussed at the presbytery meeting on 2 January 1723, when Simson and John Scot were sent to request Hervie's presence. Hervie, however, refused to appear, on the grounds that to do so would harm his reputation.[77] He was intelligent, educated, devout, and interested in state affairs, as his defence shows, but he did not initially understand the determination motivating his accusers.[78]

The libel produced at the next presbytery meeting charged Hervie with a heterogenous mixture of political and religious faults committed over four years, including the public slander of the King, the East Quarter session, Robert Wodrow, and John Gray. The libel said that Hervie had called the King an adulterer; had claimed that the recent Jacobite plot was merely a device for the government to raise money from Parliament and people, although the administration was too cowardly to mention this fact; and had said that the King and his council were like ferrymen, rowing one way while looking the other. He had called the members of the East Quarter session "Bedlamites." Finally he had said that in 1719 Robert Wodrow had given a sermon containing nonsense and that the preaching of Gray did more harm to religion than it did to sin.[79]

76 *Letter from a Ruling-Elder,* 6–7, GUL 2883.

77 GCA, CH2/171/9B, f.182–183r.

78 The courtesy title of "Mr." (i.e., Master) in the documents indicates that Hervie had an MA Alexander Milne, a Glasgow barber, testified to the Presbytery of Glasgow that he and Hervie had been members of a fellowship meeting for the previous fourteen or sixteen years. GCA, CH2/171/9B, f.201v. Hervie paid careful attention to sermons that he heard and was obviously devout, if critical of inadequate preaching. Ibid., f.209v.

79 See ibid., 184r and v; also *Letter from a Ruling-Elder.*

The vendetta against Hervie that had resulted in this incongruous collection of accusations was clearly based on both secular and religious politics and seemed to be directed at removing him from his position in the North-West Quarter session. Hervie testified that Gray had indicated that "if he would Leave the Session, there should be no more of the affair" – an offer underlined by the fact that Gray had been heard to say "That the Defender being a fashious [troublesome] man to the Ministers in the Judicatorys, he wished, or could be glade that they could be rid of him."[80] The North-West Quarter session was Argathelian in sympathy, in contrast to the Squadrone loyalty of most of the ministers, as had become clear in the call to John Anderson. After Anderson's death, John Maclaurin (1693–1754), brother of the distinguished mathematician, Colin, became the session's new minister. Educated at Glasgow and Leiden, Maclaurin was politically Argathelian and theologically conservative. On both counts he could be expected to oppose his old professor and to support an anti-Squadrone parishioner. Hervie, with his outspoken views of state and church, was a thorn in the side of the Squadrone loyalists. He also clearly believed in calling a spade a spade, at least in the privacy of his own house. Although his sympathies lay with the Argathelians, his ideals of independence and liberty were stronger. This was particularly true at a time when threats to Glasgow mercantile prosperity seemed to come from the government. Hervie's opinion of Walpole's handling of the 1722–23 Jacobite crisis was shared by many.[81] Since the Argyll–Walpole alliance had not yet been consummated, Argathelians could criticize the English minister freely. Hervie's remarks about the ministry are surely significant straws in the wind as to the temper of Glasgow's merchant community in the early 1720s.

Hervie also seemed to uphold a Whig standard of individual liberty when he was apparently supportive of the Irish non-subscribers in their bid to maintain their freedom from credal oaths.[82] The charge of insulting the East Quarter session resulted from Hervie's comments about its treatment of another merchant, Robert Boyd. The session had delayed giving Boyd a communion token on the grounds that he had "uttered some undecent and offensive words" to those raising money for a collection authorized by Glasgow's town council in aid of the subscribing faction in Belfast.[83] Hervie had told a group of acquaintances that the

---

80 GCA, CH2/171/9B, 198v.
81 See the English opinion of the anonymous writer of *Discourse*, 29.
82 For a discussion of the Irish subscription issue, see below, 216–24.
83 GCA, CH2/171/9B, 201r.

session acted as Bedlamites. When some present took exception to his words and demanded an apology, he readily "acknowledged his fault to the Company, and said That he was rash in saying, And That if he had not been in passion, he would not have expressed himself so."[84] Hervie's defence was that since his apology had been accepted and there had been an agreement not to publicize his comments, there were no grounds for a libel of scandal.

Witnesses called in Hervie's case in 1723 included Professor Alexander Dunlop, who refused to be examined on oath unless he might distinguish in his testimony between conversations held with Hervie in private and those held in public.[85] Professor William Forbes was also a Hervie supporter.[86] Faced with the opposition of these familiar academic Argathelian adversaries, Simson indulged in his customary sarcasm. He seems to have particularly objected to Hervie's criticism of sermons. When Hervie defended the rights of private Christians to praise or criticize any sermon, Simson informed him that it was proper to complain privately to a minister about weak preaching, whereas Hervie had censured sermons in "a Histrionick manner, and with an air."[87] After some acrimonious interchanges with Hervie, Simson was later heard to remark that Hervie must be drunk to talk at such a rate.[88] Simson's interjections into the evidence, and his name on the *sederunt* lists of the presbytery meetings, prove that he was an active and assiduous member of the judicatory. When a committee of three was later formed to draw up answers to an appeal by the North-West Quarter session against the sentence of the presbytery, he was one of its members.

Through February and March 1723 the presbytery, Hervie, and the North-West Quarter session battled over the acceptability of witnesses, the methods of procedure, and the right of the presbytery to act as court in the case. Appeals and counter-appeals of presbytery rulings eventually led the Session to take its case to the Synod of Glasgow and Ayr, although its grounds for so doing were disputed by the presbytery. The case was a *cause célèbre* that provided entertainment for all classes.

84 Ibid.
85 Ibid., 199r.
86 Ibid., 203v. At the suggestion of a private meeting between Hervie and a committee of the presbytery, Hervie asked that "some of my friends might be at that second Meeting, naming Mr Forbes, Mr Dunlop and Baillie Orr." Orr later supported Simson in the General Assembly.
87 Ibid., 197r.
88 Ibid., 198r.

Support for Hervie was strong. His friends, "Gentlemen of the first rank,"[89] attended the hearings with him; the mob waited outside the doors, verbally and physically attacking witnesses they considered damaging to him.[90] One anonymous pamphleteer stated plainly that Hervie's sin was his support for John Anderson and the fact that he had followed Anderson in opposing the subsequent overtures concerning kirk sessions. He was a nuisance to his enemies, presumably because of his eloquence in such causes. The writer questioned the propriety of evidence obtained from private conversations: "What Man can be safe if all the small Title Tatle he has had, in Confidence with his Friends, must be ript up, and made so many Articles of a Libel against him? ... for these we are only to answer to our Great Judge, and ought not upon every Trifle to be staged before our earthly Rulers."[91] He pointed out that Professor Simson had protested against such treatment in his written answers to Mr Webster and that in the Anderson case the Glasgow ministers had similarly complained when the magistrates quoted against them to the General Assembly words that had been spoken in private conference.[92] Had the presbytery truly been intent on preventing public scandal, it could scarcely have chosen a more ineffective technique.

In April 1723 the synod heard both sides and voted to "interpose in an amicable way to compose these differences."[93] A committee, formed to negotiate a solution, reported back that both sides were willing to refer the decision to the synod. Hervie craved pardon for his errors, in carefully chosen words that ended with the statement, "I am sincerely resolved through God's grace to keep such strict guard upon my conversation as to prevent giving offence to any, & convince the world that whatever may have escaped me in time past, was without any intention to hurt or prejudge the valuable interest of religion, or the peace & quiet of the place."[94] Eager to resolve the matter, the synod accepted

---

89 Ibid.

90 Ibid., 209r.

91 *Letter from a Ruling-Elder*, 7–8. The pamphlet ends in mid-sentence on the eighth page.

92 Ibid., 8. The reference to Simson's protest may have been to a reported conversation in 1712 between the professor and two Glasgow merchants, which Webster had used against him. Simson noted of William Harvie, one of the merchants: "he was very Diligent in Spreading, not only through this Town, but other Places what I had said to him, that he thought Erroneous, and put them in Words of his Own, which made them truly Errors." Simson, *Libel*, 276.

93 NAS, CH/464/3, 112.

94 Ibid., 113.

this affirmation, admonishing Hervie for his past conduct and exhorting him to keep his resolution. At the same time it recommended that the Presbytery of Glasgow should forgive and forget what had passed in this affair. Peace and quiet, however, were not easily attained in early-eighteenth-century Glasgow, and two years later Hervie was still complaining that the presbytery's records contained "remarks" about him.[95]

WALPOLE, ISLAY AND THE MALT TAX RIOTS OF 1725

The political in-fighting between the Squadrone and the Argathelians in Glasgow came to a head in 1725. With Scotland seething with resentment at Walpole's policies, Islay's ability to end the civil unrest caused by the malt tax helped to establish him as unofficial chief minister for northern affairs. Although John Simson was not involved in the events of that year, they are relevant to his career. While there is no evidence about the exact date or reason for the shift in his own factional loyalties, which took place in the late 1720s, Simson cannot have been unaffected by events around him in Glasgow. A major unanswered question is whether one of his reasons for re-evaluating his politics and returning to his family's traditional loyalty to the house of Argyll was gossip about his teaching by his Squadrone ministerial colleagues or whether their antipathy to him arose from his political move.

Walpole's decision to use the stronger Argyll nexus to establish his position in Scotland rested not only on the demonstrated political skills of Islay, but also on the unique strength of the Campbell name in the Highlands, where Argyll was the sole Whig Presbyterian magnate to possess vast consolidated estates. To wield this power, Argyll and Islay needed to control such fundamental elements of national life as town councils, church assemblies, and university faculties. By the end of the decade, Argathelian control had been largely perfected through a judicious mixture of patronage and threats brewed up by Islay and his intelligent subordinates. The partnership had benefits for both sides. Walpole depended on his Scots allies to keep him in power; in return they controlled Scottish patronage and directed Scottish affairs at the national and local levels.[96]

The development of Argathelian power over Scottish institutions created inevitable opposition, with repercussions on Simson's second case. At the General Assembly of 1724 there was a move that appears

95 Wodrow, *Analecta*, 3:193.
96 When Argyll withdrew his support from Walpole in 1742, the government fell.

to have been designed to limit the Squadrone influence over the church. The management of the Church of Scotland between assemblies rested on the commission, a large executive committee appointed by each assembly to conduct affairs during the year, which met quarterly to follow up on unfinished business and to deal with urgent new matters. During the previous year, the commission had made decisions that had angered some presbyteries. The Argathelian Edinburgh politician George Drummond (1687–1766), with the support of Linning and others, proposed that the members of the commission should be nominated by the presbyteries, not by the assembly. The Squadrone members, led by Robert Dundas, protested strongly that this method would create a new assembly, not a committee of the previous one. Wodrow considered the proposal "One of the boldest attacks on our constitution for these many years."[97] He feared that constitutional change might result in the Crown's withdrawing its recognition from the commission, thus reducing the ability of the Church of Scotland to administer itself between assemblies. The move suggests that the Argathelian faction was still relying on the support of orthodox or evangelical groups that had greater strength in the parishes than in the assembly. Islay had not yet fully realized that these men were too fanatical to be politically reliable.

To forestall further complaints, Drummond and Linning were appointed to the next year's commission. Wodrow worried about factional intrusion: "It's very plain party humour appears in very great measures, which will undoubtedly weaken our reputation in this church."[98] He appreciated that the issue centred on the ability of Drummond and Hugh Dalrymple to take over ecclesiastical management from the Squadrone leaders. By May 1725, Wodrow's strictures were getting more severe: until recently, assemblies had been controlled by the minister members, while now it seemed that Drummond was "set up for dictator."[99] He went on to lament "That nothing can be more hazardous than State partys coming in and wresting out of Minister's hands the management of Assemblys. Each side endeavour to drau votes to their side, and to recomend themselves to Court by their interest in directing our Assemblys."[100] This situation could result only in the church's loss of reputation and strength.

97 Wodrow, *Correspondence*, 3:128.
98 Ibid., 3:139.
99 Wodrow, *Analecta*, 3:200.
100 Ibid.

Glasgow University was also in a state of unrest in 1725. In March, the month when the rector was chosen under the original constitution of the college, sixty students signed a petition calling for restoration of their rights in this election. The participation of William Campbell, son of John Campbell of Mamore and cousin to Argyll and Islay, indicates that politics played a major role in this demand. Along with an Irish student, William Robertson, Campbell presented the petition to Stirling, who "rejected [it] with contempt."[101] Campbell had his protest notarized, and then the petitioning students marched to the house of the rector, Hugh Montgomery of Hartfield, where Robertson read the protest publicly.[102] Wodrow's version was more dramatic – the students entered Hartfield's house in his absence, opened the windows, and read the petition loudly "in very impudent terms," slandering both Stirling and Hartfield.[103] Robertson was the only student against whom the faculty took action: despite the vociferous support of Dunlop and Johnston, the faculty voted to extrude him, whereupon his tutor, Loudoun, and Dunlop composed explanatory letters to his father. Wodrow considered that this decision resulted in a drop in the Glasgow student enrolment.

Robertson left for London, where he presented a memorial to the Duke of Argyll, stating the claims of the Glasgow students and his own mistreatment by the faculty. Argyll sent him to Islay, "who was better versed in such matters than he." According to Robertson, the 1726 visitation of Glasgow University was the direct result of Islay's review of the matter.[104] To assist Robertson professionally, Islay introduced him to Dr Hoadly, then bishop of Salisbury. When, two years later, Hoadly's brother received an Irish bishopric, Hoadly presented Robertson to him. Robertson became the first man ordained by the new bishop of Ferns in early 1727.[105]

101 William Robertson, "Memoirs," 747.

102 Ibid.

103 Wodrow, *Analecta*, 3:185.

104 "[Islay] was so affected, that he applied to the King for a commission to visit the University of Glasgow, with full power to examine into and rectify all abuses therein." William Robertson, "Memoirs," 748.

105 About 1760 William Robertson was seized with doubts about subscription and Christology. He began to omit the Athanasian creed from his services, and when his parishioners took offence, he resigned his living in 1764. He returned to England, where he published his opinions. After presenting Glasgow University with one of his works in 1767, he received from it the degree of DD. His memoir stated that he had studied under Simson. Simson, however, could hardly be blamed for a change of heart forty years later.

Others groups in the west were now concerned. The alliance of Glasgow with the Argathelians, which had seemed firm after the 1716 election, became strained in the aftermath of Walpole's rise to power. The Clyde valley, territory formerly committed to Presbyterian orthodoxy, found itself with divided loyalty in dealing with the new régime in London in the early 1720s. Walpole's economic measures pleased few in Glasgow and reduced the support given to Argathelian politicians. Complaints from English merchants about unfair Scottish competition, along with the need to improve British finances, forced Walpole to reform the creaky mechanism of the Scottish customs and excise departments, thereby virtually creating a new patronage network.[106] Such complaints had been heard since 1707 and were probably unjustified. Nevertheless, the English felt that the success of Scottish merchants rested on "fraud, indulgence, collusion, corruption, and perjury."[107] Glasgow tobacco merchants were particularly indignant at the 1723 reforms, which included the suspension of many Squadrone customs officials. Daniel Campbell of Shawfield's reputation in the town was not enhanced by the general belief that he was involved in these changes, despite the fact that he was himself a tobacco merchant who had been trying to defend Glasgow trade.[108] One pamphleteer considered that animosities had intensified among the citizens of Glasgow since the Argyll faction gained control of the town's affairs, with no resulting improvement in trade. "Trading Men," the backbone of the town, should serve on council.[109] Political obstacles to the well-organized Glasgow tobacco trade were compounded by a drop in domestic tobacco prices in the 1720s, which served to keep rancour smouldering. Economic innovations produced ill-feeling, which temporarily reduced the intensity of Argathelian loyalty among the merchants of the Clyde, who were convinced that such changes damaged their commerce.

The Glasgow community at large found another economic irritant in the government's decision to impose the full tax on malt in Scotland starting in mid-1725. At the Union, Scotland had been given relief from some national taxes in view of the depressed condition of its economy. The financial policies of Walpole, however, were steadily eroding this

106 See Price, "Glasgow."
107 Price, "Rise," 302.
108 Ibid, 17–19.
109 *A seasonable Advice*, 10, in GUL 2883.

relief. Glasgow merchants were already upset by attempts to clear up corruption in the Scots Customs, since the result was an increase in duties payable. The decision to raise the tax on malt used in brewing by 6d. per bushel, effective 23 June, brought more general opposition to the government, since an increase in the price of ale affected the population as a whole. Although the lord advocate, Robert Dundas of Arniston, was firmly on the side of the Scots brewers, Daniel Campbell of Shawfield became increasingly unpopular because of his failure to support his constituents. The imposition of the malt tax was seen as a party stratagem, and politicians and ministers were damned for factional interests. Party was the "fatal Spring of all our Misfortunes," and churches had become "Oratories of Party and Faction, and some weak Brain'd Zelots Choos'd rather in the Pulpit to sound the Trumpet of their Party than preach Faith and Repentance."[110] One pamphleteer saw the malt tax as "the sole project and grand Masterpeice of the A[rgathelian] Faction, by which they promise to secure themselves in the Government, and bring into the publick Treasury a considerable Revenew levied at a small Expence."[111]

Meanwhile, Walpole was altering the political management of Scotland in a way that appeared to give substance to the Scottish complaints. To deal with any potential trouble when the new tax came into force on 23 June, at the end of May he dismissed Dundas from his post as lord advocate and appointed as his successor an Argathelian – Duncan Forbes of Culloden. His timing proved remarkable, for on the night of 24 June 1725 a Glasgow mob sacked Daniel Campbell's grand town residence in the Trongate.[112] Provost Miller, Dean of Guild James Peadie, and Justice of the Peace Campbell of Blythswood decided that might not to make a show of strength with the two companies of troops that had been summoned to the town, lest this incite trouble. When the troops were called out on the following day, the rioters appeared again in some

110 Ibid., 3.
111 Ibid., 7–8.
112 Campbell appears to have been warned of trouble and had moved his family and valuables out of town. See Eyre-Todd, *History of Glasgow*, 3:135–6. The degree of damage inflicted on the house is hard to judge. Some sources suggest that it was razed, but Andrew Brown, *History of Glasgow*, 2:38, states temperately that "a mob broke into Mr Campbell of Shawfield's house, and destroyed some furniture and liquor, but were dispersed by the magistrates and gentlemen of the city." This seems to be a more likely outcome, since even magistrates antagonistic to Shawfield would hardly have allowed a mob to demolish the whole house.

force, and several citizens died in a volley of fire ordered by the officer in charge.

The government took this opportunity to teach the recalcitrant burgh politicians a lesson. The magistrates of Glasgow were arrested and taken prisoner to Edinburgh to answer for their inaction in the face of the mob. William Stewart wrote to Andrew Fletcher, Lord Milton, in early July that all agreed that the provost should be punished "for a failure in his duety" as a magistrate.[113] The two factional legal champions, Dundas and Forbes, rushed into action, with their supporters. On one side Dundas, with the backing of the Duke of Roxburgh, endeavoured to mitigate the offence of the magistrates. On the other side, Forbes sought to bring them to trial, with the co-operation of the provost of Edinburgh, John Campbell, MP for the capital and a "Warm party man," who happened to be Daniel Campbell of Shawfield's brother.[114]

Islay wrote to Milton in mid-July asking for a list of the magistrates of Glasgow with "their character as to their party or dependence."[115] At the end of the month, John Campbell told Walpole that the situation was unusual: "The present temper of the people of Glasgow, from whence all the ferment took its rise, is a very odd one. When the general and my lord advocate went thither to enquire into the authors of the barbarous riot there, they indeed found some people who condemned the mob; but they found a combination among the citizens to conceal the actors, and they found nobody in authority there, had been at the least pains to make discoverys."[116] Campbell had not perhaps appreciated the depths of the feeling in Glasgow against Shawfield and those who had arrested the magistrates, although he noted that the Glaswegians called the Edinburgh Argathelians "betrayers of the interests of their country."[117]

The Glasgow magistrates were prepared to defend themselves against Argathelian insinuations. They published corrected accounts of the disturbance and at the end of July sent an address to the King.[118] Shortly afterwards, Islay told Milton to instruct Forbes to leave the magistrates alone for the time being. A pamphlet published in Glasgow on 1 September states that "the great Crime chargeable upon them [the provost

113 Stewart to Lord Milton, 3 July 1725, NLS, MS 16532/143.
114 Wodrow, *Analecta*, 3:213.
115 Islay to Lord Milton, 10 July 1725, NLS, MS 16531/22.
116 Coxe, *Memoirs of Walpole*, 2:440.
117 Ibid.
118 31 July 1725, Renwick, *Extracts*, 225.

and magistrates] is, That they favoured not Mr. Campbell's Interest in the late Election for Magistrates, and of a common Council for this City … This is the Crime which is not bailable, this is the sin that is unpardonable … And these Proceedings may chance to produce this desirable Effect in the ensuing Election."[119]

To add to the government's Scottish problems, the brewers of Edinburgh now went on strike, with the backing and advice of Roxburgh and Dundas. In August, a "Fyfe Gentleman" attributed the civil disorder primarily to the fallen state of mankind, but secondarily to agents of the party that had lost power. Sedition was promoted by "Men of turbulent Spirits [who] cannot bruik Disappointments" and whose aim was to weaken the position of the present government.[120] Provost Campbell wrote to Walpole at the end of June that his citizens "submit not from choice but because they believe the reins of the Government here are held tight and that it will not be cheap to rebel," although Jacobites and "another party of men" were stirring up trouble.[121]

From his viewpoint, a Squadrone adherent wrote: "The squadrone have ten friends now for one that they ever had befor…. Mr Dundass plays the divell with his successor [Duncan Forbes], cuts him down one all occasions and is at present the idol of the populace."[122] This situation gave Walpole the pretext for removing Roxburgh, but the duke's dismissal as secretary of state for Scotland on 21 August 1725 was unpopular among many who saw the Squadrone as a patriot party upholding Scots rights. The Jacobite Lockhart wrote to Lord Inverness in December 1725: "The Government of this country is intirely in Argyles or rather Ilayes hands, and the Campbells are very uppish and insolent," while the Squadrone had not made any effective response, being "a mean-spirited dastardly set."[123]

Walpole followed up the attack on the Squadrone by sending Islay north to subdue the Edinburgh brewers in person. While the case against the Glasgow magistrates was quietly dropped, Islay dealt firmly with the danger to the Edinburgh ale trade. During August he applied pressure successfully on the brewers, and, before any crisis of supplies arose, ale

119 Burgh elections were held annually in October. *Letter from a Gentleman in Glasgow*, 19, in GUL 2883.

120 "L.D.L.," *Letter from a Fyfe Gentleman*, 9.

121 Quoted in Sedgwick, *House of Commons*, 1:523.

122 Sir William Bennet to the Countess of Roxburgh, 10 Aug., 1725, HMC, *Fourteenth Report, Roxburgh*, 54.

123 Lockhart, *Lockhart Papers*, 2:230–1.

began to flow plentifully again. By the end of September James Campbell was relieved that Islay had "gone to such great length in settling the afairs of our distracted country";[124] a less partial observer, though glad of Islay's success, wondered about his motives: "for great mens ways have something very awful to us who do not understand them."[125]

Islay's work earned him the gratitude of Walpole and enhanced his position of control in Scotland. He himself, along with Walpole, attributed his success entirely to the King's wise decision to dismiss Roxburgh. As Walpole wrote to Townshend, in words intended for the King's eyes, "Without that alteration, all the art of man could not put an end to these disorders, which had their rise and support from the countenance and protection which they expected and received from hence."[126] The London politicians were evidently persuaded that the office of Scottish secretary was itself a cause of dissension. The Duke of Newcastle told Townshend that he believed there could be no peace so long as the office existed, since "parties run to that Height that each think any extravgancy tho' even against the governm[en]t justifiable and right if it is but opposing wh[a]t thee other is for."[127] The overemphasis on the removal of Roxburgh leaves a suspicion that Islay and Walpole were not above exaggerating the Edinburgh crisis in order to achieve this desired political end. Islay, though lacking the title, became *de facto* secretary of state for Scotland.

The victorious Campbells prepared to impress the Squadrone with the new reality of management in Scotland. Shawfield now managed Glasgow and the west, and his brother, John Campbell, along with George Drummond ran Edinburgh and the east. Wodrow noted, "The same people have taken on them to manage our Assemblys these two or three years; and being able to manage the Burrous and Kirk, as they pretend, it folloues the Scots administration ought to be in their hands."[128] The church courts again provided a forum in which to air factional differences, although their management was not always successful. The General Assembly papers of 1726 contain a petition from John Campbell, Esq., late provost of Edinburgh, complaining that James Richardson,

---

124 J. Campbell to Lord Milton, 22 Sept. 1725, NLS, MS 16531/77.

125 H. Dalrymple of Newhall to Lord Milton, 25 Oct. 1725, ibid., 131.

126 3 Sept., 1725, Coxe, *Memoirs of Walpole*, 2:467.

127 Duke of Newcastle to Lord Townshend, 6 Aug. 1725, Newcastle Papers, microfilm, Part 1, Additional MSS 32687, 134v.

128 Wodrow, *Analecta*, 3:214.

preacher of the Gospel in Glasgow, had spread scandalous reports about him. Richardson was said to have accused John Campbell of corrupt involvement in the Glasgow elections on behalf of his brother Daniel, which had created some personal profit.[129] The Presbytery of Glasgow had looked at this complaint and had decided that it was insufficient to incur censure on Richardson, who had probably been Simson's student at Glasgow University in the previous decade.[130] The Presbytery of Glasgow was still pro-Squadrone in its sympathy and may well have agreed with Richardson's comment. Campbell, having unsuccessfully appealed to the Synod of Glasgow and Ayr, which confirmed the decision of the presbytery, took the matter to the General Assembly.

Familiar names appear in the cast of characters involved in the case. Campbell's commissioner to the synod was Professor Robert Simson, assisted by Professor Alexander Dunlop, Thomas Hervie, and Bartholomew McCall, who was in charge of Daniel Campbell of Shawfield's private affairs. Archibald Murray, advocate, who later served as one of Simson's lawyers, was Campbell's commissioner to the assembly. He was assisted by Hugh Dalrymple, advocate, and Rev. William Miller. Prominent academics were no longer restraining the expression of their Argathelian opinions to faculty meetings.

Although Simson played no part in the events of 1725, the accompanying political changes affected the university and led to the appointment of a Campbell as principal after the death of Stirling in 1727. They may also have forced Simson to reconsider his loyalties. His personal inclinations to change sides would be fortified after Campbell became principal of Glasgow University, since he had always seen it as his duty as ranking professor to support his principal in every way. As a supporter of legitimate administrative authority, he may have felt that he ought to join his nephew, Robert, in the Argyll camp. If so, this might explain the animosity shown towards him by the Glasgow ministers in the months ahead.

These factors inevitably influenced Simson's second heresy case. Since Argyll interests appeared to dominate the church courts, Simson needed their support. If he indeed changed political sides between 1725 and 1729, it might be seen as perfectly in keeping with his philos-

129 NAS 1726, CH1/2/53, 50–4.
130 A James Richardson appears on Glasgow University's divinity roll of 6 February 1716. This would make him the normal age to be a preacher ten years later.

ophy of government, as well as being expedient for his own welfare. He had consistently given his devotion to those in power, whose task it was to maintain the stability of the nation, the rights of the church, and the administration of the university. Once the Argathelian-Walpole alliance had established itself in Scotland, Simson could adhere to it, given his beliefs about order.

9

Further Gulps of Error:
Simson and Religious Turmoil

Scots Presbyterians had to deal with religious as well as secular changes in the early Hanoverian years, with three emergent threats demanding immediate neutralization. The first was the perception of renewed Antinomianism, the second was a movement against subscription to creeds and confessions, and the third, while seldom stated explicitly, was an ideological rift between the old school of clergymen and the moderns who were updating university education. Simson and his opinions became entangled in all of these developments in Scottish intellectual life and emerged as from the third as a scapegoat.

ANTINOMIANISM, THE *MARROW*, AND THE ROLE OF QUERIES

The church managers spent the period between the conclusion of Simson's first case and 1721 taking steps against the Antinomian tendencies that Simson had decried. After rapping Simson over the knuckles in 1717, the General Assembly condemned the Presbytery of Auchterarder for demanding that candidates seeking licensing or ordination should sign clauses over and above those of the Westminster Confession. The most contentious of these read: "I do believe, that it is not sound and orthodox to teach, that we must forsake sin, in order to our coming to Christ, and instating us in covenant with God."[1] Webster and his evangelical friends saw the individual as being passive in receiving grace and regeneration, while Simson believed that prevenient grace gave man the

---

1 This and the other quotations in this paragraph are from Act 10 of the assembly of 1717 and from Act 8 of the assembly of 1718, found in Stewart of Pardovan, *Abridgement*, 136.

means with which to prepare for regeneration. Ecclesiastical leaders endorsed Simson's belief that it was the church's task to maintain morals and uphold civic obedience. The assembly in 1717 ruled that the proposition required by the Presbytery of Auchterarder was "unsound and most detestable, as it stands" – a condemnation that it reiterated in 1718. These terms were considerably stronger than those employed against Simson, because Antinomian tendencies represented an unacceptable danger to public discipline.

Almost immediately, the Scottish church found itself immersed in further debate over Antinomianism provoked by the re-publication of *The Marrow of Modern Divinity*, a seventeenth-century spiritual guide discovered by Thomas Boston around 1700.[2] In the aftermath of the Auchterarder affair, Boston showed the *Marrow* to his friend James Hogg, who reprinted it in 1718. While the early eighteenth-century Scots emphasis on a limited atonement and on the Gospel offer being made only to the elect seemed to curtail Christ's role as the Saviour of sinning men, earlier English Puritans had been more open and eclectic. Drawing largely on the work of the first Reformers, the *Marrow* stated the case for evangelical Christianity. Evangelical religion, legalism, and Antinomianism offered answers to Neophytus, who searched for truth. The evangelical message said that "here you are to work nothing ... here you are to render nothing unto God, but only to receive ... Jesus Christ, and apprehend him in your heart by faith ... and so shall you obtain forgiveness of sins ... and eternal happiness; not as an agent but as a patient, not by doing, but by receiving."[3] Scots evangelicals saw this expression of the love of God to suffering humanity as a useful pastoral tool. It conveyed the same message as the Auchterarder creed: "No man can turn to God, except he be first turned of God: and after he is turned, he repents."[4]

Opposition to the theology of the *Marrow* was choreographed by Principal James Hadow of St Andrews, who "led the Dance to the *Synod*."[5] He denounced the *Marrow* for teaching universal redemption, as well as being Antinomian. Preaching to the Synod of Fife on 7 April 1719, Hadow showed that his mind was still on the dangers of rationalism as espoused by Simson: "The divine Doctrine concerning the Salvation of Sinners can be known only by divine Revelation, Wherefore I see no

2 *The Marrow of Modern Divinity*, by Edward Fisher, had been first published in London in 1645. It ran through many subsequent editions. Boston, *Memoirs*, 160.

3 Fisher, *Marrow*, 117–18.

4 Ibid., 145.

5 *Review of a Conference*, 8.

ground for asserting, that Men, from the Light of Nature, and Works of Creation and Providence, may know that there is a remedy provided."[6] He then argued against the necessity of assurance as the essence of saving faith, noting that it was not demanded by the Westminster Confession. Hadow believed that to make assurance a part of faith implied universalism, pointing out "As our Confession of Faith denies Assurance to be of the essence of saving Faith; so it no less disowns all *Universalism.*"[7] His intention may have been to ensure that the church could include those who lacked any conversion experience or belief in assurance. The purpose of a national kirk was the provision of ethical discipline over the population as well as spiritual support for the elect.

The General Assembly of 1720 determined that *The Marrow of Modern Divinity* was a work "replete with Antinomian errors."[8] Webster stood with the evangelicals on this issue; in his final days "in the judicatory, where the matter of the *Marrow* was considered, [he] expressed his concern that they would beware of condemning it."[9] On 20 May 1720, three days after Webster's death, the assembly forbade ministers to preach or write in favour of the book and enjoined them to warn their parishioners against it.[10] The dying Webster must have been irritated, but not surprised, to see his old bugbears – faculty members of universities – leading the *Marrow*'s foes. The church seems to have accepted the arguments of Hadow regarding the *Marrow*'s heterodox spirit, although modern commentators consider them to have been ill-judged.[11] John Macleod saw the debates over the theology of the *Marrow* as an inevitable reaction to hyper-Calvinist preaching, which "fenced and hedged with elaborate restrictions and conditions the enjoyment of God's free salvation."[12] In David Lachman's opinion, the *Marrow* doctrine is compatible with the Westminster standards and the general trend of Reformed thought, in contrast to the tendency of Hadow and his friends towards legalism.[13]

---

6 Hadow, *Sermon*, 14.

7 Ibid., 35.

8 Statement by Rev. John Brown in Appendix to Fisher, *Marrow*, 344.

9 Boston, *Memoirs*, 332.

10 Stewart, of Pardovan, *Abridgement*, 186.

11 For instance, David C. Lachman; see his articles "Hadow" and "Marrow Controversy" in *DSCHT*.

12 Macleod, *Scottish Theology*, 143.

13 Lachman, *Marrow Controversy*, 491.

Twelve ministers, including Boston, Hogg, Ebenezer Erskine, and his brother Ralph, signed a representation against the assembly's condemnation, becoming known as the Marrow Brethren, or the Representers. They subsequently composed careful answers to queries that the commission of the General Assembly put to them prior to the assembly of 1722, proving that the *Marrow* was a useful spiritual manual that expressed pure Reformation doctrine. In condemning it, the assembly appeared to condemn "the precious truths of the gospel."[14]

The issues that had been in contention between the evangelical group and the "moderns," such as Simson and probably Hamilton, continued to be the basis for discussion in the *Marrow* affair. Many of the positions argued in the answers of the Representers were similar to those taken in the debates against Simson between 1714 and 1717. Thus, in the answer to query 1, the question was raised of Adam's ability to believe in Christ, which Arminians denied. If Adam did not possess it, then he could not lose it, so God must give the power to believe in Christ to all men. The Representers believed that "Socinians, Arminians, Papists, and Baxterians, by holding the gospel to be a new proper, preceptive law, with sanction ... have confounded the law and the gospel, and brought works into the ... cause of a sinner's justification before God."[15]

In a further echo of Simson's statement that men served God as a result of their quest for eternal life, query 7 asked whether the "preaching of the necessity of a holy life, in order to the obtaining of eternal happiness, [was] of dangerous consequence to the doctrine of free grace?"[16] In response, the Representers noted that although in various senses a holy life was indeed necessary, yet such words had "an appearance of evil ... [therefore] Protestant churches ... knowing the strong natural bias in all men towards seeking salvation, not by faith ... but by works of righteousness ... have industriously shunned to use ... choosing rather to call holiness and good works necessary duties of the persons justified and saved, than conditions of salvation."[17] They believed that "a persuasion of life and salvation from the free love and mercy of God ... offered to us ... is the ... justifying, and appropriating act of faith, whereby the convinced sinner becomes possessed of Christ and his saving benefits."[18] They contrasted this assurance with the Antinomian assurance

14 Appendix to Fisher, *Marrow*, 345.
15 Ibid., 347.
16 Ibid., 355.
17 Ibid., 357.
18 Ibid., 362.

that Christ's pardon for sin could be claimed prior to belief. The Representers agreed that ministers had the duty to offer Christ freely to all, although only the elect would be given grace to receive Him. The gift must be offered as "a common salvation," but "This giving ... is not ... a giving in possession ... but a giving by way of grant and offer ... and the party to whom is not the election only, but lost mankind."[19] The reprobate "do justly and deservedly perish" when they refuse the offer.[20]

The debate over the *Marrow* indicates the stresses within the Presbyterian community in Scotland. While everyone professed adherence to the Westminster standards, there was deep division as to what exactly comprised these standards. Simson and the rationalists looked to Calvin and to natural theology. They believed that the framework of the Westminster Confession could accommodate both. The evangelical group looked back to an earlier Reformed orthodoxy, when fear had not yet erected barriers to the Gospel message. Hadow and the hyper-Calvinist majority in the 1720 assembly wanted to restrict discussion and to uphold the accretions that Reformed dogma had accumulated over the past century.

In the short term, this last group appeared to be victorious. The Representers, despite the orthodox tone of their thoughtful responses to the queries, were rebuked by the 1722 assembly for their defence of *Marrow* doctrine and for their implied criticism of the decisions of the 1720 assembly. While they were not officially punished further, the representers found preferment within the church blocked. Their disaffection with the managers of the day encouraged several to secede in 1733. Hogg, however, was subjected to a lengthy persecution by the Synod of Fife, which included Principal Hadow among its members. In 1722 the synod asked Hogg to answer questions relating to his authorship of anonymous pamphlets. He declined, on the grounds that his "naturall right as a man and a Christian" prevented him from accusing himself, that he did not wish to implicate others, and that Christ refused to answer questions.[21] Hogg's doubts about the good will of his synod were justified; the case against him dragged on for over ten years, until in 1733 the frail old minister begged that it be concluded. The synod agreed to close the matter but admonished him that "he had expressed

19 Ibid., 367.
20 Ibid., 367–8.
21 NAS, CH2/154/7, 71–4, quoted in Lachman, *Marrow Controversy*, 325 n. 2.

himself in some terms and phrases which the Synod did not see altogether agree with our Standards."[22] These words must have sounded to
the evangelicals like an ironic echo of the General Assembly of 1717's
act against Simson. The condemnation of the *Marrow* theology can be
seen as the obverse of the admonition given to Simson. While Simson
may have regarded the church's disapproval of the *Marrow* in 1717–20
as encouragement to his teaching of rational moralism, later he must
have seen the mode of procedure taken against the *Marrow* supporters
as ominous.

Evangelicals were outraged at the difference between the treatment
that Simson had received and that meted out to the Representers. They
noted that Webster had been forced to libel Simson, while the assembly
and the commission had dealt directly with the *Marrow*. They demanded
to know why Simson, who was still preaching a "new Gospel," had not
been forced to renounce his errors or respond to questions about
them.[23] The anonymous writer ("Private Christian") of the *Videte apologiam nostram contra Websterum* was still angry five years after the resolution of Webster's charges against the professor. The censure of the
Marrow and the rebuke given to the Representers kept alive the anti-
Simson sentiment among the orthodox and may have stimulated their
search for new flaws in his doctrine.

The church's reaction to the answers of the Representers may also
illuminate John Simson's later unwillingness to answer questions directly. The censure of the Representers must have reinforced Simson's
reluctance to respond to queries. In 1713 he had personally seen how
Webster used his answers to formulate further accusations against him.
Whether or not he agreed with the position taken by the Marrow brethren, he learned from them that painstaking and scrupulous responses
to theological questioning failed to save from rebuke valued pastors
against whom there were no insinuations of scandal or doubt. In the
small world of the Scottish church, Simson would have known of the
grounds for Hogg's refusal to answer the queries posed by the Synod
of Fife, especially since his own nephew, Dr Thomas Simson, was
appointed professor of medicine in St Andrews University in 1722.

When Simson found himself in a similar predicament a few years
later, it is understandable that he felt disinclined to answer questions. A
man's own words might be used against him, and sincere explanations

---

22 NAS, CH2/154/7, 375, quoted in Lachman, *Marrow Controversy*, 332.
23 Private Christian, *Videte apologiam*, 5.

were insufficient to allay doubts. Simson's resistance to questioning was not unprecedented, nor were his grounds for non-compliance novel. He must have been aware that the ultra-orthodox considered his reputation tarnished and distrusted his academic colleagues. He probably saw his position as weaker than that of the twelve Representers in general or of Hogg in particular in the eyes of the average devout church-goer. His influential political and academic friends would find it easier to defend him if the opposition were given minimal ammunition.

SIMSON AND SUBSCRIPTION

A second dispute, on the merits of mandatory subscription to creeds or confessions, reverberated throughout the British Isles during this period. Many felt that it stemmed from Ireland, where Emlyn had been convicted of Arianism in 1703. Ulster Presbyterians, whose adoption of the standard of the Westminster Confession was relatively recent, were embroiled in controversy over the nature of the subscription demanded of clergymen.[24] In 1705 a group of ministers formed the Belfast Society for the purposes of biblical and literary study. By the next decade, some of its members had come to believe that there was no necessity for ministerial candidates to subscribe a confession of faith of human origin, because such a requirement interfered with Protestant free judgment.[25] Of the society's leading founders, James Kirkpatrick had been Simson's fellow student in James Wodrow's Glasgow classes and John Abernethy was probably known to both as a student completing his philosophy training in Glasgow in 1696, before he went to Edinburgh to study divinity under Professor George Campbell.[26] Several of the later members of the society were students of Simson himself.

Nineteenth-century historians attributed the problems in Ireland to the laxity of Scottish divinity schools, and held Simson, Hamilton, John Gowdie, and Francis Hutcheson responsible.[27] They stressed the disastrous effect of the Glasgow divinity programme, in which most of the Irish theologues enrolled: "Professor Simpson of Glasgow had inoculated his students with those principles which led to the separation of

24 M.A. Stewart, "Rational Dissent", 2.

25 See Killen, History, 3:158–9.

26 Barlow, "Career," 400–1.

27 Gowdie (c. 1682–1762) was professor of divinity at Edinburgh University from 1733 to 1754, when he became principal, a position that he held until his death. He opposed the *Marrow* and was known as supporting Simson during his second case.

the presbytery of Antrim; and so remiss were the judicatories of the Church of Scotland, that even after the mischievous character of his teaching had been fully demonstrated, he was permitted, year after year, to continue his theological prelections."[28] This blanket condemnation is unfair, particularly given John Smith's denunciation of Simson for suspecting him and fellow club members of non-subscribing opinions. It was certainly true that the thinking of many Irish Presbyterians had changed radically, but Scottish professors were probably blameless. Twentieth-century historians have seen the tide flowing in another direction. Roger Thomas in 1953 traced the subscription dispute from England to Ulster and thence to Scotland.[29] More recently, M.A. Stewart sees some inspiration coming from Ireland to the Scottish universities, where it advanced the new spirit epitomized by Hutcheson's teaching after 1729.

In contrast to the Irish criticism of subscription, Scottish attachment to the Westminster Confession deepened, and the terms of subscription became more rigorous in the early years of the eighteenth century. The explanation for this phenomenon is not entirely religious – between 1690 and 1715, the confession became a tool in the battle against Episcopalians and Jacobites.[30] During Queen Anne's last years, when the Tories inflicted their loathed series of acts on the church, political instability increased the significance of subscription to Presbyterians. Although the influence of Irish Presbyterians had some effect on academic institutions, it is more likely that the similar debates taking place in England raised Scots interest in the current debate. The constant contact between Scotland and London ensured that the Scots were fully aware of religious trends as well as of political events in the south.

In March 1717 Benjamin Hoadly, bishop of Bangor, preached a sermon in the Chapel Royal in London proclaiming that the kingdom of Christ was not of this world (John 18:36) and that, accordingly, the laws of the church must have only spiritual, not temporal, sanctions. Hoadly decried confessional subscription and censorship of the opinions of individuals because they oblige men "to Profess even what They do not, what They cannot, believe to be true."[31] Christians may not add to or reinterpret the laws laid down in the Bible, civil sanctions may not be used

28 Killen, *History*, 3:327.
29 Thomas, "Non-Subscription," 179.
30 See Alexander C. Cheyne, "Place," 17–20.
31 Hoadly, *Nature*, 28.

against any religious transgressions, and Christians need not subscribe to anything beyond a belief in the Bible.

These views ran contrary to Scottish beliefs. While the Church of Scotland considered Christ the King and Head of His Church, it demanded strict obedience to its discipline and saw the enforcement of that obedience as the duty of the secular magistrate. When William Wishart, Jr, was accused of heterodoxy by the presbytery of Edinburgh in 1737, denial of the duty of the magistrate to impose secular punishment for doctrinal offences was one of the charges brought against him.[32]

Discord in the Church of England was followed by controversy among English Dissenters. This divided group was also moving into the eighteenth century in its ideas and demands. Between 1716 and 1718 a series of publications called the *Occasional Papers* printed articles of progressive theology in London.[33] Politicians under the leadership of MP John Shute Barrington were working towards the repeal of the various acts against Dissenters. Their efforts received a setback in 1718 with a controversy in Exeter over the Arian tendencies of Rev. James Peirce and the necessity for subscription. This dispute led to the Salters' Hall Conference of February 1719, at which the Dissenters present voted narrowly (57 to 53) against demanding confessional subscription to words of human composition.[34]

The points raised in the English debate prompted Professor William Dunlop (1692–1720) to write in defence of his church. Dunlop's father had been the principal of Glasgow University, where his brother Alexander now taught Greek. William earned his MA at Glasgow University and then studied divinity under Simson. To prepare for ordination, he went to live in Edinburgh with his uncle, Principal Carstares, and in 1715 was appointed professor of church history there.[35] The young author had been incensed by statements made in the *Occasional Papers* and by Hoadly's comments on Scottish religion:

In *Scotland*, let a man depart an Inch from the Confession of Faith, and Rule of Worship, establish'd by the Assembly there; and he will quickly find, that, as cold

32 Wishart's case was printed in Wishart, *Answers*, 5.

33 In his article, Thomas said, "One cannot read these papers without perceiving a growing sense of liberation from ancient bigotries." "Non-Subscription," 169, n. 3.

34 Whiston in his *Memoirs* claimed that a jubilant supporter of liberal thought, Sir Joseph Jekyl, said of the vote, "The Bible carried it by four." Whiston, *Memoirs*, 220; quoted in Thomas, "Non-Subscription," 171.

35 For details of Dunlop's life, see William Dunlop, *Sermons*, Publisher's Preface, 1:vi.

a Country as it is, it will be too hot for him to live in. Infants are baptiz'd; there, not only into the Name of the Father, Son, and Holy Ghost; but into the Pure Doctrine, profess'd and settled by the Church of *Scotland*. To suppose therefore, any point of Doctrine to be Erroneous, or so much as a Subject for a new Examination, in so Unspotted a Church, is a Token of Malignity and Infidelity; and the Man who doth it, must be content to escape out of their hands as well as he can.[36]

This castigation, written after Simson's first case but well before the subsequent proceedings against him, shows how liberal public opinion in England regarded Scottish ecclesiastical discipline, and we should recall it below when Scots raise fears of English retribution during the second case.

Dunlop published a *Collection of Confessions of Faith* in 1719 and the next year produced an extensive *Preface* to the Westminster Confession, which explained its "Justice, Reasonableness and Necessity as a Publick Standard of Orthodoxy."[37] He rejected the charges of fanaticism levelled against his countrymen; Presbyterians obeyed the civil law and were by no means "a factious and licentious sect, enemies to order, promoters of confusion and an unrestrained liberty, and zealous for levelling principles in the church and the state."[38] Although the confession maintained justification by faith and attributed no part of salvation to works, the Scottish church was unequalled in its demands for proof of sanctification in the daily lives of its members. The purpose of a confession was "to secure the purity of the *christian doctrine* from the many contagious *heresies*" that endangered the church.[39]

Dunlop demolished the arguments of Socinians, Arminians, English Dissenters, Anglicans, and Swiss Calvinists against confessions, using the discourse of a Lockean Whig: "As freedom is the birth-right of mankind, any number of persons may voluntarily unite themselves, to such purposes and under such regulations as appear useful and convenient to them, provided they be agreeable to the rights of others, and the rules of justice."[40] Individuals may choose their religious beliefs, but, having done so, they may demand specific qualifications of their ministers and teachers and establish doctrinal tests for them. Dunlop strove to balance the supremacy of conscience with the confessional needs of national churches, whether established or not.

---

36 [Hoadly], Dedication, xi–xii.
37 William Dunlop, *Preface*.
38 Ibid., 20.
39 Ibid., 44.
40 Ibid., 69.

Dunlop addressed the questions of the day about the use of scriptural phrases rather than those of human composition, which were soon to be discussed in Simson's second case. Familiar with current critical scholarship, he discussed the difficulties inherent in the expression of religious ideas through translations, with their inevitable distortions. He concluded: "That 'tis simply impossible to declare our belief of *scripture-consequences*, however necessary and momentous they be, in the precise terms of the *bible*."[41] Since the difficulties in stating accurately all aspects of the Christian faith using biblical language were insurmountable, the Westminster Confession expressed these truths as clearly as possible.

Dunlop explained why he, along with so many Scots ministers of the period, believed that it gave important advantages to the Church of Scotland: "an uncommon harmony, in what we are perswaded is the doctrine of God our Saviour, flourishes amongst us: That religion hath been preserved in its purity, and a security from errors and heresies, which greatly distract other churches, in so great a measure obtained among us; together with a freedom from all the melancholy effects of disputes and divisions amongst ministers as to the established articles of Faith."[42] To have seen the first quarter of the eighteenth century as a period of "uncommon harmony" in Scots religious life suggests either considerable powers of self-delusion on the part of Dunlop or more probably the belief that subscription provided a bulwark against episcopal danger.

During the early 1720s discussions of confessional subscription resounded throughout the Scottish church. Glasgow preacher Andrew Gray visited London in early 1725 and met some of the important Presbyterian ministers there.[43] Principal Stirling had given him an introduction to Mr John Cumming, the minister of Founders' Hall Scots Kirk in

---

41 Ibid., 126.

42 Ibid., 176.

43 Andrew Gray (son of John Gray), MA Glasgow, Jan. 1723, entered in Glasgow theology register, 15 April 1723; *Munimenta*, 3:254. The minutes of the Presbytery of Glasgow record that he entered trials in the spring of 1724, after a remarkably rapid progression through the divinity course, and was licensed on 5 August 1724; GCA, CH2/171/10, 35v, 47r. Gray was presented to the Graham parish of Airth in 1727, but the presentation was disputed by the elders, who were supported by the presbytery. In 1730 he was presented to the parish of New Kilpatrick by the Duke of Montrose, and he was ordained there in 1731 despite strong opposition to the call by some heritors. Wodrow thought him "a choice, deserving person"; Wodrow, *Analecta*, 3:408–9.

London.[44] Simson had recommended him to Dr Calamy, who "had a particular concern about me." Gray noted that the London debates about confessions "are nothing so warm as they have been." Nevertheless, non-subscribing principles were spreading, with young preachers denouncing confessions as tests of orthodoxy.[45]

Robert Wodrow's young cousin "Mr Stewart" solicited his advice in 1726 about the various sermons required in his trials to obtain a licence. Exegesis topics continued to be paradigmatic of the current concerns of the church. Stewart's subject was "Num formulae fidei sunt scribendae etiamsi in expressis Scripturae verbis non concipiantur?" (Should formulas of faith be devised, even if they are not drawn up in the express words of Scripture?) In dealing with this subject, he noted in his letter to Wodrow, he would be forced "to engage in that much agitated question anent Subscriptions of Confessions. a task, Im afraid, I shall be found very unequall for."[46] Stewart hoped that the older minister would be able to advise him about the proper method of dealing with the subject. While the advice that Wodrow gave to Stewart has not survived, he might well have directed his cousin to Dunlop's *Preface* for the necessary arguments.

Meanwhile, in Ireland, the controversy over subscription had continued to grow. Francis Hutcheson, home after completing his theological studies in Glasgow, wrote in 1718 that the younger ministers there were preaching Hoadlian principles "as if their hearers were all absolute princes going to impose tests and confessions." Since this was clearly ridiculous, given the civil disabilities under which Dissenters lived, he surmised "that the antipathy to confessions is upon some other grounds than a new spirit of charity. Dr. Clarke's book [Samuel Clarke, *The Scripture Doctrine of the Trinity*] I'm sufficiently informed has made several unfixed in their old principles, if not entirely altered them."[47] Hutcheson had just completed his studies under Simson, so he was also probably echoing his professor's opinion of non-subscription.

A conviction about the biblical basis of faith was stressed by a member of the Belfast Society, who was quoted as writing, "I do not find that it is

44 Cumming (1685–1729), an Ulster Scot educated at Glasgow University (MA 1705), became minister of London's Scots Kirk in 1716, played a "prominent part" in the Salters' Hall Conference, and was a strong supporter of subscription. In 1728 Edinburgh University honoured him with a DD. He was succeeded as minister by William Wishart, Jr. See George C. Cameron, *Scots Kirk*, 25.

45 A. Gray to J. Stirling, 16 Feb. 1724/5, GUL, MS Murray, 204:106.

46 Mr. Stewart to R. Wodrow, 26 Feb. 1726, NLS, Wodrow Letters Quarto, XII, 30.

47 F. Hutcheson to W. Wright, Sept. 1718, quoted in Killen, *History*, 3:160.

required in Scripture, as a term of salvation to believe that Christ is the absolutely supreme God.– – – And therefore so long as I believe the doctrine about which I am in doubts is not fundamental, I think I may safely continue to preach."[48] This comment suggests that when, in 1721, Rev. George Lang wrote to Wodrow that there were Arians involved in the subscription controversy, he had some basis for his opinion: "The aversion of some among us to our confession as a term of ministerial communion, and indeed to all fixed tests of orthodoxy seems rather to increase: and what is far worse, we are not free of some apprehensions of Arianism having got some footing among us ... But however it be as to Arianism, I'm pretty sure that several ministers incline to the Arminian principles."[49]

Both sides in these debates sent representatives to Scotland to solicit support. The discord caused by the 1722 fund-raising visit to Glasgow of Samuel Smith, a pro-subscription Belfast merchant, was reflected in Thomas Hervie's case.[50] When, in the sub-synod of Belfast, Smith suggested a return to Scotland in 1723 to raise funds in the east, the non-subscribing minister Samuel Haliday referred to portions of a letter from Simson, "in which the professor alleged that Mr. Smith of Belfast, when in Glasgow in the previous autumn, had said, that though he did not suspect the non-subscribers of Arianism, he feared they maintained principles which might be dangerous to the Church."[51] Haliday refused to produce the letter in question, which prompted the accusation that he was unfairly refraining from substantiating insinuations against the conduct of an elder. Whereupon others suggested that if Smith had indeed said such words, they were not slanderous because they were true.

The whole incident is tantalizing; the brief comment about Simson gives no indication about the tone of his letter. He might well have used the words quoted about Smith without in any way implying condemnation of the merchant. Since Simson had opposed Hervie, who seems to have disapproved of Smith's mission, it is not inconceivable that his comment had no negative connotations and that he agreed with Smith, which might explain Haliday's reluctance to table the document.

48 Quoted from "Narrative," 23. Killen, *History*, 3:165, note.
49 G. Lang to R. Wodrow, May 1721, Killen, *History*, 3:179.
50 See above, 197–8.
51 Killen, *History*, 3:201.

In spite of rumours about Simson's approval of non-subscribing views, his verified statements never display this attitude. With his normal support for authority both in church and in state, it would seem out of character for him to have endorsed non-subscription as a desirable practice. Simson never wavered in his public claim that his teaching fell within the limits prescribed by the Westminster Confession to which he had sworn. This can be partially confirmed by a letter written to him by Robert Wodrow in February 1723, in which he passes on thanks for support from Rev. Gilbert Kennedy, minister of Tullylish in Ulster and one of the strongest adherents of subscription. Wodrow also enclosed a letter from a non-subscriber and asked Simson and Stirling to comment on its criticism of articles of the Westminster Confession. Wodrow displayed no doubts about Simson's steadfast advocacy of subscription.[52]

The persistence of rumours about Simson and non-subscription, as well as the lack of definitive evidence, appear in a letter from Charles Masterton, an Irish subscribing minister, to Principal Stirling in 1726. The letter is one of recommendation brought by a new divinity student, "Mr Allexander." After introducing the young man, it goes on to express alarm at the rumours which had reached Belfast about Simson. Masterton expressed his respect for Simson as a man, as well as for his "learning and piety," but wished that he had answered queries more directly. "Our Nonsubscribers here tryumph much in his conduct, alledging he is making his defense upon the foot of their nonsubscribing or nondeclaring principles, it is likeways supposed that he has been privatly corresponding with the Nonsubscribers here to the disadvantage of the cause of the Subscribers.... the letter from a learned min[iste]r of the Church of Scotland to Mr Boyse of Dublin ... its generally supposed here that the Rev[eren]d Professor is the author of the letter."[53]

Masterton's words show the concern of the Belfast subscribers about the possible intervention of Simson in their church's affairs. He was, however, continuing to send young men to the divinity school at Glasgow. This attitude suggests that while the orthodox in Ulster might doubt Simson's position on subscription because of his refusal to answer queries, they cannot have believed that he was teaching unsound doctrine.

---

52 Wodrow, *Correspondence*, 3:15–16. Simson did not reply to a letter from Barrington in mid-1725 (see GUL, MS Murray, 204:108) as he might have done had he been courting support from nonsubscribers.

53 C. Mastertown to J. Stirling, 7 Nov. 1726, GUL, MS Gen. 207:132.

Finally, the letter indicates that even Simson's possible correspondence with Irish non-subscribers was a matter of conjecture, not of fact.

ACADEMIC FREEDOM AND SIMSON

An indication of the church's determination to manage Scottish academic life can be found in an act of the General Assembly to promote learning of religion and loyalty in the universities passed in 1719 in the aftermath of the abortive Jacobite raid that spring made by two Spanish ships on the northwest coast of Scotland. It mandated the academic authorities to instil allegiance to the Hanoverian dynasty. The assembly may also have feared the further intrusion of political appointees into university faculties. A contributory factor may have been the dispute over Queen Anne's 1713 presentation of the episcopal layman Alexander Scrimgeour to the St Andrews divinity chair and his subsequent suspension by a committee of visitation. The assembly wished to ascertain its powers over academic appointments in the universities.[54] Throughout this period questions of control over appointments were discussed at various universities. John W. Cairns has shown how both Montrose and Islay used the possible illegality of William Forbes's appointment as professor of law at Glasgow for political purposes.[55]

Some Scots wished their educational establishments to be freed from excessive doctrinal conditions. George Turnbull, then a regent at Aberdeen, complained to Lord Molesworth in 1722 of "proud domineering pedantic Priests" maintaining control over Scottish universities to ensure that students would develop "a profound veneration to their Senseless metaphysical Creeds & Catechisms."[56] Men such as Turnbull connected the orthodox demand for subscription with attempts to restrict the content of academic instruction. John Simson must have agreed with them to some extent, since he had been undeterred by the limitations placed

54 See James K. Cameron, "Theological Controversy," 121. The 1719 assembly called on its commission to investigate how it might "contribute to the flourishing of the sciences and good literature, and to the propagating of religion and loyalty in universities; and … [to] enquire, what privileges … the judicatories of this church … have by the constitutions of the several universities and colleges, and by the laws of the land, with respect to the settlement of the masters and professors in them … to maintain inviolably, and improve towards the promoting of the foresaid interests of true piety and learning." Act 12, Assembly 1719, Stewart of Pardovan, *Abridgement*, 336–7.

55 Cairns, "Origins," 181–2.

56 G. Turnbull to Ld. Molesworth, 5 Nov. 1722; quoted in M.A. Stewart, "Rational Dissent," 10.

on his work in 1717. When asked by a "worthy" minister in 1722 if it were true that he recommended that his students read his *Apologiam contra Websterum,* Simson riposted "That he recommended to his Students the reading of *Socinus* his Works."[57] He continued to use the same curriculum in his teaching, recommending that his students read the book that he had published of his defences to Webster's libel and draw their own conclusions, rather than discussing topics vetoed by the assembly. In the following decade, Simson explored the conclusions of modern and patristic theologians in his attempt to make his teaching concur with both revelation and reason. Despite the assembly's ruling, there seems to have been little change in his method of instruction.

This third pervasive concern in the church – about academic freedom – may perhaps explain the anxiety that members of the Presbytery of Glasgow and others such as Robert Wodrow began to feel about the professional practice of the professor of divinity at Glasgow University in the mid-1720s. If they were aware, as they probably were, that there was a current of opinion calling for the liberation of the universities from all sectarian restrictions, they may have rightly seen the freedom of discussion that Simson allowed his students as the vanguard of the new independence. The success of the efforts of Simson and his followers at Glasgow may perhaps be measured by two remarks made years later by former students. Professor Archibald Campbell, reviewing his progress in Christian belief, stated that his education "was free and without any tincture of bigotry,"[58] and Samuel Kenrick, writing about Glasgow University in the 1740s to his friend James Wodrow, said that his father had told him "in the true spirit of a Dissenter, that they imposed no shackles of any sort on young minds, or if they had no son of his should ever go near them."[59]

At the time of Simson's second trial at the end of the decade, a balladeer, John Brigs, caricatured many of the orthodox hyper-Calvinists. Allan Logan, one of Simson's main adversaries, was said to see "Farer by Inspiration, / Than he, who by black Natures flees / For Light, to Education." Brigs went on to express the attitudes of such men in the next verse: "Ah! would th' Assembly make an Act, / To put down Pagan Fooling, / With College-lear, – not worth a Plack, / To Saints who need no Schooling."[60]

57 Private Christian, *Videte apologiam,* 4.
58 Campbell, *Authenticity,* vi.
59 S. Kenrick to J. Wodrow, 21/22 Jan. 1786, Dr Williams's Library, MS 24.157, 110/2v.
60 Quoted in Erskine, *Extracts,* 89.

The differences of outlook between Simson and his enemies are encapsulated in Logan's belief that ultimately the value of inspiration was greater than that of education. To Logan, "College-Lear" must always be subservient to revelation in a covenanted nation. For Simson, study and discovery could only assist revealed religion.

The debates of these years, however, also indicate the vitality of the Scottish academic institutions and the zest with which men indulged in intellectual pursuits. The increasing size of the Glasgow faculty and the wide range of John Simson's interests in philosophy and science are similar tokens of this vigour. The ideological rift between the old school and the moderns who were updating Scottish education was less a matter of age or educational affiliation than of conviction and enlightened thought. To traditional Calvinists this trend towards increasing rationalism was alarming, and the Simson cases represent part of their attempts to reverse the process. The disappointing verdict of 1717 was seen as a grievous mistake on the part of the church; as one traditionalist commented sadly in 1727, "the Opinions then vented, which appeared so much to advance humane Reason, may be supposed to have led the Pr[ofessor] into further Gulps of *Error.*"[61]

SIMSON AND "LAXITY IN GLASGOW"

Professors might be changing the nature of divinity instruction, but they were not calling for the elimination of subscription. While the Church of Scotland was anxious about the possible effects of the subscription issue, and the potential Arianism underlying it, there was as yet no sign that it was in any danger from contagion from England. Alert ministers read "the blasphemous pamphlets of the upstart Arians in England, [which denied] with the greatest air of assurance, the true and proper Deity of the Son of God."[62] Ebenezer Erskine, who wrote this in 1721, was personally at no risk from heresy, but he felt that others should be warned, and that the Church of Scotland should publicly support the orthodox in England and Ireland. In 1723–24 Robert Wodrow was confident that all was still well in Scotland. His correspondence from these years included friendly references to bibliographical discussion with Simson and to Professor Hamilton's concern for the subscribing brethren in Ireland.[63] Nevertheless, there were developments that worried

61 Williamson, *Remarks*, 33.
62 Donald Fraser, *Life and Diary of the Reverend Ebenezer Erskine*, 253–4.
63 Wodrow, *Correspondence*, 3:88, 3:122.

him: foreign influences, student laxity, political change. All these grew rapidly more disquieting.

Glasgow seemed to be a less pious place by the mid-1720s than it had been in Wodrow's youth, when a virtuous young minister such as John McLaurin would never have been propositioned by a whore.[64] Although he was only in his forties, Wodrow sounded elderly when he complained about "The younger Sett of people ... [who] continou grosly ignorant in the first points of Religion ... Lately, at the dismissing of the Synod, a company of these young racks were heard say, 'Oh! what a smell of the Gospell this day!' "[65] He deplored inexperienced ministers who lacked gravity and "love[d] to call grace virtue."[66] He grumbled that the church escaped "the present prevailing humour against humane composures and confessions" only because the law demanded subscription to the confession.[67] Wodrow's opinions of matters in Glasgow grew even gloomier in December 1724 after a conversation with John Gray, who told him that the Glasgow divinity students were openly opposing the Confession of Faith as well as displaying the same dubious characteristics that Wodrow had catalogued about young ministers elsewhere – information that presumably had come from Gray's son, Andrew. Gray's anecdotes about the discussions taking place at"private meetings"of the students suggest that they were passionately interested in all the controversies of the day and that they enjoyed taking extreme positions in debate. The young firebrands who produced plays, supported Lord Molesworth, and demonstrated for the right to elect their rector were also active in the divinity school.

Although we know that Simson did not support his students' demands for freedom from administrative authority, Wodrow suspected the worst. "I fear," he wrote, "the lightness and liberty of speaking allowed to students by the Professor at Glasgow, and his open and unguarded way of expressing himself, be a sad inlet to fearfull corruption among the youth."[68] The stark contradiction between his picture of a lax professor and Smith's description of an unsympathetic disciplinarian suggests that each exaggerated his point. Simson was blamed for permitting the discussion of dangerous subjects when the "cases" that the theologues debated as part of their curriculum continued to cause scandal. In 1725, John Millar apparently said, "He hoped there was a set

64 Wodrow, *Analecta*, 3:130.
65 Ibid., 3:129.
66 Ibid., 3:155.
67 Ibid., 3:156.
68 Ibid., 3:171.

of young men coming up that would shake off the shakles of their education, and open their eyes, and not act any more with implicit faith; and he hoped some of them in a feu years would stand before Judicatorys, and make gloriouse appearances for truth."[69] The statement is ambiguous – did he mean that Simson was encouraging these men, or was he calling for his friends to rebel against the teaching of their professor?

This was the moment at which Simson began to suffer from the recurrent ill-health that was to plague him for the next three years. The records of the Presbytery of Glasgow show that Simson's absence from meetings was excused on the grounds of sickness from October to December 1724. From January to March 1725, Simson served as presbytery moderator, but Alexander Maxwell (minister of Rutherglen 1719–41) took the chair as moderator *pro tempore* in April and May, when the professor was "under Indisposition of body."[70] During the summer of 1725, Simson managed to attend most of the meetings, but by the autumn he was again ill. Thereafter, where the *sederunt* lists are legible, Simson was excused from 29 September 1725 to 2 November 1726.[71] According to Wodrow, Simson suffered from the flux, or dysentery, but he may have had colitis or some related disorder.[72] The restrictions that this ailment must have imposed on his activities would have been much more severe under eighteenth-century conditions than they would be today with the benefit of indoor plumbing. It would not be surprising if Simson was psychologically as well as physically shaken by the experience; certainly his contemporaries attributed some of his ill-advised expressions to his illness. It is possible that continual malaise left Simson less careful in his choice of words and caused him to make slips of the tongue by late 1725. Whether the professor's physical condition slackened his control over his students, leading to their "liberty of speaking," is unclear. The comments made by Millar and Campbell on their own education suggest that Simson had always

69 Ibid., 3:179. John Millar (?–1738), son of Rev. Robert Millar (1672–1752) of Paisley, was licensed in 1727 by his father's presbytery, after some dispute about a letter written by him that had offended the Presbytery of Lanark. The Presbytery of Glasgow apparently also made representations against him. He was presented by the Earl of Dundonald and ordained to Kilpatrick in 1728. Ibid., 3:411, 430.

70 GCA, CH2/171/10, 64v.

71 The quality of the records deteriorates rapidly at this point; after April 1727, they are illegible because of fire damage. Ibid., 67–97.

72 In January 1726, Wodrow said that Simson "appears still weaker and weaker, and to be in a dying condition, his flux recurring twice or thrice a-week to a great height." R. Wodrow to Lord Grange, 26 Jan. 1726, Wodrow, *Correspondence*, 3:237.

encouraged free debate. Moreover, the Glasgow students were not alone in their behaviour. John Williamson wrote of the Edinburgh students, "I fear the laxnes of their way of thinking, by their way both of expressing themselves and their vain deportment."[73] The evidence from both cities suggests that by 1725 professors and students generally were challenging the strict intellectual discipline that their elders had thought normal.

The disapproval voiced by Wodrow of Simson's teaching bears out Turnbull's remark to Molesworth about the aim of university theological instruction as conservative Calvinists envisaged it. In Wodrow's eyes a serious problem was developing, but he could find no legally valid charge against Simson. At the end of 1724 Wodrow mused that error was creeping in, but "It's hard to prove these things; and to begin process, without clear proof, is very hard, and as hard to let things run on from evil to worse."[74] It was his opinion that Glasgow University was losing students as a result of the reputation that Simson was gaining. It is difficult to judge from Wodrow's strictures the real basis of his concern. There is a major difference between a professor's encouraging open discussion of liberal ideas by students and one personally propagating heresy. Whatever its cause, by the summer of 1726 Wodrow's disapproval had become well-known. His correspondent Rev. Thomas Mack of Terregles said, "they say none jealouse [suspects] Mr Simson more than you doe, none is more displeased with his way of doing business." Mack himself, however, freely indulged in criticism of Simson, commenting that "if he fall on any rational sceme, he is neither afraid nor ashamed to vent it."[75]

The Glasgow rumour mill, helped in its work by John Gray, continued to grind out gossip about the rise of non-subscribing principles among the divinity students, as well as about the possible Arian opinions of some. The ministerial activities of William Wishart, Jr, were also being watched.[76] The eldest son of Principal William Wishart of Edinburgh University, Wishart had been educated and licensed in Edinburgh and had been called to the Tron church in Glasgow by the burgh council in 1724. He was representative of the younger generation of ministers in his approach to his pastoral duties. Preaching at his communion services were friends such as Charles Telfer (1693–1731), minister of

---

73 J. Williamson to R. Wodrow, 13 April 1727, NLS, Wodrow Letters Quarto, XVII:243.
74 Wodrow, *Analecta*, 3:172.
75 T. Mack to R. Wodrow, 9 June 1726, NLS, Wodrow Letters Quarto, XII, 93r. and v.
76 Wodrow, *Analecta*, 3:171–2, 174–5, 176.

Hawick, Robert Wallace (1697–1771), minister of Moffat, and James Sempill (d. 1752), minister of Dreghorn, whose opinions were considered equally dubious. Hearsay accused Wishart of being unreliable on the equality of the Father and the Son, as well as of such misdemeanours as trying to make a parishioner change her seat in church to accommodate an Irish non-subscriber.[77] Wishart and his contemporaries were the fruit of the new trend in Scottish universities and would continue to distress the older generation of hyper-Calvinist stalwarts.

At the same time, student club activity continued to grow, perhaps fertilized by the quarrels among the ministers. Wishart had joined the Triumpherian Club, which later became known as the Sophocardian Club in his honour.[78] His participation was criticized by Wodrow, who felt that clubs were potential breeding grounds of dissolute behaviour. To make matters worse, student members wrote a satirical farce about Simson, whose character was called Whiffler. Lacking the text, the modern scholar can only surmise that the fears of the orthodox, the instruction of the professor, and the reactions of the students made up an amusing brew of topical concerns. The *dramatis personae* also included Principal Stirling, Coats, Gray, and Webster. Wodrow complained that "some of them are brought in as opposing reason"; he added that "Matters are come to a sad pass, when people begin openly to mock and ridicul Gospell Ministers."[79]

After dinner one day in early February 1725, members of the Presbytery of Glasgow discussed the rumours about the divinity students. Simson called Gray their prime disseminator and accused him of taking up "Mr Webster's cudgell." The spreading of "groundles storys of him throu the country Ministers" caused Simson justified concern, as the evidence left by Wodrow indicates.[80] Simson had discussed Gray's criti-

77 Ibid., 3:178–9.

78 Ibid., 3:178, 183.

79 Ibid., 3:184. Rev. John Gray seems to have been unfortunately easy to ridicule. According to Hervie, his sermons were nonsense; moreover, he had had an enlarged sense of self-importance. The records of the Presbytery of Glasgow tell of his prosecution of a Mrs Wake for breaking the sabbath and disobeying a minister. She was guilty of "profaning the Lord's Day with idleness" by gazing out of her window. Gray's rage, however, was plainly aroused less by her misdemeanour than by her refusal to obey his command to leave her vantage point. GCA, CH2/171/10, 17–20.

80 Wodrow, *Analecta*, 3:181.

cisms with him, but he had "heard him advance nothing but authority, which had no great weight with him." Charles Coats (d. 1745), minister of Govan, said that in his opinion the presbytery should be aware that Simson's scholars, "in answering cases, did go on principles which did plainly support the Arminian and Socinian errors." Simson apparently lost his temper and used "very rough words" to his two adversaries.[81] He assured the presbytery that unorthodox "cases" were corrected by himself, and even by the principal. He could see no reason for the presbytery to become involved with them.

Wodrow's version of this encounter implies a long-standing antipathy between Gray and Simson and indicates that Gray and Coats were now waiting for Simson to commit an indiscretion and present them with usable "clear proof" with which they might demand his deposition. Their complaints relate not to Arianism or subscription, but to the teaching that Webster had denounced. The presbytery's records, however, give no hint of internal discord. During the winter that this reported passage of arms took place, Simson served as moderator of the Presbytery of Glasgow. James Sloss, a student of Simson who later deposed against him, underwent trials and was licensed. At privy censures in March all members of the presbytery were well reported of and encouraged to continue their efforts.[82] This meant that the majority of Glasgow ministers believed Simson's theology to be orthodox and that his detractors could bring forward no convincing evidence to the contrary.

In March 1725, the church session of Portmoak recorded an overture calling for the session to transmit "to the superior judicatories of this Church" a wish that the Church of Scotland might testify against "these pretended Protestants in neighbouring nations, who by this damnable heresy are attempting to take away the bright jewel of our Redeemer's crown, and to bring him, even as to his divine nature, in among the ranks of created beings; whereby ... the foundation of our holy religion ... is overturned."[83] The fears of Ebenezer Erskine and his circle about standards of orthodoxy in England seemed justified by trends there, but their overture made no reference to rumours about Glasgow. Indeed, the minute continued with the comment that while Scotland was untainted, the frequent visits to London of members of the nobility and

81 Ibid., 3:182.
82 GCA, CH2/171/10, 52–63.
83 Donald Fraser, *Life of Ebenezer Erskine*, 256.

gentry gave cause for alarm. It is therefore probable that the gossip that loomed so large in Wodrow's mind was restricted to the southwest and still centred on Simson's supposed Arminian rationalism.

In April 1725 Gray preached to the Synod of Glasgow and Ayr on the text "Holynes becometh thine house," speaking of dangers to the church, corruptions of doctrine, ideas favourable to "man's naturall pouers," and the fact that dependence on the first cause was not inconsistent with the liberty of man.[84] Many saw all this as being directed at Simson, especially when Gray "faithfully rebuked the lightnes and frothynes of young men, and recommended modesty and humility: He had severall very good and necessary cautions to Students of Divinity."[85] After this introduction, the synod's moderator felt obliged to inquire at the time of privy censures whether there were any concerns about members of the Presbytery of Glasgow. Directly questioned, Wodrow replied, "We had a great deal of noise this winter of corruptions in doctrine getting among the Students at Glasgou, and casses that were answered which conteaned some things not agreeable to the Standarts of this Church; and I thought the Presbytery should be inquired what they had done as to these rumors."[86] Divisions were already forming among the ministers: one said that the synod sermon had alerted them to a need for inquiry, while another said that, on the contrary, inquiry would be hazardous in creating trouble in the church. After hearing speakers from both sides, the synod ordered the moderator to tell all members to observe the acts of assembly as to doctrine.

Clearly no proof of Simson's heterodoxy had yet come to hand, since nothing was mentioned at either the assembly of 1725 or the later synod meeting that year. The excitements caused by the malt tax riot, the charges against the town magistrates, and the subsequent political changes kept Glasgow's intellectual classes supplied with conversational staples for the summer and early autumn. Only in November, with the October municipal elections over, did they turn back to religion as a topic to enliven their evenings. First William Wishart provided them with a theme for criticism in his communion of 31 October, at which Telfer and Sempill preached. Each gave offence with sermons emphasizing societal duties and the performance of good works. Then, preaching on the text "Wisdome is the principle thing," Telfer ignored

84 Wodrow, *Analecta*, 3:190.
85 Ibid., 3:190–1.
86 Ibid., 3:192.

Christ and discussed the use of reason and reflection. The informed decided that these "incoherent discourses" had some of their roots in Shaftesbury, the *Tatler*, and the *Spectator*, not normal source material for Scottish sermons.[87]

Finally, after the new academic year began in November 1725, Simson apparently lapsed into open heresy on a new and dangerous issue. The professor had suffered a particularly severe attack of the flux and had been teaching only "nou and then," which may explain why Gray and those of his cohort had been slow to obtain definite evidence of error.[88] Simson was reported to have told his scholars in the course of a review of Pictet's summary of the doctrine of the Trinity that "Christus est Deus, sed non Summus Deus" (Christ is God, but not the most high God).[89] Given the prevailing fear of Arianism, here was a charge that could be used to remove Simson from the divinity school. Simson was said to have admitted that he had revised his opinion about the Trinity, because he had now read some of the early church fathers in the original. He now believed that in 1724 he had been verging on Sabellianism, an ancient heresy that he had come to see as the prevalent danger. Sabellius was probably a third-century Roman who believed in a divine unity with three successive modes. His heresy, known as modalistic Monarchianism, was a second- and third-century attempt to protect the unity of God. The modes or manifestations of the elements of the Trinity are only names, although they are "rooted eternally in unseen reality, so that God is always the Father, the Son, and the Spirit, although known through the threefold self-manifestation or not known at all."[90] The tendency to emphasize divine unity was natural for a generation that was particularly worried about the Arian subordination of the Son.

Simson

has defended what he said in privat conversation to ... Mr Andrew Gray, Mr George Buchannan, and others, and pretended to answer all their objections. He says he is nou reading Dr Clerk's Essay, and sees nothing comparable to it, and bids his scholars "not be affrayed to be termed Clerkians and Arrians," in conversation with them. He say the Confession of Faith will bear a safe sense,

---

87 Ibid., 3:239–40.
88 Ibid., 3:240.
89 Ibid., 3:242.
90 W. Fulton, "Trinity," in *Encyclopaedia of Religion and Ethics*, 12:461.

though it's ill worded, and the doctrine in it will be unreasonable, unles under-stood in his sense. "These Three are One, in the Catechisme, he sayes, he knoues not what to make of it: 1 John v. and 7, 'These Three are One,'" is to be understood of one consent: That the ordinary systeme is come in with the Scho-lastick Popery, that subjects reason to faith: That all the first Fathers, whom he had not read before in the originall, (till within these six weeks,) are all in his opinion.[91]

Wodrow was surprised that Simson was making no effort to hide his opinions and that they had produced so little talk. He thought that per-haps "people think he is crazed in the head, after his long weakning sicknes."[92] Wodrow had also heard that Simson's students did not accept his new views and were angry with him.

In December, Andrew Gray told Wodrow that Simson said privately that Dr Clarke had the only explanation for Christ's divinity. Simson also said "That he is not an Arrian, but perfectly of the opinion of the Council of Nice."[93] He believed that the "Popish doctrine" of the Trinity should be "throwen off" as contrary to reason, just as the Reformers had abandoned the doctrine of transubstantiation as "contradictory to sense," in order to stimulate the counter-attack on deism and atheism.[94] Some caution seems necessary in accepting Wodrow's third-hand testi-mony, given his avid reception of anything tending to Simson's detri-ment. John Gray's knowledge of Simson's students must have come mainly from Andrew. Would Simson have made any theologically indis-creet comments in the presence of the son of his presbyterial arch-enemy, or was Andrew Gray retailing hearsay evidence to Wodrow? Much of what Simson was quoted as saying, however, could be interpreted in a perfectly orthodox sense by someone who was not looking for heresy. Just what he meant by "Throwing off" the "Popish doctrine" of the Trin-ity was never fully explained. From his later statements, he seems to have been trying to disentangle Trinitarian dogma from much of its scholas-tic accretions and to reconstruct a Nicean Trinity of persons with recip-rocal relationships, stated in language that came either from scripture

91 Wodrow, *Analecta*, 3:242.
92 Ibid.
93 Ibid., 3:245.
94 One of Andrew Gray's pieces of information may have been first hand, since he and William Wishart had been licensed in the same year and must have been acquainted. He told Wodrow that Wishart was worried about the effect of the publication of Simson's new beliefs on others and had obtained a promise from the professor to cease mentioning them in public. Ibid., 3:246.

or from patristic literature. That he found Samuel Clarke an inspiration in this effort was more than enough to damn him in the eyes of most of his countrymen.

Writing to Grange in late January 1726, Wodrow was concerned about the effect of "the melancholy accounts" of Simson's errors in Edinburgh, as well as in England and Ireland, fearing that they would place the Church of Scotland in a bad light. Simson had denied

> what his scholars report, and says he never taught any thing against our Confession; that he asserts the Son to be *Summus Deus*, the Supreme God, of the same substance with the Father; that he teaches his Proper Divinity and Eternity; and yet he owns in conversation that he does not think the Son's Independency, his Self-Existence, and Self-Origination, consistent with his being begotten. Inconstancy, and frequent changes in this foundation-article, are loudly charged upon him by his scholars. At first he taught ... the ordinary doctrine with much zeal; for the two last years he seemed almost Sabellian, and upon every turn censured Dr Clarke; and this winter, they say, he is gone in in [sic] several things to Dr Clarke's scheme.... and yet he still refutes the Doctor's ... notion as to God's nature, which he takes to be the foundation of all the Doctor's mistakes.[95]

Wodrow went on to speak of Simson's apparently dying condition, which had made many feel "that his disease had affected his head."[96] This illness had also held the Presbytery of Glasgow back from inquiring formally into the affair.

Matthew Crawford wrote to Wodrow from Edinburgh on 3 February asking for information to supplement the imperfect account that he had received both of the doings of Wishart and of "Mr Simson's affair."[97] In fact the powerful Edinburgh minister William Mitchell had been in correspondence with Principal Stirling about the prevalent gossip from the beginning of the year. On 11 January 1726 Mitchell told Stirling that he believed that the reports of Simson's having openly declared himself Arian were "wholly false & calumnious." Since these reports were being spread with great assurance, he begged Stirling to explain their origin.[98] Stirling responded to Mitchell, and Simson must have written to Professor Hamilton, since Mitchell's next letter mentioned that these missives

---

95 R. Wodrow to Lord Grange, 26 Jan. 1726, Wodrow *Correspondence*, 3:236.
96 Ibid.
97 Rev. Matthew Crawford (1683–1736) succeeded William Dunlop as professor of church history at Edinburgh University in 1721. M. Crawford to R. Wodrow, 3 Feb. 1716, NLS, Wodrow Letters Quarto, XII, 27.
98 W. Mitchell to J. Stirling, 11 Jan. 1726, GUL, MS Gen. 204, 133.

had been used to "putt a stop to the gross part of the reports concerning him, viz: his declaring openly for the Arrian doctrine." None the less, Mitchell was still worried and looked forward to discussing the matter with Stirling at the next commission meeting.[99]

The correspondence continued with two notes between Stirling and Simson. On reflection, Simson felt that the rumours had started with a misunderstanding by some students of his explanation of the words *supremus* or *summus deus* in Pictet. In class he had told them that "some writers understood of being of none or unbegotten in which sence it belonged only to the father but if understood of being the creator & sovereigne governor of the world it belonged also to the Son in which sence Pictet seemd to take it as all other writers who call the son the supreme God." He had said that certain modern writers used "self-existent" to mean being of none, in which sense it could apply only to the Father. However, he assured the students that there could not be more gods than one, either co-ordinate or subordinate.[100] These letters from Glasgow allowed Hamilton to announce in March that the clamour in Edinburgh about Simson had quietened.[101]

Rumours persisted throughout the winter of 1725–26 that Simson had made unguarded remarks about the Trinity while teaching. Wodrow heard that Principal Stirling and Mr Hamilton had spoken to Simson about this and that he had admitted to some agreement with Clarke. However, he had denied teaching contrary to the Westminster Confession, assuring them that if he had wanted to do so he would have laid the matter before the presbytery. When he was told that the confession declared the persons of the Trinity to be the same in substance and nature, "he ouns they are of the same nature, and that the same substance is not to be understood of the numericall substance, which was the opinion of the Counsell of Nice."[102]

In early February 1726, John Hamilton intended to take the Simson question to the presbytery. Simson's continued sickness, however, caused him to delay.[103] Then, in Simson's words, "Upon the sixteenth *February* 1726, when Professor *Simson* was so very ill of an Indisposition, which had lasted a Year and a half, that his Life was almost despaired of,

99　W. Mitchell to J. Stirling, 22 Feb. 1626, ibid., 134.

100　J. Simson to J. Stirling, n.d., ibid., 135. This letter is difficult to read. Murray was unable to decipher the word Pictet.

101　W. Hamilton to J. Stirling, 15 March 1726, ibid., 138.

102　Wodrow, *Analecta*, 3:253–4.

103　Ibid., 3:261.

as was generally known at *Glasgow*, Mr. *Charles Coats*, Minister at *Govan, without first speaking to the Professor himself*, represented to the Presbytery, That he had heard, that Professor *Simson* had taught several Errors that Winter concerning the Doctrine of the *Holy Trinity*, to whose Information some Particulars were (said to have been) added by some other Members."[104] Here Simson was referring to the procedure laid down in the *Form of Process*. The correct order of action demanded that the accuser first speak to the minister in question and then that the alleged errors should be considered by some of the more prudent ministers and elders in the presbytery. From the beginning, Simson was conscious that the process against him was being improperly conducted.

The published official *Case* merely states that the Presbytery of Glasgow received a report that Professor Simson

hath taught erroneous Doctrine with Respect to the *Blessed Trinity*; particularly, that *Christus est verus, non summus deus, non est aequalis Patri, non est ens necessarium vel independens*; and that he refuted *Pictet*'s Arguments for the Equality of the Son with the Father; That in speaking about the title in *Pictet*'s Book, in the Chapter about Christ's being *summus Deus aequalis Patri*, he said it was to be understood, *Cum grano salis*; That disowned Christ's Self-existence; That in speaking upon *John* xvii.3. He said there was a Sense in which the words (*The only True God*) could not be applied to the Son, but only to the Father.[105]

The members resolved that "four or five queryes" should be written to Simson for delivery by the current moderator, Love, along with Scott and McLaurin.[106] The reason for this step seems to have been a desire to have an answer ready should the approaching synod ask any questions about Simson. The presbytery wanted to know what the professor had taught during the past session on the matters mentioned in the report. Wodrow's friends told him that Simson inquired who had raised the matter in the presbytery, "insinuating that he would prosecut them for slander."[107]

The approach by the presbytery gave Simson a new attack of the flux. Nevertheless he promised to give answers in writing by the first Wednesday in March. In Simson's own version of events, while "under the Tryal

104 Simson, *Case*, xi.
105 Dundas, *Processes*, 14.
106 Wodrow, *Analecta*, 3:273–4.
107 Ibid., 3:274.

of a new Medicine (all former ones having proved unsuccessful)," he sent a message to the committee of the presbytery that, although he was too ill to meet them, he would answer any charges "according to the Rules of the church," should he recover "any Measure of Health."[108] He noted, however, that the presbytery members were not following the *Form of Process*. Had they done so, they would have first inquired into whether a *fama clamosa* existed and how it had arisen. Simson also claimed that John Scott had come to him privately to say that he opposed the actions of the presbytery as being "apter to make Mistakes than remove them."[109]

At the presbytery meeting on 2 March the three emissaries reported that they had seen Simson, who was still ill, and that he had promised answers. From his sickbed the professor sent an extremely long letter of explanation, which he asked be read to the assembled presbytery, including the students who normally attended as onlookers.[110] This request may be construed in at least two ways. Simson could have been utterly open in wishing his students to hear exactly what he considered himself to be teaching. If they agreed with his words, they could support him fully, while if they interpreted his lessons differently, they could tell the presbytery their understanding.[111] On a more disingenuous level, it could be suggested that Simson wished his scholars to hear his official explanation so that if they desired they could match their testimonies to his. Just as the Marrow men had taken care with their responses, so Simson meticulously explained his teaching and stated his case. He presumably intended his long and detailed explanation to scotch the gossip once and for all.

---

108 Simson, *Case*, xiii. A 1741 recipe for treatment of the bloody flux called for 1 tablespoon of cochineal, bruised fine; ½ ounce of cinnamon; 3 ounces of loaf sugar; and a "pottle" of spring water. The reader was to bring the mixture to the boil over a slow fire and boil it, stirring, until it was reduced to three pints. The patient should drink ½ pint while it was warm and the rest one gill at a time, warm, as a "common drink." When the flux had ceased, and only stomach pain remained, the patient was to take 1–2 spoonfuls of "Daffy's Elixir" or, in its absence, a spoonful of syrup of rhubarb. Dietary instructions called for rice and milk, flour and milk, bread and milk, and poached eggs. The patient could drink warm whey but was not to consume broth or flesh. *Scots Magazine* (March 1741), 134.

109 Simson, *Case*, xiii.

110 Dundas, *Processes*, 14–21.

111 Wodrow stated that Simson asked the presbytery to read the letter "before his students, that they might see and knou that what was conteaned in it was the very thing he taught them." Wodrow, *Analecta*, 3:276.

Unfortunately for John Simson, his letter had quite the opposite effect, leading directly to the libel against him and his eventual suspension from ecclesiastical office. From this date on, the various issues of the day united in the person of Simson. First, the hyper-Calvinists returned from pursuing Antinomianism to a renewed war on rational theology and modern dogmatic interpretation. Second, the methods by which the church handled the Simson case raised anew the question of liberty of conscience and subscription to creeds. Lastly, the question of the conflicting rights of academics, politicians, and clergymen to choose university professors and determine the doctrine taught was reopened for discussion.

Part Four   Simson's Second Case and After

10

A *Crime Deeper than Crimson*:
From Letter to Suspension, 1726–1727

Convinced that his choice of terminology could be justified, Simson was not intimidated by the attacks on his orthodoxy, but he was disturbed by the threat to his work. He was not prepared to deny the importance of reason or to use an archaic scholastic vocabulary. He told his colleagues that he took "Care to keep closs by the Expressions used in Scripture and our *Confession*, being sensible of the Danger of essaying to be wise above what is written, in teaching a Doctrine so far above our Comprehension, and which we can know nothing of by the Light of Nature."[1]

The enigmatic voice of John Simson rings through the letter read to the Presbytery of Glasgow on 2 March 1726. Its opening paragraph displayed his characteristic blend of piety, self-confidence, assurance of orthodoxy, and impatience with criticism, as he complained of his "uneasiness" at being "deprived of the Comfort and Advantage of attending your Meetings ... thro' bodily Indisposition, wherewith a Holy and Righteous GOD has thought fit to exercise me." While God had granted him periods of relief from his discomfort, man had been less generous, contributing to his afflictions with a "Load of Calumny thrown upon me by false Reports ... of my having taught Heresy or gross Errors, concerning the Doctrine of the Holy Trinity," which could have been "long since wip'd off, Had I been in ordinary Health, and able to attend your Meetings."[2]

1 Dundas, *Processes*, 18.
2 Ibid., 15.

Simson proceeded to review how he had taught the doctrine of God and the Trinity from the Westminster Confession, distinguishing the true God from false deities by His attributes as eternal, omnipotent Creator. He had refuted the anti-Trinitarian views of Samuel Clarke about God's nature using texts such as John 1:1, 3, 10. Here his intention was presumably to emphasize the unity of the Father and the Son, using biblical rather than scholastic expressions. Simson had proved the singularity of God by nature and by revelation, noting that in the unity of the Godhead, there were three persons, distinguished by personal properties, the nature of which equally proved the separation of the persons and the oneness of the Godhead. Further charges against him stemmed from his teaching on the incommunicability of the personal properties of the three persons, when he had stated that the words of the Westminster Confession best expressed the doctrine of the church:

For the Father is of None, neither begotten nor proceeding, and begets the Son; the Son is eternally begotten of the Father; the Holy Ghost eternally proceeding from the Father and the Son: And the Property of each Person is incommunicable to any of the other two, as is owned by all sound Divines ... The personal Property of the Father cannot be truly affirmed of the Son ... for it would be the same as to say, The Son is of *None*, he is not begotten of the Father, but begets the Father: Which manifestly contradicts the express Words of our Confession, and of the *Holy Scriptures*.... The same holds true of the personal Properties of the Son and Holy Ghost. I also by the way took Notice, That the Father's being of *None*, is the same that many Authors understand by being *Self-existent*, taken, not absurdly, in the positive Sense, but in the *Negative* meaning, That he has his *Being* and godhead *of* None; so that he has not only Life in himself, but has it from no other Person or *Being* whatsoever.[3]

Simson denied being a tritheist – Father, Son, and Holy Ghost share the same divinity, with their personal properties making them distinct persons. As a result, "I think it evident, That the Son and Holy Ghost must needs be one God with the Father, and also Persons distinct from him, and likewise that these *Properties* are the Foundation of their mutual Relations, and of the Order of their *Being* and *Working*."[4] As well as refuting Sabellianism and Arianism, Simson taught that the Westminster Confession and the Nicene Creed were compatible, recommending

3 Ibid., 17.
4 Ibid., 17–18.

that his scholars read Bishop Pearson's *Exposition of the Creed* (1659 – Simson used the fourth edition). He ended this clarification of his teaching by saying that in their essential perfections the three persons were equal, though distinguished by personal properties, and that scripture ascribed to all three the same names, attributes, and worship.

In his letter, Simson tried to respond individually to the specific statements of which he was accused. He admitted that when discussing Pictet's text "Christus est summus Deus" (Christ is the most high God), he might have said that it should be understood "cum grano salis" (with a grain of salt), since he often used this phrase "when a Term is not to be taken in the greatest Latitude, wherein it is used by some Authors."[5] Here he intended to caution the students that if one took the phrase *summus Deus* to include the Father's personal property, one could not then properly use it of the Son. It could, however, be correctly affirmed of the Son when taken to mean all other properties of the Godhead, such as creation and government. Simson flatly denied that he had ever said "Filius non est equalis Patri" (The Son is not equal to the Father).[6] He cited Athanasius, as well as Pearson, and Bishop George Bull's *Defensio Fidei Nicaenae* (1685 – Bull argued that the teaching of post-Nicene orthodox divines conformed to that of the pre-Nicene church fathers) to support his interpretation of John 16:3, "the only true God" as not being applicable to the Son in the particular sense that includes the Father's personal property, and in that sense only.

Disavowing the use of terms such as "Christus non est ens necessarium" (Christ is not a necessary being) and "Independens," Simson pointed out that his vocabulary was that of the theological system that he taught, the Bible, and the Westminster Confession. When a student brought up the words "dependent" and "independent" in class, Simson responded,

That the Words *Dependent* and *Independent, Co-ordinate* and *Subordinate,* were never in Scripture or our *Confession of Faith* applied to the *personal Properties* and Relations of the Divine Persons, nor could we pertinently and safely apply them so, because they are ordinarily used with Respect to Creatures, in a Sense not applicable to the Persons of the Glorious *Godhead*; yet all are agreed, that if the Words *Independent* and *Necessarily-existent,* be taken in a Sense that includes the *personal Property* of the Father, they cannot be applied to the Son; but if said of

5 Ibid., 19.
6 Ibid.

him in any Sense consistent with the *personal Properties* of the Father and the Son, they will no doubt agree to him.[7]

The professor ended his letter with the assertion that he believed himself to have been maligned. If Simson hoped that the presbytery would approve his explanation and forget the matter, he was overly sanguine. Instead, to his distress, his letter was tabled until his health should permit him to attend a meeting personally. Regrettably, Simson was "threatned with a return of his loosnes" on 23 March, when the presbytery next met, and in his absence his letter was tabled once more.[8]

During these critical weeks, Simson seems to have discussed his theological ideas candidly with his friends. Wodrow heard that he had made several statements that the orthodox considered wild. In conversation with Gershom Carmichael, Simson was reported to have said that "the Council of Nice understood that the same in substance was to be taken of the same kind of nature, the same species, and not the same numericall substance."[9] Simson was correct in his belief that the early church had had problems defining the intra-Trinitarian relationship. Justin Martyr (c. 100–c. 165) felt that the Logos was "a second God in number."[10] Tertullian (c. 160–c. 225), writing against modalism, devised the Latin formula of the Trinity consisting of three persons of one substance. In the Eastern church, however, writers such as Origen (c. 182–c. 251) used the word *hypostasis* where the Latin writers used *persona*. The Greek word bore a wider range of meaning than the Latin; to Origen it allowed a numerical distinction in the persons of the Father, Son, and Spirit.

The Council of Nicaea, called in 325 to settle the problems raised by Arius, used the word *homooúsios* to mean "of one substance." The ambiguities of this word have led one modern scholar to comment, "It might have meant that the Son and Father were precisely the same being, or else it might have meant that they were the same sort of being. Probably the latter was meant, since the former is modalist and the latter good enough to rout Arius."[11] He also noted the use of such images as rays from the sun and twigs from the branch to express the Son's relation to the Father. Echoing Tertullian, Simson feared that his co-religionists

7 Ibid., 19–20.

8 Wodrow, *Analecta*, 3:279.

9 Ibid., 3:277.

10 Justin Martyr, *Dialogus contra Tryphomen*, 128.4. Quoted in *International Standard Biblical Encyclopedia*, "Trinity," 4:918.

11 C. Plantinga Jr, in *International Standard Biblical Encyclopedia*, 4:918.

were verging on modalism. He was probably explaining this view to Carmichael within a sympathetic circle of friends that included the Wishart brothers, William and George.

Wodrow, however, felt that Simson was now concealing much of his opinion from the presbytery.[12] The apparent contradiction between Wodrow's narration of open comments by Simson to his colleagues and his belief that the professor was prevaricating to his fellow ministers may reflect both Simson's fear that the presbytery's charges were personally motivated and the fact that he was not well. Simson was now almost sixty, and his indisposition had prevented him from teaching regularly for months. His ailment was debilitating physically and must have left some mark on his temperament, if not on his mind. He probably considered that, although the conclusions to which his researches had led him were entirely consistent with the most ancient Christian traditions, it might be wiser to withhold them from the more zealous of his brethren in the Presbytery of Glasgow.

Academic action on the Simson problem was ruled out at about this time. Glasgow University had considered making its own determination about the orthodoxy of its divinity professor, with the *Facultas Theologica*, comprising Principal Stirling and the dean of faculty, John Hamilton, acting as judges. This scheme fell through when it was learned that Carmichael, and possibly the other regents, had the right to judge along with the theologians. Stirling, reluctant to create a precedent for the philosophy professors ruling on the doctrine of a professor of divinity, chose to do nothing.[13] He may also have felt that the politically divided masters might use this opportunity to strike at him through his ally, Simson. While Stirling's inability to create unity within his faculty meant that he could not use internal university action to save his relative, it is unlikely that any academic finding would have silenced the calls of the zealots to remove Simson from contact with students.

When the Synod of Glasgow and Ayr met on 4 April, William Wishart was the only Glasgow member present to give the moderator the papers dealing with the Simson case and make a brief verbal report.[14] Attendance by Glasgow ministers at meetings held in Ayr was generally poor,

12 Wodrow, *Analecta*, 3:277.
13 Ibid., 3:279.
14 NAS, CH2/464/3, 180.

but this figure was unusually low.[15] The sole Glasgow member was a friend of Simson's, suggesting a calculated absence by Glasgow ministers to prevent the synod from taking action. Simson certainly saw these weeks of deferral of consideration of his letter as a deliberate attempt to force the whole matter into the national arena at the General Assembly. There had been eight weeks in which to deal with the matter in Glasgow, during which postponements of discussion were "industriously made."[16] Simson later implied that the Presbytery of Glasgow avoided dealing with his letter of 2 March but made sure that its details became public. Since his supposedly erroneous teaching had taken place in late 1725, it could hardly be the result of chance that by early spring 1726 other presbyteries were forming instructions to the assembly asking for an inquiry.

The complex system of review in the Church of Scotland entailed the frequent public washing of dirty linen. Webster's charges of 1714 against Simson became known when the Synod of Lothian and Tweeddale examined the Presbytery of Edinburgh's record book and required that the accusations against the Glasgow professor be pursued in the proper place. Once the new allegations of 1726 became general knowledge, the chance of resolving the matter quietly in Glasgow was lost. The delays, combined with the presbytery's instructions, meant that the question of Simson's teaching would reach the floor of the General Assembly in May.

THE GENERAL ASSEMBLY STRIKES A COMMITTEE

Hugh Campbell, 3rd Earl of Loudoun, royal commissioner to the General Assembly of May 1726, may have travelled north with instructions to support William Mitchell as moderator. In late March, Lord Milton had heard that Mitchell had abandoned the Squadrone, while Professor Hamilton, the other candidate for the moderatorship, had not.[17] As usual, politicians were active behind the scenes, as we know from Grange's notes of conversations with Loudoun and Islay about getting "things prepar'd to go right."[18] In the event, after a close election, Mitchell became moderator.

Prior to each assembly, the various presbyteries drew up lists of their instructions to their commissioners, which were sent to the committee

---

15 See Wodrow, *Analecta*, 3:149.
16 Simson, *Case*, xiv.
17 NLS, MS 16533/80, 183.
18 NLS, MS 1008, 19.

of instructions. The committee created a two-week timetable to include all important administrative business and allow consideration of the most common concerns. In 1726 six presbyteries asked their representatives to demand action about Simson's teaching and the "hazard of error and refined Arianism."[19] They were all in the east, north of the Forth, and included areas influenced by Hogg and the Erskines: Coupar, Deer, Dundee, Ellon, Kirkcaldy, and Perth. A subcommittee considered the Simson affair, recommending that the Presbytery of Glasgow, with help from an assembly committee, deal with the matter.[20]

This plan met opposition in the committee of instructions, some of whose members felt that the regular judicial procedure of the church was adequate. Eventually the arguments of those who called for a special committee prevailed, since the local presbytery and synod did not wish to bear the total burden, and the advice of other divinity professors and senior clerics would be valuable. Simson noted later that although the Glasgow commissioners to the assembly had no instructions to have the matter raised, "yet it is well known how diligent they were in private to persuade the Members of Assembly of the Necessity of a Committee to assist them."[21] He blamed Coats for personal attacks in the subcommittee, pointing out the danger of allowing public assaults on a man's reputation in his absence, a practice contrary to the *Form of Process*. Presumably the ruling powers in the church wanted to send the matter back to Glasgow for quiet resolution, but the "hott brethren" were determined that the issue should have a wider airing.

When the full assembly on 12 May 1726 approved formation of a special Committee for Purity of Doctrine to assist the Presbytery of Glasgow, Simson had been stricken with a recurrence of his illness, so his brother Matthew conveyed his assurances of orthodoxy and obedience to the commands of the assembly. A few days later Wodrow commented to his wife that Grange and Col. Erskine, "who are now upon the Commissioner's, and shall I call it the Court side" (Islay's side), had managed to calm upset tempers over another matter.[22] Presumably in the matter of the committee they were equally active. The committee's twenty-six members comprised a cross-section of the membership of the church:

19 Wodrow, *Correspondence*, 3:242–3.

20 This committee comprised Moderator Mitchell; Principals Haddow, Chalmers, and Wishart; Professor Hamilton; Revs. J. Alston, A. Logan, and R. Wodrow; the commissioners from the presbyteries of Ellon, Glasgow, and Perth; and Lord Grange. Ibid., 3:243.

21 Simson, *Case*, xv.

22 Wodrow, *Correspondence*, 3:256.

William Mitchell, Edinburgh; Principal James Hadow, New College, St Andrews University; Allan Logan, Culross; Principal William Wishart, Edinburgh University; William Hamilton, professor of divinity, Edinburgh University; James Craig, Edinburgh; James Ballantyne, Edinburgh; James Smith, Cramond; James Alston, Dirleton; William M'George, Penicuik; John Brand, Borrowstounness; Michael Potter, Kippen; John Hunter, Ayr; Hugh Fauside, Loudoun; Robert Wodrow, Eastwood; Thomas Linning, Lesmahago; John Curry, Old Monkland; and James Bane, Bonhill, ministers; Rt Hon. Sir Hugh Dalrymple of North Berwick, lord president of the session; Adam Cockburn of Ormistoun, lord justice-clerk; Mr James Erskine of Grange, Mr James Hamilton of Pencaitland, and Sir Walter Pringle of Newhall, senators of the College of Justice; and Sir James Steuart of Goodtrees and Mr Robert Dundas of Arniston, younger, ruling elders. A quorum was to be thirteen, of whom nine must be ministers.[23]

The assembly's act instructed the Presbytery of Glasgow to investigate Simson's opinions on the doctrine of the Trinity, particularly the passages about it in his letter or in any other of his writings and in his public teaching; it was also to consider whether he had obeyed the ruling of the General Assembly of 1717, and should it "suspect him to be unsound in any other Article of our Confession of Faith, they shall likewise make Inquiry into his Opinion and Sentiments concerning the same."[24] Simson and his supporters rightly feared that this act countenanced a full-scale interrogation of the professor, which had no justification according to the rules laid down in the *Form of Process*.

The actual charge to the Committee for Purity of Doctrine was worded differently. It prevented the committee from passing any judgment, appointing it to "prepare this Affair by all proper Ways of Inquiry" and to make its report to the next General Assembly. The presbytery and committee were warned not "to insist" on any article not contained in "the Word of God, the Confession of Faith, and Larger and Shorter Catechisms of this Church."[25] This proviso seems to have been designed to permit the investigators to circumvent the act and accept Simson's teaching as orthodox. It would allow them to avoid dealing with the doctrinal issues raised by the non-biblical terminology that Simson had refused to use.

23 Dundas, *Processes*, 21–2.
24 Ibid.
25 Ibid., 23.

As events proved, the hyper-Calvinist faction was unwilling to abide by this limitation. Perhaps foreseeing this eventuality, Simson declared the assembly's decision "hard, and an inquisition."[26] He had many friends, however, and Grange commented that they were already trying to "sense" Simson's letter to the presbytery in an acceptable way. Unimpressed by the exertions of the Simson camp, Grange damned their efforts, "Such sensing I take to be the art of teaching heresy orthodoxly."[27] His memoirs give a glimpse of how difficult it must have been to reach any consensus, mentioning the "Partyship, evil-speaking & many other things wch this Assembly gave me occasion to reflect upon."[28]

THE COMMITTEE AND ITS QUESTIONS

The committee met immediately after the assembly ended, but with the approach of summer it took little action. In late May, Simson took a country trip for his health, while "in June most of the ministers of Glasgow were out of town at the goat-milk."[29] In August the presbytery approved six draft questions (composed largely by Gray and Hamilton) to put to Simson, with the hope of discussing his response at the September meeting:[30]

1mo, Whether are there Three distinct Substances in the Three Persons of the God-head, or is it one and the same Numerical Substance that is in them all?

2do, Whether is the Son Necessarily-existent, in the ordinary Sense of the Word, so that it is impossible that he should not have been?

3tio, Whether is the Deity of the Son and Holy Ghost Self-existent and Independent?

4to, Is this Title, THE MOST HIGH GOD, in the highest Sense, used in Scripture due to Christ, as he is God?

5to, Whether is it agreeable to Scripture and the Confession of Faith, to ascribe to the Father that Title, THE ONLY TRUE GOD, in such a Sense, as it cannot be affirmed of the Son and Holy Ghost?

6to, The Presbytery desires to know, why the Professor, in teaching the Doctrine of the Trinity, has not mentioned the Terms, INDEPENDENT, DEPENDENT and SUBORDINATE, seeing Adversaries of the Truth assert the Dependence of

26 Wodrow, *Correspondence*, 3:260.
27 Ibid., 3:261.
28 NLS, MS 1008, 19.
29 R. Wodrow to Lord Grange, 19 July 1726, Wodrow, *Correspondence*, 3:266.
30 Wodrow, *Analecta*, 3:322.

the Son, and his Subordination, as to his Divinity, to the Father. And there seems to be as much need as ever to caution Students against this Subordination and Dependence?[31]

By these questions the presbytery showed that it planned to make the full inquiry that the assembly's act authorized. It also demonstrated that it had no intention of following the assembly's directions to restrict its usage to the language of the Bible and the Westminster documents, thus rendering any meaningful response from Simson unlikely.

During the summer of 1726 the Argathelians were consolidating their gains over the Squadrone in Scotland. It was rumoured that a visitation of Glasgow University was designed as a party attack on Principal Stirling.[32] In such circumstances, Simson needed to forge new alliances. Fighting for his career and his livelihood, he was prepared to use whatever means came to hand. Observant of the political scene, Simson may have felt that assisting the Argathelians in Glasgow would win him support against the presbytery. The Argyll faction needed men who would be pliant agents for use in ecclesiastical management. Looking for ministers with whom they could work, Islay and Milton were beginning to realize that this eliminated the "hott brethren," despite the traditional Argathelian sympathies of the church's evangelical wing. Signs in Edinburgh indicated increased political activity in church and university affairs. In July it was reported when the duke heard George Wishart preach, he instructed the Argathelian provost, George Drummond, to abstain from his previous support of a call to "Mr. Jardine" from the Edinburgh West Kirk.[33] Whether Argyll appreciated his sermon or, more likely, believed that this was a moderate man who understood political exigencies, Wishart received the call. Edinburgh's divinity professor was in disgrace; Islay had written to Milton in May, "Professor Hamilton will soon pay the price of his late impertinence."[34] Wodrow explained Hamilton's dismissal as royal almoner as stemming from his

31 Dundas, *Processes*, 24.

32 T. Mack to R. Wodrow, 18 Sept. 1726, NLS, Wodrow Letters Quarto, XVII, 146r.

33 The Jardine in question may have been Robert, minister of Glencairn and later of Lochmaben, who was the father of the better-known Moderate minister John Jardine. W. Stewart to R. Wodrow, 14 July 1726, ibid., 113–5.

34 Islay to Lord Milton, 14 May 1726, NLS, MS 16533/80. The penalty turned out to be the loss of his royal chaplaincy in September 1726. Islay to Lord Milton, 6 Sept. 1726, ibid., 132. By the following year Hamilton had been forgiven, and his chaplaincy was restored. Islay to Lord Milton, 26 Oct. 1727, ibid., 124.

accepting the nomination for the moderatorship at the last assembly, when the court was in favour of the Argathelian Mitchell.[35]

Searching for health and allies, Simson spent part of the summer in Ayrshire, where he recovered enough to ride twenty miles a day.[36] In September he visited Edinburgh, where he "made deep Impressions of his Orthodoxy upon several Considerable ministers," although these supporters worried about "his too great forwardnes, and want of due Caution in his manner of Expression," fearing that reaction to Simson might lead to demands for more explicit standards of subscription, including "new Coined words."[37] Simson persuaded many that the whole prosecution was based on malice arising from disagreements between himself and Gray. Whatever the original source of the rift between them, by now politics must have entered into it. Gray remained a Squadrone man, and the Graham family rewarded him for his loyalty by bestowing church presentations on his son. Simson, however, "affected much to be what they call an Argathelian, and said he was never upon the Squad side, as it's called; that still he had the highest regard for the family of Argyle, and endeavoured to gain my L[ord] Grange and the Provest of Edinburgh, by assurances he was still upon their side."[38] Influential in ecclesiastical affairs, Provost Drummond and Grange were worth cultivating, but where doctrine was concerned, Simson made little headway with Grange. While in Edinburgh, Simson was also rumoured to have been "much with my Lord Isla."[39] The professor's tactics were to impress his doctrinal soundness on his hearers, while stressing his family's traditional Argathelian loyalty.

When Simson studied the committee's six queries on his return to Glasgow at the end of September or early October, he must have felt his worst fears realized.[40] It was "impossible to reconcile" these questions

35 Wodrow deplored this infusion of state management into church affairs. He also commented that although the chaplaincies were sinecures, the post of almoner was onerous, and "not very desirable." Wodrow, *Analecta*, 3:320–2.

36 Ibid., 3:322. Wodrow noted later that in Ayrshire young students were meeting regularly to confirm each other in non-subscribing principles "and loosnes in other points." He was sure that this resulted from "Mr Simsons libertys that he gives and teaches his scholars." Ibid., 3:337.

37 J. Williamson to R. Wodrow, 13 April 1727, NLS, Wodrow Letters Quarto, XVII, 242.

38 Before the Glasgow council elections of 1725, Gray had preached a sermon "On the Evil of Parties," in which he had claimed that parties obstructed justice in Scotland. Wodrow, *Analecta*, 3:324.

39 Ibid., 3:337.

40 For dates, see ibid., 3: 324, and Simson, *Case*, xvi–xvii.

with the "express Words of the Act" of the General Assembly of 1726, which called for the committee "to proceed by all proper Ways of Inquiry" – the methods laid down in the *Form of Process*. More significantly, the committee and presbytery had been instructed not to insist on any articles not contained in the Bible, confession, or catechisms, "which everyone may see the Presbytery's Questions are not, the Terms of them not being therein mentioned."[41] The presbytery was following conservative Scottish practice in dealing with doctrinal inquiries. William Dunlop wrote: "[T]he principal things which any society will require in their publick teachers, respect his *practice*, and his *faith*; his *practice*, that it be suitable for the designs of his work ... and for this end they may use all proper means to attain a just character of him, and sufficient information of the manner of his life."[42] To a Scot versed in civil and ecclesiastical law, "proper means" included questions. Simson and others were suggesting that these methods were no longer appropriate. His indignation about the presbytery's disobedience was entirely justified and seems to have been shared by many, since "a great outcry is made against the Presbytery for them."[43]

In his preface to the 1727 edition of the *Case*, Simson discussed some of his doubts about answering the Presbytery of Glasgow's questions. To begin with, any action against a minister should follow the rules of the *Form of Process* and any other directions set by judicatories. Second, it should not demand the disclosure of private opinion. Third, inquiry by questions had problematic aspects, since the answers to one set of queries could lead to a further inquisition, "and so on without any End or Limitation that he could perceive."[44] When queries concerned matters of which the orthodoxy had never been formally determined, there could be conflicting opinions as to the correct doctrine. Simson concluded that "to answer such Queries, were very dangerous for a Professor, of whose Errors so many *Surmises* and *Reports* had arisen ... [which] had made no small Impression on the Minds of many People."[45] These doubts made it inappropriate for him to claim any authority on doctrinal points about which his church had no established position. The demand that he should answer questions was an infringement of the individual liberty promised to all by law.

41 Simson, *Case*, xvi.
42 [William Dunlop], *Preface*, 71.
43 Wodrow, *Analecta*, 3:322.
44 Simson, *Case*, vi.
45 Ibid., vii.

When Simson chose not to respond to the queries until his objections to their congruency with assembly directions had been studied, he acted against the advice of Mitchell, who had warned him to ignore the issue of liberty and to "answer all the questions discreetly, and in the termes agreable to our Standarts, the Scripture and Confession; and if you have taught otherwise acknouledge it, and promise amendment, and then we may support you; otherwise we cannot!"[46] In his decision to ignore this practical counsel, Simson may have been influenced by Edinburgh dignitaries as well as by William Wishart, Jr, who was reported to have dissented from the procedure of the Presbytery of Glasgow in September on the grounds that the queries were "against the Claim of Right and the liberty of the subject," "against the rulcs of Christ and his practise," and "an Inquisition."[47]

This language corresponded with that used by Simson in his appeal to Edinburgh church leaders to oppose the investigations that were being made against him because they "wer against human liberty."[48] Wishart was believed to have consulted with Telfer, Wallace, and Patrick Cumming (1695–1776), minister of Lochmaben, at that favourite clerical watering-place, Moffat. These young men were all Edinburgh graduates who had belonged to the Rankenian Club, where they had discussed politics, religion, and philosophy with youthful radicalism. Cumming later was closely associated with Islay in the management of the church. Commenting on Wishart's intervention, Wodrow felt that "he, and some others with him, expect a greater backing then I hope they have in this Church, otherwise they would scarce be so bold and insolent as they are."[49] His words imply that Wodrow believed that these young men had the assurance of Argathelian political support for their actions.

Over the next year, Simson came to appreciate that by his refusal to respond to the Glasgow presbytery's queries he had sabotaged his own defence in the eyes of the undecided majority of his countrymen. To one commentator it seemed, "Were he truly *sound*; he would look on it rather as a *Favour*, than a *Hardship*, in his Circumstances; seeing, thereby, he hath a fair Opportunity of satisfying the World of his *Orthodoxy*."[50] Just as it was assumed that when Irish non-subscribers refused to endorse

46 Wodrow, *Analecta*, 3:325.
47 Ibid., 3:338 and 3:325.
48 Ibid., 3:324.
49 Ibid., 3:326.
50 [Williamson], *Remarks*, 39–40.

creeds and confessions of human composition they must disagree with the tenets of those creeds, so when Simson refused to answer questions it was assumed that he was unable to do so in an orthodox way. As Simson correctly recalled: "This declining however to give a ready Answer to those Questions, had very bad Consequences with Respect to himself; and many think it was an unlucky or imprudent Step in Matter of Conduct, whatever Grounds he had for it in Matter of Law, or the Merits of the Question itself: For by Means of this the Jealousies [apprehensions] and Suspicions that had been conceived were confirmed and increased; and many People so far mistook the Professor, as to imagine that he declined to answer these Questions, as not daring to declare his real Sentiments upon the Subject of them."[51]

Nevertheless, Simson's reluctance to respond received considerable public support in educated society. The Glasgow minister Andrew Tait told Wodrow in early 1727 that he had conversed with people of all ranks who "have drunk in a notion that it is contrary to Liberty and our form of process" to force Simson to reply to queries.[52] Similar impressions of the feelings of secular society were expressed by Mr ML [McLaren?] in March and by John Williamson in April.[53]

Instead of giving direct answers, from his sickbed Simson wrote to the presbytery on 12 October 1726, summarizing the events that had transpired since the previous February. He noted that he had received no reply to his letter of 2 March, "nor have I heard so much as by Report, that you have found Fault with any Proposition in it."[54] Referring to the six questions, he said that he felt that he had dealt with the sixth in his March letter, while the others seemed to have no relation to his letter or his teaching. He reiterated his adherence to the Confession of Faith, declaring that he found the words of the Westminster Assembly more fitting to express his beliefs about the doctrine of the Trinity than those of the questions. Having missed almost two years of presbytery meetings through illness, he could not follow the reasoning behind the queries. If it referred to something other than the doctrine contained in the confession, he did not understand his involvement, unless "it were

51 Simson, *Case*, vii–viii.
52 A. Tait to R. Wodrow, 23 Feb. 1727, NLS, Wodrow Letters Quarto, XVII, 211.
53 Mr. ML to R. Wodrow, 10 March 1727, ibid., 220. J. Williamson to R. Wodrow, 13 April 1727, ibid., 242.
54 Dundas, *Processes*, 25.

to have my assistance in determining some new Articles of Faith."[55] He ended by stating that he planned to wait for an explanation for the questions before making any reply, to avoid further misunderstandings.

With better judgment, Simson would have deleted his sarcastic comment about new articles; by the next year he was admitting its foolishness. This letter demonstrated his usual curious mixture of political astuteness and indiscreet language. The shrewdness with which Simson dealt with the eighteenth-century world of interest and influence seemed to desert him when he faced church judicatories. His intellectual arrogance and his fatal ability to find retorts to use against those whom he saw as inferiors proved a trial to his supporters. While in much of the letter he made his points effectively and might have set the presbytery on the defensive, with a few words he gave his foes a breach through which to attack. While to Wodrow the letter "appears childish, trifling, and rather the banter of a desparat person than a grave man,"[56] it left the presbytery unsure as to how to proceed, beyond informing the Committee for Purity of Doctrine where matters stood.

In better health by the time of November's presbytery meeting, Simson counter-queried with four questions of his own: whether the Presbytery of Glasgow felt itself empowered by the assembly's act to demand his private thoughts on points of doctrine; whether its questions were contained in the Bible, Westminster Confession, and catechisms; if so, where they might be found; and finally, what relation the questions had to Simson's letter of 2 March, or to anything else hc had vented or taught? Once more the presbytery's members were unable to agree how to treat the difficult professor. Principal Stirling and John Hamilton exhorted Simson to answer their questions. Wishart and Ruling Elder John Orr supported his refusal.[57] They compromised by writing to Mitchell, as moderator of the Committee for Purity of Doctrine, that it was "our Earnest Desire that the Rev[eren]d Committee may give us plain directions what further steps we are to take in this affair."[58] Although the official documents of the case make no mention of Glasgow politics, the resentment of the Squadrone over the Argathelian attempts to control the town must have influenced the Glasgow ministers. Since

55 Ibid., 26.
56 Wodrow, *Analecta*, 3:338.
57 Ibid., 3:342.
58 NLS, CH1/2/56, 24.

Simson was moving in the direction of Islay, their convictions of his heterodoxy may have been strengthened by their eagerness to diminish Argyll's power in Glasgow. It is equally likely that Mitchell and his Edinburgh friends were in no hurry to assist their Glasgow colleagues.

A reported conversation with his defender, Orr, gives us a glimpse of Simson's state of mind, "I could find a way to give such answers to the Presbitry as would very much satisfy them; but I will not, for I knou a handle will be made of my answers, and forsee the next Assembly will run me doun and depose me; and I will let them run on; and though they condemn me, it shall be without convicting of me."[59] His poor health must have affected his mood, depressed as he was by belief in personal malice on the part of Coats and Gray and by fear of conviction through any word that he might let slip. The contradiction between his statement that he could satisfy the presbytery and his anxiety lest his words be used against him may be explained by the way Webster had misused his written answers.

In a letter of 7 November to the Committee for Purity of Doctrine, Simson represented himself as having approached the Presbytery of Glasgow in a "most inoffensive and modest Way" and suggested that its method was contrary to the intention of the last assembly. He exposed the proceedings against him as being in conformity with neither the *Form of Process* nor the Claim of Right and compared them to "the most mischievous Engines of Popery."[60] Unless proved guilty of error, ministers held their offices for life by both civil and ecclesiastical law, "so as they become in a Manner their *Freehold,* which they are not to be deprived of, unless *by due Course of Ecclesiastical Process* they be found guilty of a Fault deserving that Penalty."[61] He was obliged by conscience not to comply with inquisitorial methods. The presbytery had treated him unfairly, trying to silence those members who dissented from its procedure. He asked why, after eight months of inquiry into his writing and teaching, it had still not listed his errors and provided witnesses to prove them. He finally requested the committee to press the presbytery to proceed according to the rules of the *Form of Process,* which were "the only proper Means for removing false Reports and groundless suspicions."[62]

---

59 Wodrow, *Analecta,* 3:354.
60 Dundas, *Processes,* 29.
61 Ibid., 31.
62 Ibid., 33.

The Committee for Purity of Doctrine entered this document into the minutes of its meeting on 9 November. Although the committee found the letter "very Long and prolix and [it] occasiond some heavy reflexions on Mr Simson,"[63] it decided to nudge the presbytery of Glasgow into compliance with Simson's requests, agreeing to ask the presbytery to specify the phrases in Simson's letter on which the questions were founded and to which passages of the Bible, the confession, and the catechisms these words were contrary. All present "save 4 or 5" approved of the way the presbytery was acting.[64]

Nevertheless, a prevailing lack of enthusiasm for vigorous action may be deduced from the committee's attendance records. Between 19 May 1726 and 10 March 1727, it held ten meetings, seven of which lacked a quorum. After the first meeting, the only lay elders who attended were Grange and Pencaitland – the former presumably because of his doctrinal concerns, while the latter may have been present in support of Simson, since Matthew Simson was his parish minister.[65] An expression of the general unwillingness to serve can be seen in the attitude of James Alston (1679–1733), minister of Dirleton, who was a favourite of Islay and Milton. At the meeting on 9 November, Alston begged to be relieved of attendance, since he considered the difficulty of the subject insurmountable. Impervious to the moderator's persuasion, Alston excused himself and left.[66]

In Glasgow, Gray, Hamilton, and McLaurin quickly compiled the specified references. In January 1727 Simson responded with a paper of explanations and a letter, which together fill twelve printed pages of text and are much more formal in tone than his previous communications. He had composed a defence detailed enough to satisfy most accusers: gone were the personal complaints and insidious sarcasms, and in their place were careful and itemized replies to the presbytery's questions. In later hearings, Simson used the services of various advocates. The changed style of these answers indicates that he had already realized the need for professional legal advice. It must have been another source of regret to Simson that one sarcastic comment slipped through the editing, since, as so often happened, it returned to haunt him.

63 R. Wodrow to Mrs. Wodrow, 9 Nov. 1726, NLS, Wodrow Letters Quarto, XVII, 156.
64 Ibid.
65 NAS, CH1/2/56, 21–3.
66 NLS, Wodrow Letters Quarto, XVII, 154.

Simson began by explaining his teaching on the view of some theologians that the phrase "self-existent" meant "being of none" with regard to the Father. He told his students not to assume that orthodox authors were wrong but to realize that rather they expressed themselves "by an unfit or ambiguous Word."[67] He continued with this untimely question about the words "self-existent": "I should take it as a Piece of useful Caution, or Instruction, both to me and the Students, if the Presbytery would declare the true Meaning of that English Term of Art, when it is to be affirmed of the Person of the Son or Holy Ghost?"[68]

Simson may have been truly bemused about this issue. The sources all indicate that he had been engrossed in the work of Samuel Clarke for the previous year. His scholarly interest had been aroused by the questions that Clarke raised in his *Scripture Doctrine of the Trinity* and by the various published refutations of Clarke's views. The obvious shift of Simson's position over the latter half of the decade suggests that he was struggling to come to a fuller understanding of the biblical texts. When he affirmed his loyalty to the Westminster Confession, he was sincere. He did not see himself as a heretic or as one who had renounced his Calvinist heritage. His whole teaching career had been devoted to expounding sound Reformed doctrine. Both in the years of Webster's pursuit of him and during the 1720s, he believed that he was recovering truths that had become buried in the accretions of the previous century.

In the second part of the letter, Simson reviewed his use of the words "cum grano salis" with reference to Pictet's exposition of the title "summus Deus" (most high God) as applied to Christ. Once again he stressed that he was discussing the usage of other writers, rather than giving his own opinion; when an author used "summus Deus" to include the Father's personal property, it could not also apply to the Son. This interpretation was made not only by heretics, but also by orthodox theologians, who most certainly did not see the Son as in any sense lower than the Father.

Third, Simson analysed his view of the self-existence and independence of Christ. He restricted his teaching on this subject to the words of the confession and catechisms. While the presbytery and other conservative Scots took his explanations as proof of his unwillingness to attest to the self-existence and independence of Christ, it is equally possible to see them as the opinions of a theologian who had rejected

67 Dundas, *Processes*, 40.
68 Ibid., 40–1.

scholastic arguments and was moving forward to a new world of enlightened thought. Scotland stood on the brink of growth and expansion within the Hanoverian Britain. The era of the covenanters was over, and their theology deserved re-examination in the light of scientific and philosophical discoveries. Simson shared the ideas of many contemporaries in turning to "the Light of Nature" for explanations. He was not a deist; the mysteries of the Christian revelation were integral to his thought. At the age of sixty, he still found them mysteries and was still interested in the contemplation of how they might best be described. Under the influence of Clarke, he wanted to reject "terms of art." This left him with the vocabulary of the Bible and the Westminster fathers, a position that he found satisfactory. He pointed out that neither Pictet nor the members of the Westminster Assembly had used the terms "self-existent" and "independent." For these reasons he wanted to repudiate such phrases as "Christus est ens necessarium" (Christ is a necessary being), but "[T]he truths taught by them, I have always owned, and do yearly mention them in teaching, as I have often in preaching, and they are plainly contained or owned in my Letter."[69]

Simson's unusually open teaching style may have seemed odd to his ministerial colleagues. He welcomed questions and gave his class the opportunity "to propose any Difficulties." He was an experienced lecturer, aware that he might "omit several Things necessary."[70] As a result, he was prepared to deal with whatever issues might arise from questions put by his students. A strong argument against the suggestion that Simson was covertly teaching error, as his adversaries claimed, was the fact that his students sometimes demanded further explanation and contradicted his views. He stated his opinions openly, feeling free to discuss any matter raised by his scholars, while trying to confine his prescriptive statements to the language of the Bible and confession. The licensing record of his students proves that these discussions did not result in a generation of unsound ministers.

In his interpretation of John 17:3, "And this is life eternal, that they might know thee the only true God, and Jesus Christ, whom thou hast sent," Simson claimed in his letter of January 1727 to follow the examples of Athanasius and of Bishops Pearson and Bull. The introduction of Athanasius was a clever touch, since everyone knew that Clarke and his followers refused to repeat the Athanasian creed. He stated that these

69 Ibid., 46.
70 Ibid., 48.

divines took the words "the only true God" to include the Father's quality of being of none. Used in that sense alone, it applied only to the Father, and the suggestion that it was true of the Son contradicted both scripture and confession.

The letter ended with a summary of Simson's beliefs on the issues involved. His final hope, that the presbytery would find the accusations against him "groundless, false and injurious," was to be disappointed.[71]

On 18 January 1727 the presbytery voted that the professor had failed to answer its queries satisfactorily. When it asked the outraged Simson to make more complete answers, he appealed to the Committee for Purity of Doctrine. He pressed for a ruling on whether any proposition in his letter of 2 March 1726 "was contrary unto the Word of God, or to the Confession of Faith, or Catechisms of this Church."[72] His colleagues in the presbytery quickly voted to refer Simson's answers to the committee. To prove that they were not utterly incapable of coping with the difficult professor, the presbytery members then agreed to follow the recommendation of the last assembly and make inquiry into what Simson had taught or vented concerning the Trinity, by taking statements from the students in Simson's divinity class.

Simson promptly demanded that care be taken to observe the rules of the *Form of Process*. Either a *fama clamosa* should be declared, in which case he must be given all particulars of the matter before any inquiries were made, or else an individual must consent to stand behind a formal libel, on pain of censure should it be proved false. Propositions to be investigated should be given to the suspected person in writing, along with the name of the complainant, before any depositions were taken. As the subject of a *fama clamosa* or a libel, Simson would have the right to be present when any witness was being examined or any inquiry made. He was legally correct in making these requests, but the presbytery ignored them and arranged for the students to be questioned about the professor's teaching on the Trinity before the next meeting.

When two weeks later the presbytery met to approve the minutes of the meeting of 18 January, it noticed the omission of a clause in the motion denying Simson's request to be present at the examination of the students. Whether or not it had been in the original motion, it was

71 Ibid., 51.
72 Ibid., 54.

certainly against the rules of the church. In Simson's eyes, this was a miscarriage of justice, since it was necessary "for expiscating [literally, fishing out] the Truth in a Case of this nature that proper Counter-queries should have been put to the Students by him."[73] In the event, not only was Simson unable to cross-examine the students at this point, but he believed that some of their statements, which might have exonerated him, were omitted from the record.

Simson's arguments in January 1727 on the propriety of a libelled person's being present at the taking of precognitions prove how he had profited from the earlier skirmishes of his professional life. Precognitions were statements made by witnesses being interrogated in the preliminary stages of an investigation. They could be used to determine whether a case existed to answer and to prepare both the charge and the defence. During the disputes of 1722 between the Glasgow students and Stirling, James Arbuckle had been accused of visiting a brothel.[74] Stirling and Simson had investigated that incident by examining witnesses privately. When Arbuckle protested, he was assured that nothing detrimental to his honour had been found and that he should drop the subject. However, later Simson refused to give him a communion token on the grounds that he had not cleared his name of scandal. Naturally Arbuckle pointed out that he had been told not to pursue the matter and asked about the investigation of his alleged impropriety.

Upon which, (says the P[rofesso]r) "Now Jacobe, I hope you will allow me to understand these Matters much better than you, who not being a Native of the Kingdom, cannot be supposed to know the Methods of Procedure in our Courts, for you must know that the only Thing we did was by Way of Precognition, where the parties are not obliged to be present; and tho' indeed we found nothing against you, yet that was your Business, and not ours to take Notice of, and you ought certainly to have done it." To this Mr Arbuckle replied, that he was sure there never was such a Practice in any Court in EUROPE, unless it were the Inquisition, for Witnesses to be examined on any Affair, without allowing the Parties concerned to be present.[75]

73 Simson, *Case*, xxii–iii. The descriptive word "expiscating" comes from the Latin *expiscari*, to fish out, meaning to discover by investigation.

74 [Smith], *a Short Account*, 24.

75 Ibid., 26.

Five years later Simson would in effect agree with Arbuckle that taking precognitions in the absence of the accused party constituted an improper exercise of power. The Arbuckle incident shows that Simson knew the rules. When he himself was the victim, he struggled to make it his "Business ... to take Notice" of anything that might help his defence.

Simson's protest against the presbytery's actions was denied, and on 14 March he was expelled from the meeting while the precognitions from the students were read, despite his protest that he was under no formal process and was a legal member of the presbytery. During regular presbytery business, a student's exegesis on the subject of Christ's Supreme Deity was heard and approved – further proof, if necessary, that a young man could listen to the professor without lapsing into heresy.[76] Simson later described how at this meeting the presbytery moderator, in answer to a question by an elder, said that there was no further business to be dealt with and, after "he and some others went out," allowed the introduction of a document called *Remarks on the Professor's Answers to the Presbytery's References*, which was to be included in the agenda for the joint meeting to be held with the Committee for Purity of Doctrine.[77]

The professor thought this an underhand way to conduct business. The accuracy of Simson's judgment can be found in Wodrow's evidence that the *Remarks* were the combined work of Gray, Hamilton, and McLaurin. Wodrow's rationale for the way the paper was introduced does no credit to the presbytery's sense of justice. The decision was made not to adopt it as presbytery material, but simply to allow it to be produced for the committee, since "if they had adopted it as their paper, it would have gone alongst with the rest to Synods ... but then the Professor behoved to have had it to see and answer, which would have prolonged the debate."[78] When a Whig of genuine piety, wide scholarship, and simple humanity could justify such actions, one remembers how recently the Church of Scotland had burned witches and how little some of its members saw tolerance in theological matters as a virtue. The ultra-orthodox, like the witch-burners, believed that they were about the Lord's business. This belief resonates through the literature of the Simson cases more loudly than do the factional interventions, which necessarily took place behind closed doors. Not all Simson's

---

76 Wodrow, *Analecta*, 3:379.
77 Simson, *Case*, xxiv.
78 Wodrow, *Analecta*, 3:379.

detractors, however, were naive men of God. The determination of the Squadrone members of presbytery to ignore the rules laid down in the *Form of Process* is yet another indication of the political nature of Scottish justice, where a man's relationships, of blood or allegiance, might be of greater importance than his innocence. The very fact that the rules needed to be so clearly spelled out indicates the laxity with which they were often observed.

THE LIBEL OF MARCH 1727

When the committee and the presbytery met on 15 March 1727 for their first joint session, little time remained to produce a report for the General Assembly in May. The outside members provided an element of academic expertise to counterbalance Simson's rhetoric among his long-time neighbours and colleagues.[79] With Mitchell as moderator, the events of past months were reviewed and the student precognitions read. To evaluate this undigested mass of material, an eight-member committee of Gray, John Hamilton, McLaurin, and Scott from the presbytery and William Hamilton, Hunter, Logan, and the layman Grange from the committee was appointed to summarize the depositions. This group seems to have been designed to ensure that the selected depositions were as damning as possible, since Professor Hamilton was heavily outnumbered by conservative Calvinists. Simson's request to read the *Remarks* was initially refused, but, on protest, he was given a copy.

During an *in camera* session the next morning, the 16th, the eight-member group decided to base a libel against Simson on the articles in the report. It was to be drawn up by John Hamilton, McLaurin, Wodrow, and Grange – a group whose personal animus against the professor could hardly be greater. Simson was asked for further clarification of his views, but he was again unwell, and his contemporaries seem to have had no doubts about the reality of his ailments. He wrote to Mitchell, "I am rendered unable either to speak or hear Speaking, or apply my Mind attentively to any Subject, were it in my own Room, thro' the continued Indisposition of my Head and Stomach, that it is with the greatest Difficulty I am able to dictate this, or hear it read over again."[80]

79 The members of the committee present on 16 March 1727 were Allan Logan, William Wishart, William Hamilton, William M'George, John Brand, John Hunter, Hugh Fawside, Robert Wodrow, Thomas Linning, John Currie, James Bain, Lord Grange, and Sir James Stewart. Dundas, *Processes*, 61.
80 Ibid., 65.

Apologizing for his absence, he begged to be excused from answering further queries, which seemed irrelevant, since the committee planned to frame a libel against him. He felt that the most satisfactory solution would be to make his case when he answered the libel. Sick or not, Simson was still fighting to avoid answering the questions, but in reply the committee warned him that he risked suspension from teaching and preaching if he declined to respond.

Simson was now aware of the danger in which he stood. His friends tried to persuade him to provide answers, while conducting a public relations campaign among the members of the presbytery of Glasgow, using "All the arguments and importunity that they could that compassion should be sheuen to a stiff, peremptory man, who would ruin himself, and was sound enough in his principles, as he offered to evidence; but made it a matter of conscience with him, that he would not answer Queries, as being against his principles."[81] Further efforts by Simson's coterie went to ensure that he kept silent at critical times. It was felt that, regardless of his health, he should keep away from the committee meetings, since he might "spoil all the concert by his imprudence and peremptorynes, and ... disoun his declaration as an Answer to Queries."[82]

During the presbytery meeting of 22 March, Simson's nephew, John Paisley, appeared with his uncle's apologies for absence and two papers, discussion of which was postponed until the next week. Simson's friends must have kept him informed of the discussion in the presbytery, for on 29 March he produced further written "Thoughts upon the Subject of all their Queries."[83] Mitchell felt that now "the Propositions concerning the Numerical Essence & Necessary Existence are more posetive & express."[84] After an extended introduction in which he reviewed Trinitarian heresy, Simson said that to him no hypothesis fully explained the mystery of the Trinity, a fact emphasized by the absence of hypotheses in Christian creeds and confessions. The growth of new heresy had not changed the situation, since the current problems were rather "some old ones ... revived in a new Dress."[85]

81 Wodrow, *Analecta*, 3:400.

82 The previous week Simson had said that he would see the presbytery hanged before he answered its members queries! Ibid., 3:400–1.

83 Dundas, *Processes*, 68.

84 W. Mitchell to Lord Grange, 1 April 1727, NAS, GD124/15/1294.

85 Dundas, *Processes*, 70.

Simson admitted on 29 March that in the past he had used the common hypotheses, but experience had taught him that they were more likely to lead students into error than to help them. Therefore,

I have thought it more for the Benefit of the Students, and the Interest of the Truth, to observe to them, That the Father, Son and Holy Ghost, must be so far *distinct Persons*, as that the incommunicable Properties, Characters and Actions ascribed to them in Holy Scripture, and from thence inserted in our Confession of Faith and Catechisms, *must truly agree to them*: And on the other Hand, that they must be *so One among themselves*, as to be but *one true eternal God*, in Opposition to a Plurality of Gods; *of one* or *the same Substance, Power and Eternity*, in such a Way as is *consistent with the said Distinction of their Persons*, in Opposition to their being but one Person. The Nature and Measure of which *Oneness* and *Distinction* is not revealed in the Word of God, which alone teaches us this Doctrine; and 'tis probable we have not Faculties capable of apprehending it, and 'tis certain we have no Words fit for expressing it; There being no Terms applicable thereto, but such as were invented mostly by Heathens to express the Difference and Oneness of created Beings; which therefore still lead our Minds to frame Ideas of the Distinction and Oneness of the Divine Persons, like unto what obtains among Creatures, which cannot possibly agree to the Persons of the Glorious Godhead, and which, I have observed in all Ages, has occasioned endless Debates and Contentions about it.[86]

While Simson believed that one substance in number was common to all the persons, it was necessary to review the Greek terms used, such as *homooúsios*, since Sabellians misused them. He considered the Son to be a "Necessary-being"; the proofs that established that also proved "his Eternal Independency, Self-existence, and true Godhead."[87] He told his scholars that some authors took self-existence to mean the Father's being of none in order to prevent them falling into error through ignorance. Simson added a list of authoritative quotations to prove his orthodoxy, most of which emphasized the role of the Father as the fountain of the Godhead, eternally communicating His nature to the other two persons in the Trinity. Read carefully, this document seemed to be a full refutation of any perceived lapse in orthodoxy.

Reporting to Grange on 1 April, Mitchell wrote that there was division in the Presbytery over how to consider this new declaration. Some

86 Ibid., 71.
87 Ibid., 72.

members felt that, with slight changes, it might help Simson's case, while others continued to demand that the professor appear and answer the queries.[88] Even Gray, Hamilton, and Scott felt that it contained "materiall answers," although they needed amplification.[89] Indeed some supporters who had encouraged Simson to resist questioning were distressed by the lengths to which he had gone to satisfy his examiners. Wodrow felt that the non-subscribers would be particularly disappointed, since they had boasted that Simson was making "a glorious defence in favour of humane liberty."[90]

Fear of immediate suspension, which would have had a disastrous effect on his attempt to rehabilitate his own reputation and that of his university, must have forced Simson to change his tactics. His friends now realized the need for counter measures to the orthodox propaganda. "Many lauers [lawyers] and gentlmen" spoke actively on Whiggish principles against inquisitorial trials.[91] The evidence indicates that Simson's position appealed to many uncommitted Scots. Wodrow's correspondents continued to keep him in touch with feelings in other parts of the country. Mr ML [McLaren?] wrote from Edinburgh that "the great part of those I have occasion to converse with here, think that since he [Simson] adheres tenaciously to the Confession of faith; that if nothing can be naturally deduced from his writings or proven by his schollars it will be an hardship upon him to oblige him to answer questions that are not founded either upon his letters or upon writings or upon the testimonies of his schollars ... his freinds make a great clamour here against the committee who made th[i]s inquiry for their partiality."[92]

Many people hoped that the Committee for Purity of Doctrine could find an expedient to avoid the publicity and rancour of discussion at the General Assembly. This may well have been the opinion of those educated laymen who endorsed an inclusive theology that elevated the importance of moral values. Men such as Islay and Milton rightly distrusted the influence of the conservative wing of the Church of Scotland in the General Assembly. Thomas Mack, the lugubrious minister of Terregles, feared that Simson might yet "keep his chair and hiss at all th[ei]r efforts," unless the committee made certain that its libel was

88 Mitchell to Grange, 1 April 1727, NAS, GD124/15/1294.
89 Wodrow, *Analecta*, 3:402.
90 Ibid., 3:404.
91 Ibid., 3:406.
92 Mr. M.L. to R. Wodrow, 10 March 1727, Wodrow Letters Quarto, XVII, 220.

"well founded." Members of Mack's presbytery were open supporters of the beleaguered professor.[93]

Despite Simson's efforts, on 30 March the Presbytery of Glasgow approved a libel listing all the now-familiar charges against him, along with the accusation of his not having obeyed the assembly's act of 1717 forbidding the use of expressions that could have an unsound sense. The examination of the students had found little new material, so the presbytery added to the libel Simson's rash remark about English terms of art. It appended a list of over thirty students and ex-students of Simson as witnesses. Simson demanded that the students who had been examined should be called as witnesses for his exculpation, except those whom he considered to be raisers of a *fama clamosa*. Appendix B to the current volume presents the libel of 1727, the list of witnesses, and Simson's response.

THE STUDENTS' EVIDENCE OF APRIL 1727

Many of the participants at the April 1727 meeting of the Synod of Glasgow and Ayr appeared to be friendly towards Simson.[94] There was general excitement, and opinions were hardening. The light-hearted young ministers present endorsed club membership, non-subscription, and "liberty of thinking," which made synod meetings "melancholy times" to Wodrow.[95] His often-prejudiced records suggest that many of the younger generation of ministers, not merely those who had studied under Simson, were anxious to see the church approve a Christian doctrine broader than that laid down at Dort. The correspondence of Wodrow's son, James, with Samuel Kenrick confirms this impression. They had studied together at Glasgow in the late 1740s, when the memory was still green of a liberal ministerial group, epitomized by John Millar, who had studied under Simson or had attended Francis Hutcheson's lectures after his arrival as professor in 1729.[96] Half a century later the two men recalled the atmosphere of intellectual excitement in their youth. They had felt that they were looking towards a more enlightened age; a Simson victory would have signified that the dawn had broken.

93 T. Mack to R. Wodrow, 11 March 1727, ibid. 221.
94 Wodrow, *Analecta*, 3:411.
95 Ibid., 3:412.
96 See Dr Williams's Library, MS 24.157/261/5r, 264/3r.

Additional evidence of the enlightened nature of Millar's theology can be found in Robert Wodrow's correspondence. The expatriate Aberdonian Dr James Frazer wrote from London in July 1726 praising the forward-looking views of Millar, who had called on him during a visit south. In striking contrast to most of Wodrow's friends, Frazer was pleased that an open attitude was developing among the Glasgow students. In words that echo the thoughts of George Turnbull, Frazer commented, "I am glad to hear that amongst your young students of Divinity there appears a noble spirit of search after truth, without being tyed up to narrow principles as the prejudices of education, or the prevailing power of partys, has made fashionable, and confined them to." He had been delighted with Millar's account "of the hopeful progress the young students made in the study of the Scripture, and of all useful knowledge relating therunto, and are getting rid of the leading strings of arguments merely founded on the authority of men, without reason to support the same."[97] Enlightened clergymen were appreciated by a secular society that promoted the church as an ethical bulwark against public disorder, but which would not support excessive ecclesiastical scrutiny into private opinions or morals.

Among the laity, criticism was mounting against the Simson prosecution. Wodrow found in this atmosphere proof that "the generality of gentlmen are turning loose in their reasoning, mockers of Scripture; and the Arrian notions, and Mr Simson's noveltys, are greedily drunk in and defended. The Church is condemned by them for taking any nottice of these things; and they are for a boundles latitude in every point."[98] In a tone typical of many in Wodrow's circle, John Williamson passed on his fears of the prevailing temper in Edinburgh: "I find a very great coldness about maintaining the manner of expressing those articles in use in our Reputed Orthodox Systemes, and that under pretence of The Greatness of the Mystery (which indeed cannot be denied) and which therefor they say we should rest satisfied to express in Scripture terms.... Great noise is made about the fear of Enlarging Our Standard by new Coined words, &c."[99] The gentlemen thus criticized certainly saw themselves as devout Presbyterians, not as deists or atheists. Men who had rejected religion did not "greedily" absorb new theological

97 J. Frazer to R. Wodrow, 7 July 1726, letter published in Maidment, ed., *Analecta Scotica*, 1:314.

98 Wodrow, *Analecta*, 3:413.

99 J. Williamson to R. Wodrow, 13 April 1727, NLS, Wodrow Letters Quarto, XVII, 242.

ideas. The moderation against which later generations of evangelical Scots preached had its genesis in these earlier conflicts.

On 11 April Simson presented to the presbytery written objections against the form of the libel (see the last section of Appendix B). His lawyer, Mr James Graham, spoke on his behalf, "*viva voce* at great length," detailing the exceptions taken to the libel.[100] Simson professed his orthodoxy and regretted that, after a long, friendly association, mis-understandings had grown up between himself and the other ministers in Glasgow, as a result of his ill-health since October 1724. The libel contained errors and omissions that made it legally invalid, such as not mentioning the specific place and time at which the offenses were committed. There was also a problem in the ambiguous nature of the terms that Simson was accused of using. Since it was unclear whether, if he did use them, he was stating his own opinion or quoting the views of others, they were incapable of legal proof without the full context in which they were employed. "For at this Rate, he might be accused of gross Error, yea Blasphemy, or Atheism, had he been barely reciting some Texts of Scripture, of which the Hearers remembred only some Scrapes, such as *There is no God: Curse God and die; you see then, how that by Works a man is justified,* and the like."[101] The libel did not indicate the specific passages of scripture or confession to which the alleged statements were inconsistent. Lastly Simson pointed out that some of the alleged expressions were so contrary to his normal convictions that if he did say them it could only have been a slip of the tongue caused by his recurrent illness throughout the period in question. "This Libel being manifestly of a criminal Nature," Simson pointed out that being found guilty of its charges could deprive him not merely of his reputation but also of his "Office and Benefice."[102] Given the laws under which Aikenhead had been hanged, and under which Simson was at risk of punishment, his concern for strict compliance with legal procedure was understandable.

100 Dundas, *Processes,* 82. McLaurin told Wodrow that the professor used his poor health as an excuse to have his lawyer present; "& if it was an advantage to the Prof in one respect to have the Assistances some reckond it an advantage to the Presty in another respect because that Gentleman appeard carefull to hinder the Prof from such ways of speaking as tended only to irritate Members of the Presty & to occasion needless & hurtful contention." J. McLaurin to R. Wodrow, 14 April 1727 NLS, Wodrow Letters Quarto, XVII, 260.

101 Dundas, *Processes,* 81.

102 Ibid., 80.

The presbytery was less concerned with legality, rejecting Simson's objections with the single exception of the lack of specific place, which it remedied by giving the location as within the bounds of the city or university of Glasgow.

A week later, on 18 April, the presbytery met to hear Simson's response to the libel. The meeting began with Principal Stirling's statement of protest against any derogation from the university's right to judge its own members. Simson's defence followed; he expanded the arguments made in previous letters and in his objections to the libel, testified to his orthodoxy, and assured the presbytery that any witness who heard him say otherwise was either mistaken or had heard a sick man inadvertently make a slip of the tongue. There is ample justification for much of his argument. Any divinity lecture could be found to contain heretical statements, without the full context in which a given term was used. Part of the function of the eighteenth-century Scottish divinity course was to evaluate the orthodox rebuttals to various heresies and to ensure that they were adequate for contemporary purposes. Inevitably the professor and students would have to analyse the heresies themselves. Simson admitted that he recommended the study of Socinus's works. Any student arriving late, or waking after a brief doze, might hear a remark that would seem startling out of the framework of the lecture. Simson noted of one article, "This Allegation has the same Fault with most of the Rest, that it does not mention what the Defendant was then teaching."[103]

An early-eighteenth-century divinity class held a further pitfall. The Dutch theological texts, written in Latin, were reviewed and lectured on in Latin. As Simson said of one quoted phrase, "in teaching the System, he always speaks *Latin*, and a Hearer's translating any Part of his Words into *English*, can bear no Faith in Judgment, because they may be wrong translated, and his Testimony cannot be an Evidence of what was Fact, or really said by the Defendant, but only of his own Judgment about it, fifteen Months or more after the Thing happened."[104] The Latin skills of the students were of a reasonably high standard, or they would not have reached this level in their studies. Nevertheless, taking notes in another language, however familiar, must have increased the likelihood of incorrect transcription when the listener's attention drifted. Thus

103 Ibid., 89.

104 Simson was aware that students might be confused by language, as can be seen by questions that he tried to ask them. See below, note 111. Ibid., 88.

Simson's suggestion that a student copied *creare* instead of *generare* in the libelled phrase *Ni supponamus Deum non posse creare ab eterno* is more likely than that the professor changed his normal dictation vocabulary. At a time when renewed Arianism loomed as a major threat, it is difficult to conceive that Simson would have deliberately used a phrase which suggested that Christ was a created being. To an inattentive student, the enormity of the suggestion might have been less immediately apparent.

The demands made on Simson to conform to seventeenth-century Reformed scholasticism were scarcely in keeping with the pastoral needs of the 1720s. Simson said that he taught the doctrine of the Trinity from Pictet and from the Westminster Confession, using the terminology of the texts and thus explaining why he might omit the words "necessary-existence" and "independency." He added "That this Omission can be no more a Crime in his Teaching, than it is in Ministers Preaching; and he does not remember, that he ever observed any minister use these Terms in preaching, tho' he has been capable of noticing what he heard preach'd these forty Years and more."[105] Simson's memories suggest that since the Glorious Revolution the normal sermons of the Church of Scotland had been delivered in words that were comprehensible to the full spectrum of society, even those delivered in presbyteries, synods, and assemblies to largely clerical audiences. Sermons were highly dependent on biblical material and employed the vocabulary of the King James version of the Bible. Simson was too astute to use an example that could readily be disproved, so we may assume that the instruction given to his prospective ministers was in accordance with the contemporary practice of his church.

The presbytery had objected to Simson's calling various expressions "English Terms of Art." This phrase was used by Simson and his contemporaries rather as a modern writer might use the word "jargon." Simson perhaps felt that such expressions obfuscated rather than clarified the meaning of theological concepts; he certainly proposed their elimination from normal usage. He tried to clear the minefield of the meaning of "self-existent." Quoting from Dr Daniel Waterland (1683–1740) and other writers against Clarke, he pointed out that there was a difference between "necessary existence" and "self existence." The former was a property of all persons in the Godhead, while the latter could be argued as belonging only to the Father. Saying this, however, did not mean that the existence of the Son was in any way precarious or contingent;

105 Ibid., 98.

indeed to place undue stress on Christ's self-existence was to run the danger of falling into heresy. The Arians claimed that the Son could not be God unless he were "*Unoriginate* and *Self-existent* as the unbegotten Father himself," while to Sabellians the eternal nature of the Son demanded that he "must be the *Self-existent* Father himself."[106]

Each of these positions was wrong, but to Simson the latter risk was greater in Scotland. His argument about his similarity to Waterland was picked up by English Dissenters who were following the case. In 1728 Abraham Taylor wrote to Grange that "our Non-subscribers industriously give out, that you are persecuting a man who has exactly the same sentiments with Dr Waterland."[107] English perceptions such as this added to the fears that the orthodox harboured about possible reactions in London to the case.

The *State of the Processes* prints the re-examination of thirty students in April 1727 in some detail. The young men ranged in age from eighteen to twenty-nine, with the average age being 22.8 years. A few were already licensed to preach the Gospel, proving that their theology was acceptable to the presbyteries that had issued their licences. John McLaurin reported, "The committee sometimes could not but be somewhat surprizd to hear students after hearing the Interrogations proposed to them Deny th[a]t they rememberd anything about these things."[108] Part of the problem was again the matter of testifying in *ipsissima verba*, as had been the case in 1714–17. Even James Sloss, against whose participation Simson had protested as being a partial witness, known to have spoken publicly against the orthodoxy of the professor, could remember few details of heterodox teaching when questioned by the presbytery. He could not recall whether expressions came together or had explanations between them. He was not sure whether Simson had omitted to caution the students about the use of the term "person" with respect to the Godhead in the past year. In response to Simson's cross-examination he was equally nebulous, remembering little detail about the supposedly offensive classes, remarking vaguely that the professor had said many orthodox things, but also many that he had thought not orthodox.[109]

106 Ibid., 104.
107 A. Taylor to Lord Grange, 24 June 1728, NAS, GD124/15/1332/3.
108 J. McLaurin to R. Wodrow, 28 Jan. 1727, NLS, Wodrow Letters Quarto, XVII, 251.
109 Dundas, *Processes*, 111.

The examinations had proceeded swiftly; on 26 April eleven men gave their depositions and answered questions from the defence. Simson complained that he was permitted to cross-examine only those witnesses who had been called by the prosecution and not allowed to cite further witnesses for the defence. Moreover, he was "limited to put such Questions only to them as the Presbytery should find relevant and Proper."[110] Simson gave examples of disallowed questions, which certainly seem reasonable by twentieth-century standards.[111] One anti-Simson writer, criticizing Simson's published *Case*, felt that the presbytery was correct to reject one line of questioning on the grounds that Simson wanted merely "to see whether the Witness might be catcht tripping in his Discourse, or failing in his Memory, which Design the Presbytery did not think fit to incourage."[112]

The limitations placed on Simson are not surprising, since the object of questioning the students was to obtain evidence of his heresy, not to conduct a disinterested inquiry or to find proof of his orthodoxy. Once again the good intentions of the *Form of Process* counted for less than the need for the ultra-conservative ministers to prove their case. For those in the presbytery who were already convinced that Simson was a dangerous propagator of loose theology, if not of heresy, the need to obtain a conviction was more pressing than any notions of fair procedure. Anti-Simson pamphleteers tried to rebut Simson's complaints with the insinuation that "Ministers, especially Professors of Divinity, may (if they be for propagating Error) convey their Notions so artfully, and under such Disguise as their Errors cannot be clearly proven from the Words they emit, nor will Witnesses pretend to deduce the Series of their Discourse in the Variety of Expressions and Turns of it."[113] These words indicate the aggravation that some members of the committee felt at their inability to secure clear depositions of heretical words from Simson's students.

---

110 Simson, *Case*, xxx.

111 "The first Cross-question the Professor proposed to Mr. *Sloss*, was, *Whether he was teaching upon the Latin System or the Confession of Faith?* But the Presbytery would not allow him to ask it, saying it was an *ensnaring Question.* And when he proposed to ask the second Witness Mr. *Ritchie, Whether he had not heard him refute the* Arian *Heresy, and particularly that the Son of God was created or made?* They would not allow it to be asked, but refused it by a vote." Simson noted that on the following day, the presbytery relented vis-à-vis this question. Ibid., xxx–xxxi.

112 [Hamilton?] *Animadversions*, 52.

113 Ibid., 25.

Opinions differed as to whether Simson's teaching had changed. Of thirty depositions, ten said that in 1725 Simson's methods had changed, five said there was no change, and fifteen made no comment on the matter. Thirteen of the last group had not attended the divinity school prior to 1725, so were in no position to know. This means that of seventeen who had heard Simson teach both in 1725 and in previous years, ten had noticed a change, while seven had seen none.[114] This hardly suggests a change in emphasis of any magnitude.

The only other question on which a large group of the students agreed related to an interchange between William Brown and Simson on the impertinence of the terms "necessarily-existent" and "independent" with regard to the Son. Brown and his brother David appear on the list of theological students for April 1723, so by 1727 they were among the more senior men interviewed.[115] In December 1725, Simson had taught that the Son derived his perfections from the Father. The libel charged him with saying that God the Father is before the Son not in time but by causality (*Deus Pater est ante Deum Filium non tempore sed Causalitate*) and with adding, "unless we add that God could not create from eternity" (*Ni supponamus Deum non posse creare ab æterno*). The first phrase stated an accepted patristic view, held by many early Christian authors, including Augustine, who used the analogies of the source and the stream or the sun and the ray to try to explain the procession in the Trinity.[116] The second statement was potentially much more dangerous to Simson, and he consistently denied that he would have deliberately uttered such words. He would never have used *creare* in this context but would have said, or intended to say, *generare*. Throughout the case, he maintained that if indeed he said these words, they were a slip of the tongue caused by illness.

In his various explanations in March 1726 and April 1727 of the first part of this charge, Simson cited Bishop Pearson's *Exposition of the Creed*,

114 Dundas, *Processes*, 111–34.

115 *Munimenta*, 3:255. William and David Brown were presumably the sons of Thomas Brown, minister of Paisley 1698–1708. William probably became minister of Kilmarnock (Hew Scott, *Fasti*, 3:351) He received his licence from the Presbytery of Paisley in 1729 and a presentation from the Earl of Dundonald in 1732. He was ordained in 1733 and remained in Kilmarnock until his death in 1761. David (Hew Scott, *Fasti*, 3:218) was also licensed by his father's old presbytery in 1729 and was ordained to Port Glasgow in 1731, over the objections of the town council of Glasgow.

116 For the history of Trinitarian theology, see Kasper, *God.*

a work that contained references to the use of such vocabulary by authors from the early church such as Victorinus Afer (c. 362), who said, "Pater causa est ipsi filio ut sit." Pearson remarked on the terminology of the "ancient doctors of the church," who called "the Father the origin, the cause, the author, the root, the fountain, and the head of the Son or the whole divinity."[117] He said that the Father must not be denied the pre-eminence due to him, which "consisteth in this, that he is God not of any other, but of himself."[118] Simson's emphasis on the importance of the personal properties of the members of the Trinity may have had its root in Pearson, who stated that the priority of order of the three persons "doth properly and naturally result from the divine paternity; so that the Son must necessarily be second unto the Father, from whom he receiveth his origination, and the Holy Ghost unto the Son."[119] Pearson followed the views of the church fathers when he acknowledged the Father to be "the original cause of all things as created by him, so is he the fountain of the Son begotten of him, and of the Holy Ghost proceeding from him."[120] He did, however, affirm that there would be only one essence and one supreme God. None the less, Christ was the true God and was given titles that were those of the supreme God.

Simson also quoted from Dr Owen and Bishop Bull in his several written and verbal defences. John Owen, as a Puritan, had a better lineage for Presbyterians than Pearson, but his views on the Trinity were similar to Pearson's: "It is true, there is an *order*, yea, a *subordination*, in the persons of the Trinity themselves, whereby the Son, as to his personality, may be said to depend on the Father, being begotten of him."[121] Owen commented that there were disputed issues about the doctrine of the Trinity, such as the manner of generation and procession and the nature of the personal subsistence of the persons with respect to their distinguishing properties. Since a full understanding of these matters, however, was not necessary for faith, he felt that they might be passed over quickly.[122]

Bull had written that the Latin *causa* had the same meaning as *principium*. As a result many patristic writers felt that the Father was the cause

117 Pearson, *Exposition*, 58, 59 n. 2.
118 Ibid., 55.
119 Ibid., 57–8.
120 Ibid., 64.
121 Owen, *Works*, 12:201.
122 Ibid., 2:408.

of the Son. Bull quoted St Augustine [Lob. 73, Quæst. 16] as saying, "God is the Cause of all things that are. As he is the Cause of all things, he is the Cause of his own Wisdom, nor was God ever without his Wisdom. Therefore he is the eternal Cause of his own eternal Wisdom, nor is he prior in Time to his own Wisdom."[123] Simson's "*Deus Pater est ante Deum Filium non tempore sed Causalitate*" corresponded closely to the Augustinian statement.

These expressions were unfamiliar to many eighteenth-century Scots Presbyterians. An anonymous pamphleteer scorned them as he condemned Simson's concerns about the numerical unity of the Godhead:

I have heard of strange Fancys, about one commone principle, and certain emanations from it, as Rays come from the Sun, which in some sense are the same substance with it, yet not so as to be Truely or Numerically one with the Sun. Divines can tell wher severall such wild and Bold things are to be mett with. Whether any of these have Entered Into *Mr Simsons* schemes, upon his Discovery of the Insufficiency of what our most Eminent Divines have Taught upon the Trinity, I do not say; some may perhaps suspect somewhat of this nature, Is not altogether inconsistent with ane Innovating Genius, nor the expressions and Notions he has used and vented.[124]

Simson's expositions of patristic theological similes would certainly fall into the class of "strange Fancys" to this writer. Indeed, on a date possibly in December 1725, William Brown, one of Simson's students had complained that "that way of speaking seemed to derogate from the Son's Independency," to which Simson had replied that there was a sense in which independence could be taken as a personal property of the Father and thus could not be applied to the Son. When the student pursued the connection between independence and necessary existence, Simson replied that such terms were irrelevant and should not be used of the Trinity.

In a subsequent conversation with the Brown brothers, in Simson's room in the college at the end of March 1726, the professor had stated that there were three intelligent agents in the Trinity. When William

123 Bull, *Works*, 2:6. Wodrow was familiar with Bull's work and considered him "grossly Pelagian on the head of Justification." Moreover Bull's *Defensio de subordinatione Filii* "conteans many very hazardous expressions." Wodrow also believed that although "excellent Protestant Writers" had used the expression *Pater est Fons Deitatis*, current heretics had so misused the words that the orthodox preferred to avoid them. Wodrow, *Analecta*, 3:391.

124 Anonymous, *Some materials for answers to the Papers*, NLS Wodrow Folios, XLIX, 196r.

Brown asked Simson if there were therefore three beings, his reply was "Certainly there must," or words to that effect.[125] Dr Owen had called the persons of the Trinity "distinct, living, divine, intelligent voluntary principles of operation or working," the distinction among whom rests in their personal properties of generation and procession.[126] These words are similar to those that Brown deponed Simson had used of the Trinity – "Three intelligent Agents or Agencies."[127] Simson was still arguing against Sabellian modalism. John M'Alpin deponed that during "this session" Simson had said "That there was such an Unity in the Godhead, as was consistent with a Distinction of Persons, which ought always to be maintained against the Sabellians, and that there was such a Distinction of Persons as was consistent with Unity, which ought to be maintained against the Arians."[128] Although eight students remembered the interchange between Brown and Simson in class, their recollections of the words used differed.

The results of the examination of the students 19–26 April 1727 hardly constituted an overwhelming denunciation of the professor. The precognition taken from the students in early 1727 presumably said much the same as the testimony contained in the printed depositions. In March 1727 Wodrow and the orthodox found the "declarations in it wer so glaring as, when joyned with the ambigouity of the Professor's Answers ... did shoak many extremely,"[129] which proves that the orthodox were both easily shocked and actively looking for heresy. The ease with which these men found Simson's replies startling reveals their lack of familiarity with the controversial literature of the early church. It also indicates their lack of sympathy with Simson's desire to modernize divinity without parting company with the historic beliefs of the Church of Scotland.

When the hearings concluded at the end of April, the presbytery abandoned its attempt to reach a decision on the divisive problem. Its report was noncommittal, stating that Simson had changed his method of teaching without passing judgment on the change. Unable to prove error definitively from the witnesses, the presbytery included an inflammatory table that compared statements by Simson with heterodox

---

125 Dundas, *Processes*, 117.
126 Owen, *Works*, 2:405.
127 Dundas, *Processes*, 117.
128 Ibid., 132.
129 Wodrow, *Analecta*, 3:381.

propositions from Samuel Clarke's works. Finally it voted to refer the whole affair to the General Assembly in May, begging the assembly's members to "bring this Matter to an Issue as speedily as they can."[130] For a second year the Glasgow members had contrived that the assembly would take a distasteful decision out of their hands.

Wodrow's correspondents had grave doubts about the outcome. Mr ML has been quoted above; John Williamson felt the same: "I heartily wish That affair come not in to the As[sembly]: by what I can perceive, Im affriad he have too many favourers; but I must not be more plain."[131] Nevertheless, few presbyteries sent specific instructions about this matter with their delegates to the assembly. Only the presbyteries of Biggar, Chanonry, and Kirkcaldy sent their commissioners with instructions about the Simson case. The members of the Presbytery of Kirkcaldy were bothered by the fact that the views now voiced by Simson seemed to differ from the original rumours of his teaching, which "creat great Jealousies in the breasts of the members of this Presbytery." They expected the upcoming assembly to bring the matter to a "happy Issue."[132]

THE GENERAL ASSEMBLY OF MAY 1727

It is doubtful that the hopes of Kirkcaldy's ministers were realized at the General Assembly of 1727, which began on 6 May, with the Earl of Findlater as royal commissioner and Professor Hamilton as moderator.[133] Past moderator Mitchell preached the opening sermon on Psalm 122:6, "Pray for the Peace of Jerusalem," in the course of which he said that truth was more important than peace in matters of doctrine.[134] The sermon displeased the young "bright images," one of whom, currently on trials before the Presbytery of Edinburgh, told a large gathering that this was "an inflaming and villanous sermon," which is further proof that critical theological analysis was in no way confined to Glasgow.[135] Professor Hamilton was a cautious man, but by 1726 Allan

130 Dundas, *Processes*, 157.

131 J. Williamson to R. Wodrow, 6 April 1727, NLS, Wodrow Letters Quarto, XVII, 237.

132 NAS, CH1/2/55, 174.

133 Findlater seems not to have been a strong party man. He may have owed his appointment to Lord Townshend. See Wehrli, "Scottish Politics", 245.

134 Wodrow, *Correspondence*, 3:291.

135 Wodrow, *Analecta*, 3:421.

Logan and Robert Wodrow had considerable suspicions as to his ortho-doxy on the Trinity.[136] The next year Grange told Wodrow that many English Dissenters distrusted Hamilton as much as Simson, since English divinity students who studied at both Edinburgh and Glasgow became non-subscribers on returning home.[137] Other evidence of Edinburgh theological innovation lies in a letter written by Williamson to Wodrow shortly before the 1727 assembly. After commenting that there were many students currently at Edinburgh University, he went on, in words similar to Wodrow's descriptions of Glasgow students, "I fear the Laxnes of their way of thinking, by their way both of expressing themselves and their vain deportment."[138] The sum total of this criticism probably added up to the same sort of instruction that Simson had engaged in – a more benevolent and liberal interpretation of traditional Scots Calvinism than the ultra-orthodox considered appropriate.

When his case came up for debate, beginning on 8 May 1727, Simson appeared with two advocates, Archibald Murray and William Grant, while Peter Grant of Little Elchies represented the Presbytery of Glasgow.[139] Simson complained that the presbytery had withheld some of the relevant papers from him, and objected to the presbytery members' being allowed to vote, since they were parties in the case.[140] The reading of documents occupied the assembly's agenda for portions of three days. Simson refuted the arguments in the *Remarks* that the presbytery had drawn up, stating that in all respects other than the personal property of the Father, the Son shared the Father's attributes, "Whence it is manifest, that the highest Notion we can frame of *Necessary-existence*, that does not include *Being of None*, does no doubt agree to the Son,

136 Ibid., 3:302.

137 Ibid., 3:460.

138 J. Williamson to R. Wodrow, 13 April 1727, NLS, Wodrow Letters Quarto, XVII, 243.

139 Wodrow, *Correspondence*, 3:309. Archibald Murray of Murrayfield (d. 1773) became a member of the Faculty of Advocates in 1718. The identity of the various Grants mentioned by Wodrow is uncertain. Simson's counsel was presumably William Grant (c. 1701–1764), later Lord Prestongrange (created 1754), who served as procurator for the church and principal clerk of the assembly after the death of Dundas of Philipston in 1731. Grant of Easter Elchies, who supported Dundas and Drummore in legal quibbles, was Patrick Grant (1691–1754), later Lord Elchies (1732). No Peter Grant of Little Elchies is listed in Grants's *Faculty of Advocates*, 89, but since "Peter" and "Patrick" were interchangeable in eighteenth-century. Scotland, Little Elchies may simply be Easter Elchies.

140 Wodrow, *Correspondence*, 3:296.

according to which the Professor believes that the Son is *Necessarily-existent,* and that it is *Impossible that he should not have been.*"[141]

Having proclaimed his soundness, Simson commented that it was "an unfair and unjust Way of Dealing" to pick words out of his papers and compare them with similar words of Dr Clarke, in order to "continue Suspicions in the Minds of unthinking People, as if the Professor and Dr. *Clark* were of one Mind and Opinion about the Doctrine of the *Trinity.*"[142] Over the past two years, Simson had been steadily distancing himself from the taint of Dr Clarke. The excitement that he had felt when he was studying the *Scripture Doctrine of the Trinity* had long gone, leaving the unfortunate fact that he was universally believed to have "gone in to Dr Clerk's scheme."[143] By now, Simson was being attacked on the rumours of his past teaching errors, not on anything that he was currently endorsing: there was no reason for the church to be "entertaining jealousies of his Unsoundness as to his Faith on the Doctrine of the *Trinity,* nor any Reason of continuing or propagating Scandal about it."[144] Simson explained that the theoretical basis for his teaching about the divine substance hinged on his determination to avoid Sabellian or Socinian interpretations and on his desire to differentiate between words that were normally used for created matter and those appropriate for theological use. There were differences between the usages of philosophy and of theology; for instance, in divinity the word "substance" had to signify one substance in number but must avoid the Aristotelian sense of a "Substance peculiar to one single Person."[145]

The General Assembly had decided to discuss and vote on each article of the libel individually, but it quickly became evident that such a process would be too slow, so the assembly asked a small committee to organize the material for swift debate. The committee ruled that four propositions taken from the second and third articles of the libel were relevant

141 Dundas, *Processes,* 167.

142 Ibid., 169.

143 Wodrow, *Analecta,* 3:242.

144 Dundas, *Processes,* 171–2.

145 Ibid., 175. McLaurin had told Wodrow in January 1727 that one student's precognition stated that Simson had talked of "a Definition of Aristotle where he makes one Numerical Essence the same wt one person & sd in this sense th[a]t the Unity of Essence in the Trinity could not be import the same Numerical Essence, the young man sd yt the Prof did not (as he remembered) deny one Numerical Essence absolutely but with a view to this definition of Aristotle." NLS, Wodrow Letters Quarto, XVII, 252.

to incurring censure: denying the necessary existence of Christ; teaching that the necessary existence of Christ was something that human beings did not know; teaching that the independence of Christ was something that human beings did not know; and calling these terms "philosophical niceties" and "impertinent" (irrelevant).[146] These propositions came from reports of Simson's lectures and discussions with students.

When the assembly considered the proofs for the relevant articles, Dundas, speaking for Simson, argued that the students' evidence was inconsistent and unreliable. In view of their contrary assertions, guilt could be proved only by the written word. Wodrow commented, "All this is a strong proof of the necessity of queries"[147] – a reaction to Dundas's speech that underlined the prejudice implicit in the Scottish legal procedure of the day and provided justification for Simson's reluctance to answer questions.

Nevertheless, after discussing the first article, the "great majority" found that Simson had denied the necessary existence of Christ in his teaching.[148] The second article was likewise found proven by a "very great plurality."[149] The third was found "not proven," but the next day the fourth was found "relevant."

Next the statements of the witnesses were studied again. Simson recorded which witnesses he felt were most dependable. Sloss was the "Raiser and Broacher of the *Fama Clamosa*" and as such to be treated with suspicion.[150] He and Dennison were mistaken in what they thought the professor had said, while Bain was a "very young student."[151] Boyd, Chapman, and Stirling were "of the oldest standing in Divinity and consequently are to be presumed not only to have the most knowledge, but to understand best the Professor's Sentiment and Ways of Speaking on these Subjects," since they had heard him lecture on them before. The seniority of these three does not seem to be borne out by the information given with the depositions, which indicate that others had studied under Simson for as long. They might, however, have been the most faithful in attendance, when other students had been forced to take time from their studies to earn a living. Simson added that only three of

146 Dundas, *Processes*, 183.
147 Wodrow, *Correspondence*, 3:309.
148 Dundas, *Processes*, 184.
149 Ibid., 185.
150 Simson, *Case*, xxx.
151 Ibid., 117. Bain had informed the presbytery that he was eighteen. He was the youngest student from whom a deposition was taken. Dundas, *Processes*, 118.

the students attending his last session were cited: others would have testified that the professor taught the necessary existence of Christ had they been called.[152] Simson was scathing about the deposition of Alexander Barr, a twenty-year-old who had entered the divinity class in November 1725, saying that Barr had testified from a written paper giving the alleged words of the professor in execrable Latin. He questioned how Barr could have remembered his words for fifteen months when he could not remember them for twelve hours.[153]

Simson produced a new vindication of his orthodoxy with respect to the necessary existence and independence of Christ, which said:

1st, That Christ is *Necessarily-existent* in the common and ordinary Sense of the Word, as it signifies an Impossibility not to have been, which is one of the *Essential Perfections* of the Divine Nature that are equally common to all the Three Persons.

2dly, That *Independency* is to be affirmed of the Son of God, at [sic] it signifies an *Essential Perfection* of his Divine Nature, which is equally common to all the Persons of the *Trinity*.

3dly, That the Three Persons of the *Trinity* are of one Substance in Number, not taken in such a Sense as that Phrase is in common Use applied to Creatures, which restricts it to one Person, but in a Sense importing the strictest Unity of the Godhead in Opposition to a Plurality of Gods, yet consistently with their being Three Persons in Opposition to one Person.[154]

Wodrow, comparing Simson to Charles I in making important concessions too late to help his cause, felt that the whole unpleasant business might have been avoided, had Simson made such a declaration to the Presbytery of Glasgow in 1726.[155] Considering the animosity shown against Simson by some of his colleagues in the early 1720s, however, this seems unlikely.

After Simson's many orthodox declarations, the issue debated by this assembly was not heresy but whether a teacher who employed inappropriate language should be censured by the church.[156] However strongly some churchmen might feel about Simson's position, more knowledgeable members such as Grange realized that the professor's views were

152 Simson, *Case*, 129.
153 Ibid., 179–80.
154 Dundas, *Processes*, 187.
155 Wodrow, *Correspondence*, 3:318.
156 Ibid., 3:304, 307.

within the pale of Reformed thought. Furthermore, the professor had a forceful contingent of supporters led by Dundas of Arniston, who were mainly Squadrone members.[157] This fact, combined with the Argathelian management of the assembly, gave some basis to Wodrow's feeling that "party appeared as litle in this affair as I have seen any, nou for many years."[158] For once the Whig gentlemen were willing to ignore their political differences in order to work out a compromise that would prevent the deposition of Professor Simson, with whose theology they agreed. They seem to have been prepared to argue for a non-partisan settlement, although this proved difficult to achieve, because in the eyes of the ultra-Calvinists Simson had committed "a Crime deeper than Crimson," by even discussing Clarke's views on the Trinity.[159] He was guilty of causing dissension in the church and of unsettling the faithful.

The impossibility of bridging the divide between the two sides led the assembly's members to approve unanimously the report of the committee that had been studying the case and to empower the moderator, Hadow, Mitchell, and the delegates from the Presbytery of Glasgow to nominate thirty-four members for a new Committee for Purity of Doctrine to continue the investigation for another year. The membership of the nominating committee is of some interest, since Hadow and the Glasgow ministers had firmly opposed Simson throughout the assembly, and proves the strength of anti-Simson feeling in the assembled church.[160] The new committee was to consider all the articles not judged by the present assembly. Simson was to be neither absolved nor condemned, but a report was to be prepared so that the next assembly could resolve the case. In the interim, Simson was to be suspended from teaching and preaching, since some articles had been found relevant and proven.[161]

On the morning of 19 May, Simson received instructions to make himself available to the committee and to attend the next assembly. He

157 These included Alexander [?] Anderson, James Bannatyne, Robert Carrick, Principal Chalmers, Lord Drummore, Professor Hamilton, John Hunter, James Mercer, Alexander Robison, John Sinclair, and others. Ibid., 3:310.

158 Wodrow, *Analecta*, 3:420.

159 "When abandoned Mockers and Scriblers conspire, / To make impious Ballads for *Simson*, / They proclaim the profane Spirit them doth inspire, / To defend a Crime deeper than Crimson." Crawford and Stewart, 19 May 1729, Erskine, *Extracts*, 92.

160 Wodrow, *Analecta*, 3:420.

161 Dundas, *Processes*, 190.

agreed to obey the will of the assembly, assuring it that "I have always wished for, and to my Power endeavoured the Peace and Prosperity of the Church of Scotland. And will still earnestly pray for and seek her Peace and Welfare; and if I cannot live in this Church without being a Bone of Contention, I will much rather leave it, and heartily pray that Peace with Truth and Righteousness may be promoted in it."[162] Despite this profession of goodwill, when the committee held its first meeting on 22 May, Simson was absent. His excuse of ill health and family circumstances had been accepted, since his wife had given birth to their son Patrick on 16 May, and a new meeting date was set for August.

The professor may have been startled by the antagonism that had been shown to him. His conversations with gentlemen and with moderate ministers had led him to expect a more sympathetic hearing at the assembly. The lack of political tension had increased this hope. Instead, the members had accepted hearsay evidence about odd phrases taken out of context and had rejected his own assertions of orthodoxy. His long-standing lay Squadrone friends had rallied to his support, but the Argathelian managers had not been strong enough to defeat the ultra-orthodox stalwarts. In his diary Grange congratulated himself on his efforts to influence the assembly, calling himself an instrument of God in the Simson case. Modestly he added, "not that I attribute all to have been done by me, even as the Instrument."[163]

Wodrow was also surprised at the outcome of the assembly, though pleased that the feared split on political grounds had not taken place. He had expected that Simson would receive more support from Argathelian-controlled burghs, as had been rumoured. The conservatives had feared that Argyll influence would be sufficient to sway delegates from such Campbell strongholds as Inveraray, site of the duke's main Scottish residence. In the event, most Argathelians seemed to oppose Simson, "and not a feu of the Squadrone joyned them."[164] The old covenanting Campbell supporters remained true to their heritage as their leaders adapted to the ways of the new century. Even those most favourable to the professor regretted the disturbance that he had caused to the church with "his imprudence and stiffnes."[165] Wodrow's fears of a total rupture within the Church of Scotland over Simson's fate led him to urge the maintenance

162 Simson, *Case*, xliii.
163 NLS, MS 1008, 16.
164 Wodrow, *Analecta*, 3:420.
165 Ibid.

of a united front. Hence he upheld the necessity of suspending Simson, despite his apparent retraction of any error, since merely rebuking him would have led to separation by the extreme orthodox elements in the church.

John Simson's public career ended with his suspension by the assembly in May 1727. Although in 1808 James Wodrow said to his friend Kenrick that "Simpson was not expelled either from the Church or the University, but *suspended* or prohibited from teaching in public; continuing to enjoy the emoluments of his Office, & even to teach a little in his own house."[166] Whatever the truth about these private classes may have been, Professor John Simson never again lectured in the divinity hall nor occupied a Scottish pulpit. However, he did not give up the contest easily. For four more years the campaign of sabotage by propaganda, skirmishes in committee, and pitched battles in assembly continued on both sides.

166 J. Wodrow to S. Kenrick, 18 March 1808, Dr Williams's Library, MS 24.157, 259, 2r.

11

The Brink of a Rupture:
Depose? Acquit? 1727–1729

PROPAGANDA AND COMMITTEES,
MAY 1727–MAY 1728

Simson's suspension by the General Assembly of 1727 pleased neither the orthodox party in the church nor the proponents of enlightened theology. For the next four years both sides continued to make efforts to have him deposed or restored to office. The unfettered discussion that took place during this period points to a society that was informed and free to participate in debates of principle. Simson's continued suspension did not silence other liberal teachers or ministers, although his mild punishment disheartened the orthodox anti-Erastian extremists in the church. Waiting in the shadows, Scots politicians watched warily, prepared to apply the necessary pressure to avoid the serious conflict that they all dreaded. This political necessity gradually began to dominate the concerns both of those who believed Simson guilty of heresy and of those who advocated his religious philosophy.

With the hopes for an early resolution to the Simson affair dashed, the combatants turned to the printed word to press their views. As the ultra-orthodox mustered their arguments against the outspoken professor, positions hardened and publications became more frequent. As early as 1726, Allan Logan had produced a brief pamphlet explaining to the uninitiated that the significance of the necessary existence of Christ lay in the fact that modern Arians denied it.[1] Before the General Assembly of May 1727, Simson and his supporters had printed the details of the actions taken against him and his defence against the charges in a *Case*, with a preface that explained his side of the affair. By

---

1 [Allan Logan], *Countryman's Brief Remarks.*

July 1727 Simson's friends had printed a second edition of it with additions. Grange called for the orthodox to counter this propaganda, since he feared that the Simson camp would persuade the Court in London that "men of sense and breeding" approved the professor's teaching and that it was "only opposed by odd out-of-the-way people."[2] As late as May 1728 Grange lamented to his London friend Abraham Taylor, "Nothing has yet appear'd in Print against it [Simson's *Case*], but two little Pieces: One Entitled Remarks on Mr Simsons Case & it is written by Mr McLaren one of the Edinburgh Ministers ... The other little Piece I think has the Tittle of Animadversions on a Pamphlet Entitl'd, The Case of Mr John Simson, & was written by a Minister about Glasgow."[3] In his reply Taylor attributed the second pamphlet to John Hamilton and suggested that Grange's friends should focus their literary efforts on the question of the necessary existence of the Son and on Simson's shiftings and inconsistencies over this.[4]

Grange and Wodrow are known to have encouraged the publication of anti-Simson material because their papers have survived, but others must also have spearheaded crusades to present the orthodox case. By the late 1720s much of the strength of the anti-Simson movement came from east-central and northeast Scotland. Fife and Perth were the home districts of Haddow, the Erskine brothers, Hogg, and Moncrieff of Culfargie. Many ministers holding extremely orthodox views had been parachuted into office in the Aberdeen region during the purges of the early 1690s and after the Fifteen. It seems likely that such men would have encouraged their presbytery brethren to demand punishment for Simson.

Accordingly, the presses began to pour out an ever-increasing number of pamphlets and books presenting the anti-Simson point of view. Most were anonymous, but Wodrow generally put the author's initials on his copies if he knew them, permitting the identification of some. A smaller number were published by Simson supporters, who were presumably less fanatical about their cause. Over the next two years, Wodrow noted the authorship of works against Simson by James Haddow, John Hunter, Allan Logan, Alexander Moncrieff of Culfargie, and John Williamson and in his favour by William Wishart, Jr.[5]

2 Wodrow, *Correspondence*, 3:321.

3 Lord Grange to A. Taylor, 18 May 1728, NAS, GD124/15/1332/2.

4 A. Taylor to Lord Grange, 24 June 1728, ibid., 3.

5 This last pamphlet has traditionally been attributed to William Wishart, Sr. M.A. Stewart, however, believes from internal evidence that it comes from the pen of the son rather than the father.

The official collection (*Processes*) of all the relevant documents and minutes of the case was compiled prior to the 1728 assembly by the church's senior lay official, the advocate John Dundas of Philipston, clerk to the General Assembly. The publication of this volume in Edinburgh was designed to provide its members with accurate background information.

Wodrow told Grange in February 1728 that Simson had been lobbying quietly to ensure that the delegates chosen to the next assembly would be favourable to him.[6] The polarization of the more vocal members of the Church of Scotland was now well established, their theological concerns inextricably combined with church politics. Each side had invested too much time and effort in the Simson affair to suffer defeat complacently. To the ultra-orthodox, the case was further evidence of the general corruption of the church. To the moderates, it was proof of an intolerant zeal that damaged the Presbyterian image. At the same time, Wodrow and his friends began to appreciate the dangers into which the church was running headlong, reawakening in them the old Scottish apprehension lest division among Presbyterians be used as an opportunity for intervention by English politicians. There is no doubt that Wodrow and Grange saw Simson's teaching as hazardous to orthodox doctrine; by this stage, however, their immediate aim was to prevent a schism between the extreme conservatives and the proponents of modern theology that might weaken the church and have political repercussions for the nation.

In June 1727 there was a battle in the University of Glasgow over the election of the dean of faculty. Simson, Dunlop, and the Argathelians seem to have backed William Wishart, Jr, while Stirling and his faction nominated John Gray.[7] These nominations reveal conclusively the chasm between the factions within the university, since the perspectives of the two nominees could hardly have been further apart.[8] The principal managed to secure Gray's election by cajoling a vote from Forbes, who had changed sides, and by persuading Brisbane to abstain. Stirling was then in declining health, and this victory was one of his last. Writing to a Scottish Squadrone subordinate after the election, Chancellor Montrose

6 Wodrow, *Correspondence*, 3:335.

7 It is not clear from the context which Simson supported Wishart – John or Robert. Wodrow, *Analecta*, 3:429.

8 GUA 26635, 52.

regretted Stirling's illness, both for the sake of the principal and for the consequences that his death would entail. He connected Simson's problems with the appointment of a new principal: "You say Mr Smyth of Cramond, who I know is a very good man, will probably fill Mr Sympsons place if he is turn'd out, and that if he was once there, it would be naturall to apply for him to be Pri[ncipa]ll but you know it will be a year before Mr Symp[sons]'s fate is known."9 The Squadrone would have preferred the Simson case to be decided before Stirling died. Apart from his natural preference for a Squadrone member, Stirling's desire for Gray to be elected dean of faculty may have been a final attempt to persuade him to support the university and its problematic professor. At this juncture, it might have seemed wiser to co-opt an active opponent than to promote a youthful member of the Simson camp, especially in view of Simson's political defection to Argyll.

Simson himself was assumed to have political aims in the summer of 1727, just as in the previous year, since he set off for England the day after the dean's election. Rumours abounded as to the purpose of his journey. The simplest were related to health: he was going to Bath to drink the waters; he had been advised to ride for his health. The proof of the latter lies in a medical directive of 1 July signed by three of Simson's colleagues at Glasgow, Professors Thomas Brisbane and John Johnston and medical lecturer George Thomson: "It will be proper he [Simson] should ride most of the summer and harvest season taking care not to ride too much at a tyme but rather frequentlie avoiding the night air and the heat of day equally. In rainy weather he is to keep the house and if he finds anything of his indisposition return or his stomak heavie and loathing he must take the vomitoure he is used to. He must drink no malt liquor butt water or bristol water with sherry canary or port wine. And lett him observe all the rules of diet formerlyie prescribed to him."10

Some people postulated ecclesiastical motives for Simson's journey: he was looking for a post in the south; he was going to explain his case to English ministers; he had been heard to preach in Newcastle, or in Coventry; he was meeting non-subscribers, or even subscribers. Political gossip said that Simson was hoping to make his case at Court, to which he had been introduced by Lord Chancellor King and where he was favourably received as a "man of merit" who was being unfairly attacked,

9 Montrose to Gorthie, 10 June 1727, NAS, GD220/5/859, 15a.
10 NAS, CH1/2/56, 107.

or that he had been soliciting support from Islay, who had written to Grange and Drummond "to moderat their zeal against him."[11]

None of these suggestions was proved, although some may well have been accurate. While there is no evidence that Simson was acquainted with Peter King (1669–1734) personally, he had cited in his defence King's *History of the Apostles' Creed* (1702). Educated as a Presbyterian, and interested in religious subjects as well as in law and science, Lord King might well have been sympathetic to Simson. Wodrow was curious about the matter and asked Grange if the rumour were true. Grange replied that if Simson had indeed been introduced at Court, King was the man to have done so, since "he denyed all foundamentalls in religion save what ... wer in the Baptismall Covenant."[12] Up to 1727, Simson had another influential acquaintance in London, his old pupil John Montgomerie of Giffen, who was member of Parliament for Ayrshire and groom of the bedchamber to the Prince of Wales. That year financial difficulties forced Montgomerie to give up his seat to become governor of New York. Islay was also resident in London for much of the year, and if Simson visited London he would have paid his respects to such an influential patron.

Wherever his travels took him, Simson was not in Edinburgh at the meeting on 8 August of the Committee for Purity of Doctrine, since "Professor Crawford put in the Clerk's Hands, a Consultation subscribed by three Physicians, advising the Professor to ride for his Health."[13] Accordingly a new meeting date was set for 7 November 1727.

On 28 September Simson returned to Glasgow, "just about ten or twelve minutes before Principall Stirling dyed, and was with him at his death; but I be[lieve] it was the Principall's happines he did not knou him."[14] Other notable deaths that summer were those of William Mitchell and Sir James Stewart. The former died on his way to London with the Church of Scotland's congratulations to George II on his recent accession. There he had planned to inform the English Dissenters of the true state of affairs from the anti-Simson point of view. Mitchell's death left the conservatives concerned lest Professor Hamilton "have

11 Wodrow, *Analecta*, 3:444.

12 Ibid., 3:457.

13 Dundas, *Processes*, 193. On other occasions the sources noted that Simson's doctors had certified his inability to attend meetings on account of his poor health; see ibid., 236. A second medical certificate dated 10 April 1728 appears in NAS, CH1/2/56, 168.

14 Wodrow, *Analecta*, 3:444.

publick affairs mostly in his hands."[15] Wodrow worried about the effect that the loss of these men would have on the Simson committee. By now, however, it seems that the ultra-orthodox propaganda against Simson had begun to take effect, and the deaths made little difference to the deliberations of the committee.

At its November meeting, Simson tried to get the Presbytery of Glasgow to acknowledge his right to be notified of, and participate in, presbytery meetings, on the grounds that he had been suspended from teaching and preaching, but not from his other ministerial functions. This proved a difficult decision for the members; when they finally denied his request, Simson announced that he would appeal their ruling to the synod. These actions indicate that Simson was determined to profess complete innocence of the charges against him and to proclaim to the world that he was being persecuted. He was giving notice to his opponents that he would continue to monitor the legality of their actions.

The Committee for Purity of Doctrine sat for three days in November, when it reviewed the fourth article, dealing with whether Simson had called specific terms "philosophical niceties" and "impertinent," when used with reference to the Trinity. Considerable amounts of time were spent on "needles delayes and harangues" made on Simson's behalf by Lord Drummore, with Provost Drummond contributing to the delay.[16] Lord Pencaitland, Professor Matthew Crawford, and the ministers Craig of Edinburgh and M'George of Penicuik also supported Simson. Once again Argathelian made common cause with Squadrone member in the struggle against fanaticism. In the end Simson and the committee agreed to transmit to the next assembly a statement relating to the proof of the fourth article of the libel, which admitted that he had uttered the words only once and that it was unclear on what he had been lecturing at the time.[17] The committee now agreed with Simson about the lack of suitable context for his words and admitted that the students were vague in their memories of them. Convinced that evidence still existed that could clear his name, Simson called for further depositions to be taken for clarification.

15 Ibid., 3:447.
16 Ibid., 3:455.
17 Dundas, *Processes*, 198.

A new subcommittee was given the task of analysing the depositions on the second and third articles of the libel for a meeting to be held in early March 1728, when members of the Committee for Purity of Doctrine planned a two-week session to prepare for the May assembly. Prior to this, the Presbytery of Glasgow was to finish its review of Simson's compliance with the act of 1717, and Simson was instructed to attend both the relevant meetings. Meanwhile Wodrow and some kindred spirits from the committee met to discuss possible anti-Simson measures, such as making efforts to prevent the Simson side from influencing the choice of delegates to the next assembly and refuting Simson's printed *Case*.[18]

In December 1727 and January 1728 the Presbytery of Glasgow had inconclusive meetings, with many absentees. In the first week of February, it agreed on the form of questions to be put to the professor at an interrogation to be held on 14 February, but Simson declined to appear because of a legal technicality in his summons. Depositions were taken from students who had studied under Simson since 1717. The young men were "preachers, and lads of good reach and knouledge," and gave clear depositions.[19] Not surprisingly, since they were being questioned on lectures heard up to ten years earlier, some had limited recollections of Simson's words. The doctrine taught by Simson had not been condemned in 1717, only his methods of expression, so he had continued to focus on the rational basis of Christianity and on such texts as "Seek, and ye shall find" (Matt, 7:7). Indeed William Boyd testified that Simson had cited these words of Christ to prove that the Lord would give grace to all who sought it piously and sincerely.[20] The testimonies suggest that Simson did not separate grace and works in order to elevate the latter; his stress had been on man's duty to seek the gift of grace through the means provided. These statements contained little new, but they horrified Wodrow, who saw the doctrine delineated in them as dangerous Pelagianism. Convinced of Simson's guilt, Wodrow did not question how such dubious teaching had managed to produce well-educated preachers.

At the March meeting of the Committee for Purity of Doctrine, Simson showed composure and poise under attack by Allan Logan and

18 Wodrow, *Analecta*, 3:456.
19 Ibid., 3:480.
20 Dundas, *Processes*, 300. The depositions appear on pages 281–302.

Lord Grange. Although the committee was obviously in favour of orthodox opinion and against innovation, Simson showed himself neither "dashed nor sunk" when all seemed to go against him; in Wodrow's eyes he was "rash, incautiouse, and highly imprudent."[21] When asked how he had observed the 1717 act, Simson struggled to maintain legal process. Without replying, he asked if he had been accused of a breach of the act, and by whom. The response was that the presbytery was merely obeying the instructions of the 1727 assembly.

When the presbytery admitted that it had taken precognitions from his old students, while denying him access to them, Simson decided to take refuge in silence, given the prevailing ill-will. He felt that it was not "just or safe for him to give any Answer ... because he knows not what Information may have been given against him by these who have been examined; the Presbytery having refused ... to read to him the Declarations of the Witnesses that had been already examined in the Precognition."[22]

He appealed the presbytery's refusal to give him access to the precognitions on the grounds that it was contrary to the *Form of Process*, 7:3. The procedure was also against all canon law as established by Pope Innocent III and as followed by the Church of Scotland. Simson requested extracts of the presbytery's report, giving the questions asked, the answers, and the names of the students interrogated. The Presbytery of Glasgow, in a decidedly shifty move, refused his request until it had taken the advice of the Committee for Purity of Doctrine. Simson protested this refusal and appealed to the synod, explaining that, although he intended no disrespect to the committee, it was not a judicatory according to the rules of the church and so he could not appeal to *it*.

Not surprisingly, Simson and his supporters compared the manoeuvres of his accusers to those of the Inquisition. Nevertheless, a strange lack of urgency on the part of the committee members was again shown by the absence of a quorum to discuss the matter at the meeting of 12 March. Moreover, the next day, when enough members were present, it was found that the subcommittee formed to prepare a report had not met. A new group was hastily put together to study the depositions.

Even a remote country minister such as Thomas Mack of Terregles heard of the interventions of Professor Hamilton to assist Simson. He

21 Wodrow, *Analecta*, 3:481.
22 Dundas, *Processes*, 201–2.

reported that Hamilton had written to Dumfries committee member Alexander Robison, who was a Simson supporter, that "measures are to be laid th[a]t Mr Simson may not be deposed, nor condemned as a heeretick, but th[a]t he may have as fair an outcome as possible if he cannot be continued with chair and tho[ugh] deserving yet he must not be censured as a criminal."[23] At a subsequent committee meeting, Professor Hamilton apparently showed himself in agreement with some of Simson's views. Grange, who considered Simson's statements about the personal properties of the Father "a Subterfuge for him to Lurk under with a Heretical meaning," recorded that Hamilton agreed with Simson "that by this necessity peculiar to the Father he meant, the Father's being of none, wheras the Son is from the Father, & in that sense not self-originated."[24]

Since the orthodox group seemed scandalized by this proposition, Rev. James Craig, a Simson supporter, asked the professor, "Is not the Son as necessarly the only begotten of the Father, as the Father is necessarly of none?"[25] This question caused the subtle mind of Simson to reflect on the doubts that had troubled the early church, leading him to refuse to answer directly. At the General Assembly he explained this hesitation – he had been thinking of the words of the Creed of Damasus and was concerned lest the necessary generation of Christ seemed to include fatality and coaction.[26]

On 19 March 1728 a new libel accused Simson of contravening the act of 1717 and charged him with continuing to teach all the propositions considered doubtful a decade earlier, citing twenty-two witnesses in proof. The next day a report declared that Simson was guilty of having once denied necessary existence, of uttering ambiguities, and of having made omissions in his teaching. On 22 March the committee found him "highly culpable" and deserving of censure,

through his foresaid Disobedience to the Act of the Assembly, and the Orders of the Presbytery and Committee, and in that he maketh bold to justify his said Conduct, from such Grounds as tend to overthrow the Discipline, in use throughout this Church, in the Case of all Scandals, and do condemn the Practice of Assembly and other Judicatories, in their Procedure with Persons justly

23 T. Mack to R. Wodrow, 6 March 1728, NLS, Wodrow Letters Quarto, XVIII, 29.
24 Lord Grange to A. Taylor, 16 April 1728, NAS, GD124/15/1332/1, 2–3.
25 Lord Grange to A. Taylor, 16 April 1728, NAS, MS, GD124/15/1332/1, 3.
26 See below, 302. NAS, CH1/2/56, 260.

suspected of Error, or concerning whom there is a *fama clamosa* of their being erroneous. And that it will be the more needful the Assembly duly animadvert
upon this, to prevent the like Disorders in any others hereafter, and to prevent
the spreading of dangerous Errors, through not questioning Persons about
whom there is a just Suspicion or *fama clamosa*.[27]

Although the committee had determined that the professor was guilty of
errors and omissions, its findings suggest that to the members his greatest sin was disobedience, which brought the church courts into disrespect. The committee seemed to be calling for Simson's censure largely
to prevent others' using his case as a precedent for refusing to answer
queries. The Glasgow professor loomed larger as a trouble-maker than
as a heretic.

The committee ordered Simson to respond to the new libel by 9 April.
Grange had no sympathy with Simson's plea that the time was inadequate. He told Abraham Taylor that the committee had found relevant
all the articles of the libel that it had studied. Simson's defences had
been rejected, although he had wasted time through "jangling and
Quibles." Generally Simson was "the most egregious chicaneur" that
Grange had ever known.[28] On 24 April, after two weeks of delay because
of lack of a quorum, Simson's health, and legal arguments against the
libel, the defence produced a four-point paper of objections to the new
libel: the period of time from May 1717 to March 1728 was too long for
the memory of the witnesses to be accurate; the place was too vague; the
libel was founded neither on a particular complaint nor on a *fama
clamosa*; and the professor had fully observed the act of 1717. The defence also noted the differences between the act of 1717 and that of 1722
against the *Marrow*, which specified the propositions that ministers were
forbidden to teach. The lack of such specificity rendered the libel null in
law. As incontrovertible proof of his orthodox teaching, the defence
stressed that over the years Simson's students had passed trials both in
Glasgow and in other presbyteries, becoming "useful and faithful Ministers," who "by the Course of their Preaching and Gospel-conversation,
have given good Proof of their Soundness in the Faith, and of their
Christian Behaviour. Whence it is manifest that there is no Error taught
by the Defendant, which is spreading among the People, no nor so
much as even among these who have been his Scholars."[29]

27 Dundas, *Processes*, 234.
28 Lord Grange to A. Taylor, 16 April 1728, NAS, GD124/15/1332/1.
29 Dundas, *Processes*, 242.

The committee rejected all these objections. The time and place were adequate. There had indeed been a *fama clamosa*, as claimed by the General Assembly of 1726, which had found "it is notour, that there was a flagrant Report widely spread abroad," saying that Simson had continued to teach the prohibited doctrines.[30] (To this, of course, the argument that nothing had been specifically prohibited still applied.) However, the committee felt that Simson's maintenance of objectionable doctrines was clear from his answers to Webster's libel, to the letters to Rowan, and to the Committee for Purity of Doctrine at that time. A subcommittee making more careful written answers the following day added that even if, through God's grace, no scholars had been infected with Simson's opinions, his trial should continue.

In response, Simson defended the validity of many of the teachings discussed in the first case. Some might be controversial, but there could be no prohibition on discussion of them, since there was "no *Index Expurgatorius* in this Protestant Church" and the act of 1717 did not forbid the reading of any book.[31] He called witnesses for the defence, but he may have realized that his cause was lost. The committee found that all the articles of the new libel were relevant, although it allowed Simson to pose questions to the witnesses. Perhaps heartened by this small victory, on 27 April Simson again attacked the libel on the grounds that he had taught nothing contrary to scripture, to the Westminster Confession, or to the catechisms of the church; therefore "the whole allegations of this libel are irrelevant."[32] Opinions that were merely matters of speculation among Reformed theologians could not be found either true or false, so could not be used as the basis of a libel under the act of 1717. The committee rejected these objections and proceeded to examine the students. Although Simson's words were generally scriptural and to modern eyes unexceptionable, all the articles were found proven.[33] This finding was unanimous, but several of the members who normally supported Simson were absent.[34]

---

30 Ibid., 245.

31 Ibid., 264.

32 Ibid., 271.

33 We can gain a measure of how the committee looked at Simson's teaching in Wodrow, "As to the third about *ratio*, we found that it was proven, that he had used terms, used by adversaries in an unsound sense, though he explained them in a sound sense, which comes under the prohibition of the act 1717 directly, and, consequently, is a breach of the act." Wodrow, *Correspondence*, 3:342.

34 Wodrow mentions Crawford, Drummore, and Hamilton as being absent. Ibid.

Whatever Simson may have anticipated from the coming gathering, his enemies had fears about the outcome. John Williamson published a pamphlet at the beginning of May in the "Name of some Onlookers who are Trembling for the Ark of God."[35] He exhorted the members of the General Assembly to allow the Lord to direct their words with brevity, in order to prevent further delay, which might win more support for Simson. Williamson warned against the plans of Simson's friends to have the assembly pass an act prohibiting the professor from teaching using the terms found objectionable. This would merely allow Simson to "instil his dangerous Sentiments by other Words, and so shift from Time to Time under this Colour; Is it not evident from what hath been found relevant and proven, that he entertain wrong Sentiment about the Trinity and Supreme Deity of Christ; and shall this be tollerated by such a gentle Method as a meer Prohibition of the Use of Terms?"[36] The fact that the supposedly dangerous sentiments of the professor had not been proved to have been instilled into any specific student was of minimal importance to the irate and anxious hyper-Calvinist faction.

Grange worried about the views of some members of the assembly and was bothered by rumours of support for Simson in high places in London, since these would give courage to his supporters. Should the Church of Scotland fail to curb Simson, its "General character … will suddenly be quite alter'd & cruelly to the worse," and "reall Christians will be the Laughter of the world, and the wrong side will gain ground & increase. This will have terrible effects even with respect to civil matters; w[hi]ch I wish those who should, may duely Lay to heart."[37] London politicians should beware what they did in interfering in Scottish ecclesiastical affairs.

THE GENERAL ASSEMBLY OF 1728

When the General Assembly commenced on 2 May 1728, the committee hearings were still incomplete. The royal commissioner was the Earl of Loudoun, the preferred candidate of the Simson side.[38] Loudoun had told Grange the previous week that the Court desired that "the softest measures" should be taken against Simson.[39] The King's lawyers

35 [Williamson], *Speech.*
36 Ibid., 15.
37 Lord Grange to A. Taylor, 16 April 1728, NAS, GD124/15/1332/1, 4, 5.
38 Wodrow, *Correspondence*, 3:335.
39 Wodrow, *Analecta*, 3:500.

had suggested that it would be illegal to separate Simson from a living that was a Crown presentation. Grange was happy to inform the earl that Glasgow's divinity chair was not a royal presentation. Furthermore, in matters of doctrinal error, the church had legal jurisdiction. Simson's English excursion the previous summer may have been bearing fruit: a Campbell earl could be expected to act on the advice of Argyll and Islay. Simson must have welcomed such Argathelian political interference as was implied by Loudoun's pre-assembly conference with the royal lawyers.

We may deduce feelings of at least one Edinburgh citizen about the legality of queries' leading to self-incrimination from a satirical set of questions displayed publicly at the Cross, at the Assembly House, and on Lord Grange's front door on 9 May. They asked Grange: "1. Whither he be a Jesuit or not? 2. Whither he be a pensioner to the Pope? 3. Whither my Lord Grange can answer the former Queries? 4. Whither if he answer them he ought to be belived?"[40] Grange's strong stand against Simson had not made him universally popular. To calm emotions, Professor Hamilton's opening sermon called for the exercise of wisdom and the balancing of due regard for personal rights with the necessity of maintaining the fundamentals of faith.[41] William Wishart, Sr, was elected moderator, although Wodrow decided that the way men voted proved that this choice had no reference to the Simson affair. Wishart, whose early patron had been Carstares, was no extremist, though more conservative in his views than his two clerical sons.

On 6 May Principal Neil Campbell protested that the assembly's determination should not affect the rights of the university to judge its own members. The next day Simson addressed the assembly, stressing his full belief in the necessary existence of Christ. He repeated the definition that he had given to the previous assembly and tried to establish that his understanding of essential necessary existence was in accordance with the words of the Westminster Confession. He stated that he had always taught that the names "Jehovah" and "I am" – terms that some committee members believed "to be the Scripture Expressions containing their Meaning of the Word *Necessary-existence*" – belonged to the Son, "Wherefore I would be understood to mean the same Thing, when I say the Son of God is *Necessarily-existent*, or when I say he is

40 Ibid., 3:510.
41 Wodrow, *Correspondence*, 3:338.

Jehovah, or that he always was, is, and must be the same invariably, or that he is *Infinite and Unchangeable in his Being, Wisdom, Power,* &c."[42]

Advocate Murray then explained how the professor, in his classes, had tried to differentiate between the essential properties, which were common to all three persons in the Trinity, and the personal properties of each – the Father's being of none, the Son's being begotten of the Father, and the Holy Ghost's proceeding from the Father and Son. When Simson had said that terms such as "necessary existence" and "independency" should not be used in the context of the personal relations between the persons of the Trinity, it was to prevent misunderstanding, not to spread heresy.

Murray addressed the question of how to interpret the students' testimonies through an analogy: a professor of law might be libelled for saying that it was lawful for a man to kill his neighbour; several witnesses might well remember such a statement, but the professor should not be condemned if others also remembered that the context was a predicament involving self-defence. The whole conversation between Simson and his students needed to be examined to discover the context in which he had made his comments. The lawyer reconstructed the circumstances in which the libelled statements on the impertinence of words such as "independency" were made, showing that Simson asked rhetorical questions to challenge his students and tried to separate the personal and essential properties of the Godhead. Although he had said that some expressions were "Philosophical niceties and ambiguous Terms of Art," no witness was positive as to what those terms might have been.[43] Despite these arguments, however, the assembly voted that it was clearly proven that Simson had taught that the term "Necessary-existence" was impertinent and not to be used in talking of the Trinity.

The *General Assembly Papers* for 1728 contain many of the questions put by delegates and Simson's answers on the subject of necessary existence. Although to the modern reader the professor seems to have responded with expressions of the greatest orthodoxy, either his past reputation or his manner of explanation continued to irritate the evangelical wing of the Church of Scotland. On 8 May Simson clarified his teaching further by stressing that since necessary existence was common

42 [Simson], *Supplement,* 58–9.
43 Simson, *Case,* 165.

to all the persons of the Trinity, it could not be used to express the properties distinguishing the three persons. If he had ever said that the term was impertinent, it was in this context.[44] In response to a question from the floor he added that it was "a very unfitt & unsafe way of speaking to say that the Father alone were Necessarily Existent, or that necessary existence were the personal property of the Father considering the common use of the word all the three divine persons being equally possest of infinite & Divine perfections among which necessary existence & Independency are comprehended, they being all one God."[45]

The complexity of the debate is seen in a question about the statement in the fifth-century *Symbolum Damasi*, "The Father begot the Son, not by will, nor necessity, but by nature" (*Pater Filium genuit, non voluntate, nec necessitate, sed natura*). Simson was asked if he "was of Opinion that the highest notion of Necessity did agree to his Generation Excluding the Necessity of Coaction and fatality out of the Question?" He replied, "That the 2^d person of the Godhead was the Son of God by Nature, and that the Father begot him by Nature by such a Necessity even in the Highest Sense of it, as Excludes the Necessity of Coaction & fatality."[46]

To a further question posed by Alston as to whether necessary existence and divine perfections belonged equally to all the persons of the Trinity, Simson tried to append a statement on numerical oneness, an issue that was troubling many. "And seeing all these Essential Perfections, doe belong to the persons of the Son and Holy Ghost equally with the Father ... they are not different Gods tho' distinct persons from the Father but the same God of one Substance pouer and Eternity with him, so that the unity of the Godhead is one in number & not more."[47] This declaration did not satisfy his opponents, who saw it as an arranged opportunity for Simson to demonstrate orthodoxy, rather than as a reiteration of long-held opinion.

The following day Simson was forced to announce that he had no internal reservations about necessary existence's being peculiar to the Father.[48] His personal theological crisis of the mid-1720s seems to have centred on his doubts as to whether he had been teaching Sabellianism, an anxiety perhaps stimulated by his reading of Clarke. The question of

44 NAS, CH1/2/56, 238.
45 Ibid., 255.
46 Ibid., 257.
47 Ibid., 258.
48 Ibid., 259.

the numerical unity of the Godhead related to the change in the tone of his teaching. Presumably Simson had insinuated that to insist on numerical unity was to risk the creation of a unitary divinity, showing different modes of existence in a Sabellian sense, which would have challenged orthodox beliefs on the incarnation and salvation. Some assembly members were still dissatisfied, for the next day another declaration by Simson mentioned that there were doubts about the consistency of his various statements. The professor apologized for any means of expression that might have given offence or suspicion of unsoundness in faith or of intent to mislead.

The opposition to Simson, led by Haddow, John Hamilton, Allan Logan, Gray, Ogilvy, Smith, Grange, and Auchinleck, was countered by Alston, William Hamilton, George Logan, the lord president, and Drummore. The two factions met regularly in the evenings through May 1727 to plot strategy – the orthodox at the Eagle, and the pro-Simson side at Herdman's tavern.[49] On several occasions tactical decisions to postpone votes until the next morning allowed leaders of each side to determine who would speak and how the assembly would be managed. James Wodrow confirmed the existence of this strategy. His information was doubly verified, through his own family and through that of his wife, Louisa Hamilton, daughter of Gavin, Professor Hamilton's bookseller son. According to James, the Simson supporters, under the leadership of Hamilton, "met every night in a tavern before any important branch of the cause came on; appointed their speakers, to answer & ridicule some of the violent speakers of the high party, & by their talents & other measures kept them at bay."[50] Sometimes their tactics worked, but the orthodox group worked hard to foil them.

It was again essential to convince the assembly that the issue was not heresy, but the propagation of unsound opinions by a teacher. The orthodox leaders may have been afraid that if the determination should appear to rest on the question of heresy, there was little proof on which to find Simson guilty: his orthodox declarations were many, and the evidence of his students was weak. As Simson's supporters had repeatedly reminded the assembly, only three of twenty-seven witnesses had put unsound words into Simson's mouth. Moreover, he had not been found heretical in the protracted process of 1714–17. Unsoundness seems to have been a fall-back position on which the orthodox leaders might win.

49 Wodrow, *Analecta*, 3:502.
50 J. Wodrow to S. Kenrick, 18 March 1808, Dr Williams's Library, MS, 24.157, 259, 2r.

Grange made the point about heresy strongly in his address towards the end of the assembly, when he reminded members that the question was not "Whether Mr Simson was a heretic, or maintained heretical opinions as to the Necessary Existence of the Son?" Their task was merely "to judge how far the unsound doctrines taught deserved censure; that it was very certain damnable doctrines have been taught, and that deserved censure."[51] Grange was concerned lest the sound views now pronounced by Simson lead the assembly to accept his orthodoxy. Angered that Simson had refused to acknowledge errors in teaching, he feared that the professor, if not censured, would continue as before.

The majority of speeches that followed took the same line. Whether or not there had been heresy, all was now retracted, and the decision for the assembly should rest on whether or not censure was appropriate. On 14 May Simson's advocates Murray and Grant had told the assembly that their client wanted a decision as to his innocence "in express terms."[52] Attending closely to the temper of the delegates, Simson's supporters soon realized that it would be impossible to clear Simson in 1728 without creating massive dissatisfaction within the church. George Drummond, who often acted on instructions from Islay, spoke to this effect on 15 May, expressing his fear of a damaging breach and hoping that the Assembly was now reaching some degree of harmony. Some, notably George Logan and Gowdie, soon to become professor of divinity at Edinburgh University, still felt that an immediate vote should be taken on the question of censure, but an adjournment was called. These men probably helped Simson to construct his last statement of orthodoxy. Wodrow thought that Drummore, Gowdie, the lord president, and some others had a hand in it, since it was "fuller and clearer, and more distinct, than any of his papers formerly."[53] Simson said that he believed "That there is one only God, That in the unity of the Godhead there are three persons, God the father etc & that the three Persons in the Godhead are one Substance or Essence in number," and he apologized for anything that he might have said to make anyone think otherwise.[54]

The assembly's members found themselves in a quandary in mid-May. Most agreed that Simson's declarations were orthodox. However, the

---

51 Wodrow, *Correspondence*, 3:379.
52 NAS, CH1/2/56, 256.
53 Wodrow, *Correspondence*, 3:385.
54 NAS, CH1/2/56, 276.

previous assembly had found him in error, and he was guilty of casting doubt on "the great foundation-articles of our religion," thereby undermining the faith of the masses.[55] A committee was appointed to draw up an overture of censure that would explain the grounds on which it was being made. Its members came from both camps, presumably in order to ensure that any agreement reached among them would have a good chance of passing.[56] The difficulty would lie in finding common ground on which to reach a compromise. As Wodrow noted, "The one side will be content to suspend him to the next Assembly; the other will insist that he be deposed; and they are equal in the committee."[57] These fears were justified, for the next day the committee brought back to the assembly two possible overtures. While both admitted that Simson had been at fault in his methods of expression, as Wodrow had foretold, they differed as to what the outcome should be.[58]

The divisions in the assembly were clear during the debate that followed. A minister from Angus suggested that the choice before the members was between Christ and Mr Simson, while another suggested that the *Form of Process* demanded that Simson be deposed *instanter.* Smith and Professor Hamilton endeavoured to soften these statements, pointing out the correct procedure according to the *Form of Process* in cases of error. Hamilton observed, "that if the case were betwixt the glory of Christ and the person of Mr Simson, none could be in any difficulty; but he took the case to be, whether suspension or deposition were the best methods for promoting this great end of vindicating the truth and glorifying Christ."[59] He felt that either sentence would serve this purpose, but since Simson had retracted all his errors, the latter was too extreme.

When a member moved that a vote be taken, either to suspend or depose Simson, the church managers were afraid of the consequences. Since no one was sure of the outcome, there was apprehension about the possible reaction of the losing side. In pre-arrangement with the

55 Wodrow, *Correspondence*, 3:388.

56 The members were Moderator Wishart, Prof. Hamilton, Principal Chalmers, Principal Hadow, Principal Campbell, Revs. J. Alston, J. Smith, G. Logan, D. Pit — — [rest of word illeg. -cairn (?)], J. Hamilton, A. Anderson, J. Gray, A. Logan, A. Tait; elders Ld President, Grange, Drummore, Lt. Col. Erskine, Provost Drummond. NAS, CH1/2/56, 267. Wodrow gives a slightly different list. Wodrow, *Correspondence*, 3:387.

57 Ibid., 3:387.

58 Ibid., 3:388–9.

59 Ibid., 3:390.

anti-Simson forces, Haddow took the floor to express his alarm at the possible results of a vote.[60] He asked that the assembly instead agree to suspend Simson, leaving the next assembly to determine the matter finally. The Simson faction, feeling that it was in a strong position, objected to this request. Alston then proposed that the committee withdraw to produce a new overture. Simson's supporters disliked this proposal, but the consensus was for it. Two hours later the committee came back with a document expressing disapproval of Simson's conduct, proposing an interim suspension, and requiring that the printed case be sent to the presbyteries for their determination at the next assembly. The few members who still wanted to register dissents were dissuaded from doing so, and the assembly accepted this proposal without a vote.

Reaching a consensus had required careful management. Grange commented on 18 May: "The Deposing of Mr Simson was strugled against by all sorts of methods; & when honest people saw this, & consider'd the Pains taken all along to support him, even to the wounding & giving up with the great Truths of the Gospel, & the breaking of the Church in Pieces, we were on the Brink of a Rupture, w[hi]ch I'm affraid wou'd not have been heal'd in our Time."[61]

Wodrow and Grange had wanted to have Simson removed from teaching, while avoiding any outright division among the members of the assembly, since they did not feel that the Church of Scotland was strong enough to ride out the storm that a major division might produce among the politicians in England. Wodrow's description of the General Assembly of 1728 concentrated on the theological questions that were of overwhelming importance to him, but he was conscious of the political undercurrents among assembly members and condemned Neil Campbell for his partisan actions. The Glasgow principal was reported to have considerable influence in the west, although he "pretends to a great deal of modesty." With members of his own clan, Campbell was bolder; he was said to have threatened one "with the displeasure of the Duke of Argyle, if he continoued to vote as he had votted," a threat that he might have been in a position to carry out, since he was known to act as host to the duke in Glasgow.[62]

Campbell's efforts on Simson's behalf are confirmed by an anonymous letter about the assembly sent to Grange some months later.

60 Ibid., 3:392.
61 Lord Grange to A. Taylor, 18 May 1728, NAS, GD124/15/1332/2, 2.
62 Wodrow, *Analecta*, 3:511. For Argyll's visit to Campbell, see ibid., 4:68–9, 74.

Although he had not been a member of the 1728 assembly, the writer claimed to have inside information and "Attributed the keeping up of this unlucky dispute to the behaviour of some Members openly rank'd among the Friends of the Family of Argylle, had not a Certain Dignifyd Clergyman Exerted himself most Actively in favour of Simpson the Dispute had been then out of door by his Deposition. That Man had the leading of ten or a dozen of the last Assembly who certainly cast the Ballance. I do not know if he used my L[or]d Ilays Name, tho I was told he did; I should think it was great pity if My L[or]d allow'd it to be us'd again."[63] The letter went on to say that this "Dignifyd Clergyman" was the same person who dissented from the instructions given by the Presbytery of Glasgow in January 1729, along with "Simsons Father in Law" and "Young Wishart." Since Wodrow identified that third person as Neil Campbell, the anonymous letter writer was accusing Principal Campbell and the Argathelians of the political management of the General Assembly of 1728. He expressed concern lest the Argyll family, which had always been allied with the church through good times and bad, be deceived into the patronage of "One of her Apostate Sons."

Despite the political management, Wodrow found the conclusion to the assembly satisfactory, telling his wife that "we shall not hear any more of Mr Simson in public." He listed the reasons for his assessment: the peace and reputation of the church had been maintained, Simson had been prohibited from making printed statements, any danger to the royal prerogative had been avoided, and regard had been shown to Simson's family.[64]

Events over the next months were to prove him wrong. Simson did not resign, and the affair dragged on. Professor Hamilton and Principal Chalmers were unyielding over the affair, and other ministers supported them. Williamson wrote to his Eastwood friend from Edinburgh in June that he was "sorry to find so many of all Ranks so Liberall in their applauses of Mr Simson, and their Satyricall way of speaking of the Assembly."[65] Such liberals saw no empirical evidence that Simson had been spreading heresy, since none of his students appeared to be tainted. A speech by Dundas pointed out the quandary in which many now found themselves. Simson had cleared himself of any doctrinal error; his faults were now seen as tergiversation and wasting the church's time. Should he be deposed for these, it would set a precedent in the history of

63 Anon. to Lord Grange, 29 Jan. 1729, NAS, GD124/15/1350.
64 Wodrow, *Correspondence*, 3:394.
65 J. Williamson to R. Wodrow, 28 June 1728, NLS, Wodrow Letters Quarto, XVIII, 120.

church councils, which would lead to great and justified criticism in England and abroad.[66]

The General Assembly of 1728 had faced a difficult task. It did not acquit itself well by absolute standards of justice. Unable to find Simson guilty of heresy, committee and assembly members had censured him for his determination to use the terminology of the early church rather than that of seventeenth-century Reformed orthodoxy. They may have resented the professor's challenge to the faith of their covenanting fathers. They certainly objected to his refusal to answer queries, to the long-drawn-out legal battle that he had fought, and to the changes that he demanded in traditional thought. As Thomas Mack indicated in a rambling letter to Wodrow in the summer of 1728, many perhaps felt foolish because of their inability to disprove or even to understand his teaching. After listing Simson's articulate supporters, he went on, "[T]ho Mr Gray and Mr [John] Hamilton in Glasgow be as good sensible men as we have in the church, and none, more fit to reason in a judicatory, yet they are not fit to deal with a sceptical age, they want the address th[a]t Simson has, and which he improves to their detriment."[67] Above all, church leaders feared the effects of either acquitting or deposing Simson. Should they find him guiltless, the ultra-orthodox wing of the church might secede. Should they deprive the professor of his livelihood on dubious, even illegal, grounds, they might bring down the wrath of the government on their heads, apart from making themselves a laughing stock. In this quandary, the leaders chose the safe route and avoided the issue entirely. But in doing so, they ensured that the matter would be raised again the following year.

POLEMICS BETWEEN ASSEMBLIES

During the summer of 1728 contentious issues divided the masters of Glasgow University. In contrast to the previous two summers, when he had lobbied in England and the east, Simson was present at most meetings and performed various administrative tasks. He may have felt it more important to build a working relationship with his new principal,

---

66 Wodrow, *Correspondence*, 3:395.

67 Mack enumerated "Robin Stewart, & Mr Law," along with "the president, & my Lord pancaitland" and Professor Hamilton as Simson men. He also seemed to suggest that Grange was wavering. T. Mack to R. Wodrow, 8 Aug. 1728, NLS, Wodrow Letters Quarto, XVIII, 146.

Neil Campbell, than to press his case elsewhere. In June William Wishart, Jr, was elected dean of faculty, to the annoyance of Chancellor Montrose, whose fading influence at Court made him reluctant to appeal the matter.[68] This is further confirmation of the extent to which political power generated legal and administrative decisions in Scottish affairs. In October, Simson was present when Gershom Carmichael registered a protest against the legality of Wishart's election. This delayed complaint came when the faculty was in the process of appointing a substitute to teach Andrew Rosse's class while he was incapacitated by mental illness. Frederick Carmichael had been teaching Rosse's classes, but now Alexander Campbell was nominated for the post. Carmichael's father believed that the matter had been deliberately raised when the Squadrone did not have a majority in faculty.[69]

By now, the orthodox were aware that they must keep the propaganda machine in operation to ensure that Simson's friends did not gain momentum. Wodrow and his friends corresponded busily. Thomas Mack wrote in August of the need to raise awareness of the issue,

I would have a pamphlett published and the title I would is a warning to the church of scotland giving a short account of Dr Clerks principles, and th[a]t Mr Simsons new notions and Dr Clerks sceme are all one[.] it is done already a paper of remarks, th[a]t the presbytrie of Glasgow adopt as theirs, but I would have these enlarged on and set a clear light, to awaken some of us out of an Lethargy or slumber   2ndly I would represent [to] the church of Scotland the danger if Mr Simson is repond [reponed, reinstated in office] is it fit th[a]t such a man should be a teacher who has withall his airt perverted a great many youths, 3dly I would have such a pamphlet to direct ministers to proper measures if Mr Simsons a court faction shal get him repond.[70]

Mack regretted that many of his colleagues supported Simson, one calling him "a poor innocent clattering [idle chattering] thing."[71] The

68 Wodrow, *Analecta*, 4:2–3. The election had taken place in the absence of the rector, Hamilton of Aikenhead, and the vice-chancellor, John Hamilton, who had obeyed a demand from Milton that no election be held until the Lords of Session had considered the matter. John Gray, the previous dean of faculty, protested, on the grounds that two of the votes were illegal – those of John Simson and Andrew Rosse. The former was under suspension from ecclesiastical functions, and the latter was *non compos mentis*.

69 GUA 26635, 52, 60–2.

70 T. Mack to R. Wodrow, 8 Aug. 1728, NLS, Wodrow Letters Quarto, XVIII, 145.

71 T. Mack to R. Wodrow, 8 Aug. 1728, ibid., 146.

letter continued with a discussion of the political factors involved, now
that Simson had joined the Argathelians. Wodrow reported to Thomas
Linning in October that Simson's friends were planning to get his suspension lifted at the next assembly by persuading presbyteries to send
no fixed instructions and, where possible, to instruct delegates that a
two-year suspension would represent a fair punishment for someone
who had retracted all error. He believed that a current rumour, to the
effect that Simson would resign if he were provided with a pension, was
false and designed to lull the defences of die-hard Simson opponents.[72] The letter outlined Wodrow's misgivings about the actions of
other presbyteries in their own synod: only Dunbarton, Glasgow, Ayr,
and Lanark were likely to be counted on. Efforts with allies in other
parts of the country must be concerted to outwit the intentions of the
Simson group. Wodrow also proposed that a short summary of the case
be printed, which would imply that Simson's retractions had been inadequate. Writing on similar lines to William MacKnight, minister of
Irvine, he confirmed that Simson had disobeyed the act of 1717 and
that in 1728 "every branch of this retraction was wrung out of him."[73]
He thought Simson thoroughly untrustworthy, disbelieving his retractions and ignoring his legitimate concerns about the misuse of open
answers.

The polemics that survive suggest that the anti-Simson forces won the
propaganda war quantitatively, if not qualitatively. The following spring
Simson complained,

That since last Assembly there has been a greater Noise and Clamour raised
against me, than at any Time before; which seems to have been occasioned by
anonymous Pamphlets published against me ... a few of which that I have read
are filled with Misconstructions of my Words, and Misrepresentations of my
Meaning, and also with gross Falshoods and Calumny artfull mixed with great
Pretences to Piety ... some of which Papers have been industriously spread
among the People ... whereby great Numbers of good Christians and well meaning People ... were filled with the highest Prejudices and Indignation against
me. ... And no Wonder, seeing they were made to believe that I denied the Unity
of the Godhead, and the Divinity of the Glorious Son of GOD ... Which abomi-
nable Heresies I do as much detest, and have all along to my Power taken as
much Pains to confute, as any Minister of this Church.[74]

72 R. Wodrow to T. Linning, 30 Oct. 1728, Wodrow, *Correspondence*, 3:398
73 R. Wodrow to W. Macknight, 6 Dec. 1728, ibid., 3:407.

The effects of this literary battle became apparent quickly. The *Alarm* had been printed in Glasgow, to the chagrin of Simson and his friends, who threatened the printer with legal action.[75] In December 1728 the Presbytery of Glasgow agreed to instruct its commissioners to the 1729 assembly to vote to depose Simson, with only Campbell, Wishart, and James Stirling opposing the decision. By January 1729, other presbyteries were reviewing their options. In the Presbytery of Paisley, John Millar, minister of Neilston, moved that it should not make any predeterminations but leave the matter for the assembly to decide. To Wodrow, this notion, "fitt for lazy persons," was promoted by those who favoured Simson, and he was relieved when in March the presbytery met again and voted to send instructions that the assembly should declare it unsafe for Simson to teach or preach.[76] He observed that many kirk sessions were speaking to their presbyteries against Simson, which was "a considerable check upon Ministers that incline to support him."[77] This action presented some conservative ministers with a difficult choice. They appreciated lay disapproval of Simson, but they feared the consequences of secular interference in doctrinal affairs. Rumour said that only the Presbytery of Irvine, and possibly those of Dunbar and Haddington, favoured restoring the professor. It was vital that Simson's opponents be "wise as serpents and harmless as doves" in their work of persuasion.[78]

Despite Wodrow's conviction that the Presbytery of Edinburgh was likely to support Simson, on 29 January 1729 it unanimously decided that it would be unsafe to allow Simson to teach divinity because of both his subversive statements and the "unwarrantable Stiffness" in his attitude to the church processes. Furthermore, the second libel would have to be considered before any "Final Sentence" could be reached. A copy of the statement was sent to Grange, with a letter exhorting him to intercede with Islay to stop Neil Campbell from further aiding "the Subverters of the Purity" of the Church of Scotland.[79] If this vote by the Edinburgh ministers was intended as a veiled warning to Professor Hamilton that he should continue his policy of silence on controversial issues, it did not deter him from speaking warmly in favour of his Glasgow colleague at the 1729 assembly.

74 Simson, *Professor Simson's Speech*, 2.
75 Wodrow, *Analecta*, 4:24.
76 Ibid., 4:24, 33.
77 Ibid., 4:26.
78 Ibid., 4:27.
79 Anon. to Lord Grange, 29 Jan. 1729, NAS, GD124/15/1350.

In April, Wodrow assured a friend in Ireland that only three or four presbyteries had given instructions favourable to Simson and that any contrary reports circulating there were false.[80] He felt confident that the Simson party was losing heart, noting that discussions were taking place in Glasgow University over a possible successor to Simson, since the faculty feared that it would not get his suspension lifted.[81] In reality, the Argathelians were making a final effort on Simson's behalf. On 29 April Principal Campbell called a faculty meeting attended by himself, Brisbane, Dick, Dunlop, Forbes, Johnston, J. Simson, R. Simson, and Wishart to agree on the draft of a paper to be presented to the upcoming assembly. Simson read a profession of orthodoxy, in which, to counter the rumours spread by Wodrow and his correspondents that questions had been planted to enable him to make specific doctrinal points, he commented that many of his similar declarations at previous assemblies were the result of extemporaneous answers to unexpected questions from the floor.

Campbell showed the meeting his draft document for the assembly, which began by affirming the rights of the universities of Scotland to discipline their own members. Because of the royal and parliamentary privileges under which these bodies operated, the Glasgow faculty felt obliged "to declare, that we cannot allow that any Censure of an Ecclesiastical Nature upon the said Mr. Simson, can affect his Office in this University."[82] While admitting that the judicatories of the church had the power to inflict ecclesiastical censure on any member of the Church of Scotland, it noted the good behaviour of Simson since the past assembly and his renewed expressions of soundness, and it ended with the request that the suspension of Professor Simson be raised and that he be restored to the full exercise of his ministry. Some members refused to accept Campbell's statement, but in the end the Argathelian faction of Campbell, Dick, Dunlop, R. Simson, and Wishart, voted in its favour, while Forbes insisted that his abstention be recorded. Wodrow disapproved of sending out such an important declaration in the name of the university when it had been passed by a meeting lacking a quorum.[83] Both Simson and Campbell's documents were strong statements, suggesting that in the spring of 1729 Simson's supporters felt that their chances of having his suspension lifted were good.

<hr />

80 R. Wodrow to Rev. W. Livingston, 14 April 1729, Wodrow, *Correspondence*, 3:413–4.
81 Wodrow, *Analecta*, 4:28.
82 University of Glasgow, *Representation*, 4.
83 See Wodrow, *Analecta*, 4:48, and GUA 26635, 100–6.

Contrary to Wodrow's expectations, the recorded instructions from the presbyteries for the General Assembly of 1729 show no strong concern about John Simson. Since there is evidence that instructions were given about Simson's status, a decision must have been taken (by the Committee for Instructions?) not to preserve these. This indicates the existence of considerable political action before the commencement of the assembly to avert the feared rupture between the wings of the church. Simson is not specifically alluded to in any of the instructions contained in the assembly's record books, although numbers 6, 7, and 8 all refer to his cases. A group of presbyteries, largely from the central eastern area, but also including Glasgow and Ayr, called for the assembly to prepare an overture to prevent error.[84] The second and third instructions, both from Ayr, asked for renewal of the ninth act of the assembly of 1717, for clarification of its meaning, and for consideration of the proper means to uphold the authority of the Confession of Faith and the catechisms.

THE END OF THE AFFAIR

The Earl of Buchan was the royal commissioner to the General Assembly of 1729. It is not known who sponsored his appointment, although Islay is thought to have opposed it.[85] Edinburgh gossip said that the King had directed Buchan to dissolve the assembly should an attempt be made to depose Simson. Alarmed, Wodrow went to the earl and asked if such were the case. To his relief, the earl assured him that he had received no order from the throne on the matter.[86] This was probably a prevarication, since Buchan omitted to mention that he had indeed received instructions on how to deal with various eventualities, though perhaps not directly from the King. Evidence of the intimacy of the links between Buchan and the Court can be found in a letter of 13 May from the Duke of Newcastle's undersecretary, Charles Delafaye, to the solicitor-general, Charles Erskine.[87] In it Delafaye told Erskine

84 The group comprised Perth, Angus, Ayr, Dunblane, Dundee, Fife, Glasgow, Kirkcaldy, Meigle, and Penpont. NAS, CH1/2/59, 132.

85 Wehrli, "Scottish Politics," 246.

86 Wodrow, *Analecta*, 4:51.

87 The Duke of Newcastle, secretary of state for northern affairs, was nominally in charge of Scottish affairs after the fall of Roxburgh. His biographer, however, believes that Walpole, with the aid of the Argathelians, was the real master, leaving "the duke a conduit, not a pump." See Browning, *Duke*, 46–7.

that his letter of 3 May had been given immediately to the duke, "who laid it before the King." Delafaye went on to say that a letter from Buchan, praising the help given by the solicitor, "has likewise been presented to His Ma'y ... and you may believe that the pains you take for the King's Service on an occasion where your Help is so much wanted, are very acceptable to His Ma'y."[88]

The opening sermon on 6 May was preached by George Logan, an interesting choice, given his continuous support for Simson. He took his text from John 21:15–19, centring on Christ's instructions to Peter to feed His sheep. Calling for charity and forgiveness, he reminded his listeners that Peter had been forgiven for his fall from grace before the crucifixion and fully restored to office by Christ. The sermon was published after the assembly ended, presumably as a propaganda tool, since it was a powerful demand for Simson's reinstatement. Wodrow told his wife that the afternoon sermon on the opening day was by a minister from Fife called Monro (perhaps James Monro, minister of the Third Charge at Dundee), who also "spoke favourably of Mr Simson."[89] The appointment of two pro-Simson preachers demonstrates the government's desire to set the tone for the debates to follow in order to minimize the influence of the zealots.

Alston was elected moderator. He had been considered a Simson supporter, so this might be seen as another omen favourable to the professor. Charles Erskine noted that another candidate for the chair had been the Edinburgh minister James Craig, who supported both Simson and the Squadrone. Erskine indicated that the government supported Alston's appointment, presumably because of his Argathelian sympathies, and that there had been less opposition to the choice than had been expected "in a body Compos'd of very warm Members."[90] Several days later Erskine revised his opinion of the members; now they were "the most contentiously Zealous brethren in the Island."[91] On both sides, the managers would require all their skill to control such unruly troops. During the assembly those who were active against Simson met regularly after the sessions at the "Spread Eagle" tavern to plan their strategy.[92] Simson's supporters probably again used Herdman's as their meeting place.

88   C. Delafaye to C. Erskine, 13 May 1729, NLS, MS 5073, 131.

89   Wodrow, *Correspondence*, 3:415.

90   C. Erskine to [Duke of Newcastle], 3 May 1729, NLS MS 5073, 127–8.

91   C. Erskine to [Duke of Newcastle], 8 May 1729, ibid., 128.

92   Boston, *Memoirs*, 401.

The first full day of the assembly was wasted by vocal opposition to Principal Campbell's reading the Glasgow University declaration and, even after it had been read into the record, by complaints about its inappropriate nature. Pointless wrangling followed as to whether Simson had been legally summoned, since he was prepared "to be at hand, in case the Assembly wanted him."[93] The next day Simson appeared, and Mr Paisley, presumably one of his nephews, read a statement on his behalf declaring his complete orthodoxy. Asking rhetorically why so few students had testified to any unsound remarks made by Simson in class, he reiterated the telling point that no probationer had been found guilty, during trials for licensing or ordination by a presbytery, of any error of which the professor had been accused, as everyone present could attest.[94] In the previous year anonymous pamphlets had stirred up the populace against Simson with lies, but, like the Apostle Paul, he humbly accepted this divine affliction. Wodrow commented justly to his wife on "pretty sharp innuendoes" against the pamphleteers and "Scriptures pretty harshly applied" in the speech.[95]

Defiantly, even in his most careful statements of orthodox doctrine, Simson persisted in including the divine personal properties, about which he obviously felt strongly. He clung to the vocabulary of the Westminster Confession – the terminology that he had long claimed was the most scriptural and with which he always felt most comfortable.

I do believe, That in the Unity of the Godhead there be three Persons of one Substance, Power and Eternity; God the Father, God the Son, and God the Holy Ghost. The Father being of none, neither begotten nor proceeding, the Son eternally begotten of the Father, and the Holy Ghost eternally proceeding from the Father and the Son; which three Persons are one true Eternal God, the same in Substance, equal in Power and Glory, although distinguished by their personal Properties aforesaid; and our blessed Lord Jesus Christ, the second Person of the Godhead, is very and eternal God, of one Substance, and equal with the Father, who therefore is not another God, much less an inferior God, tho' a distinct Person from the Father, who, as he hath Life in himself, hath given to the Son, in his eternal Generation, to have Life in himself, which, as it is well explained by most eminent Divines, ancient and modern, comprehends all the Perfections of the Divine Nature, even all that the Father himself hath, except

93 Wodrow, *Correspondence*, 3:416.
94 Simson, *Professor Simson's Speech*, 2.
95 Wodrow, *Correspondence*, 3:420.

being the Father, namely, being infinite, eternal and unchangeable in his Being, Wisdom, Power, Holiness, and all other Divine Perfections, which comprehend necessary Existence, and true and supreme Deity, which all the three Divine Persons are equally possest of, only with this Difference, That the Father hath them from none, and the Son hath his Divine Nature and Life from the Father in his Eternal Generation, and the Holy Ghost hath the Divine Nature by eternally proceeding from the Father and the Son.[96]

There was little new to be said, so Simson and his advocate, Murray, reassessed much old ground. On 8 May, Murray closed "with a warm speech ... and addressed himself to the passions and affections of the House."[97] Debate on the issue of Simson's remaining in the chamber ended with Simson's leaving without a vote being taken. Wodrow wondered at this omission, noting that the professor's supporters appeared unwilling to sustain votes, although he was not sure why. Charles Erskine might have enlightened him. Writing that night to one of his government masters, Erskine explained, "[F]rom the first they [the assembly members] meet I saw their Complexion was hot and seeing plainly enough the Majority they had, it was my opinion there was no chance for bringing them to Temper but avoiding to show them their Majority by allowing no vote to be put and working in the mean time all we cou'd."[98] He noted that Professor Hadow seemed to be marshalling the anti-Simson forces and, having already attacked Wodrow in private, proposed to do so publicly the next day.

Ten hours were devoted to the case on 9 May, of which even Wodrow found it hard to recall details. When Thomas Linning and Alexander Anderson spoke for further sentencing of Simson, since he had by no means cleared himself of error, they were answered by Principal Campbell, who felt that on the contrary the speech of the previous day had been "a most orthodox one."[99] James Craig considered that Simson had been treated harshly by the Presbytery of Glasgow, which had resulted in his refusal to answer questions.[100] William Stewart, minister of Kiltearn, and William Stewart, minister of Perth, both spoke against Simson and

---

96 Simson, *Professor Simson's Speech*, 3.

97 Wodrow, *Correspondence*, 3:422.

98 C. Erskine to [Duke of Newcastle], 8 May 1729, NLS, MS 5073, 128.

99 Wodrow, *Correspondence*, 3:424.

100 Grange considered Craig a consistent Simson supporter: "a minr of this city who has always almost argu'd in his behalf." Lord Grange to A. Taylor, 16 April 1728, NAS, GD 124/15/1332/1, 3.

were answered by George Logan. The day continued in this way, with speakers both for and against Simson. The hack poets who engaged in repartee over the Simson affair drew attention to Hamilton: "When a certain Professor Hamilton, e'en just such another, / For *Simson* made flourishing Speeches,/The same Turn of Thought made him plead for his Brother, / With far greater Zeal than he preaches: / And what tho' his Conduct gives Ground to suspect him, / He hath grasp'd such exorbitant Sway, / As, he hopes, may suffice to defend, and protect him, / 'Gainst all his Opposers can say."[101]

The divisions in the assembly were not likely to have been healed by this rhetoric, although Wodrow felt that "decency and decorum" had been observed and that "personal hints and attacks" had been averted.[102] Wodrow's verdict on the conduct of the difficult task before the church was that the members' "speeches and reasonings wer decent, very calm, and with much feuer indecencys than I have too often seen in such a numerous meeting."[103]

Everyone seems to have agreed that it was necessary to settle the matter. The church leaders' main objective was to achieve this result with maximum satisfaction to both sides and minimum chance of public dissent, which might lead to the ultimate disaster of an open breach. The task of the compromisers was to create a settlement with which all moderates could live and that would disarm the hotheads on both sides. This endeavour was not going to be easy, since the surviving pamphlets and correspondence indicate without a shadow of doubt that the "warm brethren" preserved an unshakable conviction that Simson was fundamentally unsound, regarding all his professions of orthodoxy as typical examples of heretical dissimulation. It is impossible to determine exactly how real the risk of a breach in the Church of Scotland may have been in 1729. Wodrow and Erskine, looking at the matter from quite different perspectives, believed in the likelihood of a major crisis unless a compromise could be reached. With hindsight, we know that in the next decade such a split occurred, to which the Simson case was a contributory cause. The Secession was not immediately as disruptive as a rift over Simson might have been, but it proved that the fears of 1729 were not illusory.

101 From "An Answer to John Brigs's Ballads. By Crawford and Stewart, May 29, 1729," quoted in Erskine, *Extracts*, 93.

102 Wodrow, *Correspondence*, 3:440.

103 Wodrow, *Analecta*, 4:53.

Anticipating renewed stalemate, on the evening of 10 May the managers arranged for the appointment of a committee to work out a solution.[104] This move was opposed by Thomas Boston, but he found only one supporter in Col. Erskine.[105] The appointees represented both sides fairly equally, with perhaps a slight edge to the pro-Simson faction. That night Charles Erskine repeated his assertion that votes must be avoided, placing his trust in the committee, "which meets this night to try if it can be hit of in ane ameable manner."[106] It was his hope that the orthodox group might allow Simson to retain his ministerial office if he agreed not to teach.

While the committee deliberated, the full assembly continued to hear Simson-related speeches. By 12 May all the committee members except the die-hards, Col. Erskine and Allan Logan, had reached agreement on a possible overture to present to the assembly, which would state that Simson deserved further censure, and would declare it unsafe for him to teach divinity. The laymen who supported Simson were apparently prepared to concede this much, so Charles Erskine was willing to negotiate along these lines. Gossip said that the anti-Simson group had also been persuaded to agree by the fear that if Simson were deposed, the University of Glasgow would elect an equally objectionable professor of divinity.[107] The fact that such a threat could be effective is another indication of how unremarkable Simson's opinions must have been in forward-looking circles. The zealots realized that there were many possible candidates for the Glasgow chair with similarly pernicious views. The extreme attitudes of some lay elders, whose grasp of theology may have been shaky, contrasted with the more liberal outlook of many clergymen. The former probably constituted the majority that Erskine noted but wished to out-manoeuvre. If so, this fact may explain their inability to appreciate their own strength and defeat the wiles of the politicians.

104 The appointed committee members were listed by Wodrow as the Moderator, Professor Hamilton, George Logan, John Gowdie, Allan Logan, Principal Hadow, James Ramsay, Alexander Anderson, plus the elders, Dundas, the solicitor, Col. Erskine and Provost Drummond, "&c". Wodrow, *Correspondence*, 3:428. The "&c" was later clarified as Mr Craig, John Scot, John Gray, the Marquis of Tweeddale, lord president, Drummore, and Auchinleck. Ibid., 4:436. How many of these men actually met is unknown. Wodrow reported a speech by Tweeddale in which he apologized for not being on the committee, "not knowing he was a member." Whether Tweeddale was making excuses for avoiding a boring meeting or there was some plan concerning who received notification is a matter for speculation. Ibid., 3:434.

105 Boston, *Memoirs*, 401.

106 C. Erskine to [?Newcastle], 10 May 1729, NLS, MS 5073, 130

107 Wodrow, *Correspondence*, 3:433.

Col. Erskine and Allan Logan were determined that there should be a clause in the overture declaring that Simson deserved deposition. The professor's friends said that they would let the whole affair go to a vote on deposition rather than accept such a clause. Their aim at this stage seems to have been to ensure financial provision for Simson and his family, which would be more difficult if such direct condemnation were included. Since the object of the committee was to avoid any divisive vote, more negotiations were necessary.

When an overture was brought to the assembly on 12 May, there were still fears that the orthodox side would be unable to accept the compromise. After another day's debate, on the morning of 13 May Wodrow went to speak privately with Col. Erskine and Allan Logan but had little hope that they would agree to the consensus of the assembly.[108] When the meeting came to order that day, there was still apprehension lest the more extreme members balk at any concessions. Another long day of speeches followed, at the end of which only Thomas Boston seemed determined to prevent a unanimous decision being reached, announcing his intention to dissent in his own name and in the names of any others of like mind. Boston's open refusal to accept consensus would ruin all the careful planning that had gone into the overture and might induce the other wavering orthodox leaders such as Allan Logan to follow him into dissent. To prevent this outcome, Alston used all his powers of persuasion to dissuade Boston from action, asking him gravely, "Will you tear out the bowels of your mother?" At this, Boston, "sensibly touched," began to waver, being unwilling to harm in any way his "mother," the church.[109] Professor Hamilton quickly suggested that if Boston wished time for reflection, he might still mark his dissent at a later session, while Alston urged that he should take time for prayer and thought about the consequences of his actions, which settled the matter temporarily. After Boston's intervention, there were a few more speeches, but when Alston announced that "the Assembly acquiesced in the overture ... the Assembly went into it without a vote."[110]

The act that the assembly approved in this fashion noted both the calls for deposition and the feeling of other members that Simson deserved more lenient treatment.[111] It stated the wish of the assembly to avoid extremes and to preserve peace. Accordingly it ratified the sentence passed

108 Ibid., 3:439.
109 Boston, *Memoirs*, 402.
110 Wodrow, *Correspondence*, 3:443.
111 Church, *Principal Acts*, Act 6, 1729, 12–14.

by the previous assembly, suspending Simson from preaching, teaching, and all exercise of ecclesiastical functions until another assembly should remove the suspension. It concluded that it was not safe for Simson to teach divinity to prospective ministers of the church because of the articles found relevant and because of the offence that Simson had given by his delays in answering his critics. Simson was brought back into the assembly room, and the clerk read the sentence to him. Although he at first seemed upset, he quickly recovered and declared his acceptance of divine providence. At the same time he mentioned the falsehoods alleged against him by the pamphleteers and his own orthodox opinions. He trusted that his sentence might do no damage to the church.[112]

Boston's conscience still remained a problem to both sides. While it is understandable that Simson's friends hoped to silence Boston, the fact that his enemies agreed with them suggests that they were genuinely afraid that public dissent would entail disastrous results. Managers such as Charles Erskine worked hard to rally the moderates in the ultra-orthodox camp. That night Boston was summoned to a meeting along with some friends who were present as observers and who were considering adding their voices to his dissent. There Charles Erskine, Col. Erskine, and several others tried to dissuade him from action. Wodrow was also present at this meeting, giving the list of participants as: McLaren, Gillespie, Col. Erskine, Charles Erskine, Brown of Abercorn, Hogg, Ebenezer and Ralph Erskine, Williamson, Gabriel Wilson, Culfargie, and others. Wodrow was unsure as to the effect on Boston, although he "thought we softened him."[113]

The final act in the drama came the next day, when Boston informed Alston that he wished to speak. Erskine must have been extremely relieved when Boston merely announced that while he was convinced that it was his duty to dissent from the assembly's decision, he would not insist that it be recorded in the records. He reserved the right to use the written statement as he might later see fit.[114]

Although all efforts on Simson's behalf were not yet over, this was the point, in mid-May 1729, at which Simson's suspension became final. The chances for his restoration to office grew slimmer during the next

---

112 Wodrow, *Correspondence*, 3:444.

113 Ibid.

114 Boston noted that as the lone member of the twelve Marrow Representers, he felt that he must speak against the assembly's decision. Boston, *Memoirs*, 403–4.

two years, as more anti-Simson material was published and the conservatives worked feverishly to ensure his continued silence. Faced with the need to prove that Simson had taught error in order to depose him, the assembly had been forced to accept a compromise to preserve any reputation for fairness. Whatever indiscreet comments on the writings of Clarke Simson had voiced in 1725, in 1729 his statements were of impeccable orthodoxy. The evidence of heresy against him was weak. He had probably queried the accepted terminology about the numerical unity of the Trinity, but his explanation of concern about the prevalent risk of Modalism was reasonable. Possibly he had suggested that his students take Pictet with a grain of salt when he spoke of Christ as *summus deus*, but the lack of context left his judges unsure if he could have been referring to texts such as John 14:28, "I go unto the Father: for my Father is greater than I." He had explained his reported statements on "necessary existence" as stemming from genuine difficulties about the personal properties of the persons of the Trinity incurred through his studies. Similarly "self-existent" was seen by some earlier authoritative divines as equivalent to "unbegotten" and, if used in that sense, was unexceptionable. The *generare* or *creare* argument could be seen only as unproven. As a result, the assembly had been forced to fall back on a vague accusation of "unsound teaching" and to deny any intention of charging Simson with open heresy. Inevitably, neither side could be satisfied with the sentence. What remains clear today is that John Simson was not the heresiarch he has been made out to be.

12

Quit of him at last:
Descent into Obscurity, 1729–1740

FEARS AND ALARMS, 1730–31

By the early 1730s Simson's actual theological beliefs had become submerged under the sea of polemic directed at preventing him from ever teaching again. His attestations of orthodoxy in the General Assemblies of 1727, 1728, and 1729 had only proved to his opponents that he was shifty, devious, and dangerous. In William Wishart's hearing, "some waggish Folks" had said, "Would ever we have discovered such Keenness against this Man, have pushed at him so violently, and for so long a Time, and been at such Pains to run him down, if we had not hoped to be made quit of him at last."[1] Wishart believed that the ultra-orthodox had perhaps unwittingly stirred up a tempest of misunderstanding against Simson. In some presbyteries prior to the 1729 assembly, "not only young Ministers ... but Ministers venerable for their Age, as well as Piety, Learning, a Zeal for the Purity of the Doctrine" of the church were outvoted about Simson's case by uneducated countrymen, who lacked the knowledge to make such judgments. A rumour that Simson taught that women lacked souls naturally prejudiced many against him. Wishart "dread[ed] the most dismal Consequences to this Church" from the use of such methods by the anti-Simson faction.[2] Simson might have considerable support from his clerical colleagues, but the fears that had been stirred up against him spilled over in areas where the extremists held a majority.

The ethics of using questions remained in the forefront of men's minds. While many felt that the putting of questions concerning a mans'

1 [Wishart], *Short and Impartial State*, 50.
2 Ibid., 38–9.

private thoughts smacked of the Inquisition, to Moncrieff of Culfargie a refusal to answer questions was censurable.[3] In September 1729, the Synod of Fife, still denying the orthodoxy of the *Marrow*, demanded that a candidate for the ministry in the Presbytery of Dundee answer twenty queries about his opinions of the *Marrow*, the final one being "whither he approved of the act of Assembly 1720," condemning the book.[4] While the young man produced creditable replies to the first nineteen queries, he refused to answer the final one, saying that it was not his business to approve or disapprove of an act of the General Assembly. When pressed, he tried to remain neutral, stating that he preferred to make no public statement on the matter, but he was eventually forced to make a stand in favour of the Marrow Representers, whereupon his opponents stopped his trials. Wodrow bewailed the foolishness of the synod: to reopen the Marrow affair, and misuse inquiry by queries, seemed to him the height of folly. The use of questions to force a probationer to "give a direct consent to all complex acts of Assembly" after he had otherwise proved his orthodoxy brought the method into disrepute. "I doubt not," Wodrow continued, "but this use of Queries [will] be very satisfying to Mr Simson and his freinds, who with such keenness opposed this just method, when it's regulat prudently."[5]

Simson never ceased to feel that questions were designed to entrap the unwary. Writing (in the third person) to Archibald Campbell, who was being investigated for unsound statements some years later, he commented, "Had it not been for the vote of Assembly 28 your committee might have been empowered to put Queries as was done to P[r]of[esso]r Simson but I suppose conferring is much with the same designe to entangle you in your Talk therfore beware of their questions & ask them question about & especially let them fix a clear meaning to School Terms they may infer."[6] Evidently Simson still felt that his methods in dealing with the zealots were the safest and that "school terms" were a minefield.

The propaganda battle continued into the early 1730s, and Simson's supporters had some successes. In February 1730, after months of silence

---

3 Moncrieff of Culfargie, *Remarks*, 24.

4 Wodrow, *Analecta*, 4:79.

5 Ibid., 4:80.

6 J. Simson to A. Campbell (undated, c. 1735–6), NAS, GD461/15/14 f5. Although most of Simson's letters to Campbell are signed, a few of this period are not. Instead of "Rd & dea Br", the salutation is "Mon cher Ami," and they are unsigned or signed "Philalethes" (lover of truth)! Possibly Simson did not wish anyone opening the letters to know who Campbell's correspondent was, lest it should damage him in the eyes of the orthodox at his heresy case.

on the Simson question, Glasgow rumour mongers reported that Principal Campbell had apologized to the divinity students for the lack of attention they had received and expressed the hope that the next assembly would allow their professor to resume teaching.[7] In April, Wodrow wrote to Dr James Frazer, who had implied that the professor's declarations were perfectly orthodox, to vindicate the Church of Scotland from charges of injustice. Simson was dangerous as a teacher because of his "instability and unfixedness," so actions against him should not be seen as "the spirit of persecution."[8] Communal harmony was more important to Wodrow than individual rights. He considered that someone whose ideas were at variance with those of his fellows, "though he have fathers and first writers" on his side, constituted a hazard through his disturbance of society.[9] He asked how Simson could be seen as abused when he was enjoying his salary without teaching. The letter is a plea for understanding of the position of the church apropos Simson; it is unlikely that it persuaded many.

In Scotland, the instructions from presbyteries to the 1730 assembly prove that the orthodox, fearful lest Simson be allowed to resume teaching dangerous innovative divinity, demanded his continued punishment. The anxious presbyteries were overwhelmingly on the eastern coastal plain running north of the Firth of Forth as far as Dingwall. Twenty-three presbyteries sent one or more instructions on the twin subjects of Simson and corrupt doctrine: Aberdeen, Aberlour, Abernethy, Cupar, Shetland, Strathbogie, and Skye, one each; Aberdour, Alford, Brechin, Dunkeld, Kincardine, and Lochmaben, two each; Synod of Fife, Meigle, and Penpont, three each; Aberbrothock (Arbroath), Auchterarder, Deer, Dingwall, Ellon, St Andrews, and Stirling, four each.[10] These vigorous expressions against the return of Simson to any ecclesiastical or pedagogical function may have been the fruit of the propaganda campaign waged in Scotland's presses. They demonstrated

7 Wodrow, *Correspondence,* 3:460.

8 R. Wodrow to Dr J. Frazer, 21 April 1730, ibid., 3:461.

9 Ibid., 3:462.

10 The only exceptions to the eastern geographical location of presbyteries were Lochmaben and Penpont from the Synod of Dumfries, along with Shetland and Skye. R.L. Emerson has pointed out to me that these last two presbyteries tended to send students to King's College, Aberdeen, which would explain their similarity of opinion. The first two might be partially explained by the vehemence of such men as Mack in synod meetings. The minister of Penpont from 1693 to 1735 was James Murray, a close friend of Thomas Boston's. Lochmaben's minister was the forward-looking young cleric Patrick Cumming, who has been seen conferring on tactics with Wishart and Wallace. Perhaps the rest of this presbytery was reacting against him. NAS, CH1/2/62, 296–347.

considerable distrust of the actions of the General Assembly, demanding that any motion to reinstate the professor be submitted to the individual presbyteries for discussion.[11]

The orthodox in the northeast, who had been battle-hardened in the fight against the Arminian and mystical Episcopalians, called for maintenance of the "radical powers" of individual presbyteries. They feared the influence of fashionable ruling elders and the growing domination of the church by appointed committees whose members might hold similar views.[12]

The instructions indicate the strong feelings of the Presbyterian minority in Aberdeenshire and the geographical grouping of most of the Marrow Brethren in the other counties. The credibility of Wishart's comments about ministers' being out-voted in presbyteries is reinforced by the instructions from the Presbytery of Skye. Its fears about modern theologians led it to accuse younger ministers of "corrupt and unsound Principles" and of preaching that had degenerated from the praiseworthy methods of the past, "preferring cold harangues of morality and dry flourishes of Rhetorick to the Simplicity of the Gospel Stile, using more of the enticeing words of man's wisdom than of the Demonstration of the Spirit and of power; more like the disciples of Cicero or Seneca, than followers of the Apostles of the blessed Lord Jesus." Skye demanded that an act be passed against "this growing itch of affectation."[13]

The temper of these instructions dampened the optimism of Simson's powerful friends. When the General Assembly of 1730 opened, under the Earl of Loudoun as royal commissioner and William Hamilton as moderator, the members were given to understand that the government would frown on any discussion of Simson. The assembly thus ran its course without the Simson affair ever reaching the floor of a full session. Islay, Loudoun, and the ministry in London had come to the conclusion that feelings in Scotland still ran too high for it to be safe to try to lift Simson's suspension. Grange informed Wodrow that this group agreed to do nothing to raise the matter unless Simson's enemies voted to take further action against him. In that case, Loudoun was to declare himself in favour of the restoration of the professor.[14] Obedient to political pressure, Simson's friends avoided the issue. His opponents tried

---

11 See, for instance, the instructions from Aberdeen in ibid., 342.
12 Instructions from the Presbytery of Ellon, ibid., 346.
13 Ibid., 314.
14 Wodrow, *Analecta*, 4:143.

to get a doctrinal overture before the assembly but were outwitted in committee.[15]

The choice of preachers to the assembly is revealing and may reflect the determination of Hamilton, Islay, and their friends that Simson's ideas should not be forgotten, although it was too dangerous to restore him in person. The chosen preachers did nothing to quell factional disquiet – Cumming, J. Dick of Carluke (Simson's brother-in-law), Telfer, and Wallace. Listening to their sermons, the members from Skye must have heard their fears confirmed. Cumming and Dick were "unexceptionable," but Telfer and Wallace preached sermons that "gave no good *vidimus* of a fleece of young men notted to have been students under the Moderator, and of the vitiated tast of the youth, and young Ministry."[16] The assembly was treated to "a very wild sermon" by Telfer, "wherein he laboured to prove these times better than the former." This was a clear statement of enlightened principles, commencing with "a short, poor, and ill-grounded satyre, upon the former times in this Church," going on to consider the current advantageous conditions of peace, of trade and industry, and of law and justice.[17] "[Telfer] ended this wild discourse with an inference or two, of the duty of praise and thankfulnes, and encouragment to go on in the wayes of virtue."[18] In Wodrow's eyes, this speech did not deserve the name of sermon; he throught that it ought to have been censured, particularly since he considered its contentions quite false. The idea of progress was unacceptable to conservative Scots Presbyterians. The rhetoric of these preachers once more draws attention to the fact that criticism of young ministers focused on Hamilton's ex-students rather than on Simson's graduates.

The orthodox succeeded in passing a noncommittal act that called for all ministers to guard against the dissemination of errors that had been condemned by acts of assembly as contrary to the church's accepted standards, "particularly such as strike against the Fundamentals of our Holy Religion."[19] It is unlikely that any of Hamilton or Simson's former students were actually preaching against the basic doctrines of Calvinist Christianity, so presumably this act was directed at the dangerous spread of an Arminian emphasis on moral virtue or a belief in the reality of progress.

15 Wodrow, *Correspondence*, 3:464.
16 Wodrow, *Analecta*, 4:125.
17 Ibid., 4:131; the abstract runs 130–4.
18 Ibid., 4:133–4.
19 Church, *Principal Acts*, Act 8, 1730, 16.

Grange – who had difficulty balancing between the political parties of his time because of his Tory, then Jacobite, brother the Earl of Mar (with whom his political sympathies had probably lain at one time), his unstable wife (who possibly had information about these sympathies), and his own ultra-orthodox Presbyterian religious sentiments – feared plots on all sides. He told Wodrow after the 1730 assembly that he felt that Islay and Walpole were planning to use Simson to divide the Church of Scotland as a means of extending their own power and influence. To this end, although Islay "despises Mr S[imso]n, yet he does favour him."[20] The plot would involve the employment of the Simson case to make a breach in the church, producing inevitable consternation and confusion in its ruling bodies. Whereupon, to preserve peace, assemblies would be prohibited, and a small group of trusted ministers would be appointed superintendents to run ecclesiastical affairs on Walpole's or Islay's instructions.

Such a complicated design seems far-fetched, and there is no evidence of any such conspiracy. The fears of the ultra-orthodox were, however, based on reasonable grounds – a Scottish precedent had occurred under James VI, the Act of Union had been ignored in other matters such as the reimposition of patronage, and the convocation of the Church of England had been dissolved a decade earlier. Moreover, Scots members of Parliament had displayed little interest in preserving the integrity of the Presbyterian settlement. To Grange and his friends, Simson was heretical in his beliefs, regardless of what he might say. Since it was inconceivable that honest men could support him for upright reasons, there must be unsavoury secrets to explain his following. If a man of the world such as Grange believed in the possibility of a plot, it is understandable that the uneducated would and that Scots moderates on both sides should go to any effort to avoid a final excuse for schism.

In July 1730 Benjamin Grosvenor (an English non-subscriber who had been a major contributor to the *Occasional Papers* and had attacked Dunlop's *Preface* to the Westminster Confession) and William Wishart each received the degree of doctor of divinity from Glasgow University.[21] Wishart had resigned from the Tron church in Glasgow in December 1729, on his appointment as preacher to the Scots congregation at

20 Wodrow, *Analecta*, 4:144.
21 Ibid., 4:167–8.

Founders' Hall, London. His degree may have been a farewell gift to a departing minister and university dean of faculty, but it is unclear what motivated the award to Grosvenor. It is possible to interpret both as statements in favour of Simson's brand of modern theology.

At the end of 1730 discussion resumed about possibly bringing to the next assembly the question of restoring Simson at least to the office of minister. Simson and his circle were also claiming that he had been offered and had turned down the St Andrews chair of ecclesiastical history, which then went to Archibald Campbell. Wodrow rather doubted the truth of this rumour but was more alarmed when Simson, with his usual freedom of speech, told John Hamilton at the end of 1730 that "he and his freinds openly regrate their not applying to the last Assembly, who, they think, would have done Mr Simson justice, and restored him."

As a result, Hamilton, McLaurin, and Wodrow agreed to reanimate their letter-writing campaign "to the different corners of the Church" to make sure that their friends were on guard against such a future attempt.[22] Wodrow co-ordinated the circulation of information to other ministers, writing to one, "It's now if ever necessary that firm, honest men be sent up [as delegates to the assembly], that brethren correspond, and communicate light one with another, as to present duty."[23] Simson still claimed to have been "egregiously wronged," to be innocent of wrong-doing, and to have "the whole knowing, learned, and sensible ministers in the Church for him."[24] Wodrow wrote to Grange that there were arguments for removing the suspension on Simson's preaching, listing the facts that the libel against the professor had been concerned entirely with teaching, that his sermons had not been criticized, and that giving him a pulpit would accomplish his removal from the university.[25] Nevertheless, he felt that the preservation of peace in the church demanded that such a can of worms be left firmly sealed.

Over the next few months the anti-Simson propaganda took effect. Once again the assembly papers contain anxious instructions on the prevalent growth of infidelity. In an impassioned preamble to its instructions, the Presbytery of Deer noted,

22 Ibid., 4:190.
23 R. Wodrow to J. Warden, 17 Dec. 1730. Wodrow, *Correspondence*, 3:479.
24 Ibid., 3:473.
25 16 Dec. 1730, ibid., 3:474.

The Necessities of this National Church, the value of her Spiritual Constitution, the Divinity of her declared or Confessed Doctrine, the Sacred Ends of her Government, the malice and multitudes of her Enemies, the wounds She has lately got in the house of her friends, together with the fears and just apprehension of more, if not timely prevented, which exercise the thoughts and affect the hearts of Zion's lovers at this day, have induced us to imitate the Remnant who are resolving to apply the means of prevention & Cure, before it is too late, and to cast in our mite of endeavour among them.[26]

It went on to tell its delegates to oppose strenuously any motion to repone Simson because he had not expressed "hearty sorrow and regret, for having made so dishonourable a mention of that blessed name to his Scholars, or being so much as reputed an Adversary of his glory in that great Article [the doctrine of the essential divinity of Christ], whether justly or unjustly." The temper of Simson's antagonists is well illustrated by Deer's virulent six-page screed. Simson should have apologized for even being "unjustly" accused of any suggestion of Arianism. Furthermore, his repentance should have been couched in "the most affecting strain or manner," proving that his heart had been touched by the horror of the charge. Other northern and eastern presbyteries joined Deer in expressing either specific or general objections to the restoration of Simson. Dunfermline added a clause clearly aimed at both Simson and Professor Archibald Campbell at St Andrews, complaining about ministers who extolled natural reason and gave the name of "enthusiasts" to those who sought the intervention of the Spirit.[27]

At the same time as these instructions were being drawn up, Wodrow accused Principal Campbell and Simson of master-minding a petition circulating among the Glasgow students asking for a resumption of their divinity classes.[28] He assumed that this was a form of pressure to be put

26 NAS, CH1/2/64, 62.

27 Ibid., 73. The presbyteries that gave such instructions were Aberdeen, Brechin, Caithness, Crathie, Deer, Dingwall, Dundee, Dunfermline, Ellon, Kirkcaldy, Kirkwall, Perth, synod of Perth and Stirling, Shetland, St Andrews, and Tayne. Ibid, 62–100.

28 "That whereas the Students of Divinity at Glasgou, and the whole society, are at a great loss for want of a Professor of Divinity exercising his office, these four or five years, that therefore the General Assembly would, in their wisdom, fall upon such measures as they may be taught Divinity; and the rather, because many of the bursars there are oblidged to attend at Glasgou by their holding their bursary, and can go no where else." Wodrow, *Analecta*, 4:219.

on the assembly. Glasgow divinity students were being neglected by 1731, although it is possible that Simson gave some private lessons. Wodrow lamented the fact that "The Principall only hears discourses. He has not, this session, had above two or three prelections; he does not explain almost any thing; but only hears discourses; ther is none present but the bursars, and some feu Glasgow lads, and a few about."[29] In fact there were thirty-six divinity students at Glasgow in 1731, according to the assembly's records – a number not appreciably lower than the forty recorded in 1727–28. They included "William Lishman," the future professor. Aberdeen, Glasgow, and St Andrews all had roughly similar enrolments; only Edinburgh had higher numbers, with some 273 theologues.[30] If the younger generation of ministers preached heterodox or moral sermons, it was more than twice as likely to have been influenced by Professor Hamilton than by any other professor of divinity.

In the event, however, although Loudoun was again royal commissioner, the general tenor of the members of the 1731 assembly was seen as unfavourable to Simson. Once again the north sent many anxious instructions on doctrine and patronages with strongly orthodox leanings.[31] As a result, no application for Simson's restoration was made. Under the leadership of Loudoun and his chosen moderator, James Smith, the assembly again succeeded in stifling any attempts to bring the Simson affair back into debate.[32] Both commissioner and moderator presumably sensed the atmosphere, for each stated his opposition to any application to have Simson reponed. None the less, young ministers were again appointed to preach the assembly's sermons. Wodrow expressed his disgust at their unseemly preaching, which seemed "to please the vitiated tast of those about the throne."[33] George Wishart, who had a "decent, grave delivery," preached on "Judge Not."[34] William Robertson of Borthwick, father of the historian, "pressed peace very much," and William Armstrong, minister of Canonbie in the Merse, preached very badly "upon doing good."[35] Wodrow went to hear Archibald Campbell preach, on account of the notoriety of his published sermon proving that the Apostles

29 Ibid., 4:198.
30 NAS, CH1/2/64, 74–77.
31 Wodrow, *Analecta*, 4:237.
32 Wodrow recounts Loudoun's efforts to have Smith made a member of the assembly and elected moderator. Ibid., 4:226.
33 Ibid., 4:239.
34 Ibid.
35 Ibid., 4:239–40.

were not enthusiasts. This sermon, however, Wodrow pronounced (with disappointment?) perfectly orthodox.

The question of an overture about growing error and infidelity was discussed in committee. Despite the instructions, Professor Hamilton and others warned against any enlargement of the Westminster Confession, which would be necessary to accommodate the demands of the zealots. Lord Drummore said that the Church of Scotland should not give public notice to every pamphleteer who rediscovered an ancient error; should such errors appear in Scotland, they could be dealt with by the normal process.[36] Hamilton and laymen such as Drummore worked behind the scenes with Loudoun and Smith to avoid any overtures that could fracture the precarious unity of the assembly. Smith's talents seem to have been those of negotiator and peacemaker; on his death *A Sacred Poem to his Memory* lauded his abilities and asked, "Who now with equal warmth and equal skill / Shall heal dissension and fierce discord still?"[37] In 1731 his gifts were sufficient to prevent either side from reintroducing the Simson affair into open debate or from insisting on contentious doctrinal overtures.

UNINTENDED CONSEQUENCES: SECESSION

After 1731, Simson gave up hope of resuming his public role, resigning himself to a peaceful old age, carrying out administrative tasks for the university, corresponding with friends, and enjoying the company of his family.[38] The records of the Church of Scotland become silent about the Glasgow professor. Other issues, particularly the ongoing problem of patronage and the rights of a congregation to "call" its chosen minister, became more immediately pressing. Nevertheless, in the ultra-orthodox wing of the church, anxiety about doctrinal permissiveness combined with anger at Erastian intrusion into pastoral affairs. The first Secession of 1733 can thus be seen as an indirect consequence of the Simson cases.

36 Ibid., 4:257–8.

37 Quoted in Warrick, *Moderators*, 286.

38 John and Jean Simson's last five children were born between May 1727 and July 1735. Jean had one of her longest periods of freedom from pregnancy during John's years of illness from the end of 1724 until late 1726. Their youngest child, Jean, married Dr John Moore in 1757 and became the mother of Sir John Moore of Corunna. She survived to enjoy the victory of Waterloo, dying in London in 1820. Hew Scott, *Fasti*, 7:400. Heath, *Records*, 116–17.

There is a remarkable consistency in the geography of the support for the exclusion of Simson and in that of the group of ministers who tried to make a representation to the General Assembly of 1732 protesting against laxity in both doctrinal and administrative matters. These ministers objected to "inadequate censure of false doctrine" – an obvious reference to the refusal to depose Simson, as well as to state interference in church affairs and usurpation of authority by the commission of the assembly, factors that seemed to have influenced the treatment meted out to the Glasgow professor.[39] The forty-two ministers who signed the representation came from eighteen presbyteries: Aberdeen, Dundee, Duns, Earlston (Merse), Edinburgh, and Linlithgow had one minister each; Deer, Jedburgh, Kinross, and Selkirk, two each; Auchterarder, Cupar (Fife), Dunfermline, Dunkeld, and Stirling, three each; Brechin and Kirkcaldy, four each; and Perth, five. Apart from eight men from the Edinburgh area and the Borders, the thirty-four others all came from the eastern seaboard between the Firth of Forth and Aberdeen. The one Edinburgh minister who was out of line with his brethren in the capital was, not unexpectedly, the aged John McLaren, who had written against Simson twenty years earlier. The Committee of Overtures refused to include the representation in the assembly's agenda. When the group protested to the assembly, the other members "contemptuously" declined to hear them.[40]

In October 1733, Ebenezer Erskine preached against an act of the General Assembly of 1732 that limited the power of congregations to appoint ministers to churches where the patron had failed to present a nominee. Censured by his synod, Erskine appealed to the General Assembly, which in May 1733 upheld the synod's censure. In early December, Erskine, James Fisher, Alexander Moncrieff of Culfargie, and William Wilson left the Church of Scotland to form the Associate Presbytery. The parishes involved were Abernethy, Kinclaven, Perth, and Stirling, – all in central eastern Scotland. While the immediate cause of these four ministers' departure was the question of patronage rather than a congregational call, there is no doubt that they saw laxity of doctrine as the reason why patronage had become established. Moncrieff's nineteenth-century biographer claimed that Simson's suspension "so shook his confidence in the fidelity of the Assembly" to allow him to

39 For a discussion, see John Brown's life of James Fisher in Young and Brown, *Memorials*, 20–2.
40 Ibid., 21.

later become a Secession leader. Moncrieff and his conservative friends came to feel that "the specific doctrines of the cross" were of secondary interest to the prevailing party in the church.[41] In spite of concessions by the church over the next few years, more discontented ultra-orthodox Presbyterians joined the Seceders, who were formally deposed in 1740. The catechism taught that man's chief end was to glorify God. To the men who seceded, Simson and his fellows were not pursuing this goal. In consequence, they anticipated, ministers who believed as they did would be gradually eased out, leaving future generations without proper religious education and the "covenanted work of reformation buried in perpetual oblivion."[42]

Although only a few ministers seceded in 1733, the seeds of distrust in the judgment of the ruling ecclesiastical élite had been planted, leading to the fissiparous tendencies of the Scottish church during the next century. The Secession removed vocal opponents of Simson's teaching such as Wilson and Moncrieff of Culfargie. At the same time, the reality of the break tempered the opposition to new teaching methods by many less extreme Presbyterians. This more-restrained atmosphere prevented the censure of Simson's fellow professors in their efforts to update the Scottish divinity schools. Without the Simson cases, their work would have been impossible.

ATTACKS ON OTHER PROFESSORS

Simson lived in his university house in protected obscurity for his remaining decade, until his death in 1740. He was accepted as a useful member of faculty, sitting on committees, writing letters, and leading a busy social life. The dominant Argathelians did not repudiate him or his ideas, although educated Scots, from Islay and Milton down to the merchant elders of Glasgow, knew that the prosperity of a university depended on the ability of its faculty to attract students. In 1729, Simson's old pupil Francis Hutcheson was elected to the chair at Glasgow University made vacant by the death of Gershom Carmichael.[43] His backers

41 Ibid., xxxvii.

42 From "A Testimony to the Doctrine, Worship, Government, and Discipline, of the Church of Scotland, – or Reasons for their protestation before the commission," by the associate presbytery, May 1734. Quoted in Struthers, *History*, 2:5.

43 Carmichael died on 26 November 1729. When it was said that "all the English Students have left the University" on his death, the faculty moved swiftly to elect an equally attractive candidate on 16 December. Wodrow, *Analecta*, 4:96, 98.

counted on his blossoming reputation as an author and moral philosopher to make him an attractive successor to Carmichael, whose abilities had drawn potential students to Glasgow. The leverage exerted by Islay was also significant in this election. Dunlop, a leading Argathelian who was related to Hutcheson by marriage, applied to Islay for support in electing the new professor. Principal Campbell favoured another candidate, according to Wodrow, but "was overborn by my L[ord] Isla's orders."[44]

At the opening of the 1730 academic year, there was some doubt whether Hutcheson or Loudoun would teach moral philosophy. Some twenty English students, who had ventured north specifically to study under Hutcheson, led a revolt. Loudoun, who as senior professor technically had the right to chose which class to teach, gave way to Hutcheson for the good of the institution.[45] The necessity of finding attractive professors remained a priority for those making appointments and was accepted by all the incumbents, whose own incomes depended on student fees.

In June 1732 the issue of maintaining student numbers at Glasgow University became linked with the conferring of a doctorate of divinity on one of its most liberal alumni. Rev. James Kirkpatrick of Belfast had studied with Simson under James Wodrow. He had subsequently become a founding member of the Belfast Society, a prominent non-subscriber, and author of a study on the loyalty of Irish Presbyterians. His request for a degree caused acrimony among the Glasgow professors. Anderson, Forbes, and Loudoun all dissented from the motion to grant Kirkpatrick the doctorate.

Anderson and Loudoun gave distinctly unconvincing written reasons for their dissent. They claimed that they could find no recorded recipients other than those who were distinguished by authorship on theological subjects – a specious excuse, since William Wishart had received his DD two years earlier lacking notable written work, while Kirkpatrick was the published author of an important monograph. They also claimed that the examiner in trials for the degree should be the professor of divinity, but that since Simson was suspended his word could carry no weight. This, however, had been equally the case in 1730. More relevant were their other arguments about the impropriety of openly validating the principle of non-subscription, since this would "disoblige the far

44 Ibid., 4:99.
45 Ibid., 4:183–4.

greater part of the presbyterians in Ireland and lay them under the temptation of sending their sons and friends to other Colleges where no such opinion is countenanced."[46]

Their dissent was overruled, and on 8 June 1732 the rector, Orr of Barrowfield, Principal Campbell, John Simson, Dunlop, Rosse, Johnstone, Brisbane, and Hutcheson listened to Kirkpatrick give a discourse on "The Truth and Excellence of the Christian Religion" and unanimously conferred the degree on him.[47] The Argathelian administration felt that the problem of Irish boys' going elsewhere was less significant than the dissenters believed and that it was more important to continue to express a progressive theological stance.

Nevertheless, divinity studies at the Scottish universities did not cease to undergo the scrutiny that had led to the suspension of Simson, although the results differed. Among the under-currents of the 1730 assembly was consideration of the vacant principalship of Edinburgh University. It was common knowledge that Professor Hamilton wanted to exchange his chair for this position, and the gossip centred on whether he would accomplish this manoeuvre and, if so, who would succeed him as professor of divinity. Wodrow's opinion of Hamilton is significant in the light of Simson's fate. He had been told that Hamilton had "departed from the Calvinisticall doctrine … though he hath the wisdom to keep himself in the clouds." Hamilton had apparently recently lectured on the connection between moral seriousness and grace, the issue that Ramsay of Ochtertyre was to consider Simson's nemesis. Moreover, his students were showing the effects of his pedagogy, which Simson's never did: "It's certain that the students and preachers that are most recommended by him, and most students that have been under his lessons for some years, are very much off the principles of this Church."[48] Hamilton was also friendly with non-subscribing Dissenting ministers in London, had supported Simson, and had been peremptory in the Committee for Purity of Doctrine over the matter of queries. Despite all this, Hamilton was promoted to the principalship in 1732, although he died within a few months of his elevation.

Simson's other friends and colleagues were less immune from attack by the zealots than Hamilton. However, the purged Church of Scotland

46 GUA 26639, 19.
47 Ibid., 20.
48 Wodrow, *Analecta*, 4:139.

was no longer prepared to accede to the demands of angry conservatives to supervise the orthodoxy of clerical professors. The cases that came before the church courts after Simson's suspension indicate that Simson's views had gained widespread credence, with his opponents now a vocal minority. In the fifteen years after the end of the Simson hearings, four other professors came under suspicion and were charged with heterodox opinions. A brief review of these shows interesting parallels with Simson, except in the outcome of each prosecution.

Archibald Campbell, professor of ecclesiastical history at St Andrews, was charged with Pelagianism in 1735 after denouncing fanaticism in a sermon that proved that the Apostles were not enthusiasts. He was acquitted with a warning the following March. In early 1736 Simson told Campbell that although all his knowledgeable friends agreed that only "gross ignorance & ill will" could see his views as heterodox, this would not stop the zealots from sensing Campbell's words wrongly and spreading misinformation about his opinions.[49] Campbell and Simson agreed about the benevolence of the Creator and the possibility of grace being given to all virtuous humanity.

In response to Campbell's *Oratio de vanitate luminis naturæ* (1733), Simson had commented that the Bible gave no description of God. It stressed the facts of creation and redemption and the simple rules given to man. He noted that supreme power was not restricted to one person in its exercise, "tho' the primary direction of the whole is constantly restricted to one person. Whence I conceive that Just philosophical notions about the metaphisical Nature of God are not Necessary to all who profess or even sincerely exercise true natural Religion (as I long since writ to you) it being sufficient that they own the Supreme power, wisdom, Justice & Goodness of the first cause of all things & pay the Reverence, Love & obedience that is due to him."[50] It is most unlikely that either Campbell or Simson was tempted by Arianism. Both men, however, considered metaphysics out of place in pastoral ministry. The duty of man was to love and respect the commands of a tender Creator, rather than to ponder His ontological mysteries. Such a Creator could be known both by reason and revelation, by pagans and Christians alike.

49 J. Simson to A. Campbell, 3 March 1736, NAS, GD461/15/7, f1.
50 Ibid., f2.

Francis Hutcheson, who had initially been welcomed to Glasgow even by conservative ministers such as John McLaurin, became the next target of orthodox anger. Simson quickly approved of Hutcheson's observations about the sense of sympathy and of his ideas about the foundations of human sociability. He entreated Campbell to come to Glasgow in 1732 so that the three of them might have "some improving conversation on these subjects," since Hutcheson was of "a sweet oblidging temper."[51] In 1737 the Presbytery of Glasgow unsuccessfully accused Hutcheson of propagating heresy in his moral philosophy classes. The pamphlet war that ensued illustrated Hutcheson's liberal views and theological tolerance, but no further action was taken against him.[52]

At the same time William Wishart, Jr, had to deal with the orthodox resentment that had been building up in Edinburgh. On his nomination as principal of Edinburgh University in late 1736, he came under attack by the Presbytery of Edinburgh. Rev. Matthias Symson (?1672–1742) of London, who was related distantly to Simson, commented that "the Presbytery powerfully oppose him, because he is not a true blue, fiery, hot Zelot."[53] During a conversation with Symson prior to his departure from London, the principal-elect remarked that excessive strictness had "proved the Pest of Religion" and expressed the fear that "the Scots Kirk is in a declining Condition; for every year their General Assembly multi-plyes their Acts, which are so intricate & puzling, and executed with more warmth than discretion, it will be necessary, in time, to erect Facul-ties & Professorships in Colleges, to explain them, as the Papists have done their Canon Law."[54] Along with Simson and the other professors with modern views, Wishart saw extremist demands to legislate minutiae of doctrine as counterproductive.

The sins of which William Wishart was accused in February 1737 included denying the power of secular authorities to punish individuals for religious faults, suggesting that confessional statements may not always be necessary, demanding a non-partisan Protestant education for

---

51 J. Simson to A. Campbell, 26 Feb. 1732. NAS, GD461/15/3, f.6.
52 See Sher, "Commerce," 322–3. In May 1736 Simson tried to obtain a bursary for Hew Hugh, "a good lad," through the influence of Professor Campbell at St Andrews. By 1738 Hugh had become a virulent pamphleteer against Hutcheson. NAS, GD461/15/8, f2.
53 Matthias Symson to Revd. Dr. Grey, London, 10 May 1737, EUL, MS La.II.423/204.
54 Ibid.

children, saying that arguments of eternal reward or punishment could no more "promote a liberal Piety and Virtue ... than Whips and Sugar-plumbs,"[55] accepting the possibility of salvation for heathens or deists, and limiting the effects of original sin.

Advocate Archibald Murray, defending Wishart before the General Assembly of 1738, asked the members, "Is there not a *natural Sense of Goodness*, or of the Difference betwixt good and Evil, in all Men? and yet may not even this *Sense of Goodness* itself be in a great Measure debauched by *vitious Habits*? Before such Habits, then, have this unhappy Influence, is it not *yet in a great Measure undebauched?*"[56] The agreement of the majority of members – since Wishart was cleared of the presbytery's charges both by his synod and by the General Assembly – shows a monumental shift in Presbyterian thought since Webster accused Simson of heresy for believing that the soul was uncorrupted prior to birth.

Scots sentiment was swinging towards a form of Christianity that greatly resembled the doctrine taught by Simson in Glasgow. Undeterred, the Presbytery of Glasgow continued to try to control the lectures of the local divinity professor, William Leechman. Looking back in 1786, Kenrick remarked to James Wodrow, "A delineation of the character of the times, particularly of that spirit of bigotry w[hi]ch infested Scotland so late as 1743 when he [Leechman] was called to the theological Chair at Glasgow, would be a useful & curious lesson to posterity."[57] William Leechman himself wrote to a London friend shortly after his appointment to the post: "I don't beleive it is possible for one in your Situation to imagine to what hight bigottry & Nonsense in Religion prevails in this Country, especially in this part of it.... From this view of my present Situation you may easily perceive how difficult a task it must be to teach pure & genuine Christianity & at the same [time] not to expose myself to the fury of Bigotts: There is the utmost care taken to watch every word pronounced by me: The Zealots have always some Secret Spies among the Students to give the proper Information of what is taught on every Subject."[58]

55 Article 5 of the Presbytery of Edinburgh's charge against William Wishart, quoted in Wishart, *Answers*, 43.

56 Murray, *Case*, 16.

57 S. Kenrick to J. Wodrow, 3 July 1786, Dr Williams's Library, MS 24.157/118, 1v.

58 W. Leechman to G. Benson, London, 9 March 1744, Letters to George Benson, John Rylands Library (JRL), University of Manchester.

The system of espionage that had succeeded in bringing down Simson, however, was ineffective against Leechman. For him, "pure and genuine Christianity" meant avoiding the scholastic expressions that Simson had denounced, admitting that many might be elect, even among those who had not heard the Gospel, emphasizing trust and confidence in a generous Creator, and suggesting that threats of eternal punishment are to be interpreted as divine promptings to amendment of life.[59] Although the Presbytery of Glasgow charged Leechman with these errors, the Synod of Glasgow and Ayr and the 1744 General Assembly both absolved him from any blame. He told Benson, "The far greater part of the Assembly were freindly to me & to the Interests of true Moderation, but in such a Numerous Sett of men, there is always a considerable Number of fiery Bigots, who engage Keenly in every Cry of Heresy."[60]

Fortunately for the rising generation of academic ministers, the attack on Simson proved to be the last success of the "fiery Bigots" in the Church of Scotland against an incumbent professor. Though targets of such assaults, its members all escaped unscathed, because Secession had dissipated the forces of orthodoxy. Not only were the more extreme ministers lost to the established church, but the power of the moderate wing was also strengthened by the fears that the reality of Secession had aroused. For twenty years secular and religious leaders had haggled and compromised in ultimately futile exertions to avoid a rent in the divinely ordained order of the Church of Scotland. Although their misgivings about the political fall-out from the Secession proved unwarranted, their qualms about the ecclesiological results were fully justified. The Secession church splintered further in the decades ahead, and the established church suffered another secession in 1761 and divided yet again in 1843.

The Simson cases make it clear that the issues of liberal Calvinist theology and Erastian interference in the Presbyterian structure of the Church of Scotland were inextricably mixed in the sight of the ultra-orthodox stalwarts of the early eighteenth century. The political events of 1688 and 1707 had persuaded the moderate leaders of the church

---

59 See Leechman's explanations of the charges against him in a letter to George Benson, 5 May 1744. Ibid.

60 W. Leechman to G. Benson, 14 July 1744, ibid.

that it was in the nation's best interest to conform to government demands where possible and to avoid extremism in doctrine and practice. Simson devoted his life to the pursuit of this policy. He was truly a moderate in his generation – one whose religious views were benevolent and inclusive and whose political ideas might be seen as those of enlightened despotism.

13

Conclusion:
Scotland Transformed

A convinced Christian and a sound Calvinist, Simson had the misfortune to be a member of the first generation of enlightened thinkers in Scotland, elected to the Glasgow divinity chair at a time when political exigencies were creating an atmosphere of tension in the Church of Scotland. Intolerant of muddled thinking and scholastic obfuscation, Simson met the challenges of his day with blunt determination. His work laid the foundations for the reconciliation of philosophy and religion that was the hallmark of the Scottish enlightenment. He erred in underestimating the dwindling influence of the conservative zealots and in overestimating the willingness of politicians to incur their wrath.

The Bible was the first and definitive source of John Simson's faith. He shared with Samuel Clarke a will to return to scripture as the basis for theology. His reading also included a wide variety of Christian authorities; in his first case (1714–17) many of the theological examples given were from seventeenth-century Scottish writers such as Samuel Rutherford. Simson admitted that Clarke had stimulated his interest in patristic literature, although he certainly had some awareness of early sources before 1714. The bewilderment with which some of his adversaries read the references in his defences make it clear that their knowledge of the early church fathers, for instance, was extremely limited. Simson used his extensive understanding of Continental Calvinist and other Christian authors to argue his theological interpretations with his less-informed brethren. He disliked systems weighed down by explanations that became for apologists more important than revelation. Simson accepted the basic Protestant tenet that every man, aided by the Spirit working through reason as well as faith, must personally seek the truth in divine revelation. To the end of his days, Simson said that the Westminster Confession, with its careful scriptural citations for each clause, contained the sum of his faith; at the same time, he refused to accept that it could not be changed, should better wording be devised. Only the language of the Bible was sacred; other documents of human composition were helpful but never authoritative.

Simson's religion was simple, biblically based, and rational. Human reason had a divine purpose in establishing the truth of revelation, in helping Christians to understand the scriptures, and in assisting them to accept divine grace and struggle towards repentance and assurance. Simson believed that men had a duty to use their faculties for this purpose. Reason also was properly employed in speculation on matters indifferent to salvation. Theology students ought to be equipped for the logical consideration of such subjects as the existence of extraterrestrial life or the dietary restrictions of the Israelites. Simson's approach was cosmopolitan compared with that of many of his countrymen. In reaching his conclusions, he drew on Protestant opinion from England, France, Germany, Holland, and Ireland. His reason permitted him to accept doctrines that were also approved by Anglicans, Arminians, or Lutherans. He refused to shut his eyes to solutions to theological difficulties on the grounds that extreme Calvinists found them unsound because heterodox sects had used them.

The God of Simson and his supporters was no longer the terrible avenger of the covenanters. A more optimistic world required a benevolent Creator, who demanded of His people not fanaticism, but moral virtue and ethical life. Simson felt that Calvin's God was such a loving Creator. He wanted the next generation of ministers to preach a message of hope. His teaching in the divinity school echoed Locke and parallelled the Pufendorf-based teaching of Carmichael. Hutcheson expanded on these ideas in his own work. A probably apocryphal story tells that in 1719 he was "babbling ... about a gude and benevolent God, and that the sauls o' the heathens themsels will gang to Heeven."[1] Simson was convinced that he remained a Calvinist true to the Confession of Faith. Along with his pupils Hutcheson and Archibald Campbell, he suffered because the world in which they lived was less sure of that and less enlightened than they.

---

1 William Robert Scott, *Hutcheson*, 20.

Simson was prepared to defend his theology in front of the church courts because he believed that the Bible and the Westminster Confession contained a similar faith. To his antagonists, however, the rank heresy that he was teaching ought to be extirpated by whatever method seemed necessary. The differences between Simson and his opponents were based on his new understanding of faith, not on circumstances of age or education. The conservative viewpoint of Simson's detractors tended towards a xenophobic distrust of any departure from the extreme Calvinism of late-seventeenth-century Scotland. Observers in London and Ireland noticed and commented on the strictness of their demands on Simson. In consequence, men such as the lay elder Grange and the minister Wodrow grappled with explaining the significance of their views to uncomprehending English friends. While they were perfectly correct in seeing Simson as a danger to their preferred doctrine, their beliefs were no longer those of the wider Reformed world.

The innovations in teaching methods that Simson introduced into Glasgow's divinity school were designed to create a modern pastorate with a Calvinism similar to that of more liberal Continental churches. Simson's personal education had been typical of his generation: dependence on the dated texts used by Professor James Wodrow, followed by the broadening experience of Continental schools. This exposure to foreign thought led him to introduce new theological texts when he went to Glasgow. Like many of his fellows, he approved of the manuals produced by Marck at Leiden and used his *Medulla* as the basic text for his own theology classes. However, Simson also looked beyond Holland and found in the Genevan teaching of Pictet an authority who avoided scholasticism. Pictet's work became his secondary text.

No doubt Simson's students took dictates from his prelections, as they did from their other professors. Beyond this, however, Simson gave them a thorough grounding in controversial subjects and allowed them the latitude to argue their views in "cases." The discussion, argument, and debate that he permitted his students alarmed those who preferred the old ways. By the early 1720s the students' cases were causing disquiet to Wodrow and his orthodox friends. Simson always claimed that he and Stirling reviewed the arguments of the young men and corrected erroneous ideas. Clearly, vigorous debate took place, leading to heated personal discussions between professor and students. Some of the accusations against Simson came from private extra dialogues over contentious subjects which took place outside formal classes.[2] The professor was not afraid to act as devil's advocate on occasion, and some of the questions that led to the charges against him may well have been posed in that way. When Simson asked a student, "Now, how do you know that?" surely he was demanding that the young man cite his references, rather than casting doubt on the dogma in debate?[3]

For Simson the Bible represented the only infallible authority. He expected his classes, in reading it, to take into account the views of the church fathers, rational argument, and philological development. These demands themselves shocked the orthodox. What was worse, however, was Simson's suggestion that the Bible could not be used to prove its own truth. Here he departed from the words of Calvin and from Scottish tradition, in order to make Christian ministry more relevant to a non-Christian world. Simson did not, however, foster the growth of deism and atheism in Scotland as his opponents feared. He encouraged his enlightened younger friends to defend Reformed Christianity against the assaults of deists and Unitarians. When Archibald Campbell was accused of unsound doctrine, Simson found it strange that "Not one of our Standards of Orthodoxy has adventured to write one argument against the adversaries of Christianity but write with great zeal against the defenders of it. which would move ane honest Turk or Indian to draw ane Inference not very favourable to them & their Orthodoxy." He thought that Campbell was receiving "reproachfull & spiteful usage" in return for his efforts in defending the faith.[4] No heretic or outcast, Simson was always interested in how Reformed Christianity could best be promoted in the face of current danger, and rational argument was his chosen means.

In the northern kingdom, moderate Calvinism did not fall prey to the prevalent Unitarianism of the English Presbyterians. Roger L. Emerson has argued that the Moderates of the later part of the century retained the basic beliefs of Reformed orthodoxy and accepted subscription to the Westminster Confession willingly.[5] Principal George Campbell (1719–1796) of Marischal College, Aberdeen, and Professor George Hill (1750–1819) of St Andrews University are examples of Moderate

2 William Brown deponed that part of his conversation with Simson had been in the professor's room in the college, in the presence of his brother, David, and one other student. Dundas, *Processes*, 117–18.

3 Testimony of William Boyd, ibid., 119.

4 J. Simson to A. Campbell, 27 Aug. 1734, NAS, GD461/15/5.

5 Emerson, "The religious," 76–80.

theologians whose published works displayed sound Calvinist doctrine, though of a less hyper-Calvinist nature than those of McLaren or Flint. Despite the claims of Simson's enemies that he rejected subscription, I have found no expression of support for the non-subscribers or their principles either written or spoken by him. Even Allan Logan, one of his most formidable opponents, who noted sarcastically that in his refusal to answer questions Simson had "followed these upright and Orthodox Men, the *Antrim* Non-declarers, and adopted their very Terms; his Eloquence and Learning here is wholly *Hybernian,* and borrowed from the worst Set of Men in that Kingdom," did not accuse Simson of following their non-subscription principles.[6] The professor never renounced subscription to the Westminster Confession; rather he warmly endorsed it during the successive General Assemblies at which he was tried.

At the same time, the backward and defensive church of the covenanting period was transforming itself into a more optimistic body that would embrace and uphold the study of man and his role in society. The eighteenth-century Church of Scotland was learning to accept enlightened opinions and to find ways to incorporate them into its attitude to a world that it was seeking to understand better. Simson's tribulations taught the moderate leaders that the national church could tolerate divergent views without losing its essential Calvinism. This lesson enabled the Church of Scotland to become a patron of enlightened thought in the latter part of the century, permitting a remarkable number of its ministers and pious laymen to become distinguished in British intellectual life.[7]

We should not minimize the influence of Simson's example on the next generation of moderate Scots ministers. His modified Arminian view of the atonement, his Shaftesburian moral sense, and his vision of a benevolent Creator were widely adopted by the new leaders of the church. Hutcheson quoted his opinions, and Leechman continued his Glasgow teaching methods. His cases could serve as text books on how to respond to libels of heresy. Partially as a result of the precedents that he set, his younger friends all succeeded in evading the censures that he had received. Their escapes prove that the mood had changed.

6 [Allan Logan], *Enquiry,* 42.

7 The church drew the line only at John Home's writing of plays, and even then its disapproval centred on such matters as his sympathetic portrayal of suicide (and on his own acting)! By the 1780s, even that had changed.

Opinions that in 1715 had seemed shocking in Glasgow appeared by Simson's death unremarkable to all but a few zealots.

Simson must be exonerated from the accusation of encouraging heresy among his students. In his own words, he was a "Strange Heretick! who has never made one Proselyte among his own Disciples, nor even discover'd to them that their Master held any heretical Principles."[8] Even his enemies could not point to any heretics among his ex-students, however much they wished to blacken his name. His reputation for heterodoxy was vastly exaggerated by the vigilant evangelical wing of the Presbyterian establishment. The few controversial words that he denied intentionally uttering were not definitively proved; his admitted meditations on theological issues did not stray beyond the acceptable boundaries of Reformed Christian doctrine; his last recorded public utterances were of unimpeachable orthodoxy.

MODERATION AND THE RULE OF LAW: POLITICS, CHURCH LAW, AND PATRONAGE

The Simson cases provide an insight into the political environment in which the Scottish Enlightenment evolved. In the world of Scottish post-Union politics, church and state were closely bound together. English pressures on the kirk were alarming factors for leaders to take into consideration. The 1712 acts concerning toleration of Episcopalians and lay patronage ensured that everyone was aware of the danger. They appeared to be designed to bring the Church of Scotland more in line with English practice. The appointment of the inadequately qualified Scrimgeour to the divinity chair at St Andrews intensified the fears of many churchmen. These actions seemed both politically and spiritually threatening to the very nature of Presbyterianism. The zealots believed that God might mete out vengeance if all this activity went unchecked and unchallenged.

Political pressure on the church from England lessened gradually after Simson's suspension largely because of the Earl of Islay's political machinations and patronage appointments. One aim of his activities was to support the more theologically liberal members of the church. The effects of religious zeal on academic life also became less marked as the established church grew less fanatical and the moderate group gained greater influence. Scottish enthusiasm reached a peak at the Cambuslang revival in

8 Simson, *Case*, x.

1742; thereafter most radicals were to be absorbed into one or other of the Presbyterian splinter groups. Simson's two cases and the intervening *Marrow* affair were vital in demonstrating to Islay that he could not use the traditional Campbell "High-Flying" allies as his assistants in ecclesiastical and academic management because of their inability to compromise on doctrinal matters.

During Simson's first case, his tormentors Webster and Flint had been confident of Argathelian support because they were harassing not only a heretic, but also a Squadrone man. By the mid-1720s, Islay had become an accomplished politician, whose association with Walpole was about to make him *de facto*, though not titular, secretary of state for Scotland. He was developing a working partnership in Edinburgh with Andrew Fletcher, Lord Milton, a man related to him by marriage who had similar cultivated tastes and interests. In Glasgow, the earl had maintained an interest in the politics of the burgh and in the welfare of his old university, where he had long had an informant in Professor Alexander Dunlop. Since one of Islay's main Scottish political rivals was Glasgow's Chancellor, the Duke of Montrose, it was vital to Argathelian interests to strengthen their numbers on the faculty. John Simson needed the Argathelians just when they also needed him. In this situation, Islay reconsidered where his advantage lay. The ultra-orthodox group could not be trusted to obey directions or to negotiate compromises. Moderate men, who understood the importance of conciliating English opinion by maintaining consensus in church matters, were essential tools, through whom Islay could administer Scotland for Walpole. Islay was almost certainly instrumental in arranging for the royal commission of visitation of 1727 in Glasgow; he certainly interested himself in its proceedings. This event marked Islay's victory over the Squadrone in Glasgow University, as well as the defeat of the ultra-conservative Presbyterians – a triumph that Islay then consolidated with the appointment of Neil Campbell as principal.

In the late 1720s Islay faced a choice. He could either continue the Campbell support of the religious extremists, thereby disqualifying himself for service to Walpole, or he could transfer his patronage to the growing group of well-educated men of moderate views, who shared his outlook. A man who had little interest in doctrine, Islay was induced by events such as the second Simson case to choose the Moderates. Thereafter he assured the rise of such men, though not without experiencing resistance, as the trials suffered by professors in the 1730s and 1740s proved. Islay's protégés overcame orthodox protests to prosper in Aberdeen, Edinburgh, and Glasgow.

By overstepping the narrow accepted boundary for theological discussion among the ultra-orthodox in Scotland in the 1720s, Simson had stirred up a hornets' nest. Dispassionate politicians orchestrated committees and General Assemblies in their efforts to temper the enthusiasm of the fanatics. Islay and Walpole had no desire to see their careful manipulation of Scottish politics fall victim to religious zeal. The generous treatment that Simson received was both a reward for his consistent support for authority and an assurance to Moderates that they would be protected against persecution. At the same time, Islay was too wily to antagonize completely a substantial number of Campbell supporters. When, between 1728 and 1731, he was faced with the question of restoring Simson to his teaching duties, he knew that to do so would mean further chaos in the church. The safest course was to leave Simson's suspension in place and to use his patronage powers to place other moderates in positions of authority wherever possible. Islay's decisions ensured that the Scottish Enlightenment would have the religious and academic foundation that gave it its unique quality.

The Simson cases also produced changes in the implementation of church law. Simson's efforts helped to enforce an ecclesiastical legal process that allowed for the presumption of innocence. The notoriety that his cases acquired brought matters of law and procedure to public attention. Educated people became aware of the inherent problems of applying a Roman-based legal investigation by queries to a society rapidly becoming attuned to Whig principles derived from Locke. Discovery by question did not cease, but thinking men were obliged to consider the basis for such methods. As we have seen, even Wodrow appreciated that on occasion such investigation could be wrong. Referring to another process in 1730, Robert Wallace considered that "the method they took was unjust I mean the putting Queries to a Minister upon suspicion when nothing or no great matter can be proven against him." He added that while supreme courts could authorize a change in practice, subordinate courts should obey the existing rules: "But as this method of Querying a man suspected when little or nothing can be proven is not a stated rule of this Church I think no inferior court can take this method without the orders of a supreme court."[9] It was now a matter of common concern that due process be followed and that existing regulations be enforced.

---

9 From an undelivered speech written to give to the commission of the General Assembly in March 1730 about the suspension of Rev. John Glas. EUL, MS La.II.620, 17.

Although on procedural matters Simson was often as lacking in consistency and principle as his enemies, here too his personal experience had an impact. Simson's flexibility, and his ability to embrace effective tactics, allowed him to appropriate Arbuckle's arguments on the cross-examination of witnesses giving precognitions when he himself fell victim to comparable dubious treatment. Simson repeatedly asked to be present at the interrogation of witnesses. He was well aware that it was his business to protect his own interests, and as a result he eventually received permission to attend such examinations and to cross-examine witnesses.

The introduction of lawyers into ecclesiastical proceedings was stimulated, though not initiated, by Simson's determination to force the church to follow its own rules. As early as 1711 Wodrow had commented unfavourably on an increased use of advocates in the assembly, "pleading as warmly as if at the barr."[10] The use of secular lawyers in religious matters was considered controversial, since they were felt to be not only inappropriate, but also not conversant with theological niceties. One of the anonymous pamphleteers writing on the Simson case in 1728 claimed that the professor's representation by an advocate before the Presbytery of Glasgow was setting a precedent. He believed that it was the first time that a lawyer had been allowed to plead before a presbytery on behalf of a person charged with scandal of any kind.[11]

Simson employed several different advocates, one of whom, William Grant, in 1731 succeeded John Dundas of Philipston as principal clerk to the General Assembly and procurator and advocate in ordinary for the church. Grant's expertise in defending Simson must have impressed those who heard him. When William Wishart, Jr, was libelled in 1738, his case was presented to the General Assembly by another of Simson's advocates, Archibald Murray. Accused clergymen after Simson were careful to be properly defended. As a result, some advocates made a comfortable living dealing with cases heard in ecclesiastical courts.

The precedents set by the Simson cases left the extremists disarmed to a great extent. The outcry that the proceedings against him had produced led to greater care over the use of correct forms and appropriate charges. None of the professors accused in the decade after Simson met with the departures from due process that he had endured.

Simson's activities during his years in Glasgow suggest a man who believed strongly in the importance of firm government, with clearly stated

10 Wodrow, *Analecta*, 1:332.
11 *Animadversions on a Pamphlet*, 47.

parameters in all areas of human affairs. The fact that he sometimes exempted himself from these rules, especially in his relations with church judicatories, does not negate his belief in the jurisdiction of men of moderation and intelligence over civil and ecclesiastical society. Simson typified men of his class and education in being Whiggish by conviction, but prepared to support different factions of that party to foster his own interests, which he generally saw as similar to those of his nation. Like most other leading Scots of his generation, he believed that the Crown and its ministers should be supported as fully as was consistent with personal liberty and conviction in order to preserve the Protestant, Presbyterian establishment in the church.

The leaders of the Scottish church followed the advice of the royal commissioners to the General Assemblies in enjoining restraint in the settlement of controversy between 1707 and 1730. They believed that the preservation and well-being of the church depended on placating whichever political group was stronger. For their part, politicians used ecclesiastical and academic patronage to enhance secular power. Since loyalty required reward, an appointee in difficulties, even in church courts, had to be championed.

Because of the close connections between the church and the universities, Simson endeavoured to follow the Squadrone party line for nearly twenty years and to encourage others to do likewise. In return, Squadrone adherents took his part against James Webster in 1714–17. With a change of political control in Scotland after 1725, and particularly with a new principal in Glasgow University in 1727, Simson turned to follow the fortunes of the Argyll family, which had earlier been patron to his father. Once again he was rewarded by enough support during his second case to ensure his possession of the Glasgow divinity chair for life. Simson's story is proof that the patronage offered by the Scottish nobility was ready and able to sustain a new progressive and enlightened society.

ROOTS OF ENLIGHTENMENT: INNOVATION, MODERNIZATION, MODERATION

Scotland in 1720 was a world on which seventeenth-century tensions had left their mark. It lacked the open-mindedness, respect for law, and secular tolerance that were essential for Simson's teaching to be acceptable. The next generation, led by Cumming, Wallace, the Wisharts, and others, began to work with Islay to alter Scottish institutions through patronage and the Moderate discipline later endorsed by Principal

William Robertson (1721–1793) of Edinburgh University. Simson led the way in helping to make Scotland a more hospitable environment for new ideas and wider philosophical deliberations. For such purposes he was prepared to use the most effective vocabulary and arguments, even if they came from Arminian Remonstrants or Antrim non-subscribers. Simson's interest in religious philosophy, and his willingness to consider ideas introduced by other controversial contemporaries such as the heterodox Dr Clarke, made it inevitable that he would become the object of disapproval by those whose minds were closed to such dialogue. His open excitement on first reading Clarke's *Scripture Doctrine of the Trinity* was inadvisable in the narrow world of the Presbytery of Glasgow.

The fear that Simson's frankness inspired would be amusing, had the consequences not been so serious. Wodrow's wife clearly believed that Simson was hiding horns under his wig and possessed miraculous powers of persuasion: "Some few months ago [early 1726] she went in to Glasgou, and went to see Professor Simson. In going, she was checked in her mind for venturing to go to one who might drop somwhat that should shake her as to the Divinity of Christ, she having resolved to attack him on the storys going about his teaching."[12] Alarmed by this thought, Mrs Wodrow sat trembling on the stairs for some minutes, while she prepared a mental list of suitable texts with which to demonstrate the divinity of Christ. In the event, this was unnecessary, since a crowd of other guests frustrated her intentions. The story confirms Simson's position in Glasgow society and proves that many of its members were in favour of the new trends. It was normal for an orthodox minister's wife to call on an alleged heretic and his family, along with many others who enjoyed his company. This situation did not alter with Simson's suspension in 1729 – a fact that underlines the new liberality of religious opinion of many in educated society. Simson's letters to Archibald Campbell indicate a busy life of visits and conversation. In 1737 he recommended that his friend would find it "better for your health & work to travel & converse more than you do." He added that he "found it more profitable to both than solitary study."[13]

The few extant letters from Simson confirm the impression created by his written defences of a man with varied interests, including science, early Scottish history, modern French philosophy, and religious controversy. His opinions were shared by many others of similar middle-class backgrounds. Their educational path through Scottish and Dutch

---

12 Wodrow, *Analecta*, 3:311.
13 J. Simson to A. Campbell, 14 Sept. 1737, NAS, GD461/15/11, f.4.

universities was followed by grand tours as tutors to noble youths. They had visited England and the Continent and kept up the contacts that they had made there. *Virtuosi* of greater means put their interests in improving and modernizing into practice on their estates and in industrial projects. Simson's opportunities were financially limited; his improvements were intellectual, but his experience and circle of friends gave him the same stimulus to action. Sections of Scottish society disapproved of Simson's improvements, just as they sometimes disliked the work of other improvers. The freedom of debate that his cases engendered, however, is a sign of the progress that had been made in the previous quarter-century. Despite the unrepealed anti-blasphemy laws, no one suggested that Simson should be charged as Aikenhead had been, or hanged if convicted.

Simson's experiences were components of the change that Scottish intellectual life underwent during the first half of the eighteenth century. From aspiring to be a closed theocracy, fighting to escape from the Erastian grasp of a Crown seen as English, Presbyterian society emerged from the battles of the early decades reasonable, moderate, and engaged in the secular world. Human nature and its employment in this world, as well as in the next, were Hutcheson's concerns; they were stamped with his understanding of Calvinist faith.[14] The Enlightenment researches into societal development and economic management were the products both of Scottish religion and of the freedom from dogmatic demands that resulted from the innovations of Simson and his colleagues. John Simson would not have approved of the scepticism of David Hume or of the secularism of much of William Robertson's history, but he would have commended their methods and upheld their right to explore and to speculate. He would also have applauded their defences of freedom and their liking for order.

The striking changes in perspective on the part of educated Scots, particularly members of the clergy, during the middle years of the eighteenth century permitted a new, constructive inquiry into human society. Lord Kames, dying in 1782, was reputed to have said that one would not go to Hell for conjecturing.[15] Simson's adversaries would have censured Kames severely for investigating the development of the human

14 Emerson, "Calvinism," 19–28.

15 Henry Home, Lord Kames (1696–1782), was a judge and writer on legal, ethical, literary, and historical topics. His remark on conjecture is quoted in Phillipson, "Lawyers," 100.

condition outside the limits they thought set by scripture, just as they had criticized Simson. Even in the latter half of the eighteenth century Kames was attacked by those who denied the idea of progress on theological and historical grounds.[16] Nevertheless, real change had occurred. The freedom to conjecture was part of the legacy that the crises of the first three decades of the century left to the future.

Among the explanations for the rapid transformation of community standards, three specifically emerge from this study. The first was an innovative spirit introduced into the clergy through the teaching of Simson, William Hamilton of Edinburgh University, and their academic contemporaries. The deaths of older men, brought up with covenanting ideals that made them theologically inflexible and also unwilling to compromise for the sake of political expediency, left room in the ministry for the younger men educated under Simson and his generation. These ministers were well acquainted with trends elsewhere in Britain and on the Continent. They identified the religious requirements for the improvement of their emerging nation as rational, ethical, and progressive. They sought to define and live by a different, possibly more biblical Christianity, which stressed the beatitudes rather than the judgments of a wrathful God. Religious enthusiasm had no role in such a church. The need to preach virtue overcame the stern Calvinist stress on election and reprobation. John Simson's views and teachings were guide-posts in this direction. The accusations against Wishart and Leechman, to name only two, demonstrate that these men conformed to the ideals of Reformed Christianity enunciated by the Glasgow professor – a conformity emphasized by Wishart's opposition to the sceptical Hume's appointment as a professor.

Second, this modernization of the church leadership was facilitated by the departure of the more extreme opponents of an inclusive theology. We saw above the correlation between those who disliked Simson on doctrinal grounds and those who despised Erastian interference in clerical affairs. Professor Simson, like many of his notable predecessors in the Glasgow divinity chair, believed in the desirability of church and state's co-operating harmoniously for the good of the nation. Such a stance had frequently been unpopular; the persecution that Simson suffered was not unique. The departure of the hyper-Calvinist minority

16 See, for example, criticism by the Stirling schoolmaster David Doig, in *Conjectural History.*

from the Church of Scotland, propelled by its dissatisfaction over the Simson verdict, permitted the rise of a new, polite, and literary clerical élite, which could use the church to promote enlightened causes.

Third, Argathelian control of Scottish patronage for most of the critical years between 1730 and 1760 allowed Islay and his subordinates to install reasonable, open-minded men in university chairs and parish pulpits. While the disposing of the spoils of office may be no more justifiable when done by Argathelians than by members of the Squadrone, the men appointed by Islay tended to be not only politically but intellectually suitable for their chosen positions.[17] Although Simson's second case proved that patronage could not be used to impose an unacceptable professor or minister on a recalcitrant church, John Simson benefited from the protection of both Whig factions. During these years many men changed sides in pursuit of political gain; only Jacobitism put one beyond the pale.

Simson's use of political connections helps to demonstrate how the system worked in practice. It also reveals the limits of secular interference in ecclesiastical affairs. In 1717, the Squadrone was powerful enough to quash demands that Simson be severely punished for his espousal of rational theology and benevolent inclusiveness. By 1727, the Argathelians were in the process of establishing supremacy but were not yet in a position to resist conservative demands for the censure of a professor believed to be lapsing into heresy. It is possible that in the early stages of the case they did not make great efforts for him because he had been tainted with previous Squadrone loyalties. In the end the reality of Simson's beliefs became lost beneath the superstructure of fear and alarm that the propagandists had created, but the negotiated settlements of the late 1720s ensured his financial security. For these to be achieved, the government had to aid him. Islay was forced to break with the "High-Flyers" if he wished to continue in power. The matter had to rest with Simson's suspension, however, since political managers, both lay and clerical, were unwilling to risk the disruption that might result from a restoration of Simson's teaching privileges.

Simson's friends were perhaps disappointed by the political compromise which led to his enforced retirement, but ultimately they had won. The contribution of John Simson and his cases to changes in the church, in politics, and in culture enabled the Enlightenment to flourish in Scotland.

17 See Emerson, "Medical Men" and "Politics."

APPENDIX A
Documents re Simson's First Case

This appendix contains extracts from James Webster's libel of 27 September 1714 against John Simson, the attached list of witnesses cited, a list of ministers present at the 1713 meeting in Edinburgh at which Simson made libelled remarks, and Webster's report of the remarks that Simson made there.

The material in this appendix comes from John Simson, *Libel Mr James Webster, Against Mr John Simson Professor of Divinity in the University of Glasgow* (n.p. [?1716]), 1–11.

Extracts from Webster's Libel against Mr John Simson Professor of Divinity in the University of Glasgow, given in to the Presbytery of Glasgow.

Yet true it is, and of Verity, That Mr. John Simson Professor of Divinity hath Vented these following Errors, and, during the Space of the sixth, or fifth, or fourth, or third, or second, or first Year last past, taught them his Scholars in his Hall, Namely, Errors:

1. The end of God's Revelation towards the Heathens, is not only their Conviction, and the greater Restraining of them, but also that they may seek after further Discoveries of the Lord to themselves; for, the Heathen, by the Light of Nature may know, that God is Reconcileable, yea that there is a Remedy provided, tho they cannot know the particular Way of Salvation, and it is their Duty to seek after the knowledg of the Way how God is Reconciled: And if they would, God wou'd discover it to them, and this will be that for which the Heathens chiefly will be condemned that tho' they might have known a Remedy was provided, yet they did not seek after the Knowledg of the particular Way of Redemption.

2. As the Supralapsarian Way is intricate, and liable to many Difficulties, so neither is the common ordinary Scheme of the Sublapsarians so

satisfying, as the Creature in Reprobation is considered as a Sinner, so in the Predestination of others to the Illustration of the Glory of Mercy they are not only considered as miserable Sinners but also as invested with all those Qualities which make them meet for the Illustration of the Glory of Mercy. Therefore, this Order of the Divine Decrees in Elections seems to us more agreeable to Divine Wisdom, viz. 1mo. God decreed to give to a Number of Mankind Sinners (having also decreed to send his Son into the World for their Redemption) Faith in the Lord Jesus Christ and Repentance towards God, and Holiness, begun in Time, and perfected at their Death, 2do. They being considered as thus made meet for the Illustration of his Glory and Mercy, He pre-destinated them for that very End; And this Order seems to us less liable to the Cavills of Adversaries.

3. Our Divines do too boldly determine the Number of the Elect to be fewer than that of the Reprobate, since the Scripture is silent on this Head. The Scriptures adduced by our Author, do not prove his Assertion: Our Lord is speaking these Places of Adult Persons: And it is certain, that as many, if not mor die in Infancy, as come to the Years of Understanding and probably these make the Number of the Saved Equal with that of the Damned. If then we speak of what is most probable on this Head we think it is highly probable, that the Number of the Elect is as great, if not greater then that of the Damned, since no Reason can be given, why mor should be Reprobated, to illustrate the Glory of Justice, than Chosen to Illustrate the Glory of Mercy: Yet it seems more agreeable to the Goodness of God that his Mercy should be illustrate in as many as His Justice is. Concerning Infants dying within the Pale of the Visible Church, there is no Difficulty; for, they having received the Seal of God's Covenant, and, when dying in Infancy, having done Nothing on their Part to make void the Covenant of Grace sealed to them, it is more than probable, that they are all saved. Concerning the Infants of Heathens & Infidels, we must judge charitably of them also; for it seems very severs, and gives too great an handle to the Adversaries of truth, to say, that any poor Infants, who have never sinned in their own Persons, should be eternally punished, especially when we consider that God has provided a Remedy for Sinners, and published the same twice to the Word, first to Adam, afterwards to Noah and his Family; we think none are excluded for the benefits of this Covenant, but these who is their own Persons exclude themselves. Hence the Infants even of Infidels may be Baptized, if any Christian undertake to bring them up in the Knowledg of the Lord. We do not deny, but God may condemn to eternal Death Infants; but if He do so, it is by his Absolute Dominion; yet we doubt if His Absolute Dominion

be exerted this Way, yean the Goodness and mercy of God inclines us to think otherways. If there be any Error here, it is on Charity's Side and not great.

4. Our Author having shown wherein 'Dei Concursus doth not consist, he tells us, it lyes in 'Praevio Immediato Praedeterminanti Impulsu & Motu Creaturarum ad operandum: But he doth not satisfyingly explain it. By his Description, Rational Creatures are like passive Instruments in the hand of God. And truly, this way of Explaining it, seems to be inconsistent with the Rational Nature. Therefore, that we may the better understand it, let us observe (1mo) That God hath from all Eternity Infallibly Decreed all the Creatures Actions, both Necessary and Contingent. (2do) He has Decreed to put the Rational Creature in such Circumstances, in which being placed he Acts Certainly, yet Freely, what is Decreed. (3tio) God, in the Creation of Man, gives him such Powers, and doth still conserve them, by which man being placed in these Circumstances, doth freely produce such and such Actions as are Decreed. We are Speaking now of Humane Actions in General, Not in the way of his Concurring with good Actions in Particular. 'Concursus then is nothing else, but the Lord's (according to his most wise Decree) puting the Creature in such Circumstances in which the Creatures being placed, does without any previous or predetermining Instance upon it, freely, yet Infallibly produce the Decreed Effect. and this way the Manichean Error and Cavills of Adversaries are sooner evited.

5. The Desire of Reward, and the Fear of Punishment may not only be a Motive, as our Author sayeth, but should be the Chief motive to the Rational Creature in Worshipping the Lord; for God has so formed the Rational Creature, as Chiefly to seek its own Good and Happiness; Neither from this will follow what our Author says, That so we Worship our selves more then the Creator, for, the Lord holds forth Himself to us, to be Worshipped from this as the chief Motive.

6. Our Author speaks of God's Dispensation with Adam, as if the Lord had transacted with Adam in the way of a Proper Covenant, in which there is Stipulation, Restipulation, and Adstipulation. The Scripture goes not before us in making this Dispensation a proper Covenant: We read Gen.2.17. of a Solemn Command given to Adam with a Threatning Annexed, which Implyed a promise of Life, and God did, as Sovereign Lawgiver, require Obedience to his Commands: But if any call it a covenant by reason of the Promise of Life, it must be remembred, that it is a Covenant in an Improper sense, and so the Compilers of our Confession of Faith, use the term Chap.7th. As to the Relation in which Adam

stood to his Posterity, he was their Publick Natural or Moral Head, but not a Federal Representative; To say that he was their Federal Representative, labours with this Difficulty, viz. How it was agreeable to the Justice of God, so to Transact with Adam, when he knew he would not faithfully act the part of his Posterity? If it be said that a Federal Representation is Necessary, in order to Maintain the Imputation of Adams first Sin: We Answer the Imputation of Adam's first Sin follows clearly from his being a Natural or Moral Head; for, Imputation of Sin is nothing else, but the Connexion betwixt the sin of one and the Punishment or Loss that another sustains by it. So Adam sinning, he became Corrupt, and so we are descended Corrupt from him: This Original corruption in us is the Effect of Adam's first Sin, and thus it is Imputed to us, and thus we are to understand the Apostle Rom.5.12.

7. Our Author's Answer to the Objection of the Pelagians, is, that God is not Unjust in Commanding us to Obey tho we have no Power, because our Impotency is Culpable, and was Voluntarily contracted: But this is not so satisfying. It might well be said to Adam that had lost power to Obey, but that can't be said of us who never had that Power; Adam lost Power by his own default but we never lost it by our fault. Therefore the Justice of God in Commanding us to obey appears evidently, if we consider, He has been pleased to Reveal His Grace, and offers strength to us by the Gospel, and commands us to ask and we shall receive, and we have Natural powers and abilities to seek the Lord's special and saving Grace which if we do, He has promised to give us His Special Saving Grace Matth.7.7. God may Soveraignly prevent Sinners when they are not seeking Him, but His ordinary way of Communicating His Grace, is in the way of their seeking after it.

8. Our Divines, in Explaining the Propagation of Original Sin, say, That god in Creating the soul deprives it of Original Righteousness, upon the account of Adams first Sin: But it is hard to understand how it is Agreeable to the Lord's Justice and Goodness, to deal so with the soul, when as yet it hath Committed nothing deserving such a Sentence: Therefore we think it more safe to say, That the Soul is Created Pure and Holy as Adam's was, but by being United to the corrupted Body, it contracts wicked habits and Dispositions from it; Neither is it Inconsistent with the Justice of God, to unite a Holy soul to a Corrupt and Depraved body, since he has provided a Remedy for all who do not Despise and Reject that Remedy.

9. Our Author says, That Necessity of Eternal Punishment follows from Sin its being an Offence committed against an Infinite Majesty. but this

doth not make it Necessary; It rather flows from the Necessity of such a Sanction to the Divine Law: For, such a Punishment must be annexed to the law, as is sufficient to deter the Creature from violating the Law; and since we know by experience, that the Threatning of Eternal punishment doth not deter Sinners from violating God's law, far less would a lesser Punishment do it: Hence the threatning of an Eternal punishment is necessary.

10. What our Author saith concerning the continual Multiplying of sins in Hell we cannot approve: Since an Earthly Judge can inflict such a Punishment upon the Despisers of his Laws, as shall put them for ever out of Capacity to voilat [*sic*] his Laws in his own Dominions, Much more can the Supreme Judge Inflict such Punishment upon the Despisers of his Laws as shall keep them from violating the same: And we do not see how it is agreeable to his Wisdom and Holiness, to punish Sinners for sins they have done and yet in the mean time to suffer them to go on in Sinning against him, when it must be owned, Infinite Power can restrain them for ever from Sinning, and in this state they shall be made to acknowledge and acquiesce in the Justice of God in punishing them.

[WITNESSES CITED]

Preachers:

William Henderson,	Presbytery of Dunblane
David Stevenson,	Presbytery of Stirling
John Logan	Presbytery of Dumbarton
Robert Carrick	
James Semple	
James Leslie	Presbytery of Linlithgow
William Wilson	Presbytery of Dumfermling [*sic*]
Gilbert Craig	Presbytery of Glasgow
William Dunlop	Presbytery of Edinburgh

Students:

Archibald Campbel [*sic*]	Presbytery of Edinburgh
William Dalgleish	Presbytery of Linlithgow
John Anderson	Presbytery of Glasgow
Michael McTaggat	Presbytery of Hamilton
John Chiesly	Presbytery of Edinburgh
William Anderson	
James Millar	

[MINISTERS AT 1713 MEETING]

[Ministers present at conference at house of Mr Kello, vintner, of Edinburgh (sometime between June and September, 1713)]:

William Carstairs
William Wisheart   James Griar
John Flint   John Stirling
John McLeran [*sic*]   William Hamilton
William Millar   James Smith

[SIMSON'S ALLEGED STATEMENTS]

[At this conference, Webster stated, John Simson said:]

1. That Adam in the State of Innocence had not a Power of Believing in Christ.

2. Denyed that there was a proper Covenant made between God & Adam.

3. That Adam was not a Proper, Federal Head of all mankind.

4. That there is not a formal Imputation of Adam's first sin to this Posterity, only such an Imputation as is often of our immediate Parents Faults to us, i.e. his punishing us for the faults of our Fathers, tho we do not sin in them or fall with them in their personal sinful Actions.

5. That all the Children of Pagans, Mahometans, Jews, dying in their Infancy, before their Committing of Actual Sin, are saved.

6. That justifying Faith includes (in its formal Conception and Nature) good Works and Obedience.

7. That it is probable the Number of the Saved is as great, if not greater, than that of the Damned.

8. That after the last judgement there shall be no Sinning in Hell.

9. That there is no Immediat Previous and Physical Concurse of God with Man in all his Action.

10. That there is a certain necessary Connexion betwixt the use of Means, or Moral Seriousness, and regenerating Grace.

11. As also, the Said Mr Simson doth (in his Letters to the deceast Mr Robert Rowan, late Minister in Penningham, which I refer to for the proof of some of the Errors mentioned in this second Class) assert, that there are two Principles of Divinity, the Scriptures, and our Reason. He likewise (in 1 Letter to my self, dated Feb. 23, 1713) asserts the foresaid Connexion betwixt the use of Means and obtaining of saving Grace;

And before Mr Harvy Merchant in Glasgow and Robert Strang Merchant there, in the Professor's Chamber, a little before taking the Abjuration, did assert, that we all have a Natural Power and Ability in our selves, to seek saving Grace, which Power if we use, God has promised to give us that Grace; according to our Saviours Words, whosoever seeks shall find.

12. Likewise, before the said Mr Harvie and Robert Strang, at the foresaid time and place, he asserted, that Mans chief End was his own Happiness first and the Glory of God next; and further added that he had maintained the Said Opinion before the Presbyterie, and they condemned it, not, which they would have done, if they had not been of his Mind.

Libel subscribed at Edin. 27 Sep, 1714, before John Shaw min. of S. Leith & George Bryson, merchant in Edin.

APPENDIX B
Documents re Simson's Second Case

This appendix consists of three elements of documents related to John Simson's second case: the libel of 30 March 1727 prepared by the Presbytery of Glasgow, the appended list of witnesses, and Simson's response to the libel.

This material comes from John Dundas of Philipston, *State of the Processes Depending Against Mr. John Simson* ... (Edinburgh: Mr James Davidson and Robert Fleming, 1728), 75–82.

[THE LIBEL OF 30 MARCH 1727]

Forasmuchas, according to the Scriptures, and the Doctrine of this Church, contained in our *Confession of Faith* and *Catechisms* founded thereupon, our Blessed Lord Jesus Christ, the Son of God, the Second Person of the most Glorious and Adorable *Trinity*, is Very and Eternal God, of one Substance, and equal with the Father, and that in the Unity of the God-head, there be Three Persons of one Substance, Power and Eternity, God the Father, God the Son, and God the Holy Ghost, and Father *being of None, neither Begotten nor Proceeding*, the Son Eternally Begotten of the Father, and the Holy Ghost Eternally Proceeding from the Father and the Son; and which Three Persons are One True Eternal God, the same in Substance, equal in Power and Glory, altho' distinguished by their *personal Properties* aforesaid. LIKEAS, by the twelfth Act of the General Assembly of this Church, held in the Year One Thousand seven hundred and ten, all Persons are discharged to vent any Opinions contrary to any Head or Article of our *Confession of Faith* and *Catechisms* aforesaid, or to use any Expressions in Relation to the Articles of Faith, not agreeable to the Form of sound Words expressed in the Word of God, and the said *Confession* and *Catechisms*, which are most valuable

Pieces of our Reformation, and by the 9th Act of the General Assembly held in the Year 1717, you Mr. John Simson, Minister of the Gospel and Professor of Divinity in the University of Glasgow, are particularly prohibited and discharged to use such Expressions that do bear and are used by Adversaries in an unsound Sense, even tho' you should disown that unsound Sense, or to teach, preach, or otherwise vent Opinions, Propositions, or Hypotheses, not necessary to be taught in Divinity, and which give more Occasion to Strife, than to promote Edification: *Nevertheless* it is of Verity, that you the said Mr. *John Simson* are guilty of Impugning, or Disowning, or Denying the foresaid Necessary and Fundamental Truths of the Gospel, at least of undermining the same, and teaching, and venting, or maintaining Things inconsistent with, or tending to overturn the Belief of the said Blessed Truths, or to shake the Belief thereof, or to inject needless and ill-grounded Doubts and Scruples into the Minds of Men, and to render Men dark and uncertain, as to what they ought to believe concerning the same; at least you have in teaching, or speaking, or writing used such Expressions about the Truths aforesaid, that do bear and are used by Adversaries in an unsound Sense, or have vented such Opinions concerning the said Truths, as are not necessary to be taught in Divinity, and which give more Occasion to Strife than to promote Edification. In so far as, You the said Mr. *John Simson,* did on one other of the Days, of one or other of the Months, of one or other of the Years One thousand seven hundred and Twenty five, or One thousand seven hundred and Twenty six, or the by-past Months of the Year One thousand seven hundred and Twenty seven, Maintain, Teach or otherwise Vent the Opinion, Propositions or Hypotheses, or in teaching or Speaking, used the Expressions, and proceeded as after mentioned, or used other Expressions or Propositions directly, and not by Inference, to the same Import; *to wit,* You did alter your teaching concerning the Blessed Trinity, and Particularly, That whereas you formerly used to give your Students the following Caution, *viz.* That the Term *Person,* when applied to the Blessed three in the Godhead, was not to be taken precisely in the same Sense, as when spoken of Creatures, you forbore to give them the said Caution; as also you have owned and acknowledged, that in speaking of our Lord Jesus Christ, you use not the Terms *necessary existence* nor *independency,* and gave this pretended Reason for it, That they are not mentioned concerning Christ in the Holy Scriptures, or our Confession of Faith, or the System you teach. And further, In teaching your Scholars you have said, That the *independency* and *Necessary-existence* of our Lord Christ were Things we knew not;

That these Terms were impertinent, and not to be used in talking of the Trinity; and that they were Philosophical Niceties, we knew nothing about, and are ambiguous Terms of Art: And when your Students argued, that if the Son was not *Independent*, he was not *Necessarly-existent*, and so might not have been, and the Father might possibly have ben without him, you answered, How do you know, or how do we know that? And yet further, in teaching your Students the *Chap. de Creatione*, in *Markii medulla theologia christianæ*, you said, That this Argument against the Eternity of the World, *viz.* That if Eternal, it must be *Necessarily existent*, was not good, because *Christus est eternus, sed non ens necessarium*, or *non neceassrio existit* [*sic*]: As also, in teaching you gave it as your own Opinion, and the Judgment of the Primitive Fathers, that the Three Persons of the Trinity are not to be said to be either Numerically or specifically one in Substance or Essence; but added, they were so the same as to be one God in Three Persons; but gave not any Name to, nor attempted to give any Notion of that *Sameness* or *Oneness*; nor can there be any but *Numerical Oneness* of Substance or Essence, consistent with the Godhead, who is but One in Number, and not more; And you having asserted, That the Three Persons were all indeed one God, and had all the same Infinite Divine Perfections, you added, That whether the Subject of these Perfections was different, was a Metaphysical Question we need not determine; And you likewise affirmed, That in the *Trinity* there are Three *Intelligent Agents* or *Beings*. As also you taught, that *Deus Pater est ante Deum Filium non tempore sed Causalitate*, and added the following Expression, *Ni supponamus Deum non posse creare ab eterno*; And likewise you have taught or vented, That *Self-existence, Necessary-existence, Independency, Supreme Deity,* and the Title of *the only true God* may be taken, and were by some Authors taken in a Sense that includes the *personal Property* of the Father, and so not belonging to the Son; and tho' you said, that *Necessary-existence, Independency, Supreme Deity, and the Title of the only true God* might belong to the Son, in such Sense as included not the personal Property of the Father; yet you told not what that Sense was, but without doing so, you have inculcated the foresaid Distinction, as a Caution that may be necessary for Students, in reading both ancient and modern Authors, whether Friends or Adversaries to the Truth. And further you used to affirm, after insisting on the foresaid Distinction, with respect to the *Self-existence* of the Son, That you would take it as a Piece of useful Caution or Instruction both to you and the Students, if the Presbytery of *Glasgow* would declare the true Meaning of that *English* Term of Art, (as you thought fit to call it,) when it is to be affirmed of the Person of the

Son; and you said the same of the Holy Ghost. All, or any of which, in so far as they may respectively infer all or any of the Errors, or unsound, dangerous and unsafe Ways of Teaching or Expressing as above-libelled, being found proved. You the said Mr. *John Simson* ought to be proceeded against with the Censures of the Church, according to the Demerit and Quality of the Offence, which shall be proved; and that for your instruction and just Correction, and to prevent the flowing in, and spreading of Error, and to preserve and maintain the Purity of the Doctrine of the Gospel in this Church. At Appointment of the Presbytery, this is signed by HO. ORR *Cls. Pres.* Glasgow, March 30. 1727.

LIST OF WITNESSES

Mr. James Slos	Probationer Residing in Glasgow	
Mr. James Ritchie	" " in the parish of Campsie	
Mr. William M'Millen	" " in the Presbytery of Dumfries	
Mr. William Broun	Mr. Alexander Bar	Mr. William Millar
Mr. Edward Boyd	Mr George Meek	Mr. Alex. M'Culloch
Mr. Alex. Duncan	Mr. Tho. Hamilton	Mr. Alex. Johnston
Mr. Wil. Dennistoun	Mr. Wil Marshal	M. James Bain
Mr. William Boyd	Mr John Cleland	Mr. Fred. Carmichael
Mr Char. Jervey	Mr Dav. Bannantine	Mr. James Peden
Mr Wil. Longford	Mr. John Anderson	Mr. Alex. Campbel
Mr. Wil. Moncrief	Mr. And. Ramsay	Mr. James Stirling
Mr John Muirhead	Mr. William M'Clea	Mr. John M'Alpin
Mr Dowgal Allan	Mr. Lew. Chapman	

All Students of Divinity at the University of Glasgow and residing within the said City. Mr James Millar Probationer, Residing in the Parish of Blantyre, Mr. William Coats Probationer sometimes residing in Glasgow, and sometimes in the Parish of Blantyre, Mr. George Adam, Student of Divinity, Residing in the Parish of Renfrew.

[SIMSON'S RESPONSE]

Objections by Mr. *John Simson* Professor of Divinity in the University of *Glasgow*, against the Form of the Libel exhibited against him, and now lying before the Reverend Presbytery of *Glasgow*

The Defendant having for a good many Years lived in Peace and Friendship with his Reverend Brethren in the Presbytery of Glasgow, and having with much Comfort heartily joined with them in promoting the Interests of the Gospel, and the Concerns of the Kingdom of our Glorious Lord and Saviour Jesus Christ, he cannot without much Regrete and sensible Grief, reflect on his present unhappy Circumstances, which a wise and righteous God has thought fit in his Holy Providence to bring him unto, by Misunderstandings and Mistakes, that have crept in by Degrees between his Reverend Brethren and him for some Years past, especially during his great bodily Indisposition, since *October* 1724. And altho' he be not conscious to himself of any just Ground he has given for it, yet after several other Methods of Procedure against him, on which he makes here no Reflexion, they have found themselves in Conscience obliged, as in Charity he believes, to exhibit against him a Libel upon a *fama clamosa*, containing a Charge of his having taught or vented Errors, contrary to the Holy Scriptures, and some Passages of the *Confession of Faith* and *Larger Catechism* of this Church, relating to the Doctrine of the *Blessed Trinity*, and in Violation of the 12 *Act Gen. Assemb.* 1710, and 9 *Act of Gen. Assemb.* 1717, as the said Libel more fully bears.

To support which Charge it is alledged he has, within the Time specified in the said Libel, in teaching, speaking, or writing, used several Propositions or Expressions mentioned in the said Libel.

Concerning which Libel he must observe, *First,* That the Passages of Scripture, our Confession and Catechism therein mentioned, are what he stedfastly believes and yearly teaches; and as in former Years, so likewise these two last Sessions of the College, he has carefully taught them, acording to the plain and common Meaning of the Words, and endeavoured to prove the Truth and great Importance of them to the best of his Skill, and to confute the Errors that are opposed to them, or inconsistent with them, as it narrated in his *Letter* to the Presbytery, the 2d of *March* last Year; the Truth of which narration has not as yet been called in Question, so far as he knows.

Secondly, He observes in the Frame of the said Libel that there are manifold Uncertainties, Imperfections, and Mistakes, which render it null and void in Law, upon which no Process ought to be sustained. Such as,

1st, That in the Libel there is no Place mentioned in which 'tis alledged any of the Facts were done, or Expressions uttered. This of it self would cast a Libel before the Lords of Justiciary: And this Libel being manifestly of a criminal Nature, which would deprive the Defendant, not only of his Reputation, but of his Office and Benefice, were it proved that he had impugned or denied any of the necessary Truths mentioned in the Narrative of the said Libel, or taught any Thing inconsistent with them: Upon which Account he pleads that this Libel ought to be rejected by the Reverend Presbytery, or, at least, so reformed as to make it legal, before he be obliged to give any further Answers to it.

2dly, The Time specified in the Libel contains two Years preceeding the First of *January* last, and Three Months following it; whereas Libels before other Courts are confined to a Year. But what he chiefly observes is, That this Libel is founded upon a *fama clamosa*, which was raised, and the alledged Occasion of it happened betwixt *Martinmas* 1725, and since last Assembly, cannot be legally comprehended in this Libel, that proceeds upon a *fama clamosa*, the Defendant having taught none since last Assembly, before the 10th of *October* last, and there has been no *fama clamosa* of his having taught Error since that Time, the least Notice whereof has come to his Ears; wherefore if any Articles of the said Libel relate to what he has taught since *October* last, the Presbytery ought either to instruct there has been a new *Fama* raised, and lay before him the particular Articles thereof, or exhibite no such Articles against him, unless the Accusation be signed by an Accuser, or some Person undertake to prove it under Pain of Censure, according to the good Rules in our Form of Process, *Chap*. VII. *Sect*. 3. Unless they be Articles declared to be taken out of his Papers given to the Presbytery, which is no where plainly asserted in the Libel.

3dly, The Expressions said to be uttered by the Defendant in teaching, are laid in such ambiguous, general and incoherent Terms, that tho' it were proved he had uttered them, especially only once, which he is persuaded cannot be done; yet they could afford no certain Document, either of what was his Opinion, or what he had taught, unless the Libel did specify the preceeding and following Parts of his Discourse, and whether he spoke them as his own or other Mens Opinion, which are necessary to determine his Sense in uttering them; which not being done in the Libel, renders the Meaning of these Expressions so uncer – [page 81] tain, as to be uncapable of a legal Proof, especially after the elapsing of 14 or 15 Months since the Thing can be supposed to have happened: For at this Rate, he might be accused of gross Error, yea Blasphemy, or Atheism, had he been barely reciting some Texts of Scripture, of which the Hearers remembred only some Scrapes [*sic*], such as *There is no God: Curse God and die; you see then, how that by Works a man is justified*, and the like.

4thly, The Libel does not mention any particular Passage of Scripture, of our Confession of Faith, or Catechisms which are impugned or denied by any of the Expressions alledged, or with which they are inconsistent; nor is there any standing Rule mentioned, which is alledged to be particularly violated by any of the said Expressions, which the Presbytery in Justice did oblige Mr. *Webster,* in a former Case, to do: And they having no Interest in this Libel, founded on a *fama clamosa,* but what the vindicating of themselves and the Truth calls them to, the Defendant cannot but expect, from their Equity as Judges, that they will do him the same Justice now as formerly, in not sustaining this Libel, as a sufficient Ground of Process against him, at least, till this Defect be made up.

5thly, There are some Expressions said to be uttered by the Defendant, which are both contrary to his fixed Opinion, and what he fully taught on these Subjects; and as he remembers not his having uttered such Expressions, he is persuaded, that such Alledgances [*sic*] must either flow from a Mistake of some of the Hearers, or else from a Trip in his Expressions, mentioning one Word for another; which is no doubt incident to him, no less than it is to much greater Men, when discoursing an Hour or two on several Points of Divinity; and 'tis but reasonable to think he should have been more liable to it, the preceeding Session of the College, when he laboured under so great Indisposition and Weakness of Body, which could not but hinder his closs [*sic*] Attention, either in Thinking or Speaking.

Of this Sort is that Instance, that he said, That Professor *Mark*'s Argument against the Eternity of the World, to wit, *That if Eternal it must be Necessarily-existent, was not good,* because *Christus est eternus sed non ens necessarium*; where the Defendant was shewing that Professor *Mark*'s Argument was not good against *Aristotle* and his Defenders, who maintain, that the World was created from Eternity, and so maintained, that *mundus est eternus, sed non ens necessarium,* which Argument doth only contradict what these Authors assert; and therefore is not a good Argument to confute their Opinion, which the Defendant has been in use to notice every Year since he taught that Book, and is persuaded, that if any of his Hearers alledge, that he said *Christus est eternus, sed non ens ne*– [page 82] *cessarium,* that either he has mistaken the Word Christus for Mundus, or that by a Trip in Expression, the Defendant has said *Christus* for *Mundus,* which he is not sensible he did, the Word *Christus* being plainly impertinent to the Argument he was then upon.

Another Expression of the same Nature is, *Deus Pater est ante Deum Filium, non tempore sed causalitate*; and added the following Expression, *Ni supponamus Deum non posse creare ab eterno.* The Defendant reserving what he has to say on the first Part of this, to his particular Answers to all the Articles alledged, to be given in afterwards, if needful, he is persuaded he did not use that last expression, it being inconsistent with his fixed Opinion, and with what he fully taught on the Subject, to which the former Part of this Instance seems to have a Relation; and therefore judges, that if any of the Hearers alledge he uttered this Expression, they have thro' not hearing distinctly, or otherwise, mistaken *creare* for *generare*, or else that he has uttered the one Expression for the other by a Mistake; the Word *generare* being to the Purpose of the Argument, the other wholly impertinent.

6thly, It is alledged, That the Defendant has owned an acknowledged such or such Things, and that likewise he has taught or vented, that *Self-existence, &.* — — — without telling when, where, or what Way he has owned or vented such Things, which puts him at a Disadvantage, or renders it impossible for him to give any certain Answer thereto. From all which the Defendant pleads, that the said Libel is null and void in Law, and such as cannot be a sufficient Ground of a just and legal Process; and therefore craves, that the Libel may be either rejected, and he vindicated and dismissed; or, if the Reverend Presbytery think they have just Ground of Procedure against him, that they reform the said Libel, and make up the Defects, Imperfections, &. here justly complained of, so as a plain and certain Charge may be given in against him; which done, he declares himself willing and ready, to give distinct and particular Answers thereto.

Glasgow, April 11th, 1727. JOHN SIMSON.

Glossary

Amyrauldism: Deviation from orthodox Calvinism following the teaching of Moyse Amyraut of Saumur (1596–1664), who tried to bridge the gap between Calvinism and Lutheranism. He taught that that God's purpose of universal redemption is thwarted by human predisposition to sin.

Antinomianism: The view that Christians are freed through grace from obedience to any moral law (Gr. *nomos*); "for ye are not under the law, but under grace" (Rom. 6: 14). The heresy originated with the Gnostics and reappeared at the time of the Reformation as a result of Lutter's emphasis on justification by faith.

Arianism: A fourth-century heresy taking its name from an Alexandrian priest, Arius (c. 250–c. 336), whose denial of the full divinity of Christ was condemned at the Council of Nicaea in 325. Arians held that Christ was not the eternal Son of God but was created by the Father before the creation of the world. Although he was given the title of "Son of God," he did not share the same substance or essence.

Arminianism: Doctrine developed by Jakob Hermans (Jacobus Arminius) (1560–1609), professor of theology at Leiden, in reaction to the determinism of Calvinist predestination. In the *Remonstrance* of 1610 Arminius's followers stated that all who believed in Christ would be elect; that Christ died for all men, although only believers would benefit from this; that each believer must be regenerated by the Holy Spirit; that men may resist grace; and that it is possible to fall from grace. These propositions were condemned at the Synod of Dort (1618–19), which published five orthodox articles to counter those of the Remonstrants.

Athanasius: Bishop of Alexandria (c. 296–373) and the defender of orthodoxy against Arius. The Athanasian Creed was named after him but not written by him.

Atonement: The reconciliation of sinful humanity with God through the sacrifice and death of Christ.

Call: Between 1690 and 1712 this was a document signed by members of a Scottish congregation inviting their chosen minister to come to their parish. In the wider sense it indicated the ability of a parish to choose its own minister rather than having him imposed through a patronage appointment.

Christology: The doctrine and study of the person of Christ, particularly the relationship of His divine and human natures. The heresies of the early church frequently centred on this matter.

Communion tokens: Pieces of moulded metal about 2 cm in diameter, usually bearing the name of the church, which were distributed by the minister or elders prior to a Scottish Presbyterian parish communion. To ensure that participants in the sacrament were of good moral life, only those who had been given a token were admitted to the Lord's table. Ministers were sometimes accused of withholding tokens for political or other inadequate reasons.

Covenant: Covenant theology uses three covenants to explain the relationship between God and man. The covenant of works covers the relationship between God and Adam, as representative of all humanity, thus legitimizing the imputation of his sin to his posterity. The covenant of redemption exists eternally between the Father and the Son, by which Christ undertakes to die for the redemption of the elect. The covenant of grace exists between God and believing Christians, by which the elect receive faith and everlasting life.

Creed: Concise authorized statement of doctrine, named from the Latin opening, *credo*, I believe. The Apostles' (or Old Roman) Creed was widely used in the west as a baptismal formula. The Nicene (or Niceno–Constantinopolitan) Creed was drawn up at the Council of Nicaea in 325 to maintain orthodox faith against Arianism and was expanded at the Council of Constantinople in 381. The Athanasian Creed is a more detailed summary of the doctrine of the Trinity and the incarnation. Creeds were alternatively called symbols. The brief *Symbolum Damasi* or *Fides Damasus* is a late-fifth-century creed from Gaul called after the fourth-century pope St Damasus.

Decrees: The acts of God's will in creating and upholding the universe and determining the fate of mankind.

Heritors: Landowners possessing heritable property who shared the responsibility for maintaining the church, manse, school, and poor relief in a Church of Scotland parish.

Homooúsios: The Greek terminology (*homos,* one, *ou*sia, substance, essence) adopted at the Council of Nicaea to affirm that the Son is of one essence with the Father.

Infralapsarian: One who believes that God's decree of election took place after the Fall of man.

Justification: God's act in making the sinful individual righteous through the sacrifice of Christ. At issue for John Simson and his compatriots was whether the gift of divine grace required any human effort or whether to suggest that it might was a dangerous lapse into a reliance on "works."

Legalism: The view that the relationship between God and man is governed by strict fulfilment of God's laws. External conduct appears more important than internal motivation for action, leading to a sterile faith lacking love and compassion.

Moderatism: Historians have disagreed about the meaning and origin of this term. In this book it implies an attitude of acceptance of the Presbyterian Settlement of 1690 and of the Act of Union, despite the consequent problems in Scotland such as the reimposition of patronage. Moderate ministers and laymen acknowledged the importance of church appointments in the factional struggles of the eighteenth century and were less stringent in their ecclesiological demands than their hyper-Calvinist brethren. They were still convinced members of the Reformed tradition and accepted the necessity of ministerial subscription to the Westminster Confession. They preached the message of a benevolent God who expected high ethical standards from mankind, and they deplored both excessive legalism and antinomianism.

Monarchianism: Second- and third-century attempt to preserve the unity (monarchy) of the Godhead, which led to the pre-eminence of the Father in the Trinity.

New Light: A seventeenth-century name given to beliefs that encouraged individual choice in religious decisions, particularly in matters of church polity. The words developed different meanings during the eighteenth century, on both sides of the Atlantic. They could refer to a stress on experiential religion over the doctrine of election. In Scotland they later referred to specific church–state relationships.

Neonomianism: The belief that the Gospel represents a new law (Gr. *nomos*) that supplants the old, or Mosaic law.

Patristic: Pertaining to the era and works of the early Christian fathers (Lat. *patres*), up to the end of the eighth century.

Patronage: The role of landowners in the presentation of ministers to parishes in the Church of Scotland. Patronage was abolished in 1649, reintroduced in 1662, and abolished again in 1690 in favour of nomination by the heritors and elders of the parish. It was reintroduced in 1712 by an act of Parliament that infuriated Scots Presbyterians because it contravened the terms of the Act of Union.

Pelagianism: An early heresy named after the British monk Pelagius (c. 354–c. 420), who believed that human beings could use their free will to work towards salvation. His views were opposed by St Augustine (354–430), who insisted on mankind's total dependence on divine grace because of the corruption that resulted from Adam's Fall.

Physicus concursus: God's immediate concurrence in the actions of all created beings. Debated within the church from the time of Augustine, the doctrine divided Catholics in the sixteenth century. Dominicans and other Thomists followed the views of the Council of Trent – that divine providence governed the world and impelled all creation to action through *physicus concursus*. Jesuits held the view that God possessed foreseen knowledge of individual action (*scientia media*). Scots Presbyterians accepted the role of divine providence and disapproved of *scientia media*.

Sabellianism: Modalist form of Monarchianism taught by Sabellius (early third century), in which God has a single nature but reveals himself in three different modes or forms.

Sanctification: The gift of holiness given by grace through faith. As in the case of justification, John Simson disagreed with his extreme Calvinist countrymen and stressed the use of the means (worship, sermons, Bible reading, prayer) provided by God for people to lead holy lives.

Satisfaction: The doctrine that the death of Christ is a vicarious satisfaction made to the honour of God for the sins of the whole world.

Socinianism: A Christological heresy named after Lelio Sozzini (1525–1562) and his nephew, Fausto (1539–1604), Siennese Anabaptists who took refuge in Rakow, Poland, where a community of like-minded Protestants grew up. The Socinian God was defined in the Racovian Catechism (1605) as omnipotent free will; Christ, while conceived of the Holy Spirit and born to a virgin, lived as a mortal and became immortal only after the resurrection. Socinians placed stress on a moral life and the use of reason. Accusations of Socinianism could thus point towards both subordinationist christology and reliance on rational biblical interpretation.

Supralapsarian: One who believes that God's decree of election took place before the fall of man.

Trinity: The central doctrine of Christianity that One God exists in three per-sons, Father, Son, and Holy Ghost, who share one substance or essence. John Simson taught that each person in the Trinity had a personal property: the Father was of none, neither begotten nor proceeding; the Son was eternally be-gotten of the Father; and the Holy Ghost proceeded eternally from the Father and Son. He had some doubts about that last phrase – the *Filioque* clause in the Nicene Creed was a Western addition that had led to the schism between Rome and Constantinople, and Simson saw no need to insist on it.

Universalism: The belief that divine grace extends to all nations and peoples, not merely to the elect. The belief that Christ died for all men was perceived as Arminian heresy by eighteenth-century orthodox Calvinists.

Westminster Confession: The definitive statement of faith subscribed by all ministers and professors in eighteenth-century Scotland. The Westminster Confession and the Larger and Shorter Catechisms were drawn up by the divines meeting at the Westminster Assembly in the 1640s. The Confession was approved by the Gen-eral Assembly of the Church of Scotland in 1647 and superseded the sixteenth-century Scottish Confession.

Works: Human efforts to gain approval from God by moral living, charitable giv-ing, church attendance, and so on. Calvinist theology, with its stress on election and free grace, denied any value to such efforts, while at the same time assuming that the elect person would live an upright life.

Bibliography

MANUSCRIPT SOURCES

Dr Williams's Library, London

MS 24.157 (1–287). Correspondence of Samuel Kenrick of Bewdley (1728–1811) and the Revd. Dr. James Wodrow (1730–1810), Minister of Stevenston, Ayrshire.

Edinburgh University Library (EUL)

MS La.II.91. Letter from Jas. Stewart, Edinburgh, to C. Mackie, Leyden, 11 May 1716.
MS La.II.114–15. Papers of William Wishart, Jr.
MS La.II.407 f.13. Letter from Alexander Dunlop to William Carstares, n.d. (1709).
MS La.II.423 f.204. Letter from Matthias Symson, London, to Rev. Dr. Grey, Cambridge, 20 May 1737.
MS La.II.620 f.17. Undelivered speech of Robert Wallace, March 1730.

Glasgow City Archives (GCA), Strathclyde Region, Mitchell Library, Glasgow

CH2/171/8–10. Presbytery of Glasgow. Records of the Presbytery of Glasgow.

Glasgow University Archives and Business Records Centre (GUA)

GUA 26632. Minutes of Meetings of Faculty 1702–1720.

GUA 26633. Minutes of Rector's and other Meetings, 1717–1719.

GUA 26634. Minutes of Meetings of Faculty 1720–1727.

GUA 26635. Minutes of Meetings of Faculty 1727–1730.

GUA 26637. Report of the Commissioners of Visitation. Visitations 1664, 1680–83, 1690–95, 1726–7.

GUA 26639. Minutes of University Meetings 1730–1749.

GUA 26963. Letter from Neil Campbell to John Simson, 6 July 1737.

GUA 27130. Letter from [?] to John Stirling, 10 July 1717, re: Visitors.

GUA 27145 (f7, 9a), 27146, 27147, 27149, 27154, 27155, 27159–62, 27164. See below Documents re students grievances.

GUA 27165. Letter from James Hadow to John Stirling, 23 April 1718.

GUA 27166. Letter from Robert Dundas to John Stirling, 13 Sep. 1718.

GUA 27199–208. Documents re students' grievances.

GUA 30329. Testimonial for John Simson, Alexander Wodrow, and John Hamilton, September 1696.

GUA 43121. Inventory of the books the late Principal Stirling bequeathed to Glasgow University in his will, May 1728.

GUA 58013. Rector's election, 1717–1719. John Smith's expulsion, 1722. Documents re students' grievances.

GUA 58019. Library Accounts and Catalogue 1699–1753.

GUA 58201. Accounts for Quaestor 1682–1740.

GUA 58024. Accounts for Books bought at Auction 1701–1726.

GUA 58026. Library Documents.

GUA 58027. Library Accounts 1702–1721.

*Glasgow University Library (*GUL*)*

GUL 2883. *Collection of Pamphlets.*

M 21–d.25 Bound volume of pamphlets.

MS Gen. 204–7. Stirling Correspondence.

MS Gen. 343. "Cases answered by the Society of the students of Divinity, under Mr James Wodrow."

MS Murray 204–7. Stirling Correspondence.

MS Murray 218/64. "John How's notes on James Wodrow's methods of Studying theology, 1702."

John Rylands Library, University of Manchester

Letters to George Benson.

National Archives of Scotland (NAS), Edinburgh

CH1/1/24. General Assembly, 1714.

CH1/2/34–8, 52–64. General Assembly Papers 1714–18, 1726–31.

CH1/5/11. General Assembly Papers, *Professor Simson's Case 1715–17*.

CH2/121/8–9. Records of the Presbytery of Edinburgh 1713–1718.

CH2/154/7. Records of the Synod of Fife, 1719–1738.

CH2/252/8. Records of the Synod of Lothian and Tweeddale, 1711–1721.

CH2/464/2. Records of the Synod of Glasgow and Air 1705–1715.

CH2/464/3. Records of the Synod of Glasgow and Air 1715–1760.

GD18/5019, 41, 47. Clerk of Penicuik Collection.

GD124/15. Mar and Kellie Correspondence and Personal Papers, 1566–1941.

GD220/5/351–864. Montrose Muniments. Correspondence and Personal Papers 1566–1941; Correspondence of James, Duke of Montrose 1697–1741.

GD461/15/1–14. Lawrie Papers.

National Library of Scotland (NLS), Edinburgh

Advocates MS 29.1.2. Anderson Papers, vol. VII.

MS 1008. Memoirs of Lord Grange 1726–7.

MS 3430–1. Lee Papers.

MS 5072. Erskine–Murray Papers 1696–1725.

MS 5073. Erskine–Murray Papers 1726–31.

MS 7044. Yester Papers.

MS 16504, 16526, 16529, 16531–6, 16539–43, 16551, 16569, 16750, and 17601. Saltoun Papers.

MS 17601. Church and Ministers file. Saltoun Papers.

MS 17799. Saltoun Papers.

NLS 1.7. Pamphlet Collection nos. 25, 156.

NLS 2.246/6. *Collection of Pamphlets.*

Wodrow Folios, vols. XXXIX, XLIX, LXVIII.

Wodrow Letters Quarto, vols. I, IV, VIII, XI, XIV, XVII, XVIII.

New College Library (NCL), University of Edinburgh

Box 11.2.1–8. Correspondence concerning James Hogg and John Simson.

CHU.10.1. Register of the Actings and Proceedings of the Committee of the General Assembly for preserving Purity of Doctrine In the Process mr James Webster one of the ministers of Edinburgh against Mr John Simson Professor of Divinity in the College of Glasgow and Sentence of the General Assembly thereupon Anno 1717.

PRINTED SOURCES

Abstract of Difficulties, Occurring to a reader of the reverend Professor Simson's printed Answers to Mr. Webster's Libel against him, Humbly offered to himself for a Solution. N.p., n.d.

Anstruther, Sir William. *Essays, Moral and Divine; In Five Discourses: Viz. I. Against Atheism. II. Of Providence. III. Of Learning and Religion. IV. Of Triffling Studies, Stage-Playes, and Romances. V. Upon the Incarnation of Jesus Christ, and Redemption of Mankind.* Edinburgh: George Mosman, 1701.

Answers for the Scholars, and other Matriculated Members of the University of Glasgow, to the Petition of Mr John Simson, Professor of Divinity in the said University, and Mr John Gray, and Mr John Hamilton, Ministers of the Gospel at Glasgow. 11 June 1718.

Answers to the Remarks on Professor Simson's answers to the Presbytery of Glasgow's References. Edinburgh: Printed: and Sold by most Booksellers in Town, 1727.

Arbuckle, James. *Glotta A Poem.* Glasgow: William Duncan, 1721.

Arbuckle, James, and Griffith, Mr. *Prologue and Epilogue to Tamerlane.* Glasgow: Printed by William Duncan, 1721.

Arminius. *The Works of James Arminius.* 3 vols. Grand Rapids, Mich.: Baker Book House, 1991.

Armstrong, Brian G. *Calvinism and the Amyraut Heresy: Protestant Scholasticism and Humanism in Seventeenth-Century France.* Madison: University of Wisconsin Press, 1969.

Baillie, Robert. *The Letters and Journals of Robert Baillie, A.M. Principal of the University of Glasgow 1637–1662.* Ed. D. Laing. 3 vols. Edinburgh: Robert Ogle, 1841–2.

Bangs, Carl. *Arminius: A Study in the Dutch Reformation.* 2nd ed. Grand Rapids, Mich.: Francis Asbury Press, 1985.

Barlow, Richard B. "The Career of John Abernethy (1680–1740) Father of Non-subscription in Ireland and Defender of Religious Liberty." *Harvard Theological Review* 78 (1985): 399–419.

Barrington, John Shute. *An Account of the late Proceedings of the Dissenting Ministers at Salters-Hall, occasioned By the Differences amongst their Brethren in the Country: With some Thoughts concerning the Imposition of humane Forms for Articles of Faith. In a Letter to the Revd. Dr. Gale.* London: J. Roberts, 1719.

Bayle, Pierre. *The Dictionary Historical and Critical of Mr. Peter Bayle.* Intro. Burton Feldman. 5 vols. Reprint of 2nd London edition, J.J.&P. Knapton, 1734–38. New York: Garland, 1984.

Beardslee, John W., III. "Introduction" to Beardslee, ed. and trans., *Reformed Dogmatics.* Grand Rapids, Mich.: Baker Book House, 1981.

Bell, M. Charles. *Calvin and Scottish Theology: The Doctrine of Assurance.* Edinburgh: Handsel Press, 1985.

Blackwell, Thomas. *Ratio Sacra: or An Appeal unto the Rational World, about the Reasonableness of Revealed Religion. Containing a Rational as well as a Scriptural Confutation of the Three Grand prevailing Errors of the present Day, to wit, Atheism, Deism, and Bourignonism.* Edinburgh: Heirs and Successors of Andrew Anderson, 1710.

Bolam, C.G., et al. *The English Presbyterians: From Elizabethan Puritanism to Modern Unitarianism.* London: George Allen & Unwin, 1958.

Boston, Thomas. *Memoirs of the Life, Times, and Writings of Thomas Boston, of Ettrick.* Glasgow: John M'Neilage, 1899.

Briggs, E.R. "Mysticism and Rationalism in the Debate upon Eternal Punishment." *Studies on Voltaire and the Eighteenth Century* 24 (1963): 241–54.

Bromiley, Geoffrey W. *Historical Theology: An Introduction.* Grand Rapids, Mich.: William B. Eerdmans Publishing Company, 1978.

Bromley, James. "Correspondence of the Rev. Peter Walkden." *Transactions of the Historic Society of Lancashire and Cheshire* 36 (1884): 15–32.

Brown, Andrew. *History of Glasgow.* Edinburgh, 1797.

Brown, Callum. *Religion and Society in Scotland since 1707.* Edinburgh: Edinburgh University Press, 1997.

Browning, Reed. *The Duke of Newcastle.* New Haven, Conn.: Yale University Press, 1975.

Brunton, George. *An Historical Account of the Senators of the College of Justice of Scotland, from its Institution in 1532. Originally by Sir David Dalrymple of Hailes, Bart..* Edinburgh: James Stillie, 1849.

Bull, George. *The Works of the Right Reverend George Bull, D.D., late Bishop of St. David's, concerning the Holy Trinity. Consisting of I. The Defence of the Nicene Creed. II The Judgment of the Catholick Church of the three first Centuries, concerning the Necessity of believing that Our Lord Jesus Christ is true God, asserted against M. Simon Episcopius, and others. III. The primitive and Apostolical Tradition concerning the received Doctrine in the Catholick Church, of our Saviour Jesus Christ's Divinity, asserted, and plainly proved, against Daniel Zuicker a Prussian, and his late Disciples in England. Translated into English: with The Notes and Observations of Dr. Grabe. And some Reflections upon the late Controvertists in this Doctrine.* 2 vols. Trans. Fr. Holland. London: Stephen Austen, 1730.

Burleigh, J.H.S. *A Church History of Scotland.* London: Oxford University Press, 1960.

Burnet, Gilbert. *Bishop Burnet's History of His Own Time.* 6 vols. Oxford: Oxford University Press, 1833.

Burrell, S.A. "The Apocalyptic Vision of the Early Covenanters." *Scottish Historical Review* 43 (1964): 1–24.

– "The Covenant Idea as a Revolutionary Symbol: Scotland, 1596–1637." *Church History* 27 (1958): 338–50.

Cairns, John W. "The Origins of the Glasgow Law School: The Professors of Civil Law, 1714–61." In Peter Birks, ed., *The Life of the Law: Proceedings of the Tenth British Legal History Conference Oxford 1991*, 151–94. London: Hambledon Press, 1993.

Calamy, Edmund. *An Historical Account of my Own Life, with some Reflections on the Times I have lived in. (1671–1731).* 2 vols. Ed. John Towill Rutt. London: Henry Colburn & Richard Bentley, 1829.

Calvin, John. *Institutes of the Christian Religion.* Trans. Henry Beveridge. Grand Rapids, Mich.: Wm. B. Eerdmans Publishing Company, 1989.

Cameron, George G. *The Scots Kirk in London.* Oxford: Becket Publications, 1979.

Cameron, James K. "Theological Controversy: A Factor in the Origins of the Scottish Enlightenment." In R.H. Campbell and Andrew S. Skinner, eds., *The Origins and Nature of the Scottish Enlightenment*, 116–30. Edinburgh: John Donald Publishers Ltd, 1982.

Cameron, Nigel M. de S., et al., eds. *Dictionary of Scottish Church History and Theology.* Downers Grove, Ill.: Intervarsity Press, 1993.

Campbell, Archibald. *The authenticity of the Gospel-history justified: and the truth of the Christian revelation demonstrated, from the laws and constitution of human nature.* 2 vols. Edinburgh: Hamilton, Balfour, and Neill, 1759.

Carlyle, Alexander. *Anecdotes and Characters of the Times.* Ed. with intro. by James Kinsley. London: Oxford University Press, 1973.

Carmichael, Gershom. *Gershom Carmichael on Samuel Pufendorf's De officio Hominis et Civis Juxta Legem naturalem Libri duo.* Comp. John N. Lenhart, trans. Charles H. Reeves. Cleveland, O.: John N. Lenhart, 1985.

Cheyne, Alexander C. "The Place of the Confession through the Centuries." In Alasdair I.C. Heron, ed., *The Westminster Confession in the Church Today.* Edinburgh: Saint Andrew Press, 1982.

Cheyne, George. *Philosophical Principles of Natural Religion: Containing the Elements of Natural Philosophy, and the Proofs for Natural Religion, Arising from them.* London: George Strahan, 1705.

Church of Scotland, General Assembly. *The Principal Acts of the General Assembly of the Church of Scotland.* Edinburgh: (various publishers), 1714–34.

– *Procedure of the General Assembly anno 1728*, concerning Professor Simson. N.p., n.d.

– *Proceeding of the Committee Appointed in the Assembly 1727.* Edinburgh: Thom. and Wal. Ruddimans, 1729.

– *A Short Account of the Procedure of the Committee in Professor Simson's Affair. Taken from Original Papers For the Use of the Members of the General Assembly.* N.p., n.d. [1728].

Clark, G.N. *The Later Stuarts: 1660–1714.* First pub. 1934. Reprinted, Oxford: Clarendon Press, 1949.

Clark, J.C.D. *English Society 1688–1832: Ideology, Social Structure and Political Practice during the Ancien Regime.* Cambridge: Cambridge University Press, 1985.

Clarke, Samuel. *The Scripture Doctrine of the Trinity.* In vol. 4 of *The Works of Samuel Clarke, D.D. Late Rector of St. James's Westminster.* 4 vols. London: Printed for John and Paul Knapton in Ludgate-Street, 1738. Facsimile, New York: Garland Publishing, Inc., 1978.

Clarke, Tristram. "The Williamite Episcopalians and the Glorious Revolution in Scotland." *Records of the Scottish Church History Society* 24 (1990): 33–51.

Cobbett, W., T.B. Howell, et al. *A Complete Collection of State Trials.* 34 vols. London, 1809–28.

A Copy of a Letter from a Forreign Divine to a Minister of the Church of Scotland. N.p., 1716.

Couper, Rev. W.J. "The Levitical Family of Simson." *Records of the Scottish Church History Society* 4 (1932): 119–37.

– "The Levitical Family of Simson. II The Family of Adam Simson, 1594–1771." *Records of the Scottish Church History Society* 4 (1932): 209–40.

– "The Levitical Family of Simson. III Alexander, 1570(?)-1638, and His Descendants." *Records of the Scottish Church History Society* 4 (1932): 241–66.

Coutts, James. *A History of the University of Glasgow from Its Foundation in 1451 to 1909.* Glasgow: James Maclehose & Sons, 1909.

Coxe, William. *Memoirs of the Life and Administration of Sir Robert Walpole, Earl of Orford.* 3 vols. London: T. Cadell, Jun., and W. Davies, 1798.

Crowe, Michael J. *The Extraterrestrial Life Debate 1750–1900: The Idea of a Plurality of Worlds from Kant to Lowell.* Cambridge: Cambridge University Press, 1986.

Depositions in Professor Simson's Affair, Class'd according to the Different Articles of the Libel, With the Passages which concern it in the Professor's Papers. Edinburgh: Printed and sold in most Booksellers Shops in Town, 1727.

Devine, T.M. "The Golden Age of Tobacco." In Devine and Jackson, eds., *Glasgow, Volume I.*

Devine, T.M., and Gordon Jackson, eds., *Glasgow, Volume I: Beginnings to 1830.* Manchester: Manchester University Press, 1995.

Devine, T.M., and J.R. Young, eds. *Eighteenth Century Scotland: New Perspectives.* East Linton, Scotland: Tuckwell Press, 1999.

Dick, Stephen J. *Plurality of Worlds: The Origins of the Extraterrestrial Life Debate from Democritus to Kant.* Cambridge: Cambridge University Press, 1982.

Dickinson, W. Croft, ed. with intro. *Two Students at St. Andrews.* Edinburgh: Oliver & Boyd, 1952.

A Discourse Upon the Present Number of Forces in Great-Britain and Ireland. London: E. Moore, 1724.

Doig, David. In *Conjectural History and Anthropology. An essay on the Causes of Complexion and Figure in the Human Species. By Samuel Stanhope Smith. Two letters on the Savage State, Addressed to the Late Lord Kaims. By David Doig.* Intro. Paul B. Wood. Reprint, Bristol: Thoemmes Press, 1995.

Donnelly, John Patrick. "Italian Influences on the Development of Calvinist Scholasticism." *Sixteenth Century Journal* 7 (1976): 81–101.

Doyle, Ian B. "The Doctrine of the Church in the Later Covenanting Period." In Duncan Shaw, ed., *Reformation and Revolution.* Edinburgh: Saint Andrew Press, 1967.

Drummond, Andrew L. *The Kirk and the Continent.* Edinburgh: Saint Andrew Press, 1956.

Drummond, Andrew L., and James Bulloch. *The Scottish Church 1688–1843: The Age of the Moderates.* Edinburgh: Saint Andrew Press, 1973.

Duffy, Eamon. "'Whiston's Affair': The Trials of a Primitive Christian 1709–1714." *Journal of Ecclesiastical History* 27 (1976): 129–50.

Duncan, Richard. *Notices and Documents illustrative of the Literary History of Glasgow, During the Greater Part of Last Century.* First pub. Glasgow, 1831. Verbatim et literatim reprint, with appendix additional. Glasgow: Thomas D. Morison, 1886.

Dundas, John, of Philipston. *State of the Processes Depending Against Mr. John Simson Professor of Divinity in the University of Glasgow; Setting forth the Proceedings of the Presbytery of Glasgow, General Assembly, and Committees thereof. To which is prefixed, An Account of the Rise of the said Processes that have been carried on against the foresaid Professor, and the Acts of the General Assemblies in the Years 1714, 1715, 1716, and 1717, with Relation thereto.* Edinburgh: Mr James Davidson and Robert Fleming, 1728.

Dunlop, A. Ian. "The General Session: A Controversy of 1720." *Records of the Scottish Church History Society* 13 (1959): 223–239.

– *William Carstares and the Kirk by Law Established.* Edinburgh: Saint Andrew Press, 1967.

[Dunlop, William]. *A Preface to an Addition of the Westminster Confession, &c. Lately Publish'd at Edinburgh. Being a full and particular Account Of all the Ends and Uses of Creeds and Confessions of Faith. A Defence of their Justice, Reasonableness and Necessity as a Publick Standard of Orthodoxy.* London: T. Cox, 1720.

Dunlop, William. *Sermons Preached on several Subjects and Occasions, with some Lectures.* 2 vols. Edinburgh: Printed by James Watson for John Martin, George Stewart, Mr James Davidson, and John Paton, 1722.

Edinburgh Christian Instructor, 27 (1828): 684.

Elder of the Church of Scotland. *Memorial for the Members to be Chosen to Represent this Church, at the ensuing General Assembly, humbly offered by an Elder of the Church of Scotland.* Edinburgh, 1715.

Emerson, R.L. "Calvinism and the Scottish Enlightenment." In Joachim Schwend, Susanne Gagemann, and Hermann Völkel, eds., *Literature im Kontext – Literature in Context,* 19–28. Frankfurt am Main: Peter Lang, 1992.

– "Latitudinarianism and the English Deists." In L.A. Leo Lemay, ed., *Deism, Masonry, and the Enlightenment: Essays Honoring Alfred Owen Aldridge,* 19–48. Newark: University of Delaware Press, c. 1987.

– "Medical Men, Politicians and the Medical Schools at Glasgow and Edinburgh 1685–1803." In Andrew Doig, Joan P.S. Ferguson, Iain Milne, and Reginald Passmore, eds., *William Cullen and the Eighteenth Century Medical World.* Edinburgh: Edinburgh University Press, 1993.

– "Politics and the Glasgow Professors, 1690–1800." In Andrew Hook and Richard B. Sher., eds., *The Glasgow Enlightenment,* 21–39. East Linton, Scotland: Tuckwell Press in association with the Eighteenth-Century Scottish Studies Society, 1995.

– *Professors, Patronage and Politics: The Aberdeen Universities in the Eighteenth Century.* Aberdeen: Aberdeen University Press, 1992.

– "The Religious, the Secular and the Worldly: Scotland 1680–1800." In James E. Crimmins, ed., *Religion, Secularization and Political Thought: Thomas Hobbes to J.S. Mill,* 68–89. London and New York: Routledge, 1989.

– "Scottish Universities in the Eighteenth Century, 1690–1800." *Studies on Voltaire and the Eighteenth Century* 167 (1977): 453–74.

Encyclopedia of Religion and Ethics. 13 vols. Ed. J. Hastings. New York: Charles Scribner's Sons, 1922.

Erskine, James, Lord Grange. *Extracts from the Diary of a Senator of the College of Justice. m.dcc.xvii–m.dcc.xviii.* Ed. James Maidment. Edinburgh: Thomas G. Stevenson, 1843.

– "Letters of Lord Grange." *Miscellany of the Spalding Club.* Vol. 3. Aberdeen: Spalding Club, 1846.

An Essay to Vindicate some Scripture Truths in Five several Articles, from the Danger of being corrupted at this Time. In Answer of a Letter from a Gentleman to a Minister. Published by a member of the Church of Scotland. N.p., 1716.

Eyre-Todd, George. Vols. 2 and 3 of R. Renwick and J. Lindsay, *History of Glasgow.* 3 vols. Glasgow: Jackson, Wylie & Co., 1934.

Ferguson, William. *Scotland 1689 to the Present.* Vol.4 of *The Edinburgh History of Scotland.* Gen. ed. Gordon Donaldson. New York: Frederick A. Praeger, 1968.

Ferrier, Andrew. *Memoirs of the Rev. William Wilson.* Glasgow: Robertson & Atkinson, and Maurice Ogle, 1830.

Fisher, Edward. *The Marrow of Modern Divinity: in two Parts, with notes by the Rev. Thomas Boston.* Philadelphia: Presbyterian Board of Publication, n.d. Fisher's work first published London, 1645.

Flint, John. *Examen Doctrinæ Domini Johannis Simson S.S. Th. In Celebri Academia Glasguensi Professoris.* Edinburgh: J. Reid, 1717.

Florida, Robert E. "British Law and Socinianism in the 17th and 18th Centuries." In *Socinianism and Its Role in the Culture of the XVIth to XVIIIth Centuries,* 201–10. Warsaw – Lodz: Polish Academy of Sciences, Institute of Philosophy and Sociology, 1983.

Fraser, Donald. *The Life and Diary of the Reverend Ebenezer Erskine.* Edinburgh: William Oliphant, 1831.

– *The Life and Diary of the Reverend Ralph Erskine.* Edinburgh: William Oliphant & Son, 1834.

Fraser, William. *Memoirs of the Maxwells of Pollock.* 2 vols. Edinburgh, 1863.

Fratt, Steven Douglas. "Scottish Theological Trends in the Eighteenth Century: Tensions between 'Head' and 'Heart.'" PHD dissertation, University of California, Santa Barbara, 1987.

Graham, Henry Grey. *The Social Life of Scotland in the Eighteenth Century.* First pub. 1899. 4th ed. 1937, reprinted London: Adam & Charles Black, 1950.

Grant, Sir Alexander. *The Story of the University of Edinburgh during Its First Three Hundred Years.* 2 vols. London: Longmans, Green and Co., 1884.

Grant, Sir Francis J., ed. *The Faculty of Advocates in Scotland: 1532–1943, with Genealogical Notes.* Edinburgh: Scottish Record Society, 1944.

[Hadow, James.] *An enquiry into Mr Simson's sentiments about the Trinity, from his papers in process.* Edinburgh: printed by Thomas Lumisden and John Robertson: and sold at John Paton's shop, and other booksellers in town, 1730.

Hadow, James. *Sermon on John V 11, 12, before the Synod of Fife, April 7, 1719.* Edinburgh: John Paton, 1719.

– *A Vindication of the Learned and Honourable Author of* The History of the Apostles Creed, *from the False Sentiment, which Mr Simson has injuriously imputed to him.* Edinburgh: John Paton Bookseller, 1731.

Halyburton, Thomas. *Memoirs of the Life of the Rev. Thomas Halyburton.* Edinburgh: John Johnstone, n.d.

[?Hamilton, John]. *Animadversions on a Pamphlet intituled The Case of Mr. John Simson, &.* 2nd ed. Edinburgh: James Davidson and Company, 1728.

Hazlett, W. Ian P. "Religious Subversive or Model Christian?" In *Francis Hutcheson: A Special Symposium on the Thought, Career and Influence in Ireland, Scotland and America of the Ulster-Scots Philosopher and Dissenter.* Supplement to *Fortnight* 308 (1992).

Heath, George, ed. *Records of the Carrick Moore Family.* Cobham, 1912.

Henderson, Henry F. *The Religious Controversies of Scotland.* Edinburgh: T. & T. Clark, 1905.

Hetherington, W.M. *History of the Church of Scotland: from the Introduction of Christianity to the Period of the Disruption in 1843.* Edinburgh: Johnstone, 1844.

Historic Manuscripts Commission (HMC). *Fourteenth Report,* Appendix Part III. *Manuscripts of the Duke of Roxburgh.* London: HMSO, 1894.

– *Report on the Manuscripts of the Duke of Portland.* Norwich: HMSO, 1899.

– *Report on the Manuscripts of the Earl of Mar and Kellie.* London: HMSO, 1904.

[Hoadly, Benjamin]. Dedication to Urbano Cerri, *An Account of the state of the Roman-Catholick religion throughout the world. Written for the use of Pope Innocent XI by Monsignor Cerri ... With a large dedication to the present pope.* London: Printed for J. Roberts, 1715.

Hoadly, Benjamin. *The Nature of the Kingdom, or Church, of Christ. A Sermon Preach'd before the King, at the Royal Chapel at St. James's, on Sunday March 31, 1717.* London, 1717.

Hoare, Peter. "The Librarians of Glasgow University over 300 Years 1641–1991." *Library Review (Great Britain)* 40 (1991): 27–43.

Hogg, James. *A Letter to a Gentleman concerning the Interest of Reason in Religion.* Edinburgh: John Martin, William Brown & William Dickie, Booksellers, 1716.

– *A Letter to a Gentleman Detecting the Gangrene of some Errors Vented at this Time.* Edinburgh: John Martin, William Brown & William Dickie, Booksellers, 1716.

– *Memoirs of the Public Life of Mr. James Hogg; and of the Ecclesiastical Proceedings of his Times; Previous to his Settlement at Carnock.* Edinburgh: J. Ogle and J. Guthrie, et al., 1798.

Home, Henry, Lord Kames. *Sketches of the History of Man.* 4 vols. Reprinted, Hildesheim: Georg Olms Verlagsbuchhandlung, 1968.

Hook, Andrew, and Richard B. Sher, eds. *The Glasgow Enlightenment.* East Linton: Tuckwell Press in association with the Eighteenth-Century Scottish Studies Society, 1995.

Horn, D.B. *A Short History of the University of Edinburgh 1556–1889.* Edinburgh: Edinburgh University Press, 1967.

An Humble Address to the Right Reverend and Honourable General Assembly anent Catching of Foxes.

Hunter, Michael. "'Aikenhead the Atheist': The Context and Consequences of Articulate Irreligion in the late Seventeenth Century." In Michael Hunter and David Wootton, eds., *Atheism from the Reformation to the Enlightenment.* Oxford: Clarendon Press, 1992.

[Hunter, Mr]. *The Doctrine of the Blessed and Adorable Trinity, Stated from the Holy Scripture. With a Brief Discovery of Some Unsound and Dangerous Opinions, vented* by Mr. John Simpson, Professor of Divinity in the College of Glasgow. Edinburgh: Thomas Lumisden and John Robertson, 1728.

Innes, Cosmo. *Sketches of Early Scotch History and Social Progress.* Edinburgh: Edmonston and Douglas, 1861.

International Standard Biblical Encyclopedia. Ed. Geoffrey M. Bromiley et al. 4 vols. Grand Rapids, Mich.: W.B. Eerdmans, 1979–88.

Jackson, Gordon. "Glasgow in Transition, *c.* 1660 to *c.* 1740." In Devine and Jackson, eds., *Glasgow Volume I.*

Jubb, Michael. "Economic Policy and Economic Development." In Jeremy Black, ed., *Britain in the Age of Walpole.* London: Macmillan, 1984.

Kasper, Walter. *The God of Jesus Christ.* Trans. Matthew J. O'Connell. New York: Crossroad, 1984.

Kennedy, Thomas D. "William Leechman, Pulpit Eloquence and the Glasgow Enlightenment." In Hook and Sher, eds., *The Glasgow Enlightenment.*

Killen, W.D. Vol. 3 of *History of the Presbyterian Church in Ireland, Comprising the Civil History of the Province of Ulster, from the Accession of James the First.* 3 vols. James Seaton Reid. London: Whittaker and Co., 1853.

Klauber, Martin I. *Between Reformed Scholasticism and Pan-Protestantism: Jean-Alphonse Turretin (1671–1737) and Enlightened Orthodoxy at the Academy of Geneva.* Selinsgrove: Susquehanna University Press, 1994.

[L., Mr J.] *An Alarm to the church of Scotland, and to all Lovers of Truth against Error; and Particularly, the Damnable Error, or Denying the Divinity of the Lord Jesus Christ, the Eternal Son of God. Or a Letter from a Gentleman in the Country, to his Old Acquaintance in the City, about the Affair of Mr John Simpson, Professor of Divinity in the Colledge of Glasgow; depending at present before the General Assembly of the church of Scotland; together with the Answer to the said Letter.* N.p., 1728.

Lachman, David C. *The Marrow Controversy.* Edinburgh: Rutherford House, 1988.

"L.D.L." *A Letter from a Fyfe Gentleman, at present in Edinburgh, to The Chief Magistrate of a Burgh in Fyfe, Upon our present Situation, with regard to the Malt-Tax.* Edinburgh, 1725.

Leideker, Melchior. *A Copy of a Letter From the Learned Mr. Melch. Leideker, one of the Professors of Theology in the University of Utrecht, to the R. Mr. Ja. Hogg, a Minister of the Gospel in Scotland: Concerning the R. Mr. J. Simson Professor of Divinity in Glasgow.* N.p., 1717.

Leith, John H. *Introduction to the Reformed Tradition.* Edinburgh: Saint Andrew Press, 1978.

Lenman, Bruce. *The Jacobite Risings in Britain 1689–1746.* London: Eyre Methuen Ltd, 1980.

Letsome, Sampson, and John Nicholls, eds. *A Defence of natural and revealed Religion: being a Collection of the Sermons preached at the lecture founded by the Honourable*

Robert Boyle (from the year 1691 to the year 1732); with the additions and amendments of the several authors and general indexes. London: Printed for D. Midwinter et al., 1739.

A Letter about Professor Simpson, by Way of Appendix to the Pamphlet, called, An Alarm to the Church of Scotland, and all the Lovers of Truth, etc. By the same author. N.p., 1729.

A Letter from a Gentleman in Glasgow, to his Friend in Edinburgh, concerning the Trial of the Glasgow Prisoners now lying in the Castle of Edinburgh. Glasgow, 14 Sept., 1725.

A Letter from a Gentleman in Glasgow, to his Friend in the Country, Concerning the Late Tumults which happened in that City.... Printed in the Year M.DCC.XXV.

A Letter from a Ruling-Elder in the Church of Scotland to the Reverend Mr. Thomas Linning, Minister of the Gospel at Lesmahago, concerning the Process of Mr. Thomas Harvie, Ruling-Elder in Glasgow, before the Presbytery of that Place. N.p., 1722.

A Letter from a Student in Aberdeen to a Minister at Edinburgh Touching, the Affair of Professor Simson: The Marrow of Modern Divinity: and the new Usages among some few of the Episcopal Clergy. Together With a Postscript in answer to a Pamphlet, entitled, The Rights of Patronages consider'd. Edinburgh, 1731.

Letter to a Reverend Member of the General Assembly from a Private Christian, concerning the New Overture of the Committee for Purity of Doctrine. N.p., 10 May, 1728.

Livingstone, Elizabeth A., ed. *Concise Oxford Dictionary of the Christian Church.* Oxford: Oxford University Press, 1977.

Locke, John. *An Essay concerning Human Understanding.* Ed. A.S. Pringle-Pattison. Oxford: Clarendon Press, 1924.

Lockhart, George. *The Lockhart Papers: Memoirs and Commentaries upon the Affairs of Scotland from 1702 to 1715, by George Lockhart, Esq. of Carnwath. Secret Correspondence with the Son of James II and other Political Writings.* 2 vols. London: William Anderson, 1817.

[Logan, Allan]. *A Countryman's Brief Remarks on the Reverend and Learned Mr. John Sympson Professor of Divinity His Letter to the Reverend Presbytery of Glasgow.* Edinburgh: n.p., 1726.

[–] *An Enquiry into Professor Simson's Sentiments on the Doctrine of the Trinity, From his Papers in the Process against him.* Edinburgh: James Davidson and Company, 1729.

[–] *The Necessity of Zeal for Truth; and of Restraining Error by the Exercise of Church-Discipline.* N.p.: N.p., 1730.

Logan, George. *A Discourse on John XXI. 15, 16, 17, 18, 19. in the High Church of Edinburgh, May 4th, 1729, Before His Majesty's Commissioner to the General Assembly.* Edinburgh: Tho. and Wal. Ruddimans, 1729.

Lumsden, Harry. *Records of the Trades House of Glasgow, ad 1713–77.* Glasgow: Printed for the Trades House, 1934.

McCallum, Rev. Donald P. "George Hill, D.D.: Moderate or Evangelical Erastian?" MA thesis, University of Western Ontario, 1989.

MacCormick, Joseph. *State-Papers and Letters Addressed to William Carstares.* Edinburgh: J. Balfour et al., 1774.

(McLaren) McClaren, John. *The New Scheme of Doctrine Contained in the Answers of Mr. John Simson, Professor of Divinity in the Colledge of Glasgow; to Mr Webster's Libel, considered and examined.* Edinburgh: John Reid, 1717.

Macleod, John. *Scottish Theology in Relation to Church History since the Reformation.* First pub. 1943. 2nd ed. 1946, reprint, Edinburgh: Banner of Faith Trust, 1974.

M'Cosh, James. *The Scottish Philosophy: Biographical, Expository, Critical from Hutcheson to Hamilton.* New York: Robert Carter & Brothers, 1875.

M'Crie, Charles G. "Professor Simson, the Glasgow Heresiarch." *British and Foreign Evangelical Review* 33 (1884): 254–77.

M'Crie, Thomas. *Sketches of Scottish Church History: Embracing the Period from the Reformation to the Revolution.* 2 vols. 4th ed. Edinburgh: John Johnstone, [1875?].

Maidment, J., ed. *Analecta Scotica: Collections of the Civil, Ecclesiastical, and Literary History of Scotland chiefly from Original MSS.* 2 vols. Edinburgh: Thomas G. Stevenson, 1834.

– ed. *The Argyle Papers.* Edinburgh: Thomas G. Stevenson, 1830.

– ed. *A Second Book of Scotish Pasquils.* Edinburgh, 1828.

Mathieson, William Law. *Scotland and the Union: A History of Scotland from 1695 to 1747.* Glasgow: James Maclehose & Sons, 1905.

A Member of the Church of Christ, and a preacher of his gospel. *A Few Remarks on an Essay Designed to Expose the Reverend Mr. Simpson Prof. of Theology in the University of Glasgow.* Edinburgh: Printed for J. Webster, [1717?].

Menary, G. *Life and Letters of Duncan Forbes of Culloden, Lord President of the Court of Session 1685–1747.* London: Alexander Maclehose & Co., 1936.

The Method of Proceeding by Queries Vindicated, Particularly in the Case of Professor Simson, from Scripture, Reason and Antiquity. Edinburgh: Mr James Davidson and Company, 1728.

[Moncreiff, Alexander, of Culfargie]. *The Proper, True, and Supreme Deity of Our Lord and Saviour Jesus Christ, proved and asserted from the Holy Scripture.* Edinburgh: n.p., 1730.

– *Remarks on Professor Simson's first Libel, and His Censure considered, with a Brief Discovery of some of the many dangerous Opinions vented by him, in his Answers to Mr. Webster's Libel; and found proven by the Committee on the Second Libel.* Edinburgh: James Davidson and Company, 1729.

Moore, James. "Theological Politics: A Study of the Reception of Locke's *Two Treatises of Government* in England and Scotland in the Early Eighteenth Century." In Martyn P. Thompson, ed., *John Locke und/and Immanuel Kant: Historical Reception and Contemporary Relevance.* Berlin: Duncker & Humblot, 1991.

Munimenta Alme Universitatis Glasguensis: Records of the University of Glasgow from its Foundation till 1727. 4 vols. Glasgow, 1854.

Murray, Archibald. *The Case of Dr. Wishart, Principal of the College of Edinburgh, Humbly submitted to the Venerable Assembly of the Church of Scotland.* Edinburgh: n.p., 1738.

Murray, David. *Memories of the Old College of Glasgow.* Glasgow: Jackson Wylie & Co., 1927.

New Schaff–Herzog Encyclopedia of Religious Knowledge. Ed. Samuel Macauley Jackson. 13 vols. Grand Rapids, Mich.: Baker Book House, 1966.

Omond, George W.T. *Faculty of Advocates in Scotland from the Close of the Fifteenth Century to the Passing of the Reform Bill.* 2 vols. Edinburgh: David Douglas, 1883.

Owen, John. *The Works.* 16 vols. Ed. Rev. William H. Gould. Edinburgh: Johnstone and Hunter, 1853.

Pearson, John. *An Exposition of the Creed.* First pub. 1673. Ed. Edward Walford. London: George Bell & Sons, 1889.

Phillipson, N.T. "Lawyers, Landowners, and the Civic Leadership of Post-Union Scotland: An Essay on the Social Role of the Faculty of Advocates 1661–1830 in 18th Century Scottish Society." *Juridical Review* 21 (1976): 97–120.

– "The Scottish Enlightenment." In Roy Porter and Mikuláš Teich, eds. *The Enlightenment in National Context.* Cambridge: Cambridge University Press, 1981.

Pictet, Benedict. *True and False Religion Examined: The Christian Religion Defended; and the Protestant Reformation Vindicated.* Trans. and ed. A. Bruce. Edinburgh: J. Ogle et al., 1797.

Pitcairne, Archibald. *The Assembly.* ed. Terence Tobin. Lafayette, Ind.: Purdue University Studies, 1972.

Plumb, J.H. *Sir Robert Walpole: The King's Minister.* Boston: Houghton Mifflin Company, 1961.

Price, Jacob M. "Glasgow, the Tobacco Trade, and the Scottish Customs, 1707–1730." *Scottish Historical Review* 53 (1984): 1–36.

– "The Rise of Glasgow in the Chesapeake Tobacco Trade, 1707–1775." In Peter L. Payne, ed., *Studies in Scottish Business History.* London: Frank Cass & Co. Ltd, 1967.

Private Christian. *Videte apologiam nostram contra Websterum, &c. or a Letter from a Private Christian to A Reverend Minister and a member of the present Commission of the Late General Assembly; Pointing out several Articles of Reverend Professor Simson's new Scheme of Divinity, which he is said to recommend to his Students in the above Latine Words, referring them to his Answer to the late Reverend Mr Webster's Libel against him, to be compared with the Passages of the Marrow of Modern Divinity, condemned as erroneous by the Fifth Act of the General Assembly 1720; or with the Representation given in by the Twelve Reverend Ministers to the last General Assembly 1721, that it may be considered, whether the Reverend Professor Simson, or the Reverend Recommender and Vindicator of the Marrow … be most liable to censure.* N.p., 1722.

Ramsay, John, of Ochtertyre. *Scotland and Scotsmen in the Eighteenth Century.* 2 vols. Ed. Alexander Allardyce. Edinburgh and London: William Blackwood and Sons, 1888.

Redwood, John. *Reason, Ridicule and Religion: The Age of Enlightenment in England 1660–1750.* London: Thames and Hudson, 1976.

Reedy, Gerard. *The Bible and Reason: Anglicans and Scripture in Late Seventeenth-Century England.* Philadelphia: University of Pennsylvania Press, 1985.

Reid, H.M.B. *The Divinity Professors in the University of Glasgow, 1640–1903.* Glasgow: Maclehose, Jackson and Co., 1923.

Reid, James Seaton. *History of the Presbyterian Church in Ireland, Comprising the Civil History of the Province of Ulster, from the Accession of James the First.* 3 vols. Vol. 3, W.D. Killen. London: Whittaker and Co., 1853.

Remarks on Professor Simson's Answers To what he calls the Presbytery of Glasgow's Paper, entituled, references anent Professor's [sic] Simson's Affair. Edinburgh: Printed and sold by most booksellers in Town, 1727.

Remarks on Professor Simson's Speech to the General Assembly May 7, 1728.

Renwick, Robert, ed. *Extracts from the Records of the Burgh of Glasgow A.D. 1718–1738.* Glasgow: Corporation of Glasgow, 1909.

Renwick, R., and Lindsay, J. *History of Glasgow.* 3 vols. Vols. 2 and 3 by George Eyre-Todd. Glasgow: Jackson, Wylie & Co., 1934.

A Review of a Conference betwixt Epaphroditus and Epaphras: Wherein the very Reverend Principal Hadow's Sermon, Preached before the Synod of Fife, April 7th, 1719, Is fairly Enquired into. Edinburgh: John Paton, Bookseller, 1719.

Riley, P.W.J. *The English Ministers and Scotland, 1707–1727.* London: Athlone Press, 1964.

– *The Union of England and Scotland: A Study in Anglo-Scottish Politics of the Eighteenth Century.* Manchester: Manchester University Press, 1978.

Robertson, John, ed. *A Union for Empire: Political Thought and the British Union of 1707.* Cambridge: Cambridge University Press, 1995.

Robertson, William, of Wolverhampton. "Original Memoirs of Dr. Robertson of Wolverhampton." *Gentleman's Magazine* (Sept. 1783): 745–50.

Ruestow, Edward G. *Physics at Seventeenth and Eighteenth-Century Leiden: Philosophy and the New Science in the University.* The Hague: Martinus Nijhoff, 1973.

Schaff, Philip. *The Creeds of Christendom.* 3 vols. First pub. 1877. 6th ed. 1931. Grand Rapids, Mich.: Baker Books, 1983.

Schiebinger, Londa. *The Mind Has No Sex? Women in the Origins of Modern Science.* Cambridge, Mass.: Harvard University Press, 1989.

Scots Magazine, 1740, 1741.

Scott, Hew. *Fasti Ecclesiae Scoticanae.* 8 vols. First pub. 1866–71, revised, Edinburgh: Oliver & Boyd, 1915–30.

Scott, William Robert. *Francis Hutcheson: His Life, Teaching and Position in the History of Philosophy.* Cambridge: University Press, 1900.

Scottish Burgh Records Society (SBRS). *Extracts from the Records of the Burgh of Glasgow, A.D. 1691–1717.* Glasgow: Scottish Burgh Records Society, 1908.

A Seasonable Advice to All Lovers of their Country. N.p., [c. 1725].

Sedgwick, Romney. *The House of Commons 1715–1754.* 2 vols. New York: Oxford University Press for the History of Parliament Trust, 1970.

Sefton, Henry R. "The Early Development of Moderatism in the Church of Scotland." PHD dissertation, Glasgow University, 1962.

– "'Neu-lights and Preachers Legall': Some Observations on the Beginnings of Moderatism in the Church of Scotland." In Norman Macdougall, ed., *Church, Politics and Society: Scotland 1408–1929.* Edinburgh: John Donald Publishers Ltd., 1983.

– "St Mary's College, St Andrews, in the Eighteenth Century." *Records of the Scottish Church History Society* 24 (1991): 161–79.

Shepherd, Christine. "University Life in the Seventeenth Century." In Gordon Donaldson, ed., *Four Centuries: Edinburgh University Life 1583–1983.* Edinburgh: University of Edinburgh, 1983.

Sher, Richard B. "Commerce, Religion and the Enlightenment in Eighteenth-Century Glasgow." In Devine and Jackson, eds., *Glasgow, Volume I.*

Simpson, John M. "Who Steered the Gravy Train, 1707–1766?" In N.T. Phillipson and Rosalind Michison, eds., *Scotland in the Age of Improvement: Essays in Scottish History in the Eighteenth Century.* Edinburgh: Edinburgh University Press, 1970.

[Simson, John]. *Advertisement Concerning a short Abstract, taken from Mr. John Simson's printed Account of the Process carried on against him by Mr. James Webster. Copies whereof were given out by the said Mr. James Webster, to be sold on Thursday the 26. of April 1716.* Edinburgh: John Moncur, 1716.

[?–] *An Answer to a Paper Entituled Abstract of Difficulties occurring to a Reader of the Reverend Professor Simpson's Printed Answers to Mr. Webster's Libel against him.* Edinburgh: William Adams Junior, 1717.

[–] *Answers to the remarks on Professor Simson's Answers to the Presbytery of Glasgow's References.* Edinburgh: n.p., 1727.

[–] *The Case of Mr. John Simson Professor of Divinity in the University of Glasgow. The Second Edition. Containing, beside what was in the former Edition, and Abstract of the Pleadings, and all the Papers which were before the last General Assembly. The Preface is also much augmented, and continued to the Rising of the Assembly.* Edinburgh: James Davidson, 1727.

[–] *A Continuation of the Second Edition of the Case of Mr. John Simson, Professor of Divinity in the University of Glasgow.* Edinburgh: James Davidson, 1728.

Simson, John. *Libel Mr James Webster, Against Mr John Simson Professor of Divinity in the University of Glasgow.* N.p. [?1716].

– *Mr. Simpson's Speech to the General Assembly May 7 1727.* N.p., n.d.

– *Professor Simson's Declaration Which he gave in to the University of Glasgow, April 29. 1729. The Representation of the University of Glasgow, To the General Assembly, Concerning Professor Simson, Which was read in Assembly May 6. 1729.*

– *Professor Simson's Speech to the General Assembly, May 7, 1729.* N.p., n.d.

[–] *A Supplement to the Second Edition of the Case of Mr. John Simson, Professor of Divinity in the University of Glasgow; containing the Proceedings of the committee appointed by the Assembly 1727, and of the General Assembly 1728, with the Pleadings in the Assembly.* Edinburgh: Tho. and Wal. Ruddimans, 1729.

A Sincere Lover of Truth and Peace. *Reasons against the Restoration of Professor Simson to Teach, or Preach. With Illustrations thereof containing Several things concerning the Doctrine of the Holy Trinity.* Edinburgh: n.p., 1729.

[Smith, John]. *A Short Account of the Late Treatment of the Students of the University of G – – – w.* Dublin, 1727. In GUL, Mn 21–d.25.

Smout, T.C. *A History of the Scottish People, 1560–1830.* London: William Collins Sons & Co. Ltd., 1969; paperback, Fontana Press, 1989.

Some materials for answers to the Papers which seem design'd to handle Points of Law in Mr Simson's printed Case. N.p., n.d.

Steele, Margaret. "Anti-Jacobite Pamphleteering, 1701–1720." *Scottish Historical Review* 40 (1981): 140–55.

Stephen, Sir Leslie, and Lee, Sir Sidney, eds. *Dictionary of National Biography.* 21 vols. with supplement. London: Oxford University Press, 1921–2.

Stewart, M.A. "Berkeley and the Rankenian Club." *Hermathena: A Trinity College Dublin Review.* 134 (1985): 25–45.

– "John Smith and the Molesworth Circle." *Eighteenth-Century Ireland* 2 (1987): 89–102.

– "Rational Dissent in Early Eighteenth-Century Ireland." In Knud Haakonssen, ed., *Enlightenment and Religion: Rational Dissent in Eighteenth-Century Britain*. New York: Cambridge University Press, 1996.

Stewart, Walter, of Pardovan. *Collections and Observances Concerning the Worship, Discipline, and Government of the Church of Scotland. In Four Books. Unto which are added, The Form of Process in the Judicatures of the Church, with Relation to Scandals and Censures; and The Second Book of Discipline; or, Heads and Conclusions of the Policy of the Kirk, approved by Act of Assembly 1581.* Edinburgh: Printed for J. Dickson and C. Elliot, 1773.

Stewart, Walter, of Pardovan. (Not the above.) *Abridgement of the Acts of the General Assembly of the Church of Scotland for the Years 1638–1810 inclusive.* Edinburgh: Archibald Constable & Company, 1811.

Story, Robert Herbert, ed. *The Church of Scotland, Past and Present: Its History, Its Relation to the Law and the State, Its Doctrine, Ritual, Discipline, and Patrimony.* 5 vols. Vol. 4, Rev. T. D. Niven. London: William Mackenzie, 1890–1.

Struthers, John. *History of Scotland from the Union to the Abolition of the Heritable Jurisdictions in MDCCXLIII.* 2 vols. Glasgow: Blackie, Fullarton, & Co., 1827.

Suderman, Jeffrey M. "Orthodoxy and Enlightenment: George Campbell (1719–1796) and the Aberdeen Enlightenment." PHD dissertation, University of Western Ontario, 1995.

A Summary View of Professor Simson's Errors, Prov'd against him in the Double Process Before the General Assembly; with some Thoughts upon the Whole: In a Letter to a Friend. To which is added, An Answer to the said Letter. Edinburgh: n.p., 1729.

Sunter, Ronald M. *Patronage and Politics in Scotland 1707–1832.* Edinburgh: John Donald Publishers, Ltd, 1986.

Taylor, Samuel S.B. "The Enlightenment in Switzerland." In Roy Porter and Mikuláš Teich, eds., *The Enlightenment in National Context.* Cambridge: Cambridge University Press, 1982.

Thomas, Roger. "The Non-Subscription Controversy amongst Dissenters in 1719: The Salters' Hall Debate." *Journal of Ecclesiastical History* 4 (1953): 162–86.

Toland, John. *Christianity Not Mysterious.* Facsimile, Stuttgart–Bad Cannstatt: Friedrich Fromänn Verlag (Günther Holzboog), 1964.

Turretin, Francis. "The Doctrine of Scripture: Locus 2 of *Institutio theologiæ elenctiæ.*" In John W. Beardslee III, ed. and trans., *Reformed Dogmatics.* Grand Rapids, Mich.: Baker Book House, 1981.

(Turretin) Turretine, J.-A. *Dissertations on Natural Theology.* First pub. 1737. Trans. William Crawford. Belfast: John Magee, 1777.

University of Edinburgh. *Catalogue of the Graduates of the Faculties of Arts, Divinity, and Law, of the University of Edinburth since the Reformation.* Edinburgh: Printed by Neill and Company, 1858.

University of Glasgow. *The Representation of the University of Glasgow, To the General Assembly, Concerning Professor Simson, Which was read in Assembly May 6, 1729.* N.p., n.d.

Walker, James. *The Theology and Theologians of Scotland Chiefly of the Seventeenth and Eighteenth Centuries.* First pub. 1872. 2nd ed. Edinburgh: T. & T. Clark, 1888.

Warrick, John. *The Moderators of the Church of Scotland from 1690–1740.* Edinburgh: Oliphant, Anderson & Ferrier, 1913.

Webster, James. *Propositions taken out of Mr. Simson's Printed Book, and his Letters to the late Reverend Mr. Robert Rowan Minister of the Gospel at Penningham.* Edinburgh?, 1716.

[–] *A Short Abstract taken from Mr. John Simson's Printed Account of the Process carried on against him by Mr. James Webster.* Edinburgh: Printed by John Moncur, 1716.

– ed. *A True and Authentick Copy of Mr. John Simsons Letters to Mr. Robert Rowan, late Minister at Penningham, Taken out of the Originals.* Edinburgh: John Moncur, 1716.

Wehrli, Eric G.J. "Scottish Politics in the Age of Walpole." PHD dissertation, University of Chicago, 1983.

West, Elizabeth. *Memoirs or Spiritual Exercises.* Edinburgh: Printed for the booksellers, 1798.

"Westminster Confession of Faith" and "Westminster Shorter Catechism." In Schaff, *Creeds*, vol. 3.

Westaway, Jonathan H. "Scottish Influences upon the Reformed Churches in North-West England, c. 1689–1829." PHD dissertation, Lancaster University, 1997.

Whiston, William. *Memoirs of the Life and Writing of Mr. William Whiston, containing memoirs of several of his friends also.* London: Printed for the author and sold by Mr. Whiston in Fleet Street, and Mr. Bishop, in Little Turn-Stile Holborn, 1749.

[Williamson, John]. *Remarks on the printed Case of Professor Simpson.* Edinburgh: n.p., 1727.

[–] *A Speech without Doors: Concerning the Process Against Professor Simson, As it now lies before the Venerable Assembly of the Church of Scotland, In Name of some Onlookers who are Trembling for the Ark of God. Directed in a Letter to a Member of the Assembly.* Edinburgh: n.p., 1728.

[–] *Truth's triumph over error, in the issue of the process against Mr. John Simson, Professor of Divinity in the University of Glasgow; together with some account of the sentence of the General Assembly of the Church of Scotland concerning him, May 16th 1728. In a letter to a friend.* Edinburgh: printed in the year, 1728.

Willison, John. *A Fair and Impartial Testimony, essayed in name of a number of ministers, elders, and Christian people of the Church of Scotland ... containing a brief histor-*

*ical deduction of the chief occurrences in this church from her beginning to the year
1744.* First pub. 1744. Pittsburgh: Zadok Cramer, 1808. Microopaque Early
American Imprints, second series: 16746.

Wilson, John. *Index of the Acts and Proceedings of the General Assembly of the Church of
Scotland from the Revolution to the Present Time.* Edinburgh: William Blackwood
and Sons, 1863.

Wishart, William, Jr. *Answers for William Wishart, Principal of the College of Edinburgh
to the Charge exhibited against him before the Rev. Synod of Lothian and Tweeddale ...
of Articles of Error alledged to be contained in two Sermons preached by him.* Edinburgh: T. and W. Ruddimans, 1738.

[–] *A Short and Impartial State of the Case of Mr. John Simson, Professor of Divinity in
the University of Glasgow, As it comes before the General Assembly 1729, In a Letter to
a Gentleman, a Member of the said Assembly.* Edinburgh: n.p., 1729.

Witsius, Herman. *Dissertations on ... the Apostles' Creed.* 2 vols. Trans. Donald Fraser.
Edinburgh: A. Fullarton & Co., 1823.

– *The Economy of the Covenants between God and Man: Comprehending A Complete
Body of Divinity.* [First pub. 1693]. Trans. and ed. William Crookshank, D.D.,
2 vols. London: R. Baynes et al., 1822. Facsimile, Escondido, Calif.: den Dulk
Christian Foundation, 1990.

Wodrow, Robert. *Analecta: Materials for a History of Remarkable Providences mostly
Relating to Scotch Ministers and Christians.* 4 vols. Edinburgh: Maitland Club,
1853.

– *The Correspondence of the Rev. Robert Wodrow.* Ed. Rev. Thomas M'Crie. 3 vols.
Edinburgh: Wodrow Society, 1842–3.

Young, David, and John Brown. *Memorials of Alexander Moncrieff, M.A., and James
Fisher, Father of the United Presbyterian Church.* Edinburgh: A. Fullarton & Co.,
1849.

Index